ML.

# Indecent Disclosure
*Gilding the Corporate Lily*

*Indecent Disclosure: Gilding the Corporate Lily* captures the concerns of the business community when misleading financial disclosures of a public corporation result in an unexpected corporate collapse. Here, the authors present four main themes underpinning the crisis in a company's financial disclosures:

- A company's compliance with accounting standards does not generally produce financial statements that disclose their wealth and financial progress.
- Misleading financial statements are more the result of compliance with accounting rules, with the best of intentions, than a result of deviation from them with the intent to mislead.
- The raft of knee-jerk corporate governance mechanisms imposed following recent high profile corporate malpractice are more directed at appearances than at rectifying problems.
- There is increasing evidence that the current group structures which organise corporate activities are incapable of effective regulation.

*Indecent Disclosure* explains, explores and illustrates these themes, within the framework of an agenda for true, effective reform.

**Frank Clarke** is Emeritus Professor of Accounting at the University of Newcastle, and Honorary Professor of Accounting at The University of Sydney.

**Graeme Dean** is Professor of Accounting at The University of Sydney.

# Indecent Disclosure

## Gilding the Corporate Lily

FRANK CLARKE
*University of Newcastle*
*University of Sydney*

GRAEME DEAN
*University of Sydney*

CAMBRIDGE
UNIVERSITY PRESS

CAMBRIDGE UNIVERSITY PRESS
Cambridge, New York, Melbourne, Madrid, Cape Town, Singapore, São Paulo

Cambridge University Press
477 Williamstown Road, Port Melbourne, VIC 3207, Australia

Published in the United States of America by Cambridge University Press, New York

www.cambridge.org
Information on this title: www.cambridge.org/9780521701839

First published 2007

Printed in Australia by Ligare

*A catalogue record for this publication is available from the British Library*

*National Library of Australia Cataloguing in Publication data*
Clarke, Frank L.
Indecent Disclosure: Gilding the Corporate Lily
Includes index.
ISBN 978-0-521-70183-9 (pbk.).
1. Financial disclosure. 2. Corporate culture. 3.
Corporate debt. 4. Business failures. I. Dean, G. W. II.
Title.
332.6

ISBN-13 978-0-521-70183-9

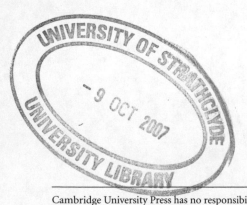

# Contents

# Illustrations

# Figures

# Tables

# Dramatis personae

**Adler, Rodney**  Chairman of FAI and non-executive director of HIH.

**Adsteam**  Adsteam was a conglomerate with the flagship company, The Adelaide Steamship Co. Limited. John Spalvins was at its helm from 1977 to 1990. It was perceived as a 1980s corporate high-flier.

**Air New Zealand**  New Zealand Government airline which acquired a 100 per cent shareholding in Ansett Australia Ltd. It subsequently allowed Ansett to be placed in receivership in 2001. Eventually Ansett was liquidated.

**Ansett**  Ansett Transport Industries Ltd, a major transport company and 49 per cent shareholder in ASL, was headed by Sir Reginald Ansett. In 1979 Ansett declined to finance further ASL's operations, thereby precipitating its ultimate collapse.

**ASL**  Associated Securities Limited (ASL group) was a leading Australian finance company in the 1970s that was not supported by its major shareholder Ansett, who 'baled out' in February 1979.

**BCH**  Bond Corp (or Bond Corporation Holdings Limited), renamed in 1993 Southern Equities Corporation Limited, was one of Australia's largest and most internationally known entrepreneurial companies of the 1980s.

**Berle, Adolf** and **Gardiner Means**  Co-authors of the 1932 classic, *The Modern Corporation and Private Property*.

**Bond, Alan**  Alan Bond was BCH founder and chairman from 1967 to 1991.

**Bosch, Henry**  Chairman of the NCSC (1985–90) and major spokesperson on corporate governance in the 1990s. He was extremely critical of the accounting practices of Westmex and Bond Corporation.

**Brierley, Sir Ron**  Founder of Industrial Equity Limited and a major antipodean investor from the 1970s to the 1990s. A takeover proved to be a major factor in the downfall of Adsteam, especially his fatal 'consolidated' account of the conglomerate's state of affairs.

**Cambridge Credit**  Cambridge Credit Corporation Limited (Cambridge group), run by R. E. M. (Mort) Hutcheson.

**Chambers, Ray**  Foundation Professor of Accounting at The University of Sydney. His iconoclastic reforms included the development of the method of Continuously Contemporary Accounting (CoCoA), entailing a completely integrated mark-to-market system that incorporates changes in both specific and general price levels.

**Dallhold** Dallhold Investments Proprietary Limited (Alan Bond's family company).

**Ebbers, Bernie** Former WordCom CEO; convicted on one count of conspiracy, one of securities fraud and seven of filing false statements with securities regulators in the $US11 billion accounting fraud at WorldCom, renamed in 2004 as MCI. Imprisoned in 2005 for 25 years.

**Enron** Enron Corporation was once the seventh largest publicly listed entity in the US, but it became one of the US's largest bankruptcies. Its Chairman, Kenneth Lay, presided over a period of intense scrutiny of its accounting practices culminating in the demise of Enron's audit firm, Andersen (one of the then Big Five accounting firms), due to its alleged document shredding at Enron.

**Fannie Mae** Founded in 1938 in the US the Federal National Mortgage Association, known by the acronym 'Fannie Mae', bought mortgages on a secondary market and issued mortgage-backed securities to the public. In 1968 the FNMA was partitioned into two operations – the wholly owned Government National Mortgage Association (Ginnie Mae) and the other Fannie Mae retaining the original name, expanding its mortgage portfolio and becoming fully private in 1970. Its operations are insured by the Federal Housing Association and is overseen by the Office of Federal Housing Enterprise Oversight (OFHEO). Its revenues were reported to be $US53.8 billion in 2003.

**Fastow, Andrew** CFO at Enron and major player in forming Enron's SPEs.

**Freddie Mac** Founded in 1970 the US the Federal Home Loan Mortgage Association, known by the acronym Freddie Mac, is stockholder owned, though government-backed and regulated by the Office of Federal Housing Enterprise Oversight (OFHEO). It offers similar mortgage-based securities to those offered by Fannie Mae, Ginnie Mae, and Sallie Mae (the 1972 founded quasi-government Student Loan Marketing Association). Its 2003 revenues were reported to be $US36.8 billion.

**Group of 100** An association comprising the CFOs of Australia's top public and private companies. The group's members are drawn from the nation's major private and public enterprises. Its declared overriding goal is to contribute positively to the development and maintenance of an Australian regulatory environment which best serves to advance the interests of Australian business in the context of international competition. Through such activity this CFO network attempts to set the agenda and lead the debate on financial reporting and management, corporate governance and regulatory issues influencing the future direction of corporate Australia.

**H. G. Palmer** H. G. Palmer (Consolidated) Limited, named after its founder Herbie Palmer. 'Palmer' refers to H. G. Palmer (Consolidated) Limited (Palmer group).

**HIH** HIH was one of Australia's largest insurance companies, one of its largest liquidations. Its founder and Chairman was Ray Williams, a leading Sydney philanthropist before HIH's collapse early in 2001.

**HIHRC** HIH Royal Commission was appointed in May 2001 with Justice Neville Owen as its Royal Commissioner. Hearings were held throughout 2001 and 2002 generating nearly 2000 pages of transcript and several million pages of submissions. The report was published in March 2003.

**HSI** Home Security International, a subsidiary of HIH.

**Insull, Samuel** Insull Utility Investments Inc., a major 1920s US utility conglomerate which took its name from its founder, Samuel Insull.

**Kozlowski, Dennis** Former Tyco CEO who was convicted in 2005 of misappropriating funds and gaoled for eight years.

**Kreuger, Ivar** Kreuger and Toll Inc., a major 1920s multinational match company, was founded and controlled by Ivar Kreuger.

**Lay, Kenneth** Enron founder and Chairman, and CEO after Skilling resigned in August 2001 until Enron was placed in liquidation.

**Maxwell, Robert** British newspaper and communications baron throughout the 1970s and 1980s, who in 1991 was found drowned in the Mediterranean thereby sparking a series of investigations that revealed a mountain of corporate debt and raised many unanswered questions about his financial empire.

**MCI** WorldCom was renamed MCI in 2004 as it exited Ch 11 Bankruptcy as MCI. It was taken over in 2006 by Verizon.

**Minsec** Mineral Securities of Australia Limited, or MSAL, refers to a loose collection of companies known as the Minsec group managed by Ken McMahon and Tom Nestel in the late 1960s and early 1970s.

**One.Tel** One of Australia's most notorious 1990s telcos. It had a meteoric rise and fall in the late 1990s and early 2000s. Its founders, Jodee Rich and Brad Keeling, and some of its financiers, Lachlan Murdoch and James Packer, were described by journalist Paul Barry in a book *Rich Kids*.

**Parmalat** In early 2003 Parmalat was placed in provisional liquidation. Its unexpected collapse revealed a 'black hole' of around 14 billion euros in its accounts, making it one of Italy's and Europe's most notorious corporate collapses.

**Reid Murray** RMH, or Reid Murray Holdings Limited (Reid Murray group), headed in its latter days by Ossie O'Grady.

**RMA** Reid Murray Acceptance Limited, formed to act as a corporate 'banker' for Reid Murray Holdings Limited.

**Rothwells** Western Australia-based merchant bank headed by the colourful financier Laurie Connell. Rothwells was pejoratively described as a 'lender of last resort' for high-risk ventures. Rothwells' and Connell's activities were scrutinised during the WA Royal Commission into WA Inc.

**Rowland, Tiny** Founder of the multinational Lonrho and a crucial player in the final downfall of Bond Corporation, especially the worldwide distribution in late 1988 of the notorious 'Financial Analysis' document detailing Bond Corporation's 'insolvent' state of affairs.

**Royal Mail** Royal Mail group, headed by the Royal Mail Steam Packet Company Ltd – the world's largest 1920s UK ocean liner group run by the former Governor of the City of London, Lord Kylsant.

**Skilling, Jeffrey** Enron CEO who resigned in August 2001 just prior to Enron being placed in bankruptcy.

**Stanhill** Stanhill Proprietary Ltd, family company of Stanley Korman, founder of the SDF group including SCL (Stanhill Consolidated Limited), SDF (Stanhill Development Finance Limited), Chevron (Chevron Limited) and SD Pty Ltd (Stanhill Development Proprietary Limited).

**Tyco** One of the new millennium corporate collapses that presaged the *SOX* reforms. Its CEO was Dennis Kozlowski.

**Westmex** Westmex Limited was a 1980s conglomerate 'high-flier' headed by Russell Goward during its brief rise and fall from 1986 to 1990.

**Whitehead, Alfred North** UK educator and philosopher. One of his insights was that a major fallacy of argument involved recourse to a proposition *as if* it was a fact, simply because others had said so many times previously. He described this as the fallacy of 'misplaced concreteness' (1919/1925).

**Williams, Ray** One-time deputy chairman and CEO of HIH.

# Abbreviations

| | |
|---|---|
| AA | Arthur Andersen. |
| AARF | Australian Accounting Research Foundation, formed in 1966 as part of the profession's response to the spate of 1960s corporate collapses. |
| AAS | Australian Accounting Standards, which have had the force of law under Australia's Corporations Law since 1992. |
| AASB | Australian Accounting Standards Board, the major standards-setting body since 1992. |
| AICPA | American Institute of Certified Public Accountants. |
| AIFRSs | Australia's modified version of the IFRSs, officially adopted in 2005. |
| APB | Accounting Principles Board (United States Accounting principles-setting body, 1959–71). |
| APES | Accounting Professional and Ethical Standards |
| APESB | Accounting Professional and Ethical Standards Board |
| APRA | Since 1998 the Australian Prudential Regulatory Authority has been Australia's national prudential regulator of the activities of the banks and other financial intermediaries. |
| AQRB | Audit Quality Review Board, a self-regulatory body formed in 2005 and funded by the two major Australian accounting professional bodies to monitor the audit practices of the four major accounting firms. |
| ASA | Australian Society of Accountants (predecessor body of the ASCPA). |
| ASAu | Australian Standards on Auditing, which have had the force of law under Australia's Corporations Law since July 2006. |
| ASC | Australian Securities Commission, the successor to the NCSC as Australia's national corporate regulator (1991–98). It was replaced by ASIC in 1998. |

| | |
|---|---|
| ASCPA | Australian Society of Certified Practising Accountants; was renamed in the late 1990s as CPA Australia. Together with the ICAA, this body represents the public face of Australia's accounting profession. |
| ASIC | Australian Securities and Investments Commission, the successor to the ASC as Australia's national corporate regulator (1998–). |
| ASRC | Accounting Standards Review Committee which was set up in November 1977 by the NSW Attorney-General, Frank Walker. It reported in May 1978, under the title *Company Accounting Standards*. |
| ASX | Australian Stock Exchange Ltd, formed in 1990 from an amalgamation of Australia's state stock exchanges. In 2006 it merged with the Sydney Futures Exchange and was renamed ASX Ltd. |
| ASXCGC | ASX Corporate Governance Council. |
| ATO | Australian Taxation Office. |
| B&M (Berle and Means) | Adolf Berle and Gardiner Means, authors of the 1932 classic, *The Modern Corporation and Private Property*. |
| BCCI | Bank of Credit and Commerce International. |
| CAMAC | Corporations and Markets Advisory Committee. |
| CASAC | Companies and Securities Advisory Committee. |
| CCA | Current cost accounting. This was one of the proposed systems of accounting examined in many countries in the 1970s to replace or supplement historical-cost accounting. |
| CEO | Chief executive officer. |
| CFO | Chief financial officer. |
| CLERP 9 | Australian Commonwealth Company Law and Economic Reform Program No 9 discussion paper, *Corporate disclosure: Strengthening the financial reporting framework*, September 2002; parts of which were enacted as legislation 30 June 2004 under the *Corporate Law Economic Reform Program (Audit Reform & Corporate Disclosure) Act*; it includes a number of reforms to the *Corporations Act 2001* (Cth). |
| Conglomerate | The type of corporate vehicle that occurs when unrelated activities (companies) are acquired through takeover or merger. |
| Enron | Enron Corporation. It was later euphemistically referred to as the *Crooked E*. |

| | |
|---|---|
| EU IFRSs | The European Union version of IFRS adopted and effective from 2005. |
| Fair Value | This method of reporting items in financial statements has become the preferred basis in most national standards and the IFRSs for reporting many assets and liabilities. It is defined by the FASB as: the exchange price (exit price) in an orderly transaction between market participants to sell the asset or transfer the liability in the market in which the reporting entity would transact for the asset or liability. The transaction to sell the asset or transfer the liability is a hypothetical transaction at the measurement date. |
| FASB | Financial Accounting Standards Board (United States Accounting Standards-setting body, 1972–). |
| *Financial Review* *(AFR)* | *Australian Financial Review*, a major daily Australian business newspaper. |
| FITB | Future income tax benefit. |
| Foozle | A supposedly short-term managerial action deemed to be on the 'grey line' of what is lawful; subsequently often followed by clearly more fraudulent actions as the perceived 'short-term' financial problems worsen. |
| FRC | Australia's Financial Reporting Council. Formed in 2001, it has oversight responsibility for the governance of corporate financial reporting practices under the *Corporations Act 2001* (Cth). |
| FRCLSE | Financial Reporting Council of the London Stock Exchange (1990–). |
| FRP | The Financial Reporting Panel, an alternative dispute resolution body in relation to the treatment of accounting standards, which alleviates ASIC from initiating court proceedings whenever a dispute arises regarding the application of accounting standards. |
| FTC | Federal Trade Commission, US regulatory agency formed in the first decades of the twentieth century. For a period it had responsibility for overseeing accounting practices. |
| GAAP | Generally Accepted Accounting Principles. |
| GAS | General Accounting Standard. |
| GEERS | Government Employee Entitlements Redundancy Scheme – implemented 12 September 2001 and revised |

|  |  |
|---|---|
|  | 1 November 2005 – provides a 'safety net' for employees made redundant, often in a group liquidation. |
| IASB | International Accounting Standards Board, formed in 2001, has carriage for the setting of International Financial Reporting Standards (IFRSs). |
| IASC | International Accounting Standards Committee, international accounting standards-setting body, 1973–2001. |
| ICAA | The Institute of Chartered Accountants in Australia (1928–). |
| ICAEW | The Institute of Chartered Accountants in England and Wales (1880–). |
| IESBA | International Ethics Standards Board for Accountants – a committee within IFAC. |
| IFAC | International Federation of Accountants. |
| IFRSs | International Financial Reporting Standards set by the IASB. Previously known as IASs. |
| INED | Independent Non-Executive Director. |
| IOSCO | International Organization of Securities Commissions emerged in April 1983 with the transformation of its ancestor, inter-American regional association (created in 1974), into a truly international cooperative body. |
| IRS | Internal Revenue Service (US). |
| ISA | International Standards on Auditing issued by the relevant arm of IFAC. |
| ISC | Insurance Supervisory Commission (1998). It was replaced by APRA in 1998. |
| JCCFS | Joint Committee on Corporations and Financial Services – a joint committee of Australia's federal parliament. |
| JCPAA | Joint Committee on Public Accounts and Audit – a joint committee of Australia's federal parliament. |
| Mark-to-market accounting | The process of stating all non-monetary assets at their current market prices. |
| Mark-to-model accounting | A method of mark-to-market accounting used by Enron. The model drew on discounting procedures to arrive at a 'synthetic' market price for Enron's asset holdings of energy (and other) derivatives. |
| Matching | A convention (sometimes referred to as a rule) within the conventional historical cost-based accrual system of |

accounting. It is the accountant's method of building into the accounts the anticipated linkages between expenses incurred and the expected future revenues.

MUA — Maritime Union of Australia.

NAS — Non- audit services.

NCSC — National Companies and Securities Commission – national corporate regulatory body (1981–90). Replaced by the ASC.

NED — Non-Executive Director.

NPV — Net present value.

NSW — New South Wales.

OECD — Organisation for Economic Cooperation and Development.

Opting-in — An *ex ante* administrative arrangement proposed by CASAC and considered (but rejected) as part of Australia's *CLERP 9* corporate law reforms.

Opting-out — An *ex ante* administrative arrangement discussed in the 1982 UK Cork Insolvency Committee as a posssible *ex ante* administrative arrangement. It was not put forward as a preferred proposal by Cork.

PCAOB — Public Company Accounting Oversight Board (a private-sector, non-profit corporation, created by the US *Sarbanes-Oxley Act* of 2002 in response to the wave of accounting and audit scandals); to oversee the activities of auditors of public companies in order to protect the interests of investors and the public by ensuring the provision of 'informative, fair and independent audit reports'.

POB — Public Oversight Board (part of the SEC Practice Section of the AICPA).

Pooling — A legislative arrangement whereby the assets and liabilities of separate entities may be pooled in an external administration. It has been recommended for adoption in the Australian Government's ED *Corporations Amendment (Insolvency) Bill 2007*.

Ramsay Report — *Independence of Australian Company Auditors: Review of current Australian requirements and proposals for reform*, prepared on invitation of the Australian federal government, October 2001, by Professor Ian Ramsay, the Harold Ford Professor of Law at the University of Melbourne.

| | |
|---|---|
| SAC | Statement of Accounting Concept, issued by Australia's standards-setting body, AARF. |
| SEC | Securities and Exchange Commission, formed in the US in 1933 during the Depression as part of the New Deal. It assumed many functions previously held by the Federal Trade Commission. |
| SEESA | The Australian federal government established the Special Employment Entitlement Scheme for Ansett employees for the purpose of making these safety payments to Ansett employees if there was a shortfall in asset realisations. |
| *SMH* | *Sydney Morning Herald*, a major Australian daily newspaper. |
| *SOX* | *Sarbanes-Oxley Act, 2002.* |
| SPE | Special Purpose Entities. |

# Acknowledgements

We publicly acknowledge our gratitude to Angelika and Nicole Dean, and to Jeanette Clarke, for their continued encouragement and forbearance over the many years it took to bring our examination of corporate collapse and accounting to this point, and to the accounting iconoclast Ray Chambers, without whose mentorship and inspiration (even following his death in 1999) it would never have commenced or have continued into this third book in the series.

Hopefully through this work Ray Chambers' ideas will remain, in his words, 'an irritant to the accounting profession to ensure that it continues to seek ways of continually improving its practices', and concomitantly to improve the products on which users of accounting information so desperately rely. Only then will the market system be able to eliminate the continuing indecent disclosures, restore the public trust that has been so shaken over the years by events like those post-2000 at, say, HIH, One.Tel, Harris Scarfe, Enron, WorldCom, Parmalat, Vivendi and more recently at Fannie Mae, Westpoint, Fincorp, James Hardie, Sons of Gwalia and other *causes célébrès*.

This is the third in a series advocating the 'Sydney School' of accounting's push for reform of the law of company accounts, first proposed by Chambers in his 1973 *Securities and Obscurities* monograph – later published as *Accounting in Disarray*. It augments the ideas and evidence detailed in the first and second editions of our *Corporate Collapse* by drawing on some material therein, on subsequent works published by the authors, and on new material and ideas. By bringing these matters together, by connecting the pieces of the jigsaw into a complete picture, the historian, as Jordanova (2000) observes, 'bears witness' to decades of writing, comment, and debate, and reveals an issue of public importance that requires atttention.

We gratefully acknowledge permission to reproduce modified extracts of the following articles: Clarke, F. and Dean, G., 'Corporate officers' view on cross-guarantees and other proposals to "lift the corporate veil"', *Company and Securities Law Journal*, Vol. 23, 2005b, pp. 299–320; and Dean, G., Clarke, F. and Houghton, E., 'Corporate restructuring, creditors' rights, cross-guarantees and group behaviour', *Company and Securities Law Journal*, Vol. 17, 1999, pp. 73–102. With permission by the © Lawbook Co., part of Thomson Legal & Regulatory Limited, http://thomson.com.au. Blackwell Publishing is also gratefully acknowledged for permission to reproduce extracts from the following: Clarke, F. L. and Dean, G., 'An evolving conceptual framework?', *Abacus*, October 2003, pp. 279–97, and several *Abacus* editorials 2002–2006 written by Graeme Dean. A modified extract from the article Clarke, F., Dean, G. and Houghton, E., 'Revitalising group accounting: Improving accountability', *Australian Accounting Review*, November 2002, pp. 58–72 is reproduced with the kind permission of CPA Australia.

We wish to thank Carl Harrison-Ford for his superb guidance generally, specifically on literary style and matters of expression. Also the Cambridge University Press copy editor Lee White for her patience and professionalism in her final editing, Glen Sheldon, Cambridge University Press Commissioning Editor for suggesting that we submit a proposal, Kate Indigo for keeping us to schedule, and to Cambridge University Press for their continuing support of our work.

# Prologue: Gilding the Corporate Lily

> We should speak ... of the immorality of accounting; for it has been the quirks of accounting that have provided many of the opportunities for misdemeanours of ... corporate officers.    (Chambers, 1991, pp. 16–17)

This book is set against a background of inquiries into discrepancies between what has been disclosed by corporations about their trading affairs and the financial outcomes of them, and what is more likely the 'truth' in respect of both – corporations gilding the lily. Matters that are its focus are currently being played-out across several continents.[1]

In this regard 2006 may yet have proved to be a pivotal year. In Houston in the middle of the year, the world witnessed the lengthy trials and convictions of Kenneth Lay and Jeffrey Skilling on charges relating to alleged wrongdoings that resulted in misleading the investing public about Enron's financial health. Prior to its collapse the utilities giant could claim to be the seventh largest corporation in the nation.

Both men were convicted of having caused the downfall of the company they built into that colossus, but more importantly because they had misled the public, auditors and regulators about its financial health. Lay was also convicted in a separate trial on four charges that he misused bank loans to buy Enron stock. Prosecutors successfully contended that Lay and Skilling directed a conspiracy that hid billions of dollars in debt in dubious off-balance sheet deals, illegally shifted funds to hide losses at poorly performing units and tapped reserve accounts to impress Wall Street. The convictions emerged after 54 government and defence witnesses, including Lay and Skilling, had their say in the witness box. In a dramatic twist, the court adjourned till 11 September 2006 (9/11) for sentencing to occur, only to then delay it for another month.

Being convicted specifically on 19 of 28 counts of fraud, conspiracy, insider trading and lying to auditors, on 23 October 2006 Skilling was sentenced to serve 24 years and 4 months gaol for misleading the investing public about the financial health of a company. Kenneth Lay had a different fate. Initially found guilty on counts of federal fraud and conspiracy that carry a maximum custodial penalty of 165 years, Lay suffered a fatal heart attack in early July. In

1

mid-October 2006, in accord with legal precedent, Judge Sim Lake vacated Lay's conviction and dismissed the indictment against him. Other officers of Enron were not so fortunate – several were also imprisoned including: Richard Causey, chief accountant (5.5 years), CFO Andrew Fastow (after turning state's witness and assisting the prosecution in the Lay and Skilling trial he received six years in prison, two years community service), and several other lower level officers for various lesser terms.[2]

Just prior to Skilling's sentencing (and as this book was nearing completion), other notorious figures were also imprisoned, including: Bernie Ebbers of WorldCom infamy who began a 25-year gaol sentence; and Dennis Kozlowski, Tyco CEO who was convicted of misappropriating corporate funds and sentenced to a minimum of eight years gaol.

As the dust settled, the 'Crooked E's' ordeal was nearing its end, but not before it had emerged as a watershed in corporate affairs, insofar as it was the catalyst for the Bush administration's sudden interest in corporate America's dubious record of living up to its financial reporting claims and its dismal performance in meeting its quarterly earnings disclosures. Notwithstanding previous experiences with Sunbeam, Cendant, Waste Management, Tyco, Adelphia, Qwest, WorldCom and (say) Vivendi, and the frequency of restatements downward from quarterly earnings predictions, Enron was possibly the straw that broke the *corporate* camel's back, too big and too well connected with Capitol Hill to ignore, and all the more so when WorldCom collapsed soon afterwards. However, as a commentator noted, this period and events had all been seen before – 'with their Gilded Age predecessors, combining financial legerdemain and political influence peddling'.[3]

As in the 1930s, the regulatory response was swift. Mimicking Roosevelt's New Deal 'truth in securities' mantra of the early 1930s, 'corporate governance reform' would dominate in the first decade of the twenty-first century. New corporate *rules of engagement* for the US were set out in the 2002 *Sarbanes-Oxley Act (SOX)*, and this supposedly was 'problem fixed'!

In Australia, with its Enron equivalent dramas in the form of the collapses and subsequent revelations at HIH and One.Tel, the regulatory response also was swift, though of questionable wisdom. Once again corporate governance matters were to the fore – this time the plea was to ensure auditor independence. In mid-2001 the federal government commissioned an inquiry which produced the Ramsay Report, *Independence of Australian Company Auditors: Review of current Australian requirements and proposals for reform*. It was submitted for ministerial approval in October.

But follow-up legislative initiatives would take longer than in the US. There was greater resistance to endorsing government-imposed black-letter law prescriptions. The proposed independence and other audit-related reforms from the Ramsay Report eventually would be included in deliberations by the federal government as part of its ongoing corporate and economic law reform program (CLERP). After a lengthy submission and review process legislative reforms would be proposed in the September 2002 *CLERP* 9 Discussion Paper, *Corporate Disclosure – Strengthening the Financial Reporting Framework*. The enactment of the *Corporate Law Economic Reform Program (Audit Reform & Corporate Disclosure) Act* on 30 June 2004 included a number of reforms to the *Corporations Act 2001* (Cth).

Drawing on such developments, the contestable claim being made by some is that corporate governance is no longer a *fad*, that the altered system has teeth. But it will be shown below that attempts to water-down the regulations were just over the horizon.

Concurrently with the Enron fallout, European courts and regulators were busy untangling the Parmalat failure in Italy. There, the somewhat different corporate ownership structure, a 'closely held' pattern in contrast with the diffuse US, capital-ownership pattern, revealed that misleading disclosure is a critical ploy in befuddling not only regulators, but financiers and the investing public at large. Members of the well-placed Tanzi family emerged as corporate malefactors with alleged deeds rivalling those in Italy a quarter of a century earlier by 'God's bankers', Michele Sindona and Roberto Calvi,[4] and in the US three-quarters of a century earlier of the likes of the household names, Ivar Kreuger and Samuel Insull; and of the many other financial rogues in the decades in between, everywhere. Particularly significant is that neither the different legal framework underpinning (say) Parmalat's incorporation, different board structure, nor rules relating to auditor appointments of the kind injected into the Sarbanes-Oxley regime, prevented a stark similarity between the alleged acts of deception by Parmalat and those by contemporary US corporates.

In Australia, having achieved minor convictions of HIH's Ray Williams and Rodney Adler on charges not directly related to the causes of HIH's collapse in 2001, ASIC's action to recover $90 million from One.Tel's Jodee Rich and Mark Silbermann for overseeing One.Tel's alleged trading when it was insolvent rolls on. A judgment is not expected until the end of 2007. Of particular interest have been the insights into the workings of non-executive directors in the revelations by Lachlan Murdoch and James Packer that they are able to recall very little about their involvements with One.Tel, other than that they were 'profoundly misled' by the disclosures to them of the company's financial performance and position: a *performance* and *position* so poor as to cost their companies in the order of $900 million. Amongst other things, their experiences raise a cloud over the corporate governance movement's claim of the invaluable monitoring role of independent, non-executive directors.

Concurrently, nearby in another part of Sydney, throughout 2006 other matters involving corporate groups and transactions that were difficult to unravel were being examined. Evidence was taken at the federal government's Cole Commission of Enquiry into alleged bribes associated with the Australian Wheat Board Ltd's contracts for the sale of wheat to Iraq under the United Nations' 'Oil-for-food' program. Under scrutiny are allegations that the alleged bribes were reported as 'trucking fees' so as to not disclose alleged kick-backs to Saddam Hussein's Iraqi government in contravention of UN sanctions under the program. At issue is who knew what, and when it was known. Disclosure again is the issue. On the final days of the Cole Enquiry directors and other witnesses would reveal contrary disclosures to those previously in the public domain for years.[5]

On the other side of the country, the Western Australian Supreme Court was considering two major corporate group imbroglios. In the first, ASIC claims that the directors of the Westpoint property group had misled investors about the use of funds raised by its 'mezzanine' finance companies and an apparent use of a loophole in the corporate reporting regime. Westpoint allegedly used investment schemes to seek funds from investors via $2 companies rather than licensed responsible entities. In this context, questions have emerged in respect of the corporate regulator's supposed inaction, evoking questions such as 'Did ASIC fail over Westpoint?'. Legitimate grounds are raised here for asking whether the national regulator's role should be that of an essentially *ex post* corporate policeman, apprehending and prosecuting, or of a more proactive agent bringing pressure to create an orderly commercial environment.

Westpoint's particulars evoke memories of the notorious early 1990s Estate Mortgage Trusts real estate property saga, with convoluted shuffling of funds between trusts which then invested in several property projects that already had obtained supposedly secured finance. Commonalities include complex corporate structures and equally complex financing arrangements, factors that eventually facilitated the ensuing suffering of the unaware investors, many of whom were pensioners.

In the second case before the WA Supreme Court, *The Bell Group Limited (In Liquidation) & Ors v Westpac Banking Corporation & Ors,*[6] began in 1995 with interlocutory hearings when the Bell Group liquidator, with financial backing from the WA Insurance Commission, sought legal action to the tune of up to $1.5 billion (which includes interest on the amount being sought over more than 15 years). This action concerns the allegation 'that when the [twenty major – Australian and overseas] banks took security for [the $250 million] loans in 1990 they knew the companies were close to insolvency'.[7] By the time the main case finished in October 2006, it was the longest running court case in Australia's history with over 400 days of evidence in three years, a legal cost estimated at $300 million, 63 000 items of evidence and more than 36 000 pages of transcript, not to mention the many trees that had been felled in response to the legal discovery process.[8]

**Illustration 1:** Alan Bond
*Source:* Caricature of Alan Bond, *Australian Financial Review*, 16 January 1995, p. 14. Courtesy of David Rowe.

Briefly, the *Bell* action relates to financing arrangements entered into as the Bell Group of around 80 companies sought loan refinancing from six major Australian and overseas banks, in response to what some have described as a financial meltdown in 1989 and 1990. The liquidator has argued that the banks agreed to extend (restructure) loans to the Bell group of companies, provided they obtained security over assets relative to other unsecured creditors. It needs to be understood that, previously, nearly all debt had been arranged primarily on a negative pledge basis.[9] At issue is how to assess solvency or insolvency from internal and reported financial information within a group setting.

Meanwhile, back in the US, all of the above interest in Enron *et al.* had emerged on top of claims by the New York Attorney-General, Eliot Spitzer, that many large financial intermediaries had engaged in creative financing practices, resulting in companies reporting healthier balance sheets than were justified – as at Enron. This included several large insurance companies that allegedly failed to disclose the full particulars of so-called reinsurance contracts. Specifically, undisclosed side-letters arguably have reduced the claimed reinsurance to that of loans. Indecently, those loans were not disclosed as such to the public. In late

5

September 2006 the US Department of Justice indicted four former executives of Berkshire Hathaway's General Re Corp. and a former executive of the American International Group Inc. on charges that they participated in a scheme to manipulate AIG's financial statements. At issue, reportedly, are two reinsurance transactions between AIG and General Re that allegedly were initiated by an AIG senior executive to quell criticism by analysts of a reduction in AIG's loss reserves in the third quarter of 2000, prosecutors claimed. 'The indictment alleges that the aim was to make it appear as if AIG – one of the world's largest insurance companies – increased its loss reserves, pacifying the analysts and investors and artificially boosting the company's stock price.'[10]

Interestingly, similar claims had featured in the 1930s US Pecora Hearings into the practices of financial intermediaries and investment trusts in the years preceding the Great Depression.

Further group actions involving transaction masking are evident in taxation investigations in the US and Australia. Recently it was reported that the US Internal Revenue Service has been engaged in a long-running battle in respect of the tax years 1989–2005 with pharmaceutical giant, Glaxo SmithKline Holdings Inc., and the company's foreign subsidiaries. At the end of 2006 a transfer pricing case in the US Tax Court was pending. Reportedly the issues relate to transactions 'between GSK and its foreign affiliates relating to US profits of pharmaceutical products and payments made by the US branch for products and trademarks developed by the company's UK-based parent company. It has been reported that the IRS and Glaxo have reached an historic settlement whereby Glaxo has agreed to pay the IRS approximately $3.4 billion (including interest).'[11] Similar tax issues also resonate in Australia, where ATO chief Michael D'Ascenzo, while acknowledging that tax 'havens [are] not all bad', reportedly stated that the ATO was increasingly aware of companies making complex transactions with foreign companies to avoid paying withholding tax, typically using 'hybrid entities and hybrid securities'.[12]

It is worth contemplating how the advent of IFRSs, AIFRSs, or EU IFRSs will supposedly change this position. Regarding insurance, it is suggested by some in the industry that the position may be worsened. Two-thirds of respondents to a KPMG survey of Australian insurance companies perceived that the 'adoption of IFRSs had actually increased the risk of inaccuracy in financial reporting'.[13] In the areas of accounting for taxation, derivatives, goodwill impairment and business combinations (merger accounting), various parties including financial commentators, bodies representing directors, shareholders and analysts (*inter alia*) are raising serious questions about implementation and interpretation issues with the IFRSs. Some are suggesting that directors should report to shareholders in a myriad of ways, resulting in 'the annual report being less relevant'.[14] Others are concerned about the volatility in earnings associated with applying IFRSs.[15] Other concerns have been expressed, including those in a recent set of empirical papers on the impact of IFRSs.[16] Still others view the IFRSs as an unnecessary intervention, overly prescriptive, and argue that the market should be allowed to determine which voluntary disclosures will prevail.[17]

Central to those discussions are questions regarding the reliability, accuracy and overall probity of corporate information disclosures. Contestable phrases or words, often touted by regulators and standards setters, imply a desire either to achieve *quality accounting information* or *transparency*. Such issues are supposed to be at the forefront of those seeking to produce an international conceptual framework, viz the IASB and FASB who are jointly undertaking such an exercise. While not questioning the motives, elsewhere the current authors have provided an assessment of the less than fruitful outcomes accompanying earlier national exercises that were underpinned by similar desires.[18]

The above illustrations are important for the light they throw on the role of financial disclosure in creating the orderly commercial environment, essential to the proper functioning of market economies. Importantly, whereas the reports of defaults and anomalies might be taken to be indicative of the new corporate governance mechanism biting into and exposing corporate wrongdoing, on closer analysis they emerge to be repeat performances of the *indecent disclosure* by companies over the past 160-odd years. They frequently are the product of their compliance with standards and rules issued by professional bodies with the best-of-intent result. Matching the current corporate governance regimes against those of the past offers little comfort, for it serves to indicate that, for the most part, the current regimes contain 'more of the same'. Little that is new has been introduced. It would seem unlikely that the matters currently under judicial review would have been prevented (or disclosed) had the latest IFRSs been in place in their current formats.

In fact, the current talk of corporate governance and the various codifications, schema and recommendations might be doing more harm than good. For if, as we argue here, the rules they specify are impotent, the representation of them as panaceas for corporate ills is likely to lure investors into a sense of false security. There is a burgeoning literature reporting research associating compliance with the various governance regimes and 'superior corporate performance'. In contrast, there is little addressing the problems of the modern corporation in this age of globalisation. 'Legacy thinking' draws upon experiences in the different corporate environments of the past, seducing would-be reformers into massaging the ways of dealing with corporate problems of the past, without much explicit recognition of differences between the past and the present. A critical issue is whether the conventional corporate form with which most are familiar (and in respect to which the current governance regimes are directed) can indeed be governed adequately, if by governing we are referring to its original notion of controlling or *steering*.[19]

7

The relatively easy access to international capital markets and the ease with which companies might move between alternative jurisdictions to exploit perceived advantageous trading, labour, stock exchange listing, and financial disclosure rules, militate against exercising control over conventional corporate structures with updated versions of past regulatory mechanisms that failed to override less sophisticated and less complex arrangements than those to which they are currently being applied. There is little ground to expect that they will be any more successful in the future.

The now Netherlands-based James Hardie group's contemporary, worldwide ongoing battle with governments, unions and the victims of asbestos-related diseases has provided a salient example of the problems with the conventional perceptions of the corporate structure. That the form of the corporation, as it is generally understood and blithely accepted, has a legitimate *place* in modern society is contestable. Doubt that the corporation as we know it – with its grouping of subsidiaries under the umbrella of 'limited liability within limited liability' – can function for the benefit of modern commercial society is evoked by the conflict between commercial and legal realities inherent in the notion of a sacrosanct *corporate veil*. That situation is exacerbated by the seeming inconsistency between the traditional notion of the corporate objective to maximise shareholder wealth and the now popular notion of corporate social responsibility, the limitation of financial statements compliant with conventional accounting practices to show present financial position and past financial performance in terms of what the public expects, the potential conflict between legal obligations and alleged ethical responsibilities and the frequent misunderstanding of public perceptions regarding the nature of the corporate vehicle and the reality of it.

Possibly, the Hardie asbestos affair has better served to highlight those matters than various other failures. The series of transactions in 1997/98 involving the Lang Corporation (loosely described as the Patricks/MUA Waterfront affair) perhaps comes a close second.[20] And whereas the legislative likes of the US's *Sarbanes-Oxley*, Australia's *CLERP 9* and the ASX Corporate Governance Council's *Corporate Governance Guidelines* (and their overseas equivalents) have poured out rules in particular for the internal management of corporations, the Hardie affair has drawn an outpouring of proposed rules regarding companies' interactions with the public at large. Of particular interest is the manner in which the debate regarding Hardie's alleged misdeeds has renewed the personification of corporate ethics. But whereas the artificial persona of the corporation has been translated (as we noted above) into an almost human equivalent, in a twist its true fictional character has been reinforced by the NSW state government's threats to 'lift the corporate veil' were Hardie to not meet its perceived financial obligations to those suffering from or having died as a consequence of the toxic effects of its asbestos products. The NSW Attorney-General in mid-2006 proposed to have a federal inquiry examine ways to prevent the type of episode at James Hardie, where a wealthy (solvent) parent company could avoid picking up 'the personal injury compensation obligations of insolvent subsidiary companies'.[21] That proposal is partial. It involves only considering issues related to this corporate group type of limited liability related to compensation for personal injury and death.

In a curious way, the plight of those victims of asbestos-related diseases has made it clear, possibly the clearest in 160-odd years, that the corporate structure (especially where groups are prevalent) is not sacred; that, at the end of the day, if it is no longer serving commerce in the way the UK Gladstone Committee and those 1840s politicians intended when pressing the British Parliament to enact the *Companies Act of 1844*, the present company structure can and ought to be changed.

That possibility doesn't seem to have been contemplated by those reacting to the successive waves of corporate collapses and crises over the past century, and over the past several decades in particular, when shareholders', finance and trade creditors' and (more recently) employees' financial woes have been to the fore. It is no surprise then, that the solutions being presented in the form of corporate governance rules have been framed with an underlying assumption that the current form of the corporate vehicle with its 'limited liability within limited liability', shareholder sovereignty and corporate veil framework, is untouchable.

A peculiar feature of the current debate over corporate shenanigans in the recent past is the similarity they bear to those revealed following the worldwide 1929 crash and ensuing Depression, to the effect that the financial statements of many companies were grossly misleading: grossly misleading, not only by virtue of deliberate acts of deceit, but also as a consequence of following the prescribed accounting conventions (rules) of the day, possibly with the best of intentions. Now, as then, few seem to appreciate the prospect that the reported financials of the companies that have not failed, those deemed the current high-fliers and 'travelling swimmingly' so it seems, are possibly as misleading as those that have crashed or are noted to be in trouble.

In the early 1930s the general lead taken in the US was to specify accounting 'rules' (incorrectly labelled then, and now, as 'principles') for the processing of financial aspects of business transactions, and disclosure rules for reporting the financial outcomes of them. That push for rules (enabling the tick-a-box mentality) to govern accounting practices has been pursued for the best part of 70 years, underpinned by the idea that comparability would be achieved were each company's financials prepared in accord with the same rules. The mistaken proposition is that uniformity of essentially input and processing rules would produce uniform, comparable financial statements. Yet the falsity in the reasoning of that proposition was clearly demonstrable, and clearly evidenced by the variances in the outputs in the form of financial statements of companies following the same rules.

Few seem to recall that, just as in the 1920s when the UK Royal Mail's drawing upon past profits to pay current dividends accorded with the *rules* of the day,[22] in the new millennium Enron's use of special purpose entities to hide debt was facilitated by a professionally prescribed ownership *rule*. Nor do they recall that the mark-to-model valuations to bring prospective profits to account had regulatory approval; as did Cambridge Credit's front-end-loading mechanism to calculate current profits in 1970s Australia; while in the new millennium WorldCom's expense capitalisation was arguably the product of the conventional accrual system, differing little from Australia's Reid Murray's capitalisation of development expenses in 1960s Australia.

Little has been recalled in the context of WorldCom's woes of the UK's Rolls-Royce's 1970s fall following its capitalisation of the costs of developing its innovative RB-211 engine. Waste Management's alleged depreciation charge scam is as much a product of accountants' contestable idea that depreciation is 'an allocation of cost', rather than a 'decrease in price'. Again, that the same problem had arisen with US airline companies in the 1950s passes without mention. Perversely, following the rules has emerged a legitimate, often as well-intentioned as intentionally deceitful, means of misleading accounting, a simulacrum of a quality mechanism.

Significantly, the practices causing the shaking of heads in outrage now, in one form or another have all happened previously. In other disciplines the habitual recurrence of undesirable events would provoke thoughts that perhaps there was something awry with the system within which they were being repeated. And certainly, failed means of preventing the repetition of unwanted outcomes would be abandoned. Curiously, in business matters the response of legislators and professional standards setters has been precisely the opposite. The failed remedies of the past have not only been repeated, in most instances they have been multiplied – more rules of the kind known to have failed in the past have been heaped upon existing ones, even though their deterrent effect and their clout to back up imposing penalties on individuals for wrongdoing have dismal histories.

Throughout all this the ways and means of lessening culpability have been encouraged by regulators, including plea-bargaining which has become the norm in the US and seems to be growing in Australia. Regulators have traded-off their responsibility to apprehend and penalise wrongdoers with the prospect of potentially easier convictions of others. Plea-bargainers have become primary witnesses for prosecuting regulators. Andrew Fastow was thus a primary witness against Kenneth Lay and Jeffrey Skilling in the Enron case. His evidence shows that the case against those officers rests more upon what their previous collaborators disclose than what the regulatory machinery has uncovered from examining public data. In the Australian cases against HIH offenders, an HIH executive Bill Howard turned Crown witness in return for indemnity against conviction. It may not be unkind to suggest that the sentiment underlying Roosevelt's quip that 'you have to set a thief to catch a thief' still prevails. Roosevelt was responding to criticism that he had appointed Joseph Kennedy (then considered by many to be a modern-day robber baron) to be the first head of the newly formed SEC in 1934.[23]

Lack of transparency, misleading disclosure – *indecent disclosure* – has characterised traumatic failures of the Enron, HIH variety. In particular, annual statements of financial performance and financial position have not presented accurate, reasonably reliable, portrayals of companies' dated wealth and periodic progress. In today's and yesterday's jargon they have not ensured 'transparent', 'truthful' financial reporting. Were they to have done so, for the most part the financial outcomes disclosed would have facilitated informed evaluations, signalled the appropriate questions to ask of managers and executives, alerted those with an eye for wrongdoing. It would have been irrelevant how company directors had acted – with propriety or with deception, in their own best interests or in the interests of the shareholders or a wider stakeholder cohort, with or without regard for social and environmental wellbeing, with or without business acumen. Fair dealing is a hallmark of a civilised society. It is grossly *indecent* that the commercial environment lacks the *order*, the *framework*, necessary for fair dealing. There is lack of trust by participants that the regulated market system is actually fair game. It is consistent with many participants' view that the market fails to operate *as if*, as Oscar Wilde's Sir Robert Chiltern quipped in *An Ideal Husband*, it has a 'commercial conscience'.

Still, the current hullabaloo has not been without its benefits. Misleading reporting of financial outcomes has been at the centre of the numerous inquiries into and prosecutions for corporate wrongdoing. Inappropriate disclosures have been noted. Earnings management practices were alleged to have facilitated companies like Enron, WorldCom, Tyco, Vivendi, Waste Management, Sunbeam, Disney and the like in the US to meet analysts' quarterly earnings predictions, to have underpinned many of the analysts' questionable 'buy' recommendations uncovered by Attorney-General Eliot Spitzer, and to have assisted the alleged tactics of some, like the US analyst guru, Jack Grubman, to push up WorldCom's share price.[24]

A spotlight on financial disclosure has evoked the questioning not only of the rules directing how companies account and report, but also whether the system should remain *rules-based* or become a more *principles-based* system.[25] A primary claim by the regulators has been that the rules are followed frequently, but the intention underpinning them is not. But there has been little compelling argument to support the proposition that the principles said to underpin IFRSs (of whatever persuasion) differ from the earlier described rules (sometimes

11

labelled principles) prescribed by national accounting bodies. That convoluted debate has witnessed those promoting the International Financial Reporting Standards to argue that they are, in contrast with the practices in accord with the rules promulgated by (for example) the US Financial Accounting Standards Board, principles-based. But there is not any undergirding, primary principle identified, suggested or specified in that debate.

The latest (albeit) preliminary discussions related to the joint IASB/FASB Conceptual Framework exercise which began in mid-2006 continue to fail to accept that any accounting conceptual framework needs to be grounded in the realities (principles even) of commerce, linking accounting with the ethical, legal, financial, economic, metrical and other foundations of business. Achieving this on an international basis is a huge challenge. Consider one such principle, the legal (based on ethical) *true and fair view* principle. Whereas one might presume that the British (and European generally) true and fair criterion governing the quality of financial disclosures has the historical and potential technical credentials to fit that role, it is not universally accepted as a basis for overriding a required compliance with the accounting standards specified.

It would appear that, ultimately, rules will prevail. This is a situation which possibly, in the present climate, best satisfies auditors' responsibility to form and report an opinion as to whether a company's financials are truly and fairly indicative of, or fairly present, its wealth and progress. For whereas auditors' performances have been criticised in the fallout from company failures, given the faulty foundations of accounting, their task is all but an impossibility.[26] We note with interest as this book is going to press, the following: 'KPMG to be sued for 2 billion by Fannie Mae in the US'.[27] To which a KPMG spokesperson has indicated that the firm will counter-sue. The Fannie Mae claim reportedly is based on an argument that there is a need for auditors to do more than adopt 'tick-a-box' mentality and to use professional judgment. This is a major theme in our book. Another theme is that it is problematic whether extant accounting standards (and the proposed IFRSs) facilitate or hinder the making of such professional judgments about whether accounts show a true and fair view (chapters 4 and 5).

It will be fascinating to see KPMG's defence as the Fannie Mae case unfolds over the next few years.

These and their related issues are addressed in *Indecent Disclosure*. In corporate matters all that glitters is certainly not gold. Accordingly, several themes course through what follows. First, that financial disclosure in accord with conventional accounting generally fails to disclose a company's wealth and progress and that the newly heralded IFRSs will do little to remedy that; second, that the corporate governance regimes currently in place are misplaced and do not offer remedies for the corporate ills evident in history and repeated in the recent past; third, that auditors' near impossible task is alleviated neither by the prospect of companies' compliance with the IFRSs nor by the implementation of the general features of the corporate governance regimes; fourth, and most importantly, though it runs counter to the thinking underpinning the current corporate governance regimes, there is increasing evidence that the prevailing corporate structure needs radical modification to cope with, and be governable in, the modern business environment.

# 1

# Indecent Disclosure: Omitted Factor in Unexpected Failure?

the story . . . [is about the] 'System' of which [the fraud] is the most flagrant example, . . . it shows that through the workings [of the System] during the last twenty years there has grown up in this country, a set of colossal corporations in which unmeasured success and continued immunity from punishment have bred an insolent disregard of law, of common morality, and of public and private right, together with a grim determination to hold on to, at all hazards, the great possessions they have gulped or captured.

(Thomas Lawson, *Frenzied Finance – The Crime of Amalgamated*, 1905, p. vii)

That could be a description of the particulars at HIH, Enron or any of a dozen other corporate failures in the recent past. It well captures Australia's latest alleged corporate antics under scrutiny at Westpoint. But of course it isn't. Thomas Lawson was writing over a century ago describing events in his 'crime of the century' at Amalgamated Copper.[1] Its resonance with the current state of affairs serves to highlight that over 100 years of ever-increasing regulation, all the ensuing corporate governance measures have achieved limited investor and public protection.

*A bad new beginning* accompanied the early months of the twenty-first century with several cataclysmic events. The world of commerce teetered on an abyss as the dot.com collapse triggered stock market collapses, some by as much as 40 to 50 per cent. For example, the Wiltshire Total Market Index (the *Wiltshire 5000*), claimed to be the broadest market index as it measures the performance of all US-headquartered equity securities with readily available price data) had declined from the 24 March 2000 high approaching 15 000 points to just over 8000 on 16 July 2002. In dollar terms more than $US7 trillion had been 'lost'. The world's wealth had nearly halved, with financial tremors felt around the world. At the time of this book going to press the index was approaching but had still not regained its pre-April 2000 levels.

During the two-year interregnum shocking images of the two towering World Trade Center infernos of 9/11 took centre stage. This had a devastating impact on US commerce and it fatally struck down an Australian airline icon, Ansett, and one of Australia's largest insurers, HIH (see pp. 148–54). But worse was to come. Just over a month later came Enron and 'Enronitis', which supposedly captured the penchant of companies to engage in so-called 'earnings management', a practice referred to in previous decades as 'window dressing', 'creative accounting' or 'cooking the books'.[2]

Almost unbelievably, shortly thereafter the world's largest bankruptcy occurred when WorldCom collapsed with a deficiency of assets of over $US11billion.[3] Newspaper headlines worldwide would focus on these events in corporate America for many months and confidence in stock markets around the world was shattered, as indexes fell to their lowest levels since the 1929 Depression.

Lawson (1905) captured the view of the populace at the turn of the century and what would prove to be a similar view in the 1930s. His observations (see quote at head of this chapter) suggested a deep malaise in the 'System'.[4] Much hubris and groupthink were aptly captured in Arnold's (1937) description of the corporate setting at the turn of the twentieth century, as a 'fairyland where men pretended that organisations *were men* who owned property . . . sheer fantasy', and equally so 'the notion that a corporation had the rights of a citizen of the state which incorporated it'.[5] Also, Brooks in his account of the 1920s UK Royal Mail affair wrote about the System 'maintaining the power of those . . . who had . . . become mere personal money-spinners, their personal position and gain being secured to them'.[6]

Interestingly for our *leitmotif*, Lawson's description of Amalgamated's early 1900s collapse as the 'crime of the century' is but one of many since that might rightly claim that mantle. Consider the 1920s' Kreuger and Insull financial imbroglios noted already and discussed later (chapters 2 and 5) with their intertwined investment trusts and companies and equally complex financing arrangements, which had prompted the quote by Arnold in his *Folklore of Capitalism* and underpinned Sir Collin Brooks' *Royal Mail*.

Corporate complexity and concealment are recurring features of corporate activity, confirmed by similar accounts each decade from the 1930s up to the present. Previously, we noted that the issue of groupthink continues to be integral in modern day commerce – at least of the twentieth (and as Enron so aptly illustrates, now the early twenty-first) century form of corporate capitalism.[7] Primarily Anglo-American examples were given there of the corporate entanglements during various decades throughout the twentieth century.[8] What is not often well understood by an outsider is the seemingly 'mission impossible' faced by directors, auditors and regulators, not to mention investors, creditors (including employees) and other interested parties, in unravelling the financial and other affairs of such Byzantine monoliths.[9]

Fast-forwarding a century after Amalgamated, another major contender for the corporate 'crime of the century' duly emerged. Enron's incredible fall from grace confirmed what many had suspected, that all was patently not well on Wall Street.[10] The dot.com fallout had yet to be properly assessed when earnings restatements, *à la* Enron, became the norm.[11] Accounting restatements and irregularities and auditing crises became premier media front-page issues. It had taken years for accounting to make it to the front pages of the *New York Times, The Financial Times,* even *The Times!* Now the world's stock markets were in free fall, as corporate commentators invented another buzz word – 'Enronitis'. That focus has proven to be another deflection from the real issue of addressing the systemic problems in corporate disclosure.

Several accounts of the Enron affair capture well many aspects revealed so compellingly in the movie *Enron: The Smartest Guys in the Room.* They canvass the chilling impacts of unfettered corporate power, the propensity for unethical behaviour by market participants, the inadequacy of the purported checks and balances within the 'system', and unqualified audited opinions on dodgy financial statements. But they have also inadvertently invited several misconceptions regarding both the uniqueness of the event and its possible impact on the corporate world. The point is, there is nothing **new under the sun**.

Despite the prominence given to it, Enron is merely a standout amongst the most recent of the many similar corporate crimes of the previous 160-odd years since general incorporation by registration in the UK, notwithstanding increasing rules-based regulations of the **genre** now being promoted under the corporate governance flag. Consider the UK skullduggery in the late 1840s by the Eastern Counties Railway Company boss, George Hudson (the 'Railway King'),[12] the US's Jay Gould's and other 1870s financiers' manoeuvrings giving rise to the notorious 'robber barons' tag; Ivar Kreuger's massive 1920s International Match Monopoly fraud where millions of investors and governments around the world (including the supposed corporate-savvy US) were duped,[13] and Samuel Insull's 1920s Insull Utilities Investments fiasco (coincidentally, like Enron, dealing with energy[14]); William DeCoster's (alias Philip Musica's) 1930s McKesson & Robbins' massive drug inventory fraud; Bernie Cornfeld's 1960s Investors' Overseas Services worldwide financial fraud – so powerful was his conglomerate it was said that the value of the US dollar was affected by its activities; the 1960s/70s Equity Funding of America insurance scam; the 1980s US Savings and Loans real estate property scandals; Italy's Banco Ambrosiano involvement with the Vatican's *Istituto per le Opere di Religione,* and those embroiled in the alleged murders of Roberto Calvi and Michele Sindona; the worldwide games played by Agha Hasan Abebi in the early 1990s at the Bank of Commerce and Credit International; and Nick Leeson's 1990s bank derivatives scam that brought down the historic House of Barings.

In relative terms (either with losses being expressed in real dollar terms or relative to national GDPs, or number of employees affected) even the Australian collapses – Bond Corporation and HIH – rank with Enron, WorldCom and others noted here.[15] While the type of asset and whether fraud was involved varies across the cases, there are many commonalities that we focus on below.[16]

Despite over 160 years of companies' law inquiries (culminating most recently in Australia's 2004/05 *CLERP 9* legislation and in the US's 2002 *Sarbanes-Oxley Act* [*SOX*]), it is contestable whether current regulation is any more likely to be in a better position to prevent the 'commercial crimes' of the kind listed above. However, Enron's collapse and the spate of earnings revisions by US companies that followed it are being hailed as the catalyst for a major breakthrough, once and for all 'fix-it' regulatory governance reforms. Claims that the modern response is different are debatable.

It will be argued later (chapter 5) that the current legislative efforts (e.g. *SOX* and *CLERP 9*) are a repeat of history. That the 1929 crash, in which companies' balance sheets were exposed to be 'full of water' and reported profits greatly inflated, was likewise, the catalyst for Roosevelt's 1930s 'once and for all' fix-it New Deal 'truth in securities'. This supposed 'fix-it legislation' would set up the US corporate regulatory agency, the Securities and Exchange Commission, as the corporate overseer. And other countries many years later would follow suit – such as Australia's states' Companies Commissions and then the National Companies and Securities Commission.

Regulation of the kind underpinning the current variety of procedural governance reforms has a record of failure. Yet, for the most part Australian regulators (and their counterparts overseas) appear to be embracing many aspects of the US-style 'more of the same' governance regimes. Regulation is directed at imposing more about how directors and auditors do, rather than what they do, apparently without much regard for the inherent defects in the system in which they have to function, and the emphasis remains on rules not principles.[17]

It is worth noting that Enron's financial manipulations are presented as being facilitated by its alleged use of mark-to-market accounting. Many claimed that one of the problems in the late 1920s and early 1930s was the abuse of asset revaluations ('appreciation' was the label then) to produce creative accounts. Showing the money's worth of items was not the cause of the problems in either era. The 1930s asset valuation critique was shown to be falsely based.[18] Regarding the current position, it is well documented that Enron's 'futures' contracts were valued under its 'mark-to-guess' or 'mark-to-model' techniques for which (perhaps foolishly) in 1991 it had been granted approval by the SEC. Enron never valued assets directly at market prices, never had any recourse to exchange prices. It injected its accounts with 'synthetic' prices expressly conjured-up for the purpose – amounts inherently non-corroborable, non-auditable. Yet these practices were approved by the corporate watchdog – the SEC – and endorsed by the auditors. Hence, contrary to the lore, Enron did not use mark-to-market accounting.

Enron functioned in a flawed regulatory environment; an environment in which the techniques used almost ensured that without any intention to mislead, financial disclosures would be misleading. It is questionable whether Enron's executives – Lay, Skilling, Fastow, *et alios* – really had to be all that smart. Thus, it is curious that the regulatory search for answers has focused almost entirely on 'patching up' a failed rules-based system.

Whereas there has been action on the part of the regulators, business interests and the professional accountancy bodies, it has lacked the appropriate focus. The reasons why were rehearsed in the Prologue. First, financial disclosure now compulsorily pursued in accord with conventional accounting generally fails to disclose the wealth and progress of companies, and the recently fanfared IFRSs will do little to remedy that; second, prior and current corporate governance regimes are misplaced, do not offer remedies for the corporate ills evident in history and repeated more recently; third, auditors' extremely difficult task of providing a quality control assurance is not alleviated by either the prospect of compliance with the IFRSs or by the implementation of the general features of the corporate governance regimes; fourth, it may be that the prevailing corporate structure needs modification to cope with, and be governable in, the modern business environment. Accordingly, the message of chapter 1 is that existing regulatory and governance initiatives, while having many virtues, are unlikely to mitigate the recurring underlying features that have emerged in the autopsies of so many large, essentially *unexpected*, corporate failures.

Whereas most of those failures over many decades have entailed some deviant corporate behaviour, inasmuch as there were departures from the conventional or approved practices, for the most part, the accounting generally complied with the Standards.[19] At the margin, there are always likely to be deviations. In some instances deviations from the approved practices exhibited more common sense and possibly produced better data than would have compliance with the Standards. Consider, for example, Adsteam's tactics in Australia in the 1980s to avoid misleading consolidation techniques, and many decades earlier in the US, Samuel Insull's alternative to 'depreciation' in respect of accounting for long-life assets. A reasonable analysis of consolidated data in accord with the Standards is easily shown to be grossly misleading, based upon false premises, employing senseless procedures, and inducing analyses that contradict company law, financial fact and financial common sense.[20] Spalvins was lampooned by the profession for booking Adsteam's 'capital gains' as part of his profit calculation, but that made more sense than excluding them, and Insull had argued the eminently sensible proposition that long-life asset depreciation based on changes in market prices made more financial sense than the profession's view that depreciation be charged as an 'allocation of cost' irrespective that the market selling price of the asset had increased.

Even with the advent of the IFRSs, this perhaps unintentional misdirection of society persists. This is especially evident as the IFRSs have introduced questionable rules on impairment and allow only some capital gains to be recorded. This partial aspect is considered further in chapters 4, 5 and 9.

To continue this theme consider the particulars at Enron briefly noted above – much of their supposed manipulation of SPEs to record periodic gains on energy contracts was shown to be in accord with SEC-approved practices and approved by Enron's auditor. Of course, some other practices were not, as have been detailed in many accounts of the Enron failure.[21] But, even the *compliant* might produce misleading data. What is clear is that the major corporate governance changes introduced everywhere in the 1990s, and seemingly adopted at Enron, proved ineffective.

Taking Enron's hotly criticised inclusion of gains under mark-to-model accounting, consider it against the current general rules for bringing into account periodic gains on construction contracts (for example, the percentage of completion method) – how different are they really from what Enron did? Consider also the allegations that WorldCom had deviously *capitalised* some of its expenses. Perhaps WorldCom overstepped the bounds of common sense, but conventional accounting practice has been essentially an expenditure capitalisation system. In part this persists in the IFRSs. Think about the general reasoning underpinning matching within accrual accounting – the accountants' way of building into accounts the anticipated linkages between expenses incurred and the expected future revenues. It is an exercise fraught with the risk of error. WorldCom's manipulations could just as easily have occurred without any intention to deceive, mislead, or improperly massage the outcomes. And similarly, consider Waste Management's alleged manipulation of depreciation policies in relation to its vehicle fleet. But the actual practice followed convention to the extent that the mechanics of the depreciation calculations were legitimate. By simply increasing the 'useful life' assumption related to fleet vehicles, hundreds of millions of dollars were removed from the P&L – profits were increased accordingly![22] And this was at a time when Waste Management's business was deteriorating. Consider the equal scope for genuine error and deviant manipulation in estimating the useful lives of assets – a matter all the more senseless considering that the accountants' 'allocation of cost' notion is an 'accounting invention'. This is so, since 'depreciation' is taken to be the 'decrease in price' (*de pretium*) everywhere it seems other than in accounting – a matter of *indecent disclosure*, at possibly its most bizarre.

Regulatory initiatives in the decades before and after the beginning of the twenty-first century by Australia's ASIC, APRA, the US's SEC and like organisations in other countries are structured to effect *external* control of corporate affairs – how they function, what they report, what documents they file, what is disclosed in them, etc. These are 'patched up' from time to time in response to company crises. One might have presumed that the latest (almost tidal wave of) crises would have convinced governments that this form of 'control' had failed. It was the catalyst for governments' external agencies to switch their focus to imposing on companies *internal* mechanisms for controlling their affairs. These have taken the form of 'corporate governance regimes' intended to impact companies' internal workings and structures, to discourage wrongdoing, and to embed a more ethical corporate culture. In some countries the imposition is mandated; in others it is more subtly introduced by self-regulatory persuasion.

While corporate governance as a notion has been around for aeons, we argued elsewhere that it has become a fad in recent years.[23] Unfortunately, emphasis at present is on the integrity of the process – emphasising, *ad nauseam*, side matters such as director and auditor independence, or whether CEOs are receiving too large a remuneration in the form of options. Meanwhile consideration of the quality of the outputs of the financial reporting system takes a back seat. Such a switch in emphasis fails to recognise the importance of addressing fundamental matters related to disclosure. As well as structural and other disclosures, there needs to be a rethink of the financial data disclosed by corporate entities, especially when aggregated as a group. As this book goes to press we are somewhat heartened by recent press concerns over how the CEO options are disclosed in accounts – headlines like 'Tell the truth about CEO pay: Reported salary totals do not reveal all'[24] suggest that perhaps there has been a change and that the accounting measurement and disclosure issues are receiving their deserved attention. This matter will be explored later.

Earlier corporate reformers, such as Hawkins,[25] were definitely on the money in suggesting that by the end of the nineteenth century the real issue was not about 'whether disclosure' *per se* was important, but rather 'what and how much should be disclosed'. What Hawkins observed then would be repeated in the period after the revelations of financiers' and companies' malpractices in the lead-up to the Depression, that '*disclosure* is the *true disinfectant*', '*publicity* is the *sine qua non*' of the 1930s US New Deal's *Truth in Securities* legislation. Decades later Chambers was almost a sole voice speaking of the need for the 'reform of the law of company accounts'.[26]

Today's reformers continually argue the need for *transparency* and *quality* accounting information. While no one can argue with the intent conveyed by the *transparency* and *quality* descriptors, the basic nature, the substance, of companies' accounts remains largely unchanged. Hawkins' and others' critical position still holds – it is essential to address 'what' and 'how much' should be disclosed in the phantasmagorical world of corporate group accounting. In chapter 6 we show a great opportunity was lost in the late 1970s in Australia to redress a parlous state that existed.[27]

We are told that this will change with globalisation and the likelihood of universal compliance with the IFRSs. There is said to be a strong desire to move from the mixed accounting system, that couples the capitalisation of expenditures to value-based data, to a system based on 'fair values'. Whether this will produce more serviceable financial data is problematic for the several reasons expounded throughout this book, not the least of which is the pervading unwillingness of the reformers to link accounting numbers to companies' present control over money or its equivalent. Whereas companies' structures and their social roles have changed over time, the canons of financial calculation are the same now as when the modern corporation was conceived in 1844.

## Corporations and change

Events at the beginning of this century suggest that perhaps the modern corporation is 'ungovernable' in its present form. Throughout this book it is argued that:

- The case for corporate reform should pursue less detailed regulation of the integrity of processes and more effective consideration of whether their outcomes are serviceable;
- Regulatory mechanisms should emphasise *ex ante* protection, rather than *ex post* penalty;
- In general, accounting standards should be more *principle-based*, less *rules-compliant*. The current fixation on IFRS compliance as a panacea is misplaced and misguided, given the perception that the IFRS is a principles-based system; and
- Specifically, there is need to address the fundamental structure of accounting and auditing for the corporation. Conventional views regarding recourse to the separate legal entity and group accounting ought to be reassessed.

*Incorporation and privilege* proves to be a critical point of departure in economic activity in many countries. And the ongoing argument for differential reporting is an excellent setting in which to illustrate the difficulties in controlling the emerging modern corporate vehicle and to better appreciate our argued positions. Debate persists as to whether society should contemplate different accounting rules for different types of corporations – small and large, public, private, not-for-profit. Should a 'one-size-fits-all' financial reporting approach be applied by the national regulators in considering what accounting standards to impose on those myriad types of corporations?

Debate on differential reporting has regained centre stage as the proposed international IASB's 2006 ED 48 *Presentation of Financial Statements* would mandate that companies required to provide regulatory reporting filings by national regulatory bodies like the SEC and ASIC must file general purpose financial reports, as defined in relevant national conceptual frameworks, such as Australia's SAC 2.[28] They will thus be subject to the burden of complying with IFRSs. Some suggest that to apply those all-embracing accounting standards, designed for general purpose financial reporting by publicly listed companies, would create a reporting schema that is unreasonably onerous on private companies.[29]

Requiring all regulatory reporting companies to be financially transparent and to file general purpose financial reports is society's *quid pro quo* for granting the benefits of incorporation (whether to be enjoyed through a public or private company status). Recent debate in Australia's financial press aptly captures the ambivalence to the reality that incorporation is a privilege, not part of the natural order of 'things commercial'. Talking as part of Australia's standard-setting machinery, David Boymal appears to perceive reality as disconcerting: 'We've got a bit of a dilemma', he notes, grappling with the notion that the financial affairs of private companies are nonetheless public matters. 'One cost' of incorporation, he opines, 'is that how [financially] the company is going should be on the public record'.[30]

It has been suggested that the problem lies not with a proposed IASB ED 48 standard, but with the possible interpretations of what is meant in the SAC 2 definition of 'general purpose financial reports' when referring to 'providing information to meet the common information needs of users [presumably broader than just shareholders] who cannot command the preparation of reports tailored to meet their particular information needs'.[31]

Others claim that many users do not require investment-type information predicated under IFRSs; rather, they need information pertaining to 'governance, management and accountability issues'.[32] Australian financial observer and valuation commentator, Wayne Lonergan, citing pragmatism, observes that 'in the vast majority of cases international comparability of SMEs' financial statements is not relevant to the needs of the preparers of and users of those reports'.[33] Possibly so.

But, as part of the orderly financial framework, it might reasonably be counter-claimed that the financial position and the financial performance of companies trading and employing in the public arena are little different from the point of view of creditors, customers, employees, government departments and the like. The 1978 Report of the NSW Accounting Standards Review Committee noted that, under the Private and Public Interest in Company Accounts, judgments are made by 'creditors and investors, [those involved in] maintaining and improving efficiency of businesses' in the pursuit of 'fair negotiation between companies and their employees, customers and suppliers'. Notions of fairness in dealings, trust engendered by being informed, would seem critical no matter the type of corporation.

Ignorance of the history of incorporation by mere registration beginning in the 1840s, and particularly of the subsequent granting of limited liability in the 1850s, gives unwarranted reasonableness to the distinction being drawn between the rights and disclosure obligations of public and private companies. It is to be noted that incorporation of a privately owned corporation is not a natural or common law right, but is conferred by legislation (in the UK, for example, originally by the 1844 UK *Companies Act*) as the 1978 Report noted '*so that the public interest may be served through the exercise of private initiative*. . . . And limited liability (in the UK post-1855) *was a primary reason for the [quid pro quo] that companies shall periodically prepare balance sheets indicating their assets, liabilities . . .*' (emphasis added). In that context, the notion that private companies' affairs are private and those of the public companies are public is utter nonsense. The ASRC Report notes 'the accounts of companies cannot be regarded simply as a *private matter*, a matter between directors and the shareholders' (emphasis added).

Notably, issues raised in that extract apply equally to private and public (including publicly listed) companies. It is the act of incorporation – with its many ensuing benefits granted by the state – that results in the *quid pro quo* publicity obligations being imposed on the directors of companies.

*Overregulation – going private – 'going dark'* is a topical issue. An Australian newspaper editorial, 'Governance can be overdone',[34] addresses regulatory issues as they relate to private and public corporations. It laments that public companies have *gone private* (or in the modern patois, 'gone dark') to avoid what many believe to be excessive regulatory constraints. Companies are reported to be de-listing in the US for much the same reasons.[35] Similar headlines could be found in other jurisdictions. Comparing Australia to the US, a Melbourne University Centre of Law study of the evidence questions whether this phenomenon is as strong in Australia.[36]

Suggesting there is a need to balance legitimate regulatory intervention when markets fail, with a recognition that there will always be unintended consequences, the Editorial cited in note 34 concludes that it is essential not to place too tight a regulatory straightjacket on public companies' activities:

> This [apparent trend of the replacement of public companies by private equity companies] can't have been the intention of the fine citizens and politicians who campaigned for tougher corporate governance after every share market bust since the early 1970s [see Clarke *et al., Corporate Collapse*, 2003]. Yet . . . waves of corporate regulation – culminating most recently in souped-up governance codes . . . [fosters] a model of corporate capitalism that avoids most of this.[37]

Perhaps so – it is a matter we have more to say about below. But, it is nothing new, 'twas always so! The main issue is whether, as the recent law study suggests,

The *UK Gladstone Committee of Inquiry*, and ultimately the *1844 UK Companies Act*, with its general incorporation by *mere registration*, illustrates the awareness of the corporate privilege. Special granting of incorporation by charter would decline in importance after the 1844 Act. A few charter companies, however, persisted. As was noted earlier, the initial general incorporation benefits provided under registration (including separate persona, the ability to sue and be sued, perpetual succession, etc.) were somewhat offset by mandatory *quid pro quo* publicity requirements and other checks on corporate activity. The limited liability benefit was not associated initially with general incorporation, as the costs and benefits associated with the State granting limited liability to the corporation were not well specified and debate ensued in parliament. The deliberations would last for over a decade. The differential reporting and other modern day debates about the corporation show that little seems to have changed in that respect.[48]

Limited liability was granted with general incorporation under the *1855 UK Limited Liability Act*, but interestingly, this benefit would take around another 50 years to be available generally, in UK and US State corporations laws. *The 1856 UK Companies Act* relegated many of the previous corporate controls (enacted since 1844) to a voluntary set of Articles of Association (Table A of the *UK Companies Act*). A codifying Act in 1862 sought some order in respect of sections contained in all the prior Acts.

There is compelling evidence that the corporation has continually adapted. For what follows in this book, the most important corporate regulatory developments, especially in the US in the latter part of the nineteenth century, were the ability of a corporation (having acquired a legal persona) to acquire shares in another corporation; contiguously, several US states (most notably Delaware) had relaxed takeover and merger constraints, at a time when stock markets had become much more developed – with an increased number of small shareholders providing finance for corporate activity; and concurrently, banks had now become incorporated and they would continue as the major suppliers of finance for merger activity and economic growth.

The last decade of the nineteenth century and first of the twentieth produced what is now referred to as the world's first merger boom. In the vernacular of the time it became known as the 'trust movement'.[49] Perhaps the modern equivalent is the private equity movement that is stumping up today's merger mania.

At the turn of the twentieth century a scenario emerged of many groups of companies, often extremely large, like Standard Oil and US Steel, with 'limited liability within limited liability' becoming more prominent. This was something presumably not contemplated by the 1844 draftsmen. Major scandals involving corporate groups, like Whitaker Wright's London & Globe Group and the US Amalgamated Copper Group, would make press headlines.[50]

Economic boom with concomitant corporate and economic dilemmas produced differing approaches to controlling corporations in the UK and the US. The UK opted for essentially more self-regulatory disclosure, while the US opted for regulation – the so-called States' 'Blue sky laws'. But it is questionable how effective those State laws were. The first two decades of the twentieth century, punctuated by World War I, culminated in the increased activity through reparations payments associated with the Treaty of Versailles. For many countries this initially produced further growth, but it would be followed by the devastating 1922–23 hyperinflation in many European countries (especially Germany, Austria and Hungary). Price inflation peaked in November 1923 when 4.4 trillion Deutschmarks were said to be equal to one US dollar.[51]

But for America, it was to be the Roaring Twenties. Captured appositely in novels like Scott Fitzgerald's *The Great Gatsby*[52] and in the iconoclastic economist Thorstein Veblen's prescient 'conspicuous consumption' observations underpinning his *Theory of the Leisure Class*.[53] The 1920s heralded the 'second merger movement' of the twentieth century. It was accompanied by a massive increase in corporate activity generally, and contiguously by substantial stock market activity fuelled by myriad investment trusts. This *laissez-faire* period created the right setting for the corporate operators, Insull and Kreuger (pp. 34–7).

## Corporate regulation – advent and purpose

Due to the increasing complexity of company structures, their financing and operations, the 'rules and sanctions' *modus operandi* of successive regulatory regimes through the twentieth century has been found wanting. And, whereas the inadequacy of the regulatory rule-based machinery to cope with the current structure employed by the likes of HIH, One.Tel, Westpoint, Enron and WorldCom is now apparent, the history of regulatory development exposes that those same rules were necessary if the co-regulatory system of accounting and corporate structuring were to survive. Rules are amenable to a transparent tick-a-box strategy, with little need of any regulatory agency intervention, whereas *principles* might require official adjudication as to whether specific practices are compliant with attendant resource costs.

Depression in the 1930s coincided with or created the forces leading to several national stock market downturns and finance sector manipulations revealed in examinations, like Ferdinand Pecora's US Senate and Banking Inquiry.[54] As noted, the New Deal's SEC emerged as the US corporate cop. 'Big Business' would be subjected to greater controls as its purposes were reconsidered within a regime of greater social scrutiny. After a brief regulatory surge in the first half of the 1930s, the business professionals (accountants and lawyers especially) responded by taking over the running. Self-regulation would re-emerge as dominant in what has been described as an extended co-regulatory environment.[55] The initial regulatory response and counter deregulatory initiatives are understandable if one considers the differing theories of regulation.

While not definitive, the early 1970s and 1980s accounts by Posner, Zecher and Phillips, and Cranston,[56] provide sound summaries of the public interest and private sector pushes for regulation and deregulation. That framework aptly explains how (for example, in more recent times) the US *SOX* legislation is being criticised for being overly burdensome on companies, how the Australian corporate regulator ASIC is being attacked for its performance – as indeed is the financial services regulator APRA. 'Where were the regulators?' is a commonly asked question today – as it was in the 1930s. Perhaps the regulators continue to employ remedies designed for corporations of a different variety, operating in a different commercial environment. Or perhaps it is not unreasonable to suggest that regulators then and now are employing trade-off tactics to secure convictions of prized scalps – the immunity from prosecution of Crown witnesses, for example, with the SEC for Enron's Fastow in the US, Radler in the Conrad Black case and Howard in HIH in Australia, where deals were done to reduce imprisonment for Fastow and Howard agreeing to give evidence against their respective corporate officers under scrutiny.

The SEC has entered into several financial settlements as a means of 'moving on'. It is not suggested here that there should not be deals entailing fines – but the imposition of them seems to be supported on the questionable grounds that they will be a deterrent. Really, they amount to small-beer for a lot of these companies and individuals. But, a legitimate concern of such deals is whether the shareholders really benefit from such tactics. They initially lose through the wrongdoing on the part of suspect actions of some executives, then lose again as the company is fined for the wrongdoing *per se*.

*Regulating the regulators* perhaps is an apt focus of attention.[57] An amalgam of theoretical frameworks encapsulates well the complexity of regulations imposed on those governing the modern corporation and securities market participants. Commentators have proposed that a mix of the 'public interest' theory (especially the branch known as the 'crisis theory' of regulation) and 'capture theory' is descriptive of initial bursts of regulation after any boom/bust period, and the inevitable deregulatory push after the regulatory bursts have subsided. Oscillation has typified the recurring regulatory–deregulatory manoeuverings by business, managements, politicians and market participants during each boom/bust cycle. Recent developments in the US to wind back supposed excessive aspects of the 2002 *Sarbanes-Oxley Act* (e.g. related to the s.404 Internal Controls measures) are apposite. A similar re-evaluation by government of the perceived excessive regulatory cost of doing business is under way in Australia.

Major events influencing the regulation of the modern corporation over the last 80 years support this view.

Big Business in the US dominated the first three decades of the twentieth century. Major corporations like Standard Oil and US Steel emerged as major economic-cum-political players. Often they grew by takeover. Tensions emerged at the political level as to whether corporations were playing too prominent a role and whether their 'economic genius'[58] had been usurped by the political and social impacts, causing concerns for many. This was the beginning of an extended period of nearly a century in which corporations and securities market participants would be subjected to increased, then reduced, controls over their activities. This toing and froing was predicted by Alfred Berle (a lawyer) and Gardiner Means (an economist) in their 1932 classic, *The Modern Corporation and Private Property.*

The Great Crash of 1929 and the ensuing Depression would portend the end of significant stock market activity for several years. It led to a period of increased corporate regulation of both stock market participants and those governing the activities of corporations. Major legal, stock market and accounting regulatory developments in the US, UK and Australia in the aftermath of the Great Crash and beyond have been described by many financial commentators.[59]

Ferdinand Pecora's US Senate and Banking Inquiry pursued a public interest (crisis) theory of regulation, suggesting that after the 1929–30 stock market collapse and the finance sector manipulations (allegedly by leading financiers, like J. P. Morgan), increased regulation in the public interest was inevitable. Amongst other reforms were the New Deal's 1933 and 1934 *Securities Acts* and the associated formation of the SEC. Big Business would be subjected to greater controls as its purposes were reconsidered within a regime of greater social scrutiny. Prominent legislation (for our purposes) included the *Public Utility Holding Company Act* of 1935 prohibiting holding companies operating subsidiaries across state borders, and the *Glass* and *Steagall Acts* which imposed restrictions on financial institutions to minimise potential conflict of interest situations with their clients. Those restrictions have proved to have had limited impact as similar issues resurfaced in the 1970s, 1980s, and two decades later at Enron and with many other public company financings. Regarding those more recent financings, several major institutions have agreed to substantial damages payouts in (no acceptance of liability) out-of-court commercial settlements to actions by the SEC and the New York City Attorney-General.[60]

After a brief regulatory surge in the first half of the 1930s, the accounting profession (especially in the US) responded by taking the running. Self-regulation would re-emerge in the new co-regulatory setting.[61] Accounting rules initially were administered in the 1930s by the governmental agency, the Federal Trade

set of regulations, including s.404 of the *SOX* Act requiring auditors to certify the adequacy of their clients' internal controls. Other matters to be investigated include class actions, shareholder rights, and overall regulatory effectiveness in ensuring that such regulations do not 'dull the allure of the US capital markets'.[72] Similarly in Australia, the April 2006 government-sponsored *Rethinking Regulation Report* was set up to examine concerns that present regulatory responses have gone too far.

The federal government acted on that Report in late 2006 by undertaking a review of all current business regulations. A deregulation response is most likely – if history is any judge. And we can then await the next crisis!

# 2

# Independence: A Misplaced Quest for Honesty[1]

Responses to the Enron and HIH collapses provide a sorry tale. Overdosing on governance rules, and the public's seduction by flimsy evidence in support of them, characterised those responses. Common sense has been outplayed by the false appeal of swift regulatory action. Appearances of good governance have outvalued the reality of achieving it. Seemingly, a regulatory desire to seek heads on poles directed attention from seeking to fix the system, especially as it relates to financial disclosure.

Failure by the regulatory agencies to pursue effectively the ethos underlying the existing laws relating to corporate directors, accounting and auditing, for protecting the general public from losses of the Enron and HIH variety, was probably the prime catalyst for switching the focus of government intervention in corporate affairs. Reactive outbursts by the regulators and the promulgation of a raft of new rules have not too subtly replaced the proposed tactics intended to make companies responsible for internal mechanisms to frustrate malpractice. Corporate governance regimes have been imposed on companies to create structures and inject management arrangements claimed to inhibit the alleged anti-social, unethical antics by corporate executives. In this the malpractices of the likes of Lay, Skilling and Fastow at Enron, Ebbers at WorldCom, Kozlowski at Tyco, and Dunlap at Sunbeam in the US, and the proven illegal behaviour by Williams and Adler in Australia's HIH affair and alleged misleading actions of principals, Rich, Keeling and Silbermann at One.Tel featured strongly.

*Independence* has been anointed the commercial virtue to underpin the governance rules. Independent auditors, independent directors, independent decision-making, independent audit, and independent director appointment, remuneration and succession committees, are seemingly the order of the day. But there hasn't been any demand that those undertaking such roles, serving on those committees, must either have the requisite skills or demonstrate relevant track records. Being 'independent' is the almost sole criterion for entry. The Arthur Andersen audit firm in the US has emerged the poster boy of a supposed lack of auditor independence. Lay, Skilling, Ebbers and Kozlowski have been identified as salient examples of directors, supposedly *sans independence*, while perhaps HIH's and Enron's audit committees emerge as exemplars of how not to run one. All that was decided, treated as a matter of fact, by both the regulators pushing governance regimes and the financial press encouraging them before any *real* evidence was presented to justify the presumptions. It was without any clear enunciation of what independence actually entails, what it means as an operational concept in the context of commercial affairs, without any serious debate regarding why it was such an imperative characteristic, or how it might best be manifested in the ordinary course of corporate affairs.

Human nature is strange. And, when commercial affairs become entangled with politics, it is even more so. If something is said often enough the mantra assumes the mantle of dogma.[2] Yesterday's virtues become today's vices; heroes morph into today's villains. The rise of independence and the demise of Arthur Andersen are cases in point.

## From hero to villain

Enron's fall greased the way for Arthur Andersen's slide into oblivion. But whereas mention of the Andersen audit firm now evokes an image of all that is perceived to be bad in the world of professional auditing, AA previously evoked the opposite response. Through the 1960s and 1970s it was identified as the very paragon of professional virtue, the leader and seminal example of how auditing was to be practised. It had had its heroes, like Leonard Spacek. It had its envied in-house (former seminary) training school, at St Charles just outside Chicago. But from 2001 it has its alleged villains such as David Duncan, who led the Enron audit for Andersen, and Joseph Bernadino, the head of AA at the time of Enron's crash and AA's initial conviction for 'perverting the cause of justice' for shredding documents. While that judgment was overturned on appeal, the damage had been done. The mud had stuck. AA was no longer.

AA's quick demise is curious, primarily because it had earned its previous lead reputation thanks to a longstanding stance against unwanted external influences, resistance against the unwanted pressure from clients wanting their way. It was renowned for its deference to *internal* rules – the Accounting and Auditing Standards of the accounting profession. The AA publication 'A search for fairness in financial reporting to the public' was known throughout the industry as was Andersen's motto, 'Think straight, talk straight'.

Back in the 1930s few could have sensed the place in corporate history of Samuel Insull's death in the Paris metro in 1938. No one could have predicted the connection between Insull's death and the fall of Enron and Kenneth Lay's death, another energy giant and energy leader, seventy years later. As Thomas Edison's 'right-hand man', Insull worked assiduously alongside the pioneer 'electrifying' the US. Insull had a strong technical background and an astute business mind. Not surprisingly, when he had learnt the business he went it alone. In the 1920s Insull established Insull Utilities Investments (IUI) and competed with Edison. There was plenty of business for both of them, for the anti-monopoly legislation ensured a fragmentation of the energy business. For Insull, the various states' legislation in the late nineteenth century that allowed companies to own shares in other companies opened the way for accounting manipulation on a grand scale. Thus, in a curious twist, energy distribution gave both Enron and Insull their footholds in US corporate life, and likewise the inherent scope that group structures give for accounting manipulation.

Funnelling business through corporate group structures has long been a medium for commercial manipulation. Insull perceived this early, building an empire comprising hundreds of related companies by 1928, through which he shuffled his assets in a manner not significantly different from the way others have done it since. By 1928 those companies controlled nearly $3000 million worth of utility properties, had around 600 000 stockholders, 500 000 bond-holders and 4 million customers. Figure 2.1 highlights the 'top-heavy pyramid' that comprised the IUI group – at its apex being two major trusts.

It is not difficult to see how exploiting the separate legal entity principle in such a complex group enterprise to isolate particular liabilities from the assets from which they might otherwise be met could have occurred at IUI. Elsewhere (Clarke *et al.*, 2003) we have shown how years later in 1960s Australia this was also achieved by Stanley Korman's 'round robin transaction' through his Stanhill Consolidated and related family companies, and how twenty years on, Alan Bond allegedly used his Bond Corporation group and 'family companies' to access the cash milked from Bell Resources.

Isolating of creditors for unpaid employment benefits from the assets of the employer company is further illustrative of the technique of utilising the capital boundary. It was the *modus operandi* in the late 1990s in the Cobar, and Woodlawn Mines cases in Australia; and in Patrick Stevedores' attempted retrenchment of employees in the 1988 Waterfront dispute, and the later cases at Steel Tank and Pipes, and that alleged of Bay Building. By exploiting much the same techniques general investors were separated from their monies in Estate Mortgage Trusts in Australia in the early 1990s, and more recently in 2006 allegedly by property developer Westpoint. The potential mischief of the group structure is aptly illustrated by the quarantining of assets alleged to have occurred in the James Hardie affair.[3]

Insull's exploitation of the loopholes for manipulating group structures was provided against a background lacking a prescribed accounting mechanism to prevent or expose it. Thus, unfettered, he was able to transfer assets between the related companies at ever-increasing amounts to 'pyramid' their values as

35

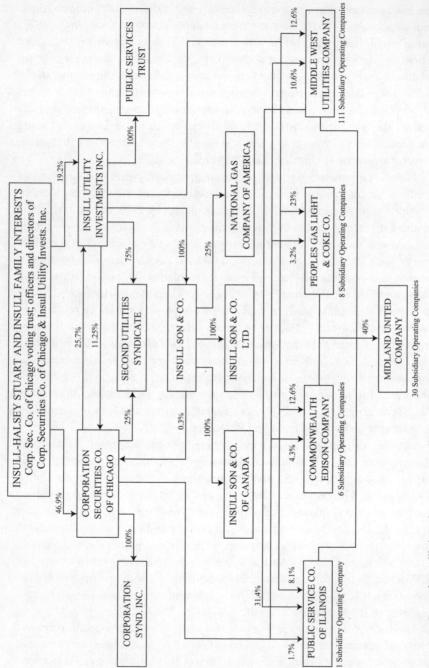

**Figure 2.1:** Samuel Insull's 'top-heavy pyramid' (extract)

they travelled through. Consolidation accounting of the kind currently in force is supposed to eliminate that kind of double counting.[4] As demonstrated in Clarke, Dean and Houghton (2002 and Clarke *et al.*, 2003) it does not ensure seviceable asset values are disclosed. Nor is it likely that it would contribute much either to expose the impact of the Enron-like use of Special Purpose Entities or prevent their keeping liabilities off the balance sheet. We shall return to the mischief of consolidated financial statements in chapters 7 and 9.

Insull, like others since, used the group structure and the accounting for it to create the asset-rich impression of an asset-poor empire. It was an exemplar of 'gilding the corporate lily'. When stocks generally fell in the 1929 crash, his companies were found to be 'full of water', with grossly misleading accounting values ascribed to their assets. With insufficient assets to meet creditors' claims, Insull was brought to trial for suspected fraud in 1932 but McDonald (1962) brilliantly recounts the reasons Insull was acquitted on all counts. Much of the argument depended on the construction placed on matters in the accounts. It was alleged that stock dividends were improperly taken in as income; but the prosecution was forced to admit the question was controversial and that reputable accountants were divided on the issue. It was alleged also that 'organisation expense' was improperly capitalised; but Insull's point had to be conceded when the practice was supported by a Michigan accounting professor. To clinch the matter Insull was shown to have complied substantially with the tax rules. The embezzlement and fraud charges were found to be baseless. And of course, the question of what are appropriate forms of infrastructure valuation and depreciation – other contentious accounting areas where Insull went against convention – remain hotly debated nearly three-quarters of a century later.[5] Significantly, some of what Insull proposed is now the accepted wisdom.

President Bush's post-Enron knee-jerk response to 'fix corporate America' through legislating corporate governance reforms, and the Australian Howard Government's leap onto the corporate clean-up wagon with the mid-2001 Ramsay inquiry and 2004/05 *CLERP 9* governance measures, are reminiscent of the post-Depression vow by President Roosevelt (stung by the unexpected nature of the Insull, Kreuger and other collapses) to put 'truth in securities'. Part of that process was appointing the fledgling Arthur Andersen firm (then known as Arthur Andersen & Co.) to unravel the wreckage of the Insull empire. This was achieved with professional assiduity applauded by the newly created Securities and Exchange Commission. AA had entered the big league, with all the trappings of a natural leader.[6] Insull did not fare nearly as well. After being found not guilty of charges against him in the mid-1930s, he died several years later a broken man.

Paradoxically, Arthur Andersen's work on the failed Insull energy juggernaut made the AA firm a household synonym for auditing expertise and professionalism. However, in the 1990s it was its alleged role in the collapse of the 1990s

Enron energy giant that made it a household name for the alleged lack of such qualities.

## If you say it often enough . . .

Repetition may be indicative of truth. But, casual observation shows repetition as likely to be capable of deluding – that if one says or even implies something often enough, many will treat it as if it were an axiom.[7] That aptly describes the pervading focus on the separation between ownership and control of the Berle and Means[8] variety in the discussions following the more recent US and Australian collapses, especially those by Enron and HIH. That focus spawned the idea that compulsory corporate governance regimes were imperatives in attempts to improve corporate regulation. First, there was the impression that those corporate governance prescriptions were novel solutions to a perceived opportunistic behaviour by professional managers for their own rather than their companies' shareholders' benefit. Second, there was an imbedded impli-cation that the opportunistic self-interest of managers, auditors and the like cannot be engaged for the shareholders' benefit. And third, that the more the system of internal corporate governance is micro-specified, failures of the kind that have attracted public outrage in the recent past will be avoided.

Whereas there are elements of likely validity in each of those presumptions, the collective focus of them diverts attention from the most insidious aspect of many of the larger corporate failures, in particular the element of surprise when an apparently stable, reportedly successful company unexpectedly crashes. Surprise occurs insofar as the systems of accounting failed to disclose the true financial outcomes of whatever professional managers had done and failed to disclose reliable data for deriving indicators in the drifts in financial affairs over time. That is most damaging to public trust and confidence in the corporate way of engaging in commerce,[9] and most damaging to the pursuit of an orderly com-mercial setting. Misleading disclosure militates against the informed risk/return assessments so important for orderly commerce being made.

Spawned in the maelstrom of public outcry following unexpected corporate collapses, corporate governance reform has been thrust centre stage. Myriad proposals have emerged for better controlling the activities of those given the responsibility for managing corporate resources. They have entailed mecha-nisms intended to monitor and control the undesirable aspects of the agency problems arising, as predicted by Berle and Means[10] over seventy years ago, in consequence of the separation of ownership and control of modern corpora-tions. What Berle, in particular, continued to forecast for decades is that there is no longer an effective entrepreneurial factor when corporations become the vehicle of economic activity. The 'corporation man' loses that function.

It is worth contemplating the 1900 to 1930s corporate world when *The Modern Corporation and Private Property* and another of Means' works, *The Holding Company: Its public significance and its regulation* (co-authored with J. C. Bonbright), were written. In the former Berle and Means had noted the emergence of the professional agent-manager in the aftermath of the large consolidation of corporate activity through the activities of the robber barons in the decades prior to, and at the turn of, the century.[11] Trusts had quickly emerged as dominant vehicles. No doubt B&M exhibited considerable prescience, although whether they really sensed the manner in which corporate activity would develop, especially since World War II, is questionable. Berle's (1965) revisit to the issues that he and Means had addressed many years earlier suggests, perhaps, it is more that he thinks they 'got it right', though possibly for the wrong reasons.

In the current setting, global corporations are the norm rather than the exception (Bakan 2004; OECD, 1999). Corporate America in the period during which B&M made their observations was characterised by the growth in utility companies and the railways, against which the few Carnegies, Vanderbilts, Morgans and Goulds stood out. Corporate America was virtually an island. Multiple and dual listings of company shares on the international exchanges, and the number of significant international mergers and acquisitions of the magnitude witnessed by the modern mergers of, for example, AOL and Time Warner, or Daimler-Benz and Chrysler, are unlikely to have been envisaged. While B&M documented an increasing concentration of power in the hands of a few, corporations of the size of Enron, WorldCom, Sunbeam, Fannie Mae, Waste Management or Vivendi are unlikely to have been in their focus. Nor could they have envisaged the potential for several companies to operate with political connections, of the kind demonstrated by those of the Halliburton ilk. Only occasional examples like Kreuger and Standard Oil existed in the 1920s and earlier.

Possibly also outside B&M's thinking were repeated collapses of the proportions that could individually shake public confidence, such as occurred following the fall of Europe's Vivendi and Parmalat, the US's Enron and WorldCom, or that rattled the insurance industry in Australia with the fall of HIH (with estimated losses of $5.3 billion). It is unlikely that B&M had envisaged cases of losses of the magnitude of approximately $4 billion (incurred by the National Australia Bank in its US 'Homeside investment') could be followed so quickly by the losses in its unfettered forex 'rogue trading' affair, or the commercial dismay when the sixth largest company in Italy in 2003, Parmalat, fell from grace (with losses approaching 14 billion euros).[12] All of these were singular events, rather than part of a wholesale economy and worldwide collapse such as underpinned the 1929–32 crisis. Even more unlikely is that B&M would have had in their minds the possibility that the latest spate of relatively sudden collapses[13] could have come after similar recurring spates of financial crises (and often failures) of household corporate names in preceding decades.[14] But those outcomes are not inconsistent with the potential implications of the separation between ownership and control that they noted.

Repeated assertions regarding managerial opportunism appear to have paid off. There have been assertions that managers left to their own devices will act in their self-interest. There is a widespread phobia that commercial order is threatened by the incapacity of directors and auditors to form honest judgments, independent of undue influences. Linking directors' remuneration to external evaluations of their company's stock and by implication to its performance, is reportedly said to make them less honest. Claims are reportedly made that the more closely auditors are involved with the day-to-day affairs of the clients, the greater the range of non-audit services they provide, the less likely they are to form honest opinions on the financials. Those assertions are undeservingly accorded commercial authority to underpin the often lauded, but seldom challenged, concatenation of governance regimes.

## Invisible hand of self-interest

Events attending company failures frequently supported Adam Smith's observation around 230 years ago. He appears to have been 'on the money' with his prediction that non-owner managers would likely be more cavalier with 'other people's money' than with their own, that the *invisible hand of self-interest* would function in a positive manner, despite the associated moral hazard. Bearing in mind the findings in the cases made against Lay and Skilling, perhaps also in the criticisms of the actions of HIH's Rodney Adler and Ray Williams, Smith's assessment appears extremely well founded.

Perceptions of self-interest underpin the allegations of wrongdoing by those at the helm of Australia's latest surprise corporate wrecks, Westpoint and Fincorp. Yet it does not necessarily follow that financial reward is the primary motivation for corporate foozles[15] or malpractice. Samuel Insull did not appear to have amassed any particular fortune from dubious guidance of his utilities empire into bankruptcy. Indeed, he died penniless.[16] Nor did the search for financial reward overly influence John Spalvins' leadership of Adsteam in 1980s Australia.[17] Understandably, however, the managerial self-gain thesis has driven most of the modern governance regimes.

Coursing through the original 1932 Berle and Means thesis is the central theme that: 'The separation [in the modern corporation] of ownership and control produces a condition where the interests of the owners [of the enterprise] and of [the enterprise's] ultimate manager may, and often do, diverge.' Of course, their assessment was made against the backdrop of the fallout from the corporate and individual excesses of the three decades prior to the 1929 crash – especially the proliferation of share ownership leading to it, the practices of the share-hawkers (Galbraith, 1971), and the exposure of the false impressions that financial statements had given of the wealth and progress of companies that failed. That evaluation was of the hazards attending the pursuit of commerce, indeed of Western capitalism, through the medium of the relatively primitive corporate structures of the time. They were primitive insofar as nothing as large in absolute terms (nor certainly as complex) as an Enron existed. The extensive legislation and other matters of company regulation that have emerged since the Great Depression, frequently of a catch-up nature, are suggestive of an underlying belief of a possibly intractable problem.

In the context of their concern for the potential problems arising from the separation of ownership and control, Berle and Means' assessment that large public companies were the dominant institution in the modern world, might (perhaps with hindsight) be taken as a warning. That, were the trend to continue, modern corporations could become progressively more (if not totally) ungovernable, the US lawyer, Bakan (2004) asserts. If we read into their assessment a prediction of how corporate matters would eventuate over the next seventy years, they were extremely prescient.

That connection has not been missed by some observers of the fallout from the most recent of US 'corporate scandals'. Culp and Niskanen in their *Corporate Aftershock* (2003), for example, note how the reliance upon an 'independent board' emerged as the favoured governance mechanism to protect the shareholders. They allude to that consensus view of corporate governance having failed on some notable occasions. In 1973, 117 of the *Fortune 500* US companies were found to have engaged in serious misconduct.[18] These were mainly accounting and auditing irregularities, despite audit committees having been recommended by the SEC as long ago as 1939 and by the NYSE in 1940. By the 1970s such committees were said to be not uncommon.[19] Such observations and revelations are mostly made in the belief that the US's Financial Accounting Standards Board's responses and the US Foreign Corrupt Practices legislation would curb similar actions in the future.

As the almost never-ending evidence shows, accounting defaults have persisted. Not only have there been continued unexpected failures or shenanigans making front-page headlines, but there have also been continual announcements of earnings restatements. There have been repeated admissions of accounting errors, SEC prosecutions and no-fault settlements by US companies,[20] and allegations of certain outlays being claimed to be 'facilitation' payments or in Australia's AWB case, 'trucking fees'. On 4 October 2002, the GAO issued a report entitled *Financial Statement Restatements: Trends, Market Impacts, Regulatory Responses, and Remaining Challenges.*[21]

That report included a listing of 919 restatements identified as having been made because of accounting irregularities between 1 January 1997 and 30 June 2002. It was updated in 2003.[22]

A curious aspect of Culp and Niskanen's inquiry is that they appear to have an expectation that the system will self-correct, that it will become functional. Yet a diagnosis outside of the commercial setting exposing those and the similar events recurring on a progressively grander scale over some thirty years, despite increasing regulation, would prompt serious questioning of whether the remedy was exacerbating the problem. There should be a questioning of whether the proliferation of accounting and other rules was the panacea implied, and whether compliance with the rules produced data any more indicative of a company's wealth and progress than those driving the SEC penalties and settlements.

Virtually none of the brouhaha surrounding the recent collapses have questioned whether the modern corporation is governable, or at least governable through the current mechanisms that are being reshaped continuously. Because it has been said often enough that it can be, it has become dogma. But the hope placed in the rules-based response to the alleged abuses of managerial opportunism is contestable. Indeed, the dogma of corporate governance is mostly a product of repetitive assertion of its validity.

Revisiting the corporate scene forty years after Berle and Means sowed the seeds of the idea that corporate mayhem would emerge from the separation of companies' ownership and control, Berle confirmed that little has occurred to change his view. But he acknowledged that corporations have changed and that the corporate setting now differs from that when he and Means outlined their case which spawned (with help from others, like 1930s to 1960s economist Ronald Coase[23]) agency theory. In particular, he noted that neoclassical economics no longer holds. Shareholders are no longer owners of the kind depicted in B&M's earlier thesis. A notion of property rights attaching through the holding of shares was no longer a valid, practical proposition. We might reasonably wonder then what they would have made of almost all the waves of corporate collapses being accompanied by alleged malpractice by directors, managers of one kind or another, accountants and auditors – all agents supposedly in place to advance the interests of their principals. We might likewise ponder their likely surprise at the regulators' slow learning in the wake of successive waves of what in current terms amount to corporate governance revisions that for the most part have merely increased the specificity of what already existed – in reality, perhaps more tweaking, patching than reforming.

Berle's rethink has implications for the potential usefulness of the governance mechanisms currently in vogue, for they are underpinned strongly by an assumed validity of the agency theme – the idea that without them shareholders' rights are likely to be impugned. However, if those rights are as uncertain

**Table 2.1:** Categories of restatements and category descriptions

| Categories of Restatements | Category Description |
|---|---|
| Acquisitions and mergers | Restatements of acquisitions or mergers that were improperly accounted for or not accounted for at all. These include instances in which the wrong accounting method was used or losses or gains related to the acquisition were understated or overstated. This category does not include in-process research and development or restatements for mergers, acquisitions, and discontinued operations when appropriate accounting methods were employed. |
| Cost or expense | Restatements due to improper cost accounting. This category includes instances of improperly recognising costs or expenses, improperly capitalising expenditures, or any other number of mistakes or improprieties that led to misreported costs. It also includes restatements due to improper treatment of tax liabilities, income tax reserves, and other tax-related items. |
| In-process research and development | Restatements resulting from instances in which improper accounting methodologies were used to value in-process research and development at the time of an acquisition. |
| Other | Any restatement not covered by the listed categories. Cases in this category include restatements due to inadequate loan-loss reserves, delinquent loans, loan write-offs, improper accounting for bad loans and restatements due to fraud, and accounting irregularities that were left unspecified. |
| Reclassification | Restatements due to improperly classified accounting items. These include restatements due to improprieties such as debt payments being classified as investments. |
| Related-party transactions | Restatements due to inadequate disclosure or improper accounting of revenues, expenses, debts, or assets involving transactions or relationships with related parties. This category includes those involving special-purpose entities. |
| Restructuring, assets or inventory | Restatements due to asset impairment, errors relating to accounting treatment of investments, timing of asset write-downs, goodwill, restructuring activity and inventory valuation, and inventory quantity issues. |
| Revenue recognition | Restatements due to improper revenue accounting. This category includes instances in which revenue was improperly recognised, questionable revenues were recognised, or any other number of mistakes or improprieties were made that led to misreported revenue. |
| Securities related | Restatements due to improper accounting for derivatives, warrants, stock options, and other convertible securities. |

*Source*: GAO (2003). Note: we excluded announcements involving stock splits and changes in accounting principles, as well as other financial statement restatements that were not made to correct mistakes in the application of accounting standards.

as Berle implies, the motivation of most of the current governance regimes is contestable.

Despite the incremental creep of governance regimes, continued incidents of corporate malfeasance may well be indicative of the former being focused on conditions that no longer prevail, or at least they no longer prevail as the primary problem. Independence continues to be cited as an essential objective of reforms relating to auditors and directors,[24] when it could equally be argued that the expert knowledge required in an ever more complex corporate world is more likely to be characteristic of those immersed in, dependent for their welfare upon, the affairs of their corporation. Rigging board structures, as some have suggested, to comprise half NEDs continues to be a sought after ideal, though how part-time directors can and will monitor executives' work effectively is yet to be demonstrated. Virtues attributed to having audit committees comprising only NEDs continue to be promoted, notwithstanding the fact that audit committees have been in existence for over sixty years, and have been features of companies involved in spectacular collapses at, for example, Enron, HIH and One.Tel.

But is independence such an unequivocal virtue?

## Independence phobia

Against the background of confusion regarding the general notion of independence, it is no surprise that despite the connections claimed between governance compliance and good performance, empirical studies find, at best, equivocal support for them, and at worst, good reason for a healthy skepticism.[25] First, there is the technical problem that attends all empirical work of that kind, there is the need to assume that commonly present commercial factors that are not, or that cannot be, controlled are either not present, or did not, influence events. Second, there also are the unknown commercial factors that will not be taken into account, and third, invariably questionable proxies have to be used to represent the independent variables under scrutiny. For example, in respect of examining the connection between board independence and superior corporate performance, something such as a majority of INEDs is taken to proxy board independence. Of course, that may or may not be indicative of the overall honesty of the board. And, of course, in any event a statistical association, correlation, is not necessarily indicative of *causation*, and must thus be of limited use in policy formation. We might also consider the Popperian notion of falsification, which invalidates a theory – for example, that there is a connection between complying with the governance regimes and a superior corporate performance – with one negative instance.

Despite the intensity with which it is heralded as a virtue, as a necessary qualitative characteristic of directors' judgment and decision-making, and of auditors' forming and reporting their opinions on wealth and performance of corporations, the notion of independence is virtually useless, operationally bankrupt. But it remains the key characteristic permeating the discussion of directors' and auditors' duties. It is useless because it doesn't faithfully describe or reinforce how essential it is that both directors and auditors in going about their tasks are extremely well informed,[26] and operationally bankrupt because it is, at best, functional only as a reactive rather than proactive tool, and of dubious benefit in either event. Macquarie Bank Executive Chairman David Clarke observed appositely: 'I'd like to see some of the black-letter law dismantled, particularly the stuff that seems to have almost no purpose whatsoever, and more focus on people who think and act independently rather than the tick-a-box mentality'.[27]

Circumstances in which independence is deemed to be at risk appear to get more attention in the governance literature than explanations of exactly what it is that might, as a consequence, be missing. Professional independence according to CPA Australia and the Institute of Chartered Accountants in Australia[28] requires their members to observe integrity in and an objective approach to professional work – so independence is presumably the outcome of acting honestly. But they then continue to declare that that must not only *be*, but also *be seen to be*. A similar line is pursued by the International Federation of Accountants as expressed in its July 2006 Code of Ethics for Professional Accountants (APES, 110).[29] 'Independence in Appearance', the professional accounting bodies explain in their 'conceptual approach to independence', means the avoidance of circumstances which would suggest that 'integrity, objectivity or professional skepticism have been unacceptably impaired'.[30] Both the Joint CPA Australia/ICAA and the IFAC Codes proceed to outline where objectivity and integrity are at risk.

Against that background it is understandable that the governance regimes have been so focused on limiting retired auditors' capacity to take employment with previous clients, requiring auditor rotation, prohibiting or at least constraining auditors also providing non-audit services to improve appearances. In some jurisdictions that focus has been bolstered by superimposed regulatory committees to have oversight of the auditing of public companies. But those governance rules possibly have little impact on the quality of the end product of the audit process, namely a meaningful audit opinion. Insofar as the intention is to improve the quality of auditing, the common requirement, such as the legislative prescription in Australia that auditors declare their independence, is a non-event.

A similar focus on appearance seems to be built into governance mechanisms applied to corporate boards. There is the specification of INEDs comprising

45

minimum percentage membership of boards, and compulsory audit committees comprising only INEDs, in some jurisdictions expensing stock options included in executives' remuneration packages, separating the CEO and board Chair functions, and requiring CEOs and CFOs to sign the financials. Why such signings will result in them showing the wealth and financial progress of the companies complying with the Accounting Standards any more than they previously did, is unexplained. The point is that *appearances* and *declarations* count for little if the reality is missing. Indeed, they are likely to evoke confidence when none is justified, exacerbate the false sense of security, and increase the surprise when reality dawns.

Not only is independence a fuzzy notion to which equally fuzzy preventative measures are applied, but it has also been wrapped in an unnecessarily complicated rigmarole, clouding rather than elucidating the fundamental idea of honesty that lies at the heart of the matter.

It might well be argued that the way in which independence has been pursued in the governance regimes – the *SOX Act*, the 2001 SEC requirements, the 1996 Federation of European Accountants legislation, the 1989 UK *Companies Act*, the UK *Combined Code*, and the *ASXCGC Guidelines*, for example – is likely to constrain auditors' capacities to undertake audits and to form their opinions on whether the financials show their clients' wealth and progress. For whereas the general drift of the propositions driving the governance regimes is that relationships formed between an auditor and client – for example, by virtue of a longstanding audit engagement, or perhaps through the client's employment of one previously on the audit team – increase the risk that an auditor might allow that familiarity to influence judgment improperly in the audit process, the opposite outcome is equally feasible. It might equally be argued that the greater such an association, the greater the opportunity for the auditor to understand the client's business. It is equally feasible that the longer the audit engagement, the more frequently and more widespread the non-audit services provided, the greater the linkages between current employees of the client with the auditor – then the greater the auditor's knowledge and understanding of the client's affairs and, as a consequence, the better positioned the auditor is to undertake an informed audit.

At issue then is not that it is an imperative for the auditor to have the appearance of independence, but that being honest is. And not that it is not being exposed to potential compromise, but *being* compromised that is improper. It is being professional in making judgments, not simply being a member of a professional body, that is important.

Interestingly, empirically the position has been found to be problematic. Numerous studies using large-scale aggregate databases have adduced mixed evidence as to whether the existence of NAS fees impairs auditor independence.[31]

Ambiguity regarding such issues arose also in Australia's HIH Royal Commission. For whereas Royal Commissioner Justice Neville Owen explains being 'independent both in fact and in appearance is fundamental to an effective audit' (section 21.4), he goes on to explain that as 'many people judge books by their covers . . . [it is a matter of] . . . the confidence that the user of accounts may place on the audit opinion'. Thus, the appearance has nothing to do there with the conduct of an effective audit, nothing to do with the technical competency or professionalism of the auditor, but everything to do with whether those who use companies' accounts are well served when they are deceived, when disclosures are misleading, when they are exposed to 'being surprised' by the trappings of false propriety, as so often is the case.[32]

Conclusions were drawn by the SEC that Arthur Andersen's audit independence was necessarily compromised because the firm was receiving consultancy fees amounting to something in the order of $US27 million from Enron. Unquestionably, those fees were large, and equally it has subsequently been alleged that the consultancy revenues were a vital factor in the firm deciding to keep Enron as a client. But equally, the $US25 million audit fees AA received from Enron could be viewed to have influenced its consultancy behaviour. It might be imagined that Andersen would have been no more enthusiastic to risk losing its audit fees by virtue of upsetting Enron management with whatever consultancy advice it gave than it would have been to jeopardise its consultancy fees by the way it conducted or reported on its Enron audit. The penchant for alleging that Andersen lacked independence rests upon a presumed necessary connection between offering non-audit and audit services to the same client, rather than on any established linkage.

Of course it may well be that Andersen was intent on protecting its lucrative consultancy business in Enron, though some have challenged that proposition. *Appearance* was given equal status with *actual*. Assisting Enron's income management through its use of the mark-to-model mechanism and keeping liabilities off its balance sheet through its use of SPEs appear to underpin the complaints against Andersen in respect to its independence offences. But of necessity it must be noted that the mark-to-model accounting mechanism by which Enron had rigged its earnings for nearly ten years had received SEC approval, and the SPEs through which it shuffled assets around the economic group was not only an approved SEC mechanism, but was also disclosed in the Notes accompanying Enron's financials.

Auditors cannot be completely without financial attachments with their clients.[33] They are paid by the company they audit, negotiate their fee with it and sign engagement letters specifying exactly what they are to do to earn that fee. The pervading regulatory wisdom appears to be that some point is reached beyond which the size of the fees is presumed to influence an auditor's judgment, diverting it from being objective and based solely on an observation of the facts, to being subjective in and influenced by the client's way of thinking. But, in any event, in the ordinary course of events auditors are precluded from using professional judgment of the kind demanding objectivity, requiring a correspondence with the facts, and satisfying the professional prescriptions.

Compliance with the Accounting Standards is the profession's conventional criterion for whether the financials are 'true and fair'. Curiously, the auditor's opinion on whether the financials disclose a 'true and fair' view of a company's affairs, its wealth and progress, is taken to be formed on the basis that the prescribed Accounting Standards have been complied with, and not according to any observations by the auditor, not according to how financial position and financial performance are almost certainly understood outside of accounting and auditing. One ought to recall Oscar Wilde's view of the importance of making observations in *An Ideal Husband*: perhaps they have had all the experience but not had the privilege of 'making the observations'. Auditors are thereby directed by their professional bodies and schooled in their education within hallowed universities to understand financial truth as the outcome of a dubious process, rather than an observable set of facts, capable of corroboration. Hence auditors are thus neither financially nor technically independent. Corporate governance claims that the prohibition of appointment longevity and restrictions on post-audit employment enhance auditor independence are little more, at best, than superficial humbug. At worst, they are contrivances that rob audits of the benefits of track record and corporate history.

Curiously, the primary point made by commentators draws upon the seriousness of Andersen's alleged lack of independence in each case, rather than the failure to apply their purportedly unique understanding of the US energy business and the Australian insurance industry. An assumed lack of independence was made the villain, rather than perhaps in some cases an alleged lack of the professional use of the unique skill and knowledge that every audit textbook instructs students to be essential for undertaking a competent and professional audit. To the contrary, the corporate governance regimes' auditor rotation, post-audit employment moratoria, (in Australia) the prohibition of multiple ex-auditor board appointments, and NASs prohibition, generally prohibit the acquisition of independence. Auditors confront a paradox. Those best equipped to undertake an informed audit are denied the role, and those least able to do so are thrust into the role in a setting frustrating their acquisition of the necessary professional skill and industry knowledge. In the extreme, the most independent in those regimes' terms, the inexperienced, the professionally and industrially rank-ignorant, best meet the prescribed governance criteria.

In a most interesting literary entanglement, independence is more often described as the outcome of particular circumstances than it is explained – and particularly more so by pointing to when it is most likely to be absent than to what it is, so that one will recognise it when it's in sight. It is like explaining a motorcar by pointing to a ship and declaring it an example of what a car isn't. True, but useless!

For the most part, independence is defined by default to descriptions to circumstances in which auditors and directors are likely to be tempted to act in their own interest rather than that of their clients' or companies' constituents. This tactic dominates not only the general corporate governance literature, but the auditing literature in particular.

Circumstance appears to have played an accidental political hand in this. When HIH collapsed, the Enron affair was already unravelling. Arthur Andersen had already been accused of having allowed the prospect of future lucrative consultancy fees to influence its judgment on how it viewed Enron's accounting practices, the structuring of its business and how it accounted for the outcomes. That is, its independence was questioned to the point that it was facing prosecution, though not for lacking independence but for frustrating inquiries into its affairs by allegedly shredding Enron-related documents. Independence was the whipping-boy, though, in keeping with tradition, other forms of professionally endorsed dependence were ignored. And just as the Bush administration in the US went after AA in its push to demonstrate its resolve to 'clean-up corporate America', it was no surprise that AA's Australian arm attracted speculation that it too had lacked actual independence in its audit of the failed HIH. No compelling evidence has emerged to support such a claim.

In an equally knee-jerk reaction, the Australian Government embarked upon an inquiry into auditor independence under the chairmanship of Professor Ian Ramsay. While the focus was primarily the independence of auditors, the Ramsay Report's coverage is illustrative of the ideas pervading the overall notion of independence in business affairs. A general theme to be drawn from the Ramsay Report is that where auditors and directors are in relationships that have the potential to influence their judgment, they lack independence.

All of that possibly explains independence in appearance's dual billing – the general exhortation for an 'avoidance of the facts and the circumstances' of the kind that a 'reasonable and informed third party . . . would reasonably conclude . . . integrity, objectivity, or professional skepticism had been compromised' (CPA Australia and ICAA, 2004), and why the Australian, US and UK professional accounting bodies prescribe professional independence to entail both actual independence and the appearance of it. In contrast with independence of mind, 'in appearance' in the terms explained is capable of *ex ante* monitoring. Ordinarily, 'circumstances' can be readily observed. But of course there is no guarantee that what 'appears' to be corresponds to what 'is'. What appeared to be the financial performances and financial positions of HIH, Enron, WorldCom, One.Tel, Harris Scarfe and the like and the lesser reality attest to that. They induced false and costly inferences. An inoperable system of dual criteria prevails. The imperative 'state of mind' can only be inferred after the event. It is impossible to police *ex ante*. In contrast, 'in appearance' back-up criterion applied *ex ante* is as conducive to the making of misleading as to the making of reliable inferences.

In the auditing literature *independence* is implied to evoke *honesty*, and dependence *dishonesty*. Why, is not explained. Honesty is a personal virtue, itself truly unrelated to alignments regarding the sources of individual wellbeing, financial reward and the like. Contrasting honesty with dishonesty seems a more fruitful line to pursue. Auditors' Accounting and Auditing Standards in effect prescribe that the auditors be influenced by them in forming their opinion and the form in which it is expressed. Indeed, auditors who comply with the professional prescriptions are dependent on (rather than influenced by) them for the implied authority they give to their work. Curiously, though that dependence underpinned AA's status in the US from when it emerged as the paragon of audit virtues through its work on the failed Insull group in the early 1930s, its dependence on similarly authoritative mark-to-market and SPE prescriptions employed by Enron, earned it the suspicion of lacking independence.

Circumstance is thus the primary evidential matter generally relied upon in support of allegations of directors and auditors lacking independence. That some circumstances are thought to place auditors' independence at risk is the rationale underpinning the promulgation of governance rules prescribing independence. Despite the equivocal evidence of a lack of board independence having been a dominant factor, or lack of auditor independence contributing to corporate shenanigans, government-inspired governance regimes have played the independence card. A heavy hand has been used to achieve appearance, when arguably, with effective enforcement, a simple prescription that directors and auditors 'act honestly' would suffice.

# 3
# Governance Overload:
# A Contestable Strategy

Corporate governance is not a term of art. At its broadest sense, the governance of corporate entities comprehends the framework of rules, relationships, systems and processes by which authority is exercised and controlled in corporations.                                                   (HIHRC, 2003, p. 101)

Curiously, despite the hullabaloo surrounding the governance movement, nothing in the regimes introduces principles by way of controlling devices that have not been in the corporate legislation for over 160 years.

The current governance regimes take a negative approach to governance. They proscribe settings presumed to increase the likelihood that managers will act dishonestly and for their own benefit. As such they assume that auditors, directors, boards overall, and the like will act without professional probity and without restrictions or particular committees in place, rather than promote the benefits from acting honestly.

Few commentators seem to perceive the recent focus on corporate governance as a replay. Few appear to recall the circumstances recounted in the previous chapter prompting Roosevelt to make *truth in securities* the poster theme for part of his New Deal program with its governance legislation of the *Securities Act* of 1933 and the *Securities and Exchange Act* of 1934 as the platform for his agenda to reform corporate affairs. *Sarbanes-Oxley* is simply the latest revision of the US corporate governance mechanisms that stress compliance with rules as the panacea. The London Stock Exchange's *Combined Code: Principles of Good Governance and Code of Best Practice* (1998) is merely one of the latest in the follow-up from the 1992 UK *Cadbury Code* following, *inter alia*, the Maxwell and the Polly Peck scandals in the early 1990s and related events in the next decade.[1] Their major antecedents were the 1844, 1929 and 1948 *Companies Acts*.

Similar codes have mushroomed. Consider the following summary by Monks and Minnow (2004, pp. 297–8) of worldwide corporate governance initiatives:

By the close of the [twentieth] century, there were more than 60 governance codes in 30 markets, as well as numerous international codes [like the OECD Principles, 1999] . . . The Cadbury Committee had latched on to a formula of governance progress . . . [to] become the industry standard – it developed a list of 'best practice' governance standards to which companies were encouraged to aspire. Companies were then required to disclose how they measured up to the code, giving any explanations for any areas of non-compliance.

For Australian companies, *CLERP 9* and the *ASXCGC*'s Guidelines merely thump more heavily themes that had their early exposure in the responses (especially by the accounting profession[2]) to the Australian failures in the 1960s – essentially in each case, more of the same.[3] That is to be expected, for the prevailing view has been that the problem lies solely with the individuals who manage corporations, who, particularly with auditors, undertake their tasks without the level of independence thought appropriate. That the fundamentals of the corporate system might need rejigging, and that the way in which the outcomes of company affairs are communicated to the market is grossly faulty, attract little comment.

Continuous incantations implying that the commercial and corporate systems are sound seem to have paid off.

That the corporate structure has nurtured an opportunity for management to act more in its own interest than in the interest of the shareholders had been noticed long before the genesis of the modern corporation in the *Companies Act* of 1844. It was not accidental that the Act required annual accounts, and that they be audited by *a shareholder* (as noted, chapter 5). Who would better protect shareholders' property than one who shared a common interest in it? In contrast, once there is a separation, once a steward is appointed, mechanisms have to be implemented, inducements held out, to forge common interests between the owner of property and the stewards of it. This was exacerbated in the latter part of the nineteenth century when companies were granted the power by legislation to be shareholders of other companies. Ideally, effective stewardship relies upon the justified trust of the owners in, and the probity of, the stewards. In reality, inducements have been the mechanism to achieve that. Perceptions of how those inducements have had an opposite effect to what was intended, evoking and exacerbating self-interest rather than capturing and exploiting it, have not aligned managers' self-interests with those of the shareholders.[4] Accordingly, they underpin a considerable part of the current corporate governance debate.

Nor is it accidental that over the past 160-odd years regulatory mechanisms have increased dramatically. Successive company law reform committees have 'topped-up' governance regimes through tinkering with legislation, gradually specifying the form and the content of financial disclosures, the audit of them, and the duties of company directors and other officers. Often each has received further injection after a series of corporate collapses or other crises (such as following takeover periods with associated asset stripping and other events or periods of rising prices and price levels) evidencing sometimes wrongdoing, always market disruption and always a loss of confidence.

We take that to be indicative of the failure of each addition to the regulatory armoury. However, by virtue of the cumulative effect of those changes the modern corporation differs substantially from its predecessor, and the battle to align managers' interests to those of the shareholders (and other stakeholders) is being waged in a corporate setting different from that in which Berle and Means (1932) conceived the agency problem. The change process does not appear to have evinced an understanding that perhaps curbing managers' self-interest is impossible through the current governance regimes. Complex corporate structures, 'directors' schizophrenia' when seeking recourse to the separate legal entity doctrine to underpin their decisions, the fuzzy notion of *independence* applied to directors and auditors now function, against a background of accounting for their actions in a corporate reporting framework chock-full of *rules* but virtually devoid of *principles*.

Limiting auditors' provision of Non-Audit Services and expensing stock options in executive remuneration packages are illustrative of rules devoid of convincing principles.

## Auditor restraints – a two-headed serpent?

AA's receipt of $US27 million from Enron for NASs clearly clinched the case against audit firms having consultancy operations under the same roof. Indeed, Toffler in her *Final Accounting: Ambition, greed and the fall of Arthur Andersen* (2004) pursues the line that the mix of consulting and audit was fatal. In a similar vein Culp and Niskanen (2003) argue that getting into consulting undermines public confidence in accounting. Levit and Dyer (2006) pursue the same line as they *Take on the Street*, while Jennings (2006) in her *The Seven Signs of Ethical Collapse* makes a big play of consulting contributing to 'Andersen and Enron: Cultures of conflicts galore for both'. And of course that may have been the case.

Andersen is alleged to have set up Enron's mark-to-model revenue recognition scheme with the SEC in the early 1990s. It is said to have mostly designed Enron's internal control system. Conventional wisdom is that such actions create settings in which a conflict of interests is inevitable. Against that background the certainty of *SOX* banning most NASs by audit firms to their audit clients was the catalyst for the remaining audit firms allegedly cutting loose their consulting from their auditing arms. But curiously Andersens had done so years earlier. Indeed, Andersen Consulting separated from AA by agreement in 1997, primarily because of conflicts between 'AA' and 'AC' regarding their different work cultures.[5]

It is not surprising that the Ramsay independence inquiry in Australia following the HIH collapse noted that some commentators argued strongly for the banning of NASs by audit firms to their audit clients. It was an internationally common theme and clearly the way matters were heading in the US.

But the equally valid case (chapter 5) is the useful insight to be gained from the audit firm being intimately involved with a client's other business affairs. It is not surprising that studies of the consequences of auditors providing NASs are mixed, or that some regimes, such as Australia's *CLERP 9* reforms and the *ASXCGC Guidelines*, despite the Ramsay recommendation, have avoided the prohibition route that underpinned *SOX*.

Knowledge of the client's business is generally accepted to be an essential in the evaluation of a client's internal control, the planning of an audit and the prosecution of it. Contrary to the idea that the greater the detachment from the client, the greater the auditor's independence and the better the audit, it might equally be argued that the greater the auditor's independence (in that sense) the less will be the auditor's knowledge of the client's industry and the client's place in it. Independence without honesty and integrity is useless. In contrast, honesty and integrity irrespective of the level of association or appearance of independence are sufficient to achieve what independence the promoters want.

Substituting independence for a demand for honesty also underpins frequent governance rules requiring auditor rotation and the moratoria on the employment of ex-audit personnel by previous audit clients. Each of the trade-offs between the familiarity risks arising from long associations and the audit benefits to be obtained from an auditor's intimate knowledge of the client's affairs is an empirical matter rather than one of definition. Those trade-offs with general approbation in governance circles, possibly amount at the end of the day to what is being gained on the roundabout being lost on the razzle-dazzle.

## Poor option?

How repeated governance ideas have become set in concrete is well illustrated by the campaign to expense equity components of executive remuneration packages, as part of the post-Enron reaction against the perception that executive remuneration was excessive, and overly short-term in orientation. Interestingly, a similar campaign in the mid-1990s had run out of steam fairly quickly. That post-Enron episode also demonstrates how unrelated matters became entangled in the governmental responses to a public outcry that had developed from a mere whimper. Again, the circumstances of large corporate failures were the catalyst. Lay, Fastow and Skilling at Enron, Ebbers at WorldCom, Dunlap at Sunbeam, Forbes at Cendant, Williams and Adler at HIH were perceived to have wealth, property and other assets, lifestyles and perks consistent perhaps with business acumen and success, but irreconcilable with the ultimate failure of the companies they ran. Yet, there was no evidence that the levels of their remuneration directly contributed much towards their companies' shortfalls.

But an indirect linkage was identified. There was the general proposition that short-term and seemingly excessive incentive components of executives' remuneration packages encouraged them to manipulate their companies' affairs, engage in earnings management and misleading reporting of their companies' financial performance and financial position to exceed the benchmarks qualifying them for bonuses. Unquestionably there was an element of validity in the argument that the remuneration system was flawed. The level of many executives' remuneration was set by their fellow board members, and the qualifying benchmarks somewhat set by themselves 'in-house', particularly in the US where the executives mostly controlled the preparation of the quarterly earnings predictions made to the SEC. So, whereas a tightening of remuneration-setting protocols was possibly justified, the means chosen were highly contestable.

Table 2.1 clearly shows that the misstatement of quarterly, and frequently annual, earnings has been a feature of the recent and prior US corporate reporting scenes.[6] Possibly, some of that is due to the necessity for predicting future earnings for the quarterly statements. For even with the best of intentions, nobody can predict the future with certainty. Some of the misstatements, no doubt, are also due to applying the questionable US accounting *rules* that fail to 'tell it how it is', despite the superlative claims made regarding the quality of the FASB's standards relative to those used elsewhere.[7] Some was no doubt due to rank dishonesty. Indication of the extent of the misstatements in the US from whatever cause is given by the level of earnings restatements in the period 1997–2003. Restatement almost became fashionable. If a restatement wasn't made, it was viewed with the suspicion that the financials were misleading in an unknown dimension.

Restatement of previous misstatements, by implication at least, has been no less an institutionalised feature of Australian corporates' financials. This is evidenced in the past by the practice of reporting prior period adjustments and extraordinary items, and more recently under accounting rules that replaced 'below the line' adjustments of those kinds by adjustments 'above the line' – almost all of which amounted to under- and overstatements of amortisation charges that came home to roost as profits or losses on the sale of fixed assets and asset write-downs.[8] This occurred without any necessary intention to mislead by the accountants (chapter 4).

**Illustration 2:** 'Executives rush share options'
*Source:* 'Executives rush share options', *The Australian*, 15 September 2004. Courtesy of Peter Nicholson, www.nicholsoncartoons.com.au

Stock options at the centre of the remuneration storm have a long history in the US. In the 1920s and 1930s issuing stock options to employees lost momentum with the 1929 crash. Unquestionably, in the US post-World War II it has been a primary mechanism seeking to overcome the agency problem. Its capacity to induce performance without incurring a cash payout has had obvious attractions. An early illustration of its potency as an aligning inducement was well illustrated in the rewards to Charles Lazarus to return to and help turn around the ailing Toys R Us that he had founded.[9] US governments gave the issuing of options in remuneration packages implicit encouragement.[10] That kind of quick talking is aided by the dramatic disclosures of the extent to which companies' bottom lines would be reduced were options to be expensed. Standard & Poor's, for example, estimated a 17 per cent negative impact on US companies in 2002. Spurred on by such 'revelations', spurious accounting arguments have been used to make options unattractive by hitting companies' bottom lines.[11]

It is to be recalled that this discussion was set against a background of disputation regarding the performances of executives and their remuneration and whether the appropriate benefits flowed in terms of increased shareholder value.

Empirical evidence of the impact of remuneration packages on the former is equivocal.[12] Vitriol attaching to the spectre of disgraced executives receiving huge sums from cashing in options in happier times, and of 'dismissed' and 'resigning' executives receiving payouts disproportionate to their performances of the companies they were leaving, has been substituted for serious inquiry. Enron, WorldCom are simply contemporary cases. And the theme continues.[13] It motivates the recent revelations such as the $US72 million payout that Australia's Telstra CEO Sol Trujillo received upon leaving US West, which understandably upset employees whose K401 pension fund holdings of US West dropped in price from $US69 to $US1.11 following the consummation of its merger with Qwest. Trujillo's stock options were apparently vested immediately upon exit. That is consistent with much of the complaint and the general themes coursing through commentaries on CEOs' behaviours and rewards, translating from the lack of communication with shareholders regarding the latter into a general criticism of what executives are paid.

In that setting historical, legal and financial facts have fallen victim to the options verbiage. Public and private debate over executive share options has been seduced by the temptation to translate a get-tough attitude to disclosure into a compulsory accounting technique. Ruling that companies *expense* the *value* of the options they issue was the US Government's solution post-Enron. It was a ruling that the SEC and the FASB willingly embraced, perhaps a little surprisingly, bearing in mind the SEC backdown on the issue in the early 1990s. Though dispute pervades the expensing ruling, it has found its way into *SOX* (2002), and IFRSs, but curiously it was not legislated as part of *CLERP 9* culminating in changes to Australia's *Corporations Act 2005*, or the AIFRSs.[14] Companies issuing options have mostly cowered under the barrage. The loudness of those assertions again has drowned out contrary analyses.

The misplaced focus on how options should be accounted continues. While the intention of a recent Australian survey of options practices in respect of CEOs of some listed large companies is laudable, for example, to have the appropriate 'cost' of the options package revealed to shareholders, the emphasis in reports on the survey again slips into discussing the implications for the companies' 'bottom lines' of the appropriate cost – namely, the 'grant' value or the 'realised' value when the options vest.[15] The real issue is that the relevant value should be disclosed, not that it should be expensed.

It is interesting to note that few of the pro-expensing advocates deny the virtue of the strategy underpinning the issue of options – to align the presumed interests of executives with those of the company owners, to maximise corporate wealth,[16] and to harness managerial opportunism rather than curb it. Equally interesting, few of them allude to evidence of successful uses of options in the past. How options substituted for cash components of salary had permitted high-tech startups to recruit the best of graduates from MIT,

Stanford, Harvard, and fuse their futures with those of the companies they were developing,[17] is rarely mentioned. Nor are the studies[18] indicating that the general body of shareholders benefited in companies issuing options to employees, though admittedly primarily by those issued to executives.[19] They refer to the experiences of companies, especially to those involved in the recent scandals, in which an association is drawn between option issues and poor performance.

The pervading implication is that the inducement did not work for the benefit of the stakeholders. But, statistical correlation does not prove causation. So, those linking options with poor performances ought to make a corresponding mistake of linking them to good performance. That does not appear to happen.[20] Nor is it usually noted that stock options have not been given exclusively to executives, though undeniably they have been the major recipients.[21]

Recall that the current furore and resurrection of the call to expense options has arisen only following notable collapses in which executives had received massive option inducements – for example, Sunbeam, Enron, Waste Management, Tyco, Adelphia, WorldCom. There was no outcry when the options inducements were accompanied by buoyant share prices; when Enron's stock was over $US90 and WorldCom's $US64.50. Nor, was there any outcry of 'foul play' when Australia's AMP was riding high in the 1990s. An inference might be drawn that shareholders are not averse to the options being granted in 'good times'. The quest for accounting transparency, a legitimate concern at all times, appears more potent in bad times.[22]

Reformers have not seen it necessary to establish 'causation' between the issuing of options and the accounting scandals. They have merely asserted it. Nor have they established that the cost of the options is an expense of the company. They have asserted that, too. But now that assertion has been accepted by many regulators as a rule to be followed. Contrary to the financial characteristics attributed to expenses elsewhere in conventional accounting (for example, in Australia's SAC 2) – a diminution of assets or an increase in liabilities – the costs of options are deemed expenses because the company receives or has the potential to receive the benefit of executives' increased efforts without any decrease in assets or increase in liabilities.[23]

Several questions deserve answers. Is the current disclosure of share options in executive remuneration packages adequate? Do the options entail a cost and if so, to whom? Should the granting companies *expense* them? Possibly not. Possibly yes. To the existing shareholders? Unquestionably 'no'.

In the executive options debate metaphorical utterances that the 'shareholders are the company' have underpinned confusion between the company and its shareholders. The *Salomon v Salomon* case established the dictum that companies are separate entities, have separate legal personalities, separate property rights and separate obligations, enjoy separate benefits and incur their own separate costs. Those matters (that were discussed in chapter 1 and will be examined again in chapters 7 and 8) are swept aside by the option-expensing advocates. Yet the legal status of companies is that it is the commercial reality that counts, not the misleading impressions evoked by the repetitive use of imprecise language.[24]

Certainly, when executives exercise share options they receive their money's worth from the company. But the critical point is *at whose expense?* Whose financial welfare changes as a consequence of the exercise of the options?

Exercising executive stock options dilutes the holding of non-participating shareholders. On the face of it, that possibly entails a loss to them. First, once the options are granted there is the potential that existing shareholders' proportions of the issued share capital will be diluted. Accordingly, when exercised, they are diluted. Second, almost certainly the inflow of capital at the exercise price will be less than had the shares been allotted in a public issue at that time. Whether shareholders individually or the company are better or worse off 'financially' depends upon whether the share price after the exercise of the options and the consequential capital inflow offset the aggregative financial effects of the dilution. Shareholders potentially stand either to gain or to lose from the dilution. But the shareholders are not the company.

Only the second leg of that scenario entails what might be viewed a potential cost to the company. There is an *opportunity cost* occasioned by the difference between the strike price and what could possibly have been received in the ordinary course of events from a public issue.

But, if the increase in the price of the shares to the strike price is deemed to be the consequence of achieving the performance benchmark, then an opportunity to make a public issue at that share price must also be considered a function of that performance. So, if an excess of the then current price over the strike price is regarded an *opportunity cost* incurred by the company, then the inflow of cash from exercising the options must also be regarded an immediate *opportunity gain*, available for offset against the presumed opportunity cost. And, once caught in that entanglement, any other net increase in the company's wealth attributable to the achievement of the benchmark performance might likewise be attributed, and offset.

Governance reformers have campaigned long and hard that because the stock options are valuable and given in lieu of cash salary components, they are a 'cost to the company' and must be expensed in the same manner as a cash salary component. But that proposition cannot be sustained from legal or accounting perspectives, for there is neither a diminution in the issuing company's assets nor an increase in its liabilities. Nothing has changed when they are vested, other than to make what was hypothetical (a net inflow of capital) more likely. And it cannot be sustained when they are exercised, for ordinarily the company's net assets will be increased (directly by any cash injection from the exercising and indirectly through the performance that triggered the exercise point) rather than diminished at that point. If the options are exercised the company stands to gain.

Perversely, potential costs and benefits accrue to shareholders. The potential costs, from the diminution of their proportional shareholdings; potential benefits by virtue of increased company net wealth from the additional capital inflow when the options are exercised.

Whereas the debate has been heated, no compelling case for expensing the options has been made that is consistent with the realities of the legal or financial settings in which companies operate. It is reasonable to conclude that the governance prescriptions that set the 'expensing options rule' in concrete have the potential to disadvantage shareholders. Expensing options does not reduce the cost of diluting shareholders' investment, and reduced earnings (from expensing the value attributed to the options) may adversely impact the share price. Shareholders are exposed to being hit by a double-whammy.

## Governance by numbers – mainly for appearance

Ticking the boxes appears to be a valued aspect of many governance regimes. If a company can tick all the boxes in a regime it is declared to 'have good governance'. And if it also reports profits, then some kind of association is usually claimed between the good governance status and performance. Numerous studies take this line. None however show that the same companies were less profitable before they could tick the boxes or have established that their performance would be lower were they unable to do so. The usual line is that the 'good governance companies' outperform the 'bad' or 'not so good' companies on the governance scale. But for the most part the 'high-roller' companies were there without the governance regimes in place and might well be expected to continue to perform well without them. With a curious reasoning, those promoting the governance tick-a-box and good performance nexus pass off, for example, Enron, WorldCom, Sunbeam, HIH, One.Tel and Ansett, having many of the popular governance regime components – audit committees, NEDs, separate CEOs and Chairpersons, and the like – as aberrations in the functioning of those mechanisms. Or they point to those governance mechanisms being overridden by the unsavoury features of the auditors providing non-audit services or the presence of other perceived governance-risk factors. Australia's One.Tel is a salient example of the presence of high-flier non-executive directors drawn from world-leading media companies. Yet, the then News Corp's Lachlan Murdoch and Publishing and Broadcasting Ltd's James Packer claimed that they were 'grossly misled' in their capacity as directors regarding the firm's financial status.[25] The point is that there is always an excuse why the governance mechanisms failed to perform their magic. In most analyses it would seem that the thought does not cross the advocates' minds that none of the mechanisms, either separately or collectively, can overcome the impact of either managerial incompetence or dishonesty, especially at the board level.

Eliminating the appearance that corporate managers will act in their own interest to the detriment of shareholders underpins the content of the well-known national and transnational governance regimes. Virtually all push the independence barrow in respect of directors and auditors, requiring board composition to be heavily weighted towards INEDs, directors' declarations to the effect that they are 'independent', audit committees comprising non-executive directors, independence declarations by auditors, the compulsory rotation and the moratoria over the employment of ex-audit staff by previous clients. Yet apart from the tick-a-box exercises claiming superior performance by regime-compliant companies – requiring the heavy discounting of the outliers that buck the rule, and the lack of explanation of how, for the most part, the same companies had commendable performances before the arrival of the current regimes – no explanation is forthcoming as to how any of the promoted governance measures could eliminate dishonesty. *Appearance* of circumstances in which companies' businesses will be conducted honestly, with no guarantee that it *is*, appears to be the most likely outcome. But the sense of false security that that is likely to evoke is possibly more harmful than the one where shareholders remain skeptical of the performance and motives of management.

Governance overload suggestions are unpopular. To the contrary, governance breakdown has been presumed on the grounds that some of the companies at the centre of the scandals had questionable internal checks and balances, because there appeared to be circumstances in which conflicts of interests may have arisen for directors, auditors and the like. Despite the flurry of knee-jerk responses to the so-called corporate scandals, evidence that they were caused by a lack of compliance with governance rules of the kind contained in the current governance regimes has not been forthcoming.

A most noticeable feature of many of the provisions contained in the UK *Combined Code*, Australia's *CLERP 9* and the US *SOX* is that they are merely reformulations of what existed previously. Most of the key measures already existed in one form or another prior to the recent crop of failures. Those mechanisms have been little more than tweaked.

It was argued above that not only is independence of the kind being promoted through the governance regimes impossible to achieve, but also that its desirability in many settings is problematic. The necessity that auditors maintain an independent mental attitude when forming their audit opinion clearly has been a fundamental theme coursing through the principles of audit company practice for over a century; and if *independence of mind* is equated with acting with great probity and honesty as a fiduciary, it has long been understood to be a fundamental ethos for directors and senior executives, too. Most companies

61

have had audit committees for a substantial period of time. There is nothing new in that, and their perceived functions have been much the same as those implied in the current governance bromides. And if we take the push in *CLERP 9* for the adoption of the AIFRSs to be the *modus operandi* for achieving comparability in financial statement data, that too reflects a long-established pursuit. Nor is the oversight of financial communication by Australia's Financial Reporting Council new in concept – the FRC and the equivalent oversight boards in the US and the UK are merely new versions of similar bodies that existed previously. For the most part little is really new. While in some instances legal status and the labels have changed, compositions and functions have expanded, and perhaps operational issues given more detailed articulation, but overall, it is simply more of the same.

Revamping and rebadging existing arrangements is a common political ploy by professional bodies, governments and their agencies when in crisis. It gives the appearance of there being a positive response to the public discomfort.

In taking the current governance push at face value we are justified in assuming that those promoting governance matters of the kind just noted believe that they will result in a commercial setting less likely to incubate corporate malpractice. We are equally justified in presuming that those driving the reform proposals are cognisant of the abject failure in the past of most of what they now propose to strengthen, or reinforce, in effect to double-up on. That invites the inference that a strong belief prevails that the proposed governance mechanisms are sound, that the problem lies only in their past implementation. Nonetheless it is an admission that in the past they did not work as effectively as desired.

That the improper behaviour of a few 'corporate bad eggs' has caused the problems, imperfect individuals messing up a perfectly good system, is implied by the tacit endorsement of the regulatory mechanisms in the governance discussion.[26] Accordingly, whether the collection of regulatory measures has been coordinated, or indeed can be coordinated, to bring about an orderly corporate commercial environment does not appear to be on the radar of company-watchers, professional bodies, regulators or government.[27]

Contrary to the way in which those in other disciplines – medicine for instance – might have addressed the perceived breakdown in governance, corporate reformers do not appear to have considered whether fewer, rather than more, of the current regulatory measures might be the answer. In medicine, if a therapy doesn't work, thought would normally be given not only to increasing dosage, but also to decreasing it, to the manner in which it is administered, and to its functioning within the combination of therapies of which it is part. It may be, in fact, that there have been too many governance mechanisms in place. It may also be that the different, perhaps conflicting, governance mechanisms were not coordinated so as to avoid frustrating the functioning of one another.[28]

That we propose to have fewer rather than more governance rules and mechanisms may not be a popular suggestion. It certainly goes against the universal trend, and in particular against both the current approach in Australia giving the *CLERP 9* proposals legislative backing and the endorsement of the approach by the professional bodies. Yet it may be that the prevailing view in this regard is a popular delusion.

Viewed against the background of an unrelenting rhetoric popularising and entrenching preferred perceptions of good corporate governance and how to achieve it, perhaps it is not surprising that the current governance regimes contain more of what has failed in the past. For there, failure of the regulatory processes has been mistaken for failure of governance *per se*. Despite numerous prescriptions of how to obtain it, those promoting the regimes have not explained what good corporate governance is, except for the implication that apparently it is what we do not have. Generally, government agencies and professional associations have been endorsing processes without any explicit consensus on the commercial condition to which the processes are directed.

Consider the definitions of corporate governance made respectively in the *ASXCGC's Guidelines*, and by Justice Owen in his Report into the collapse of HIH:

the ASXCGC has published its principles of good corporate governance and best practice recommendations . . . providing a set of reference points [processes] for the best practice aspirations . . . [it is] a 'comply or explain philosophy' . . . (p. 106)

Viewed at a high level, corporate governance is all about accountability and stewardship. The funds and assets that a corporation collects are to be held and grown for the ultimate benefit of those who have a stake in the success of the business. Those in whom responsibility is vested to control and direct the business have stewardship of those funds and are accountable for them. One critical objective of a system of corporate governance is to ensure that those people hold the confidence of those having a stake in the success of a business . . . confidence gives context to the search for a benchmark against which the exercise of judgment can be measured. A corporate governance practice can be assessed by asking how it would affect the degree of confidence that the class who have an interest in the company's success would repose in those persons who carry out the practice [or] what would the former class sensibly expect of the persons responsible for putting the practice into effect? If the way in which the practice was or was not carried out (as the case may be) falls materially short of the sensible expectation of the class, it would not engender confidence and would be undesirable. (HIHRC, Vol. 1, pp. 106 and 103.)

The *ASXCGC Guidelines* present good governance as if it were a set of processes. Justice Owen perceives it to be a framework created by similar processes. Both, perhaps the former more so than the latter, entail the substitution of the processes by which governance is to be achieved for governance itself. Justice Owen comes close to declaring corporate governance the concept of an ideal commercial environment in which authority is exercised with absolute probity with regard to the welfare of corporate stakeholders in general and the shareholders in particular, rather than a set of processes. This requires directors, executive and non-executive, to ensure that they ask awkward questions – and for the chairman to take the responsibility of ensuring a proper flow of relevant information to the Board.[29] Regarding that financial information the implication is that what is disclosed by the entity is that it satisfies the truth and fairness criterion of the *Corporations Act 2001* (Cth) rather than simply the process-oriented accounting and auditing standards underpinning its preparation.

Looking at governance as the absolute, uncompromising probity with which authority is exercised in respect of corporate affairs places in focus the objective, rather than the processes to achieve it. In contrast, the promoters of various governance regimes have committed the fallacy of substituting the means for the end in mind. Perhaps, were they to have distinguished the desired end from those preferred processes, they might have seen that the former and the latter are not necessarily linked in the way the conventional and repetitive rhetoric assumes.

Alfred North Whitehead's *fallacy of misplaced concreteness*[30] explains how repetition entrenches notions to the point at which they are accepted as unquestionable dogma. It is an apt explanation of the curious way in which corporate governance is perceived, the features attributed to it, and the continual allegiance given to processes that have failed to deliver in the past. Whitehead's *fallacy* offers an explanation of why a questionable focus on individuals has been allowed to divert attention from the objective assurance of a commercial environment in which corporate affairs are orderly and predictable; why, in the examination of corporate distress, failures and collapses, processes have been accorded more attention than their objective; and why, in those inquiries, well-established understandings of fundamental concepts have been replaced with perversions of them.

We do not appear to have learned much from successive episodes of corporate collapse. Enthusiastic, repetitious, and increasing support for contestable notions of what corporate governance entails has replaced observation and reason throughout those episodes. Corporate governance reformers appear to labour under the popular delusion that if you say something erroneous long enough it will become a commercial truth.

# 4
# A Very Peculiar Practice:
# Accounting Under Scrutiny

With the passing of the dot.com and telco hype the new millennium heralded the end of an eighteen-year bull market in many capitalist economies – one of the longest of the twentieth century. Significant turbulence, loss of confidence in corporate financial markets generally, and unease with corporate governance in particular, emerged.[1] The Long Term Capital Market's rise and fall in 1998 was to portend the demise of many dot.coms in early 2000. Financial difficulties were also the lot of several large, old and new economy companies including HIH, Harris Scarfe, One.Tel, Pasminco and Centaur in Australia, and Enron, WorldCom, Waste Management, Qwest, Freddie Mac, Fannie Mae, Ahold and Adelphia Communications in the US.

Contrary to the views of regulators (like ASIC's Jeff Lucy) and others, our view is that corporate accounting and the auditing of it are in crisis. Both are in a chaotic state, as the evidence in this and other work demonstrates.[2]

Two of the so-called 'golden age' accounting thinkers, Ricco Mattessich and Bob Sterling, are also quite adamant that accounting has been, and still is, in crisis. Mattessich (1995) noted several symptoms of the current crisis drawing on studies by Demski, Dopuch, Lev, Ronen, Searfoss and Sunder,[3] in contrast to other disciplines:

> Accounting research has failed to lead practice, [it] lags behind; . . . [it] does not have periodic cycles of innovations; . . . The research and teaching efforts during the last two to three decades did not bring accountants any closer to any solution of its fundamental problems (such as optimal choice of account-ing standards and institutions) . . . there seems to be hardly any demand for academic researchers or their product in industry or the profession (with the possible exception in auditing) . . . Accounting is considered to be a mere service area, and during the recent decade or so [1970s or 1980s], the MBA majoring in accounting has almost become an endangered species.[4]

While Sterling, upon being inducted into the Ohio Accounting Hall of Fame in 2006, lamented that his career had to be described as a failure since:

Accounting is very nearly the same in my end as it was in my beginning . . . what was being put in accountants' minds . . . [in the current texts are] the same useless concepts, invalid claims and senseless numerals that I studied in my first accounting class circa 1952 . . . Strike one . . . the careless use of language . . . If avoiding equivocal terms requires jargon, invent it. Jargon is undesirable but it is better than equivocation. In my beginning I identified this error and its solution. In my end I am still identifying it. Strike two.[5]

Other testimony to the crisis being longstanding is borne out by the 1990s' settlements of claims lodged many years earlier against several audit firms, companies and their officers, including one over $135 million (Tricontinental), $120 million related to the State Bank of South Australia, and the reported $110 million 2002 out-of-court settlement of the nearly $1 billion damages claim by the liquidator of Bond Corporation, $20 million at Adsteam post-2000 and a similar amount at Harris Scarfe post-2000. These all preceded the large out-of-court (without admitting fault) settlements post-2000 at Global Crossing, Enron, WorldCom. Waste Management, Xerox, and others in the US (see table 4.1).[6]

As in those earlier cases, it remains impossible (other than by chance) to assess the wealth and progress of a company from the published financial statements, and virtually impossible to calculate reliable indicators of solvency, rate of return, asset backing, gearing and the like from the data in published financial statements prepared in compliance with the Accounting Standards – whether the national or the IFRSs. Companies' financial statements contain data which are mere artifacts of the processing rules imposed upon accountants through the compulsory imposition of Accounting Standards. Some of the data are pure fiction. They are not merely unrepresentative of what they describe, they have nothing to describe – no real-world referent. The discussion on creative accounting in Clarke *et al.* (2003, especially chapter 2) and the instances of *creative* and *feral* accounting described in the other chapters covering the 1960s to the 2000s demonstrate the continuing unserviceable state of accounting information. Data in chapters 5 to 7 below provide more contemporary evidence. No wonder Mattessich, Sterling, Chambers and others claim that there is a crisis.

Compelling evidence needs to be provided by various governments, professional bodies and the corporate regulators to support the idea that the quality of accounting data and financial reporting can be guaranteed through mandating compliance with IFRSs. The evidence points to the opposite. Regulation is intended to protect the users of the data in company accounts from financial peril, not expose them to it. Inexplicably, faced with evidence of the kind produced here and previously by the authors and others, the accounting data emerging under the existing regulatory process fail to inform and hence protect stakeholders in the manner championed by the regulators in their push for more of the same.

In a reasonably well-ordered society, one would expect, indeed demand, regulation be directed to achieving quality, reliability, fitness for use – serviceability – of the product rather than mere standardisation of the input and processing rules. That standardisation is a virtue *per se* is a contestable proposition at the best of times. Yet the accounting profession appears to have led the field in the pursuit of standardisation, and as shown here, divorced from the pursuit of serviceability. That push has been for standardisation of input, processing, rather than of the output – namely the data emerging in audited corporate financials.

The latest international moves for the adoption of the IFRSs indicate the malaise is universal. Accountants would do much better for themselves were they to adopt the current vogue and have mission statements and the like prescribed by their professional bodies with the view towards producing serviceable data in financial statements – data that provide a true and fair view of an entity's wealth and progress. As it is, they have 'mission impossible' forced upon them through compliance with thousands of pages of Standards.[7]

Compliance with prescribed processes through the Accounting and Auditing Standards is assumed to be an effective regulatory mechanism. Linkages between the prescribed practices and the quality of the end product are missing. Not one of the Accounting Standards, nor the omnibus Australian Statement of Accounting Concepts No. 4 (SAC 4), specifies a common, necessary, general quality characteristic which the emerging data are to possess, singly or in combination. Like its predecessors in the AASB series, none of the AIFRSs explain how the input and processing rules prescribed will produce data that are serviceable in showing the company's wealth and progress or for deriving its financial characteristics. This is at a time when the quality of outcomes in particular is the general *desiderata* virtually everywhere. The notion of quality is somewhat like the Holy Spirit; except that whereas the Holy Spirit is everywhere, output quality is the characteristic pursued everywhere – except (it seems) in accounting.

With some justification, we might also question whether compulsory compliance with prescribed processing standards is compatible with the notion of a profession, where professional activity is differentiated from that of the artisan. Artisans ply their craft according to hands-on experience, and use regular and proven technology known to all in the craft without necessarily understanding why it is used. Methods are handed down from artisan to artisan. Their knowledge and skill, though considerable, is a common matter, rarely idiosyncratic. By contrast, the distinguishing feature of a professional is the exercise of the accumulated skill and wisdom, the out-of-the-ordinary, extraordinary

67

expertise applied equally to both the ordinary and out-of-the-ordinary, the extraordinary circumstances. Professionals and their professions are distinguished from others by the exercise of the *differentia specifica* of their practices that set them apart from the rest of the community. But in those settings concern is always with the product of the professional actions. There is also recognition of a social obligation, to apply one's skill and wisdom to serve also the public interest. It requires independent judgment as to how best to proceed. Perhaps it is not surprising that some leading accounting *éminences grise* are alleging members of accounting firms are no longer professionals.[8]

Specifying compulsory rules (Standards) for processing accounting data, without also specifying necessary end qualities or characteristics to be achieved, and demonstrating that they are satisfied by the outputs of the prescribed processes, poses a serious threat to accountants' claims to professional status. As does, one might imagine, the pursuit of limited liability for the consequences for their actions.

That leads to other propositions: compulsory compliance with Accounting Standards, the IFRSs, which concentrate on processes not outcomes is not necessarily conducive to producing serviceable financial data. Compulsory compliance with the prescribed processing standards is incompatible with professional activity. Conventional accounting practices complying with the prescribed Standards have masked impending failure, exacerbated losses and provided regulators with a recurring dilemma. Regulators of corporate activity have not heeded the lessons of history. The wailing, gnashing of teeth and the rhetoric of indignation at the sequential episodes of corporate failure have been recurrent but ineffective responses. Though HIH's goodwill accounting, WorldCom's capitalisation of operating expenditures, Waste Management's lengthening of its truck fleet's assets' lives to decrease amortisation charges, Enron's and Xerox's front-end loading of revenues certainly hit the headlines (often front pages of dailies), few commentators noted them to be repeat performances. It is surprising that the financial press failed to note that the accounting conventions that WorldCom, Waste Management, Enron and Xerox stretched, almost certainly have induced errors in the accounts of every company that complies with them.

We do not accept the view of those who claim that matching is no longer practised. The conventional accounting system is essentially expenditure capitalisation with an impairment override in which expenditures are capitalised and gradually leeched into the income statement as an everyday application of the accrual-based 'matching' system. All that WorldCom, for example, did was overstep the mark according to the regulators.

However, the system would not only have endorsed but also demanded a less extreme application of the rule. As such the accrual and matching rules are demonstrably defective. Contestably some even argue that they are no longer applicable if the Standards are applied. But the unqualified (generally) audited practice suggests the contrary. Waste Management appears to have exploited the rule that depreciation is 'the allocation of a cost of an asset over its useful life'. In earlier decades US airlines 'manipulated' their profits using the Waste Management device of lengthening the 'expected lives' in conventional accounting's depreciation algorithm. But, of course, to everyone other than accountants, depreciation is not an 'allocation of cost', it is the 'decrease in price'. Enron's and Xerox's front-end loading, too, can be seen to be a product of the matching rule. It differs little in style from H. G. Palmer's accounting for hire-purchase profits (in Australia in the 1960s – see Clarke *et al.*, *Corporate Collapse,* 2003, chapter 5). But the matching rule, applied as it is on a temporal basis in conventional accounting, invariably induces error and invites manipulation.

Accruing revenues and expenses to match with presumed future expenses and revenues almost ensures errors, even if not on Enron's or Xerox's scale. It is not difficult to imagine that somewhere, somehow, some day, an alert judge will question the serviceability of conventional accounting data. In 1996 a NSW Supreme Court judgment by McLelland CJ suggested the time is close when he described the untangling of one Standard prescription on goodwill as 'almost a metaphysical problem'.[9] Against financial common sense, the financial nonsense promoted in the Accounting Standards will ultimately prove impossible to defend.

The likelihood of this happening appears greater given the January 2007 High Court of Australia (HCA) ruling in the *Sons of Gwalia* case.[10] There, a class action initiated by a shareholder claimed that the shareholder had invested on the basis of information provided by the company about Sons of Gwalia's gold reserves. The action relied upon the *Trade Practices Act*'s misleading or deceptive conduct sections, specifically to claim that the shareholder had been induced to purchase shares based on an inaccurate report as to the company's going concern status. The HCA held that, where misleading information about the company was provided by the directors, some shareholders could seek to be ranked equally with creditors in seeking damages in any liquidation. It is possible that such a line of reasoning under the *Trade Practices Act* about misleading information might one day be extended to accounting information provided in accord with the standards.[11]

## Bubbles, accounting restatements – present and past

For many, events in the capital markets in April and May 2000 portending the crash of the dot.coms were to change their way of thinking. Large falls in share price indexes for technology stocks across various capital markets saw billions of dollars wiped off corporate market capitalisations. It was a particularly hard knock for those who were eulogising new economy companies. Six years on (as this book goes to press), those indexes, though still slightly lower than the 2000 levels, are definitely rising strongly again. In early 2007 the 'Shanghai Shock' saw the exchange drop 10 per cent.

Dot.coms became part of the tech-wreck as many either went into liquidation or were taken over by the surviving 'old economy' companies. Within a year or two the associated financial meltdown had also affected many old economy, merger-driven conglomerates, like Enron, Vivendi, WorldCom, Waste Management, and Global Crossing. As before, few appeared to see the similarities between the difficulties experienced by those companies and the crises of preceding generations. The boom/bust era generated new labels, like 'new economy' companies, and, rather than creative accounting, reference was to 'aggressive' accounting, 'pro forma earnings' and the ubiquitous 'earnings management'.

In this setting the old cries for better quality, 'more transparent' accounting have re-emerged. Disputed claims that some countries had better accounting standards, adoption of principles-based rather than a rules-based system, have enjoyed popular currency.[12] Much of this criticism was ill-informed, without foundation.[13]

## Regulation – self- or government-imposed?[14]

It is instructive to contemplate in general terms the similarities between the tactics of the regulators of accounting practices in the 1930s and 1970s. The promise to 'clean up accounting's act' on those earlier occasions was to be achieved by more clearly articulating the fundamental ideas – often described as 'the search for the principles' underpinning accounting practices and financial reporting disclosure and monitoring mechanisms. In each decade, the drive appeared to be to protect the essentially co-regulatory mechanism, with its retention of the accounting profession's significant influence.

Under scathing attack from the likes of Ferdinand Pecora, Price Waterhouse & Co. partner George O. May's professional oratory cut the accounting profession in for its share of Roosevelt's New Deal measures to put 'truth into securities' – the ultimate of corporate governance sentiment. The profession went to great lengths to establish its self-regulatory status and the importance of it being a major player in the emerging co-regulatory regime.[15] But the threat of government regulation, were the profession to fail to inject accounting statements with Roosevelt's 'truth', nurtured attempts to articulate the main *principles* underpinning accounting. *Accounting Principles Underlying Corporate Financial Statements* issued in 1936 by the academic American Accounting Association and Sanders *et al.*'s 1938 *A Tentative Statement of Accounting Principles* are indicative of the perceived need to show that the thinkers of the accounting discipline were as much on the job as its practitioners.

Similar to the effects of the sentiment that drove the profession's defence of its primarily self-regulatory regime in the 1930s, the impact of the faulty accounting has fuelled measures to purge corporate activity of its present ills in more recent times. Chapters 2 and 3 revealed that the corporate governance push now drives the current debate, emphasising the need for principles- rather than rules-based accounting standards – seemingly general support for some of the corporate governance mechanisms put forward in *SOX*. The requirement that CEOs and CFOs attest to the truth of the data contained in financial statements has comparable requirements in Australia's *CLERP 9*.

In this setting what the 'principles' ought to be, and any possible distinction with 'rules', appears as uncertain now as it was in the 1930s.[16] Further, in the past the profession's resolve to define the underpinnings of conventional practice – to search for what were described each time as 'principles'[17] – seems to diminish once the threat of unwelcome external intervention in its business has dissipated.[18]

Events pre- and post-2000[19] were poles apart. Just prior to 2000 Greenspan's 'irrational exuberance' and Galbraith's 'inventory of undiscovered embezzlement' were deemed appropriate metaphors.[20] Then, in early 2000 as the 'cash spigot' was suddenly turned off,[21] several major Australian corporate casualties emerged – including HIH, One.Tel, Ansett, Pasminco, Harris Scarfe and Centaur. It was a similar story in the US, where hundreds of dot.coms[22] and leading telcos, such as Global Crossing and Qwest Communications, became financial flotsam. More significantly, some of the US major mainstream companies like Enron, WorldCom, Tyco, Xerox, Fannie Mae and Freddie Mac either collapsed or suffered financial embarrassment on a gigantic scale, after disclosing alleged 'accounting irregularities' entailing billions of dollars. Several executives would be forced to resign, some would be sent to gaol for their actions, and still others would say that they were misled by the accounts.

Questionable accounting and auditing practices were daily media fodder. Arthur Andersen's fall from grace and its conviction that turned the Big Five into the Big Four swapped the 'dull and boring' image of accountants for 'bad guys', in league with 'dirty rotten CEOs' (Flanagan, 2003). Once lost in the middle pages, accountants and their antics became the brunt of talk-show hosts' jokes, especially in the US, while caricatures adorned mainstream and business media. Questionable audits of Enron, WorldCom, Waste Management, Sunbeam, the Baptist Foundation of Arizona and others in the US meant that Andersen had to be (reportedly) 'cut loose' by its Big Four surviving colleagues.[23] Guilt by association (at least) ensured a similar fallout in Australia for Andersen's involvement with HIH. Prominent was its reported $110 million May 2002

**Table 4.1:** Company losses* in nominal and scaled dimensions, and % of losses to GDP*

| Year | Company | Loss in nominal $m* | CPI $^{2000}$m | Loss in $^{2000}$m | GDP $ billion | Losses as a % of GDP |
|---|---|---|---|---|---|---|
| 1963 | Reid Murray | 47 | 14.1 | 416 | 17 601 | 0.00027 |
| 1990 | Adsteam | 2,100 | 100.0 | 2,619 | 351 933 | 0.00060 |
| 1990 | Bond | 5,330 | 100.0 | 6,647 | 351 933 | 0.00151 |
| 1990 | Qintex | 1,260 | 100.0 | 1,571 | 351 933 | 0.00036 |
| 1990 | Hooker | 1,960 | 100.0 | 2,444 | 351 933 | 0.00056 |
| 1990 | SBV | 2,700 | 100.0 | 3,367 | 351 933 | 0.00077 |
| 1991 | SBSA | 3,150 | 105.3 | 3,730 | 384 710 | 0.00082 |
| 1993 | CBA | 2,976 | 108.4 | 3,423 | 406 427 | 0.00073 |
| 1993 | Westpac | 6,367 | 108.4 | 7,324 | 406 427 | 0.00160 |
| 1993 | ANZ | 4,690 | 108.4 | 5,395 | 406 427 | 0.00115 |
| 2001 | HIH | 5,300 | 124.7 | 5,300# | 593 311 | 0.00089 |
| 2001 | One.Tel | 650 | 124.7 | 650 | 593 311 | 0.00011 |
| 2002 | Ansett | 1,500 | 124.7 | 1,500 | 593 311 | 0.00025 |
| 2002 | NAB | 3,900 | 124.7 | 3,900 | 593 311 | 0.00066 |
| 2002 | News Corp | 12,800 | 124.7 | 12,800 | 593 311 | 0.00215 |

*Sources:* CPI and GDP data are taken from Catalogue item 6401, ABS (2000); 1990 base year = 100.
# HIH's estimated losses and 'write-down losses' for One.Tel, Ansett, National Australia Bank and Newscorp are in 2001 dollar terms. Other amounts in this column have been restated in $^{2000}$m equivalent purchasing power terms.
*'Loss' data are taken from Sykes, *The Bold Riders* (1996), and Clarke *et al.*, *Corporate Collapse* (1997); and financial press regarding asset write-downs.

out-of-court Bond Corporation settlement. 'Perceived deficiencies' in accountability fuelled claims of a loss of confidence and that the securities market was not a 'fair game'. The trust that is the essential trait of an orderly market was severely tested. Accounting and auditing were said to be in a 'state of crisis'.[24] There was an epidemic of 'accounting phobia'.

However, such laments have a long history. With respect to accounting information published by companies, generally it has never been fair or truthful. Anyone who had bothered to look into the earlier episodes of corporate failures should not have been surprised by the anguish. The accounting issues that emerged in the 2000s (leading to restatements as in table 2.1) included the capitalising of expenses, revenue recognition issues, disputes about solvency, questions of inappropriate asset valuations. The current complaints are the same. And assertions that, especially in Australia, the scale of the financial dilemmas is different this time are also contestable (Table 4.1). The correspondence between the misleading financial disclosure that has fuelled the corporate problems and the scales of the fallouts shows how ineffective and inept regulatory reforms have been. Yet as in the past, the response to the recent wave of corporate malpractice has been to prescribe more of the same rather than radical surgery on the system.

Regulatory responses have varied across jurisdictions. In 1998 amid the fanfare of increased resourcing, Australia's major corporate regulator, the ASC, became the ASIC. Action increased with numerous investigations. Chapter 14 of *Corporate Collapse* detailed some of them.[25] It noted that at the beginning of 2002 the Australian press led with the claim that Australian 'judges face a busy time as watchdogs pounce'.[26] Again, for regulatory agencies, finding a scapegoat was possibly crucial. In the US, New York Attorney-General Eliot Spitzer's inquiries into corruption in the securities industry exposed the collaboration between analysts and the merchant bankers fuelling accounting misstatements to meet companies' quarterly earnings predictions. One might query the integrity of a system of accounting that is so easily manipulated.

The legislative responses have been predictable. In Australia the Joint Committee on Public Accounts and Audit (JCPAA) released *Report 391* in August 2002 that followed inquiries into 'noteworthy collapses both in Australia and overseas ... to explore the extent to which it may be necessary to enhance the accountability of public and private sector auditing'.[27] Contiguously, the federal Treasurer, Peter Costello, released a discussion paper *CLERP 9* with the proviso that more changes may follow the likely release of the HIH Royal Commission Report early in 2003. They did.

Proposed changes related to auditor independence, the interaction between audit and non-audit services, auditor liability, accounting standards, analyst independence, continuous disclosure, and fundraising. In 2005 the *CLERP 9* reforms became law. Claims were made that Australia's legislative responses were 'lighter' than their *SOX* US counterparts, but that they were, however, 'principles-based' rather than 'black-letter-law-based' (see chapters 2 and 3).

Revisiting the observations made in the Prologue, the paranoia of today's commentators has again clouded the focus of the corporate observers. It continues to blind them to some real issues, and generally lets the regulators and the accountancy profession off the hook. 'Bankers, lawyers, accountants and directors', the dishonest and the innocent alike, have been judged through the false perception that most regulatory mechanisms were apt.[28] To this might be added the ineffective and seduced financial media, the mutual fund managers, and the share analysts whose assessments in the US allegedly were affected by conflicts of interest. In such an atmosphere, investing is more likely to be part of the process that John Maynard Keynes described as being more a 'casino' than what efficient marketers claimed is an 'efficient allocating mechanism'.

In an earlier work we asked: 'Has there ever been a greater opportunity for accounting to act as a countervailing force – as the impartial disclosing mechanism?',[29] one that would act as a brake on what appears now to have been the unfettered market activities of various vested interests? The answer is 'Never!'

That denial is now strengthened by further evidence demonstrating that reforms to accounting need to address many of the inequitable commercial practices that have emerged in the recent boom/bust period. Corporate structures and financing arrangements are shown to be so complex they are difficult (perhaps impossible) to monitor and govern effectively. Complexity includes: mixing financial affairs of public and private companies within complex group structures (as alleged in respect of recent Australian instances, Westpoint, Bay Group and Auto Group collapses); undertaking property dealings and other asset transfers via extensive use of related party transactions (sometimes entailing 'round-robin transactions'); using share options to reward managers with the hope of aligning longer term interests of shareholders and managers; and using debt and off-balance sheet financing in the form of financial derivatives – like Enron's so-called 'structured financing'.

Unfortunately, within this scenario conventional standard accounting practices have proved no more able to cope effectively than they have been in the past. Somewhat serendipitously, the current bankruptcies at Enron and World-Com, and HIH in Australia, involved the same major auditing firm, Andersen. That has fuelled the suggestion noted earlier that perhaps auditors become too close to their clients when they offer non-audit services. It heightened the considerable talk of a need for inquiries into audit independence.[30]

In that environment, parliamentary and regulatory agencies' inquiries emerged on cue, premised on a desire for better, higher quality information for investors, greater transparency in today's jargon, which repeated the demands characterising late 1920s and early 1930s. In the latest kerfuffle, executives have been made more accountable and additional disclosures been required to ensure transparency. Stronger, more accountable auditing systems were to be developed. But, as in the previous upheavals after big name corporates crashed, the major push has been for more rules and regulations of the kind already non-performing. Chapter 2 noted the calls to prohibit the joint provision of audit and non-audit services, calls to mandate audit committees, the prohibition of multiple ex-auditor board appointments and calls for auditor rotations. The tenor of many of those demands mimics the rhetoric surrounding Roosevelt's New Deal following the 1929 crash, and received with approbation by those in the UK still miffed at the time by the Royal Mail scandal.[31] Similar financial affairs include: the US Penn Central, National Student Marketing and Equity Funding crises of the 1970s and the Savings and Loans fiascos in the 1980s and 1990s; the unexpected collapses of Minsec, Mainline, Gollins and Cambridge

Credit Corporation in Australia in the 1970s and of the Bond Corporation, Westmex, Qintex and Adsteam cases in the 1990s; and in the UK collapse of Pergamon in the 1970s, and the Maxwell Corporation, Polly Peck and BCCI debacles in the early 1990s. In respect of all those matters, sheeting home the blame has pre-occupied governments and the regulatory agencies keen to show they are on the job, to demonstrate their resolve to be tough, not tolerate corporate hanky-panky. Almost always this is supported by business lobbyists and the accounting profession fighting a rearguard action against outside interference, with assurances that they can fix the problem with what amounts to additional layers of internal self-regulation.

However, some newer reforms have emerged post-Enron and HIH. These include: (i) additional supervisory boards of accounting and audit practices (presumably to augment existing regulatory oversight) that took the form of government-mandated exercises such as the PCAOB reviews under *SOX*, those by the Canadian equivalent Board and self-regulatory mechanisms in other jurisdictions such as Australia's professionally sponsored Audit Quality Review Board; (ii) audit firms voluntarily instituting in-house monitoring committees to ensure ethically based best practices are being undertaken by all auditing staff; and (iii) stiffer criminal sanctions against fraudulent reporting and negligent auditing practices.

Autopsy-like examinations of corporate collapses have led many to question the usefulness of audited accounting data as a basis for the regular, ongoing financial assessments and evaluations made by investors, regulators and other interested parties: to a questioning, but to little real action. For the best part of a century misleading or untrue financial statements have involved balance date adjustments, deferring expenses, advancing revenue recognition, and judicious use of complex business group structures. These practices were described in the post-2000 euphoria as being 'aggressive', and they were justified again by managers who argued that they were better able to assess their appropriateness. Of course similar claims of business omnipotence had been made by managers in the 1970s and the 1920s. The quality control and neutrality aspects of a professionally qualified accountant subject to a regulatory enforced serviceability criterion in determining how to account for transactions seem to have taken a back seat. Directors remain the scorekeepers.[32]

But perhaps there was another factor. Had the accountancy firms become too close to their clients? The Chairman's foreword to the JCPAA 2002 *Report 391* observed that 'there has been a change in the profession over time from an emphasis on professional ethics to a more business-oriented focus'.[33] Evidence to the hearing supports such a claim.[34] Yet again in early 2000, on the cusp of an economic bust, the common experience was the sudden collapses of large public companies. While many have argued that no necessary relationship exists between accounting and corporate collapses, few fail to be alarmed at an accounting system that repeatedly does not report on a timely basis downward drifts in corporations' financial positions prior to their collapse. This inability of conventional accounting to be a reliable financial instrumentation was again called into question.

## A sense of urgency

It is really only *a sense*. In the wake of the most recent wave of corporate collapses, and the so-called accounting restatements and irregularities in the US in particular (GAO, 2003, 2004), a new-found sense of urgency has emerged. It is an urgency in professional and business circles that seems sourced more in the fear that governmental intervention might further threaten self-regulation than in a resolve to improve the quality of companies' financial disclosures. In government circles it is sourced more in its political than its commercial dimensions. Under the banner of a general push for enhanced corporate governance, corporate financial disclosure and auditing have been scrutinised with an implied intent to again 'clean it up'.

But though the rhetoric has taken on the mantle of serious reform, the capitalisation-of-expenditure-based system (subject to an impairment test) that underpins conventional historical cost-based accounting has remained. Is there likely to be a change with the advent of the global IFRSs regime? Not in our view.[35]

Under the proposed IFRSs regime the existing system is patched up by the addition of some partial fair-value adjustments for certain assets and liabilities. It comes under the mantle of asset impairment. This is instead of the fundamental underpinnings of accounting and reporting being worked over to have companies' financials disclose only data indicative of actual money or its equivalent received or expended, money to which the company reasonably has access or unequivocally owes. But standards-setting processes and the monitoring infrastructure of the system are what have been more in the sights of the governance measures being promoted 2001–02: in official reports, the *Ramsay Report*, the JCPAA *Report 391*, CPA Australia's *The Way Ahead – A New Financial Reporting Framework* (2003), and the myriad self-regulatory oversight proposals of the Big Four firms – like the PCAOB and AQRB initiatives.

There is no evidence, for example, that the 'principles' that underpinned Enron's front-end loading of 'profits' expected from its gas supply futures, WorldCom's alleged overcapitalisation of expenditures, HIH's capitalisation of expenditures, Waste Management's revision of its truck fleet amortisation practices, or HIH's, One.Tel's, Sunbeam's or Xerox's revenue recognition practices, will be raked over. No evidence that if they are found wanting they will be excised from conventional practices.

**Table 4.2:** Major US accounting investigations/lawsuits (as of June 2002; updated as at 31 December 2006)

| Company | Auditor | Action date | No fault settlements |
|---|---|---|---|
| Adelphia | Deloitte & Touche | 6 November 2002 | Ongoing |
| Computer Associates | Ernst & Young | February 2005 | Ongoing |
| Enron | Arthur Andersen | 20 December 2002 | Ongoing |
| Global Crossing | Arthur Andersen | January 2002 | US$25 million |
| MicroStrategy | PricewaterhouseCoopers | 21 May 2001 | No enforcement action taken against PwC. Settle at US$51 million plus interest |
| PeopleSoft | Ernst & Young | May 2002 | Action dismissed by judge |
| PNC Financial Services | Ernst & Young | 8 February 2002 | several million (on appeal by E & Y) |
| Qwest | Arthur Andersen | March 2005 | Ongoing |
| Waste Management | Arthur Andersen | 26 March 2005 | US$20 million |
| WorldCom | Arthur Andersen | March 2005 | US$65 million |
| Xerox | KPMG | 19 April 2005 | US$22.5 million |

*Sources:* Columns 1 and 2 are from *Business Week*, 10 June 2002, pp. 42–3; updated with data in columns 3 and 4 as at 31 December 2006 from web sources accessed by the authors. As well as settlements and judgments against auditors, directors and financial institutions have paid damages amounting to billions of dollars in these cases.

Surprise – the unexpectedness of the collapses when those bubbles burst because the companies' financial disclosures failed to show their trajectory towards failure lies more in accounting failure than in audit negligence. It is to be recalled that Andersen was convicted on the grounds that it had perverted the course of justice, not because it failed in the Enron audit, though many have held the view that it had. And it is to be remembered that no charges have been laid against the Andersen auditors of HIH. Where litigation is pending, as at Fannie Mae, we await with interest to hear what arguments are developed.

Auditors continue to be in a no-win situation. The count is over before they enter the ring. Curiously, no claims with respect to relying on the Accounting Standards have arisen in the litigation surrounding corporate collapse.

Table 4.2 shows the leading audit firms experiencing investigations. Several inferences are reasonable: first, it is to be expected that the leading firms appear, for only the top-flight audit firms have the experience and expertise to undertake the audit of the major corporates of the kind whose collapse hits the headlines; second, that the top-flight firms are exposed in this fashion is redolent of the hazard endemic in the systemic defects in accounting to which auditors are shackled.

Financial commentators have referred to the crisis in accounting.[36] Concerns have been expressed about all the elements of accounting – assets, liabilities, revenues and expenses, income. A major cause of those concerns is the accounting use of the asset, liability, revenue and expense descriptors in respect of data arising in the accounting process that do not accord with, or are contrary to, the manner in which the terms are used in the ordinary everyday commercial dealings of the public at large. It is not a matter of accountants using a technical language, but their application of commonly used descriptors to items whose characteristics do not accord with the public's everyday understanding of such things in a commercial setting. Perhaps the greatest confusion arises when numbers that are mere products of accounting processes or numbers are imputed without any real-world referent. These might be explored through contemplating the ripple-through consequences of just a few such items (of dubious parentage though in accord with the conventional rules) commonly reported in companies' financials as *assets* and *liabilities*.

For example, consider when a financial fiction is disclosed as an *asset*. We might imagine that the general commonsense notion of an asset implies something that exists – to which there are distinct and severable property rights. Few would find that difficult to understand. In contrast, we might expect considerable skepticism if the *asset* label were to be attached to pure creations, fictions of the accounting system, or to amounts of money spent and gone or legally owed. Yet, casual observation reveals how the notion of asset is applied in conventional accounting to any debit balance left over at the reporting date from the transaction processing system. First, there are those amounts emerging from the processing of transactions – expenditures carried forward, the amounts not completely charged against revenues. These are the so-called 'capitalised expenditures' of WorldCom notoriety, the unamortised amounts paid for physical assets and the like, even though they are more indicative of money the company no longer has or has yet to pay. Then there are the injected fictions of the system, amounts conjured up by the system and unrelated to any transactions: the deferred tax debits, and goodwill (such as raised by HIH on its purchase of FAI) for example (chapter 5). The former are the outcome of counterfactual assumptions about the company's income tax obligations, and the latter the difference between what was paid for assets and what is deemed the current worth of what has been received. Both of those amounts are mere products of the bookkeeping system. Reporting those amounts as 'assets' distorts virtually every key financial characteristic. The point can be demonstrated by recourse to just a few illustrations. Consider the ripple-through, offsetting and confounding effects on the reported profits (and losses), rate of return on equity and total assets, capital gearing, asset backing, and implied solvency of expenditure carried-forward, raising a tax effect asset and raising purchased goodwill on the purchase. Whereas describing such amounts in accounts as assets contradicts the everyday understanding of the notion, they are nonetheless book items in nearly every listed company's balance sheet.

Holding everything else as it is, the *capitalised expenses* understates expense and that overstates profits, which: overstates rate of return on equity and total assets, but increases assets. Now, that in turn decreases the rate of return on equity and total assets, decreases gearing, but increases asset backing and increases implied solvency. The *deferred tax asset* understates profits and that understates rate of return on equity and total assets, (most likely) decreases gearing, increases total assets, net asset backing, and the implied solvency position. The *purchased goodwill* increases expenses (amortisation of goodwill), understates profits, decreases rate of return, decreases gearing, increases net asset backing, and increases implied solvency.

Now consider when a financial fiction is disclosed as a *liability*. In virtually all commercial settings we might expect that the notion of *liability* carries the connotation only of an amount legally owing.[37] But in conventional accounting it is not the case. As with the notion of *asset* there are items appearing in the financials as left-overs from the processing of the transactions data – in a sense capitalised liabilities, and there are the injection of pure fictions such as *deferred tax liabilities* (the counterparts of the 'deferred tax assets'), and the imputation of 'provisions' for obligations that might accrue.[38] The first arises by virtue of the accrual system being based upon revenues being allocated on the basis of time rather than receipt, the second by virtue of the tax effect system of accounting, and the third from bringing to account expected obligations before they arise. As with the asset fictions, the examples of liability fictions have myriad offsetting and confounding impacts on the derivation of the usual financial characteristics. The *accrued payables* understates profits, decreases rate of return on equity and on assets, but also increases rate of return on equity and assets (as the liability decreases the equity denominator of the ratio), increases capital gearing, decreases net asset backing, and decreases the implied solvency position. The *deferred tax liability* overstates profits (decreases losses as the deferred tax credit decreases the tax expense in the income account), increases the rates of return, increases the capital gearing, decreases net asset backing, and decreases the implied solvency. The creation of a *provision* decreases profits (as the provision is charged against revenues) which decreases rate of return on equity and total assets, but the lower profit decreases equity and thus increases the rate of return in the subsequent year, increases gearing, decreases net asset backing, and decreases the implied solvency position. Provisioning difficulties have been reported in respect of many things in both the public and private sectors, involving the estimates to restore mine sites, quarries and the like, amounts set aside to cover expected merger costs, costs of funding superannuation. In the US the issue of underfunding pension funds was reported as this book was going to press. Under a reported (non-fault) settlement, the SEC, after investigating San Diego's financial reporting, found that the city had misled investors in municipal bond documents about the health of its pension plan when it issued $260 million of debt in 2002 and 2003. Assets were alleged to be overstated by about $500 million, resulting in San Diego's unfunded liability to its pension plan projected to increase to an estimated $2 billion in 2009 from $284 million in 2002. San Diego also didn't disclose that it was liable for retiree health-care costs estimated at $1.1 billion.[39] In Australia such underfunding is reported to be common (for example, in the public sector including universities and private companies).

In some situations the separate impacts offset each other to a greater or lesser extent. Raising the deferred tax asset, for example, has the implication that the actual income tax payable is less than the income tax charged against revenues, reducing the profits from what they would otherwise have been, reducing (on that score) the shareholders' equity that will be the denominator of the rate-of-return calculation for the subsequent year. Assuming the most likely case of there being a deferred tax asset carried forward implies that the rate of return denominator for a current year is understated relative to what it would have been without tax effect accounting in the previous year. That means that the RoR for the current year is relatively overstated; but, of course, that is only if the tax effect adjustment in the previous year was not greater than it is in the current year, or the current RoR would be relatively overstated. We say *relatively*, for the absolute change depends upon the respective amounts of the tax effect adjustments on the profit calculation in the previous and the current year. What a schemozzle. And all that is in accord with the existing standards.

Of course, analysts really up to the task will attempt to neutralise many of those impacts by removing the capitalised expenses, by removing, then adding back the amortisation on the goodwill, getting rid of the tax effect impacts, readjusting the tax expense, etc. How successful that will be is problematical. A deliberate massaging of the accounting data in an attempt to neutralise the distortions' effect shows them for what they are – accounting fictions having no relevance to the sort of financial characteristics being derived for various decision-making purposes.

The implications of bringing assets and liabilities to account clearly have considerable ramifications not only for the determination of financial perfor-mance and financial position, but also for the uses made by those who are adept in deriving indicators of the company's financial features. Above, we looked at only a few matters to illustrate how the bewildering and consequential impli-cations thread through. It may well be that the financial impacts substantially cancel each other out. But if they do, it is merely by chance. And in any event

**Illustration 3:** 'Welcome to Wombat's Crossing'
*Source:* 'Welcome to Wombat's Crossing', a cartoon by R. Petty, appeared in the ASRC Report (1978), p. 11. State of New South Wales through the Attorney-General's Department, 1978.

many of the potential offsets can only occur over time. That still means that the reported financials for contiguous years are almost certainly misleading, although whether they are is virtually impossible to determine.

The BHP write-offs (1996–99), see pp. 114–15, are a good example of the ripple-through effect. To the extent that the write-offs related to loss of real value in previous years, amortisation on the plant write-offs would have been overstated in those years, profits understated on that score and rate of return understated as far as assets and equity were overstated but overstated insofar as the profits were overstated because of less amortisation, and the impact in the previous year on the current year's RoR denominator. Those and the related financial entanglements are almost impossible to untangle. To the extent investors gained or lost is anyone's guess. But it is virtually certain that to the extent that those losses (in asset value, however calculated) didn't occur entirely in the year of write-down, then investment decisions such as whether to buy, not buy, sell, not sell, were undertaken on less than reliable financial data.

Consider the following indicative AIFRSs-compliant consolidated financials of an ASX-listed company for the year ended 30 June 2006.

The data in figure 4.1 relate to a notional group comprising hundreds of subsidiary companies, of which near to 20 per cent have a closed group bound by a Deed of Cross Guarantee from which several companies exited during the year. Figure 4.1 shows the consolidated balance sheet items. These data

**Figure 4.1:** Indicative ASX listed company: 2006 consolidated balance sheet items

| ASX listed company 2006 consolidated balance sheet items and notes | Accounting basis | Financial performance | Financial position | Assets worth | Amount of liabilities | Solvency | Rate of return | Debt/equity | Net asset backing | Current ratio |
|---|---|---|---|---|---|---|---|---|---|---|
| **Current assets** | | | | | | | | | | |
| Cash & cash equivalents | Cash | Yes | Yes | Yes | | Yes | Yes | Yes | Yes | Yes |
| Receivables | Cons. estimated collectible | Yes* | Yes* | Yes* | | Yes* | Yes* | Yes* | Yes* | Yes* |
| Inventories | NRV, cost | No | No | No | | No | No | No | No | Yes* |
| N/c assets held for sale | Cost | Yes* | Yes* | Yes* | | Yes* | Yes* | Yes* | Yes* | Yes* |
| Derivative financial assets | Estimated fair value | Yes* | Yes* | Yes* | | Yes* | Yes* | Yes* | Yes* | Yes* |
| **Total current assets** | Mixed measurement | No | No | No | | No | No | No | No | No |
| **Non-current assets** | | | | | | | | | | |
| Receivables | Cons. estimated collectible | Yes* | Yes* | Yes* | | Yes* | Yes* | Yes* | Yes* | |
| Inventories | NRV and cost | No | No | No | | No | No | No | No | |
| Investments – equity method | Cost | No | No | No | No | No | No | No | No | |
| Other financial assets | Cost | No | No | No | | No | No | No | No | |
| Property plant & equipment | Cost, cost less amortisation | No | No | No | | No | No | No | No | |
| Agricultural assets | Fair Value, cost | No | No | No | | No | No | No | No | |
| Intangible assets | Cost, cost less mortisation | No | No | No | | No | No | No | No | |
| Deferred tax assets | Accounting calculation | No | No | No | | No | No | No | No | |
| Derivative financial assets | Estimated fair value | Yes* | Yes* | Yes* | | Yes* | Yes* | Yes* | Yes* | |
| **Total non-current assets** | Mixed measurement | No | No | No | | No | No | No | No | |
| **Total assets** | Mixed measurement | No | No | No | | No | No | No | No | |
| **Current liabilities** | | | | | | | | | | |
| Payables | Cons. aggregate owing | Yes* | Yes* | | Yes* | Yes* | Yes* | Yes* | Yes* | Yes* |
| Borrowings | Cons. aggregate owing | Yes* | Yes* | | Yes* | Yes* | Yes* | Yes* | Yes* | Yes* |
| Current tax liabilities | Amount owing | Yes | Yes | | Yes | Yes | Yes | Yes | Yes | Yes |
| Provisions | Estimated to accrue | Yes | Yes | | Yes | Yes | Yes | Yes | Yes | Yes |
| Liabilities re:assets for sale | Estimated | Yes | Yes | | Yes | Yes | Yes | Yes | Yes | Yes |
| Derivative fin. liabilities | Fair value | Yes* | Yes* | | Yes* | Yes* | Yes* | Yes* | Yes* | Yes* |
| **Total current liabilities** | Mixed measurement | Yes* | Yes* | | Yes* | Yes* | Yes*No | Yes* | Yes* | Yes* |
| **Non-current liabilities** | | | | | | | | | | |
| Payables | Cons. aggregate owing | Yes* | Yes* | | Yes* | Yes* | Yes* | Yes* | Yes* | Yes* |
| Borrowings | Cons. aggregate owing | Yes* | Yes* | | Yes* | Yes* | Yes* | Yes* | Yes* | Yes* |
| Deferred tax liabilities | Accounting calculation | No | No | | No | No | No | No | No | |
| Provisions | Estimated to accrue | No | No | | No | No | No | No | No | |
| Derivative fin. liabilities | Fair value | Yes* | Yes* | | Yes* | Yes* | Yes* | Yes* | Yes* | Yes* |
| **Total non-current liabilities** | Mixed measurement | No | No | | No | No | No | No | No | |
| **Total liabilities** | Mixed measurement | No | No | | No | No | No | No | No | |
| **Net assets** | Mixed measurement | No | No | No | No | No | No | No | No | |
| **Equity** | | | | | | | | | | |
| Shareholders' equity interest | Mixed measurement | No | No | No | No | No | No | No | No | |
| Minority interests in controlled entities | Derived proportional Mixed measurement | | No | No | No | No | No | No | No | |
| **Total equity** | Mixed measurement | No | No | No | No | No | No | No | No | |

*Note:* Yes* indicates a reserved Yes. In respect of 'receivables' and 'payables' – owing to the likelihood that because of the elimination of intra-group indebtedness as part of the consolidation process the *receivables* and *payables* data do not indicate aggregate internal and external indebtedness. From consolidated data it usually is impossible to determine which companies are *net internal borrowers or lenders,* or *net external borrowers or lenders.* This is important, bearing in mind that without cross guarantees members of the group are not obliged to donate assets for the discharge of each other's debts. In respect to other items: the '*' is inserted to indicate that the item has been accorded the 'benefit of the doubt', though it is difficult to be certain from the Notes of listed companies whether the data include hypothetical calculations, discounting and the like.

are unequivocally in accord with the AIFRS, duly signed-off by the directors as showing a 'true and fair view' and given a clean audit report from one of the Big 4. Ignoring for the moment the inherent fiction of consolidated financials (chapter 9), in the columns to the right of the consolidated data we have indicated whether those data would otherwise be serviceable for determining the group's financial performance and the financial position, solvency, rate of return on equity, debt to equity ratio, asset backing, and its current ratio. Directors and auditors are required by the *Corporations Act 2001* (Cth) to look to the first three. The others are noted by the company's financial history, so it is reasonable to suspect that they are considered by the company to be important financial characteristics. Only the 'cash and cash equivalents' earns an unequivocal 'Yes'. Others earn a reserved 'Yes*'.

We take it that a company's *financial position* refers to the relationship between the nature, composition and money's worth of its assets, and the nature, composition and amount of its liabilities; that *financial performance* refers to the change in the net money's worth of its assets (other than the input of new capital) during the year; RoR to the rate of increase in the money's worth of its net assets (other than from new capital) during the year, and *return on assets* to be the rate of increase in its total assets on the same basis; *solvency* – the capacity for it to pay its debts as they fall due; and its *asset backing* – the proportion of its net assets attributable to each issued share.

Figure 4.1 shows that most of the individual balance sheet items fail to be serviceable for deriving those characteristics. Only those that are verifiable amounts of money or its equivalent satisfy the serviceability test. Of particular importance, it is contestable whether the new AIFRS-compliant data fare any better than would have been the case with the AASB-based data. It is still the case that the amounts for the physical assets, inventories and plant and property, are a mixture of net realisable values, cost, amortised cost, recoverable amount (the higher of the NRV and the estimated discounted cash flows from using the asset – their value in use). But as some of the plant and property items have been subjected to an impairment adjustment, the AIFRS data include the impact of discounted estimated revenue flows from lumped assets, not necessarily part of the calculations under the previous AASBs. The intangibles (goodwill and the like), and the tax effect, deferred tax assets and deferred tax liabilities remain accounting fictions that do not refer to any amounts of money the company has control over; and as the provisions are a mixture of discounted and non-discounted estimates their relationship to amounts actually payable (currently or in the future) is contestable.

All those data have been massaged in conformity with the highly questionable rubrics of consolidation accounting. They are not straight aggregations of the amounts appearing in the accounts of the companies comprising the group. Against that background – the aggregates for *current assets*, *non-current assets*, *current liabilities, long-term liabilities,* and for *shareholders' equity,* and most of the components of them, bear an unknown relationship to the magnitudes they are held out to represent. Yet, directly or indirectly, they or the changes in their amounts are components of each of the financial characteristics noted above.

## 'Not a pretty picture – but an inconvenient truth'[40]

A verdict that the data in companies' financials are generally not serviceable, not fit for uses generally made of them, is certainly inconvenient. But unless financial statements are serviceable for calculating financial performance, showing financial position and deriving the usual raft of financial indicators, what function do they serve? Compliance with the Accounting Standards is invoked as a kind of credentialism. But credentialism implying a professional *technical status* devoid of usefulness is utter humbug.

What chance do auditors have to report it as it is when they are directed to presume that complying with the Standards of the day will show a true and fair view?

# 5

# A Most Peculiar Practice: Auditing Under the Microscope

Interpretational uncertainties within existing accounting standards expose auditors to difficulties in their task of verifying what is reported by managers. Recent reforms to auditing practices create the impression that the problems lie with auditing processes, rather than with the inherent defects in the accounting data that auditors confront. Changes have been recommended and implemented by professional and legislative bodies set up to inquire into and to monitor how best to mitigate the perceived declining confidence in assurances given in audit opinions on companies' financial statements.

Major changes in Australian (ASAu) and international (ISA) auditing standards have occurred in the last five years. In some jurisdictions, like Australia, they have the force of law. Within Part 2M3 of Australia's *Corporations Act (2001)* Section 307A requires since early 2006 that auditors comply with the Australian Auditing standards promulgated by the APESB. This was introduced as part of the *CLERP 9* reforms. The changes have focused on processes – structural issues – and not, as Australian financial journalist, Bartholomeusz (2006) noted so appositely, on improving the effectiveness of the audit opinion as a quality control device.[1] Using a different context Taylor *et al.* (2003) have argued there is no need to concentrate on 'independence' in the relationship sense, but rather to consider what is needed to ensure that the auditor's opinion is reliable. Each would require the serviceability of the accounting as a pre-condition.

Currently 'accounting is auditing's devil'.[2] How the IFRSs interrelate to the 'true and fair' view legislative criterion is often the critical issue.[3] Legislators have confirmed their support for the override criterion as part of the new reporting regime, but generally the professional bodies tend to deny it. In this context it is curious how individuals use ordinary words without any discomfort in respect of their ordinary personal affairs, but as accountants have difficulty using the same words in respect of their clients' affairs. 'True' and 'fair' are cases in point.

Whereas it seems that few in a business setting had much trouble with those words used either singly or collectively in the English language for at least

120 years and informally for much longer,[4] from about the mid-1960s accountants, regulators, analysts and the like discovered that they didn't understand what the 'true' and 'fair' meant. Perhaps that was not surprising, for about the same time those groups found that they also did not understand what *financial performance*, *wealth* and *financial position* meant in the context of accounting.

Corporate disclosure reforms have sought to balance the rules-based approach of imposing more standards of the IFRS type with overarching principles in existing companies legislation – like the recourse to 'true and fair'. Considerable debate has occurred. In 2005 Australia's Parliamentary Joint Committee on Corporations and Financial Services finalised its inquiry into whether the Australian versions of the AIFRSs met the objectives of the *Corporations Act 2001* (Cth), including the need to comply with the 'true and fair' view override. Compliance with the new regime is likely to produce data in the post-2005 reporting periods contradicting those prepared under the AASB Standards previously endorsed as disclosing a 'true and fair' view of companies' 'financial performances' and their 'financial positions'.

This leads to an interesting dilemma. Complying with the new AIFRSs is now said to, *prima facie*, produce a true and fair view. That implies that what was signed-off on by directors pre-2005 – to which unqualified audit opinions were appended, accepted by ASIC and APRA as satisfying their regulatory requirements, meeting the ASX Corporate Governance Council's financial reporting guidelines, and backed by the professional accountancy bodies – was incorrect. And presumably, it was neither true nor fair.

Those who acted on what appeared in companies' financials have good reason to feel aggrieved by the implication that their decisions were based upon seemingly misleading financial information. Self-congratulations all round by those who have pushed so grandiloquently for the introduction of the AIFRSs provide cold comfort for those presumably 'misled' by what was disclosed to them in the past. How will those penalised in the past for deviating from the previous standards feel now that they are forbidden to comply with them? Will they let bygones remain bygones? Imagine the prospect of court deliberations relying on those older, now discredited, AASB standards.

Despite the best of intentions that those earlier reported profits and losses attested to were incorrect, the reported rates of return were wrong, as were the other salient financial characteristics of firms that are habitually calculated, circulated, commented on, peddled by analysts, brokers, and commentators were wrong, the nature, composition of assets and liabilities, the worth of assets, gearing ratios, asset backing, assessments of solvency, and the like. The disclosed financial performances and financial positions were wrong. It is not just a matter of a need of tweaking at the margin. It is that the data used in the calculations were defective, in error, on the wrong track. They are the result of conforming to rules rather than applying principles.

Most submissions to that JCCFS 2005 Parliamentary Inquiry suggested that adopting AIFRSs will produce comparability; that they are principles- rather than rules-based. But nowhere has a general qualitative principle, such as the serviceability principle explained above (chapter 4), been declared. And frequently those who promote the principles-based claim express an inconsistent desire for 'interpretations' to avoid variations in the way those standards are implemented.

There is uneasiness over practical issues such as the impact for Australian companies of excluding many intangibles, moving to the asset impairment regime and its use of fair-value measurement and recourse to compulsory estimating of future cash generation units and their discounting. Yet, surprisingly, there has been little concern that what was reported in the past as a consequence of compliance with the (now outlawed) AASBs amounted to a form of 'compulsory creative accounting', possibly as misleading as the 'feral' practices of those intending to mislead.[5]

A persistent downplaying of the 'true and fair' criterion for nearly twenty years has characterised the profession's championing of the idea that compliance with prevailing accounting standards would have financial statements meet the 'true and fair' quality criterion specified in the *Corporations Act 2001* (Cth). The current rejection of the previous AASBs exposes the compliance fallacy. A company's financials are to reflect the true and fair view of its financial performance and financial position – that is, the most supportable overriding 'principle' that accountants, auditors and directors can observe by drawing upon their professional experience, knowledge and skills, and accumulated commercial wisdom. Interestingly, in their submission the Group of 100 noted that apparently the AIFRSs had to be complied with even if that did not result in a true and fair view, contrary to the intention of the International Accounting Standards Board's aim. Their point hits the spot directly.

If the AIFRSs are taken to be other than general guidance to be pursued in the absence of disclosures considered more likely to achieve a 'true and fair view', little will have been achieved. That would be as 'untrue' and as 'unfair' as it can get.

We have noted the disenchantment with the misleading financials of Enron, WorldCom, Sunbeam, Waste Management, HIH, One.Tel, Westpoint, Disney, Health South, Fannie Mae, Freddie Mac, Vivendi and (say) Parmalat. It more than illustrates that accounting disclosure in significant instances has misled and deluded. Frequently, it seems this has occurred within the framework of the rules, if not in keeping with the spirit of them. In a curious twist, in many instances the outcomes of following the rules, designed to protect, have emerged as the means by which their frailty has been most exploited.

That some time, somewhere, somehow, someone – such as a director or an auditor – will be put on the spot, quizzed in court proceedings regarding what they have meant when they used the phrase 'true and fair' has been noted above. And falling back on the notion that it means whatever the outcome is as a result of complying with the prevailing Standards, it is quite likely that they will be nailed to the wall once 'true and fair' is expected to have some sensible implications. This suggests that auditing is also in crisis.[6]

The following brief case particulars (taken from fuller analyses in Clarke *et al.*, *Corporate Collapse*, 2003) of Bond, Adsteam and HIH provide the persistent setting within which such a claim occurs decade after decade. They highlight the intertwined nature of accounting and auditing – and illustrate the inherent difficulties faced by auditors seeking to comply with the accounting Standards and ensuring that accounts provide a true and fair view.

## Bond Corporation

*Corporate Collapse* noted that 'the real sting in the BCH tale is its similarity with many of the previously described (and subsequent) failures and the associated regulatory, accounting and ethical deficiencies' (2003, p. 196). It was noted that corporate complexity regarding structure and financing, the interposing of private and public interests and the pervasive schizophrenic recourse to the separate legal entity were evident. Further, we observed that

> The use of accepted accounting techniques, especially in the context of *enterprise* action, masked the true failure path which BCH was travelling. Further, our overview of selected publicly disclosed accounting treatments, in respect of foreign currency, deferred tax and convertible notes, suggests considerable compliance with the specifics of individual Accounting Standards ... How serviceable was BCH's accounting compliance, especially in producing the 1987 and 1988 consolidated accounting data? The complex BCH corporate structure, with over 600 subsidiaries, many registered overseas, facilitating dealings with related parties including family companies of the founder, again raises the question of whether society is well served by such structures and the conventional, standard accounting for them. (p. 197)

The accounting and financing manoeuvrings at Bond had many intrigued, and resulted in a now well-known ABC TV *Four Corners* program exposé that is well described in Paul Barry's book.[7] An early critic of Bond Corporation's accounts was accounting professor Bob Walker. His observations exposed the perverse nature of conventional accounting.

> [O]ne could not expect to find many gains or losses from the sale of businesses treated as extraordinary items because Bond Corp specifies that the 'primary operations' . . . include 'the disposition of assets acquired during the period or held for trading purposes from prior years . . . 'normal operations of the group' . . . include operations . . . of material once-only transactions'. Readers are advised that 'while relatively few of these transactions may be completed in any one year, their effect on the group's results is not regarded as being abnormal nor outside the principal operations of the group' . . . extraordinary items which to Bond Corp are just ordinary items.[8]

It was observed in *Corporate Collapse* (pp. 190–1) that:

> Terminological niceties were used to veil what was occurring, all under the rubric of compliance. . . . Two weeks later, under the caption 'Window dressing at Bond Corporation', Walker this time commented on two other technical accounting matters – one relating to tax effect accounting, and the second relating to the treatment of convertible bonds. Both these items were accounted for in a manner which, according to Walker, maximised 'the impression of growth and liquidity'. Another accounting treatment having a further positive effect on BCH's financial outcome related to foreign currency. These three treatments and their effects on the 1986/87 and 1987/88 accounts are of great significance, for they invited inferences regarding BCH's financial stability from the only publicly available financial information at the time – BCH's published financial statements. They provided valuable insights into the role of accounting information and, in particular, with respect to the matter of compliance with Australia's Accounting Standards.

Reminiscent of the reliance placed upon usual or standard practice in the 1920s Royal Mail accounting saga in the United Kingdom, there was no categorical claim that BCH had not complied with the Standards. Certainly the accounts were duly audited as such. No doubt they would be claimed to offend 'the spirit' of the Standards – but 'the spirit' resides as much in the opportunity for alternative interpretations, the looseness of and omissions in the Standards, as in what they state. With H.G. Palmer the court also revealed 'omission of material particulars' – specifically, failure to make *adequate provision for bad and doubtful debts*, which produced a reported profit of £408 371 in 1964 and a year earlier a profit of £431 624. Whether accounting at BCH was creative or feral, whether material particulars were omitted from the accounts, whether parties are brought to book for any actions, has still not been definitively determined by the court deliberations, judicial actions and the out-of-court settlement. The published accounts from those inquiries imply a mixture of all.

## Adsteam

The accounting matters discussed in the Adsteam litigation go to the heart of some of the major questions in accounting and auditing: What is profit? To what entity does the profit relate? Is there such a thing legally as a group profit from which a separate company dividend relates? Can asset revaluations be included in such a profit? And so on. In respect of Adsteam, these and other issues, especially a long-running class action initiated by the ASC on behalf of Adsteam, were examined by ASIC. In *Corporate Collapse* we summarised these matters:

> [The] ASC investigated several transactions between Adsteam and related companies during the 1989/90 period, as well as the propriety of certain asset valuations. This eventually resulted in the ASC launching its class action in December 1994 in the Federal Court against the Adsteam auditor and several of its directors on behalf of Adsteam.
>
> The ASC alleged that related-party transactions between Adsteam, several subsidiaries and other related parties (loans, investments, sales with put options, etc.) were used in order to present the financial state of affairs of the Adsteam group in a better light than it really was. And, that individual entity asset revaluations, related entity profits and dividend transfers, were not in accord with existing Accounting Standards. Specifically, it was alleged that the directors of Adsteam should not have permitted payment of the interim dividend of $131 488 000 and the $97 313 000 final dividend for the financial year ending 30 June 1990. They should have been aware that 'Adsteam's profit for the six months ending 31 December 1989 was overstated in the 1990 interim accounts at least by the sum of $449 985 498', and that 'Adsteam's profits for the year ended 30 June 1990 were overstated in the Adsteam's accounts at least by an amount of $518 981 000'.
>
> Several reasons were advanced by the ASC to support its contentions. ASC's claim suggested that loan asset balances should have been written down and FITB balances written off, and that asset revaluations were selective and not in accord with approved Accounting Standards. Contested was whether a surplus arising from an asset revaluation related to a particular company could be used to allow a cash dividend. The ghost of the 1961 UK case, *Dimbula*

*Valley (Ceylon) Tea Co Ltd v Laurie* appeared in the discovery process. There, Justice Buckley had ruled that, while it may not be prudent, *under certain* circumstances such a cash dividend was legal.

Reportedly, the ASC's argument drew upon the proposition that those related-party transactions masked the true state of the financial affairs of Adsteam as at 30 June 1990. The question of entity versus group enterprise immediately surfaced. Arguments presented in the process of discovery concerned whether 'group' profits were appropriate. This raised the issue of whether 'group' profits exist *per se*.

Also, we would argue that no FITB balance ought to be raised in the first place, physical asset valuation under the Standards is always selective, and related party transactions do not so much 'mask' as does the conventional accounting for them. The successful appeal by the auditors against the validity of the ASC bringing the class action was overturned on a further appeal by the ASC. Years later a settlement was reached.

In November 2000 ASIC released a press statement *Media Release 00/452* to the effect that several of the directors and auditors agreed to a settlement of the class action that ASIC had brought on behalf of Adsteam. The reported settlement figure was $20 million. The settlement contained the following covenants that have significant implications for the future actions of directors and auditors:

6. The auditors acknowledge the importance of accounting and auditing standards, and agree that compliance with those standards is essential to the presentation of *true and fair* financial statements. [emphasis added]
7. The directors and auditors note that in the 1990 Adsteam financial statements they adopted some accounting treatments which they believed were technically available. The directors and auditors note ASIC's views that the 1990 Adsteam financial statements did not present a true and fair view of the position of the company and fell outside of the accepted accounting principles and practices of that time. While they are unable to agree with this view, including for legal reasons, with the benefit of hindsight, the directors and auditors accept that a different accounting treatment would have been appropriate.

This may prove to be a watershed. The settlement is reinforced by developments post-Enron, the HIH Royal Commission, the Ramsay Report on Auditor Independence, the *CLERP 9* and JCPAA *Report 391* Discussion Papers.

It is worth considering in detail some accounting matters referred to in the above *Adsteam settlement* covenants. They are central to accounting issues

91

**Illustration 4:** 'FAI men puff profits of HIH'
*Source:* 'FAI men puff profits of HIH', *The Australian*, 13 July 2004. Courtesy of Peter Nicholson.

generally, *inter alia*: Whether asset revaluations were valid? Whether they generate a profit, especially distributable profit? Had indeed dividends been paid out of capital swelled by the increased asset values recorded as asset revaluation reserves? Further, debate centred on which entity those accounting questions related to – to the individual company, in this case the Adelaide Steamship Company Ltd, or to the Adsteam Group? The uncertainty surrounding the issue aptly illustrates the confusion for both accountants and observers, directors and regulators when discussing financial performance and financial position. They allow their reference to vacillate between the *notional group* of related companies and the *separate companies* comprising *it*.

## HIH

It is not unreasonable to ask: How is it that the directors of a publicly listed company are able to report in its financials that an entity has net assets approaching $1 billion when only a few months later, in liquidation, it is revealed that there is a deficiency of assets relative to liabilities of over $5 billion? Curiously to some, the auditors had provided an unqualified, but for the layperson an intriguingly named, 'emphasis of matter' opinion on the financials for the year immediately preceding the collapse. Perhaps even more curious to some, after more than five years there have been no litigation claims suggesting the auditors were acting in a negligent fashion in issuing an unqualified opinion. In *Corporate Collapse* (2003) this matter is discussed in depth (pp. 227–38) including reproducing and analysing the audit report. That material was preceded by a discussion of the 'emphasis of matter opinion':

HIH was placed into provisional liquidation in March 2001. Initial estimates of the maximum losses by the administrator were $4 billion, subsequently revised to more than $5.3 billion. The administration occurred, incongruously, not long after HIH had reported the 'apparently' successful purchase of FAI for $300 million in 1999, followed by a 112 per cent rise in profits in the first half of 2000. Although detailing an 'emphasis of matter' opinion in note 13 of the *Notes to the Accounts*, HIH's auditors had provided an otherwise unqualified opinion in respect of the financial accounts in June of that year, showing a surplus of net assets of $939 million. That exposes the curious state of the auditing game. An 'emphasis of matter' of opinion, though obviously indicative of a reservation entertained by the auditors, is not regarded as a *qualified* opinion. But clearly, it is entering a caveat that could be drawn upon as a defence if the need arises, were the 'clean' report to be challenged later. Auditing is a very peculiar practice, indeed. Not that such anomalies had not been exposed before. Consider the examination of 'Mr Moreland', the Price Waterhouse auditor of the Royal Mail company, in Lord Kylsant's trial in the early 1930s, which provides the greatest insight to the way in which conventional professional thinking runs on such matters. [It seems such thinking persists.[9]] At issue there was whether 'secret reserves' were a legitimate source from which dividends might be paid. The short answer was 'yes'. The long answer was 'yes and no!' Lord Plender (the president of The Institute of Chartered Accountants in England and Wales, and chair of the London-based firm of Deloitte, Plender and Griffiths) offered the opinion that the 'materiality' of the amount is what mattered. We might take it that in the same way that non-disclosure of the source of the Royal Mail's dividends did not negate a true and fair appellation by the auditor, nor does the 'emphasis of the matter' comment negate an unqualified audit opinion today. In respect of a clean audit report, Lord Plender's 'materiality' safe harbour played the same role as the current 'emphasis . . .' plays today. Putting this audit matter into context, it is worth considering the financials of HIH for the financial years 1999 and 2000 . . . [which are shown in Table 15.1 in *Corporate Collapse*].

There is a view that the 'emphasis of matter' opinion should have alerted any interested parties to possible risks at HIH. Counterbalancing this, the Royal Commission inquiry appears to have revealed questionable accounting [and related financing] practices. . . . The lore is that HIH was under-reserved. The issue of assessing the amount of an insurer's liabilities is inherently difficult – as many witnesses to the HIH Royal Commission have attested. HIH's provisioning policy did not provide for an adequate prudential reserve margin in respect of its future claim obligations, but rather it sought reinsurance to cover the risk. Allegations before the HIHRC suggest there were undisclosed (at least to many), questionable 'reinsurance side letters' that may have meant that certain reinsurance rearrangements would have been, in effect, loans. If so, reported profits would have been reduced and liabilities would have been higher.

Attention then turned in the following to matters of HIH's solvency or the lack thereof:

[T]he financial management literature in general, and the accounting literature in particular, are replete with explanations of solvency. Notwithstanding the debate over what are the critical tests ('balance sheet' or 'cash flow' tests) of solvency and insolvency, there is general agreement that the notion of being solvent entails having the capacity to meet 'debts' as they fall due. Laypersons might properly expect that in an orderly, well-regulated corporate environment, the data set out in a company's financial statements would be pertinent to, and serviceable for, such an assessment.

*Financial* position, like all *positions*, is unique to a specific date. In most circumstances only the present financial position can be determined and therefore only the current state of solvency. The prediction of future states of solvency requires estimations of likely future financial positions. No reasonable prediction of future financial positions, or of the cash resources likely to be in hand, or to which there might be access through pledging or selling physical assets, is possible *without knowledge of the present financial position* from which all future such positions will be departures. For the most part, a comprehensive use of the Accounting Standards does not produce data from which financial position in those terms can be determined. (at p. 239) [emphasis in original]

In sum, those cases cover limited circumstances, but they highlight the inherent deficiencies in accounting and the difficulties they create for auditors undertaking their verification exercise.[10]

The failure of the international accounting community to explain the function of accounting (and hence auditing) so that such key notions as financial position and performance are defined and articulated in an unequivocal way provides a challenge to the continuing acceptance of accounting and auditing as professional activities. Imagine as we speculated earlier what might happen were a judge to demand that *true* and *fair* 'as ordinary words' be given their 'ordinary meanings'. Indeed, since in respect of financial disclosures they are being used in the ordinary course of commercial events, how could anyone defend any other usage? And since the function of accounting is to inform, to 'enlighten'[11] and provide information about the financial characteristics of firms, how might the explanations turn were the judge to inquire whether the data in financials complying with the Standards are generally *serviceable* for deriving reliable indicators of an entity's wealth, financial performance, rate of return, earnings per share, debt to equity, solvency, asset backing, and the like. Suppose the answers to such an inquiry were affirmative, and that further questioning elicited the inevitable agreement on the financial nature of those characteristics. Contemplate were it then to be asked whether the data in compliant financials generally were indicative of actual amounts of money or its equivalents possessed, accessible, and owed by the entity. And when the reply was 'no', imagine the consternation and utter disbelief were attempts made then to argue, in defence, that those financial characteristics differed in the accounting context from how they are understood outside of it.

Outside of accounting, the overall requirement is that goods and services are fit for the uses ordinarily made of them – that they are *serviceable*. That is the overall catch-all consumer quality criterion. Accounting provides a service. It produces financial data that are used – as a minimum – to determine and evaluate the wealth and financial progress of business entities and to derive their financial characteristics. Those characteristics indicate businesses' vital financial signs, provide insights into how they are faring financially, and where their financial strengths and weaknesses lie. The notion of 'fitness for use' or 'serviceability' is what the *relevant, reliable, comparable* and *understandable* criteria frequently set out in conceptual framework exercises coalesce into. Unless accounting data are serviceable they cannot inform, cannot enlighten. But they certainly can confuse, mislead, befuddle and delude. That is exactly what financials generally do when certified as 'true and fair', merely because they have been prepared in compliance with the general run of Accounting Standards.

Virtually nobody has difficulty using 'true' or 'fair' in everyday discourse. And recent work suggests that there is little difficulty either on the part of those who *try* to do so, in the special setting of accounting.[12] Outside of accounting, we certainly never seriously use 'true' to mean grossly misleading, incorrect, non-existent; or to imply something in the present when it existed in the past; something here and now, when it was never anywhere. Nor do we use 'fair' to describe what we perceive to be unjust, inequitable or unfair.

More importantly, in those areas there is an automatic understanding that we are acting within a framework of what is *workable* for the purposes at hand, accepting that it is within a practicable tolerance for error. We never honestly say 'true' when we mean 'untrue', or say that something is 'fair' when we know it is unreasonable, hurtful or damaging in some way.

It is absurd that attempts are made in auditing to use 'true' and 'fair' in other than their ordinary everyday sense. Absurd, for example, that money spent is accorded the label of 'asset', that make-believe accounting numbers such as 'deferred tax debits' and 'capitalised expenses' are likewise labelled, or that 'deferred tax credits' are labelled 'liabilities' when they are the mere creations of the accounting processes – artifacts of the system. Elsewhere in human endeavour the convention is that the standard everyday meaning of words in common use is the process by which social communication proceeds in an effective and orderly manner.[13] That abuse of everyday language is tolerated in accounting partially explains the ongoing crisis in auditing.

## Auditing and the expectations gap

A persistent proposition is that the general public has it wrong in their expectations of what auditors do, and that there is an 'expectations gap'. Professional bodies in many countries have set up major inquiries to consider how to eliminate the gap.[14] Two major aspects of the gap are the persistence of unexpected large collapses (see chapters 7 and 8 below) and the debate over whether auditors should be responsible for detecting material accounting misstatements or fraud.[15] Insofar as the public expectation is that auditors will detect every instance of it, they possibly have got it wrong. But insofar as the expectation is that when auditors report the financials are true and fair they mean what 'true' and 'fair' ordinarily mean in everyday discourse, then they are surely justified.

Unless the *Australian Corporations Act 2001* (Cth) intends that the audited financials are *true and fair* as ordinarily construed in everyday discourse, then when it requires explanations and information where compliance with the Standards does not show a true and fair view, the provision serves no purpose. Amongst others,[16] leading Australian corporate lawyer Mark Liebler and Professor Bob Walker clearly hold that view. Liebler suggests:

> comparability and objectivity are enhanced by the requirement to ensure that the body of the accounts comply with accounting standards. On the other hand, the integrity of corporate financial reporting is preserved by the requirement to include in the notes to the accounts such information which

may be necessary to give a true and fair view of the company's financial position and performance.[17]

And Walker contends:

> a true and fair view . . . means a representation which affords those who might reasonably be expected to refer to those accounts . . . information which is relevant to the decisions which may be made by those persons in relation to the purchase, sale or other action in connection with their securities or interests.[18]

That the expectations gap has persisted for many decades is cause for concern for the profession. While we have suggested auditing is in crisis, it is not universally agreed that the persistence of the expectations gap is enough to support the claim. In 2006 Australian auditing instructors, for example, have asserted that the post-*SOX* and *CLERP 9* reporting environments have seen auditing (and presumably accounting) greatly improved:

> When we wrote the second edition of *Auditing and Assurance* . . . in 2003 we referred to a crisis of confidence in the underlying financial system, resulting from a number of corporate collapses (for example, HIH Insurance and One.Tel in Australia) [and presumably Enron and WorldCom in the US] and the demise of the auditing firm, Arthur Andersen. The auditing profession, an integral part of the financial reporting process, was at a crossroads.
>
> By the time we wrote the third edition in 2005, the auditing profession had gone from strength to strength. With society recognizing the need for a strong, independent auditing and assurance profession over this period. To aid in this process a lot of reform activities were undertaken.[19]

And, of course, there are continuing concerns expressed by regulators that auditors are still not independent enough. That 'independence' attack is shown above to be misdirected.

Ongoing concerns about the serviceability of audits is a function of the misconception as to the audit function. Over 30 years ago, the iconoclastic accounting critic Ray Chambers posed and answered the question 'Why audit?'

> directors and managers . . . may select and change rules to meet *their* circumstances; the evidence in Chapter 8 [of *Securities and Obscurities*] strongly suggests that the directors of many companies have done so. Ideally, an independent check of the balances of assets and equities would eliminate

97

the possibility of concealment or manipulation, even if innocent or with the best of intentions; for the object of audited accounts is to inform, not to conceal.[20]

Drawing on those moral hazard ideas it is apparent that the recognised function of an audit is to act as a quality control mechanism in verifying that the financial accounts prepared by directors (managers) do in fact provide a true and fair view of an entity's state of affairs, performance and cash flows. To quote Chambers again:

> To err is human. Hence the practice of one man checking the work of another, particularly where the consequence of error may be serious or costly. In the command of aircraft and seacraft, in medical diagnosis and surgery, in building construction and industrial processes, in scientific inquiry, testing or checking is commonplace . . . tested is the *result* of some previous action, not that action itself . . . [it is] to do with the way in which the thing tested will 'fit in with' other things, or will do what it is expected to do [that is, how 'serviceable' or 'fit-for-use' is that thing]. In effect all testing is a form of quality control . . . The tests that auditors should apply, therefore, are tests of the fitness of the financial figures for use in further calculations and in making judgments about the past or decisions about the future on financial grounds. (p. 145)

Such a view underpinned Chambers' advocacy – and of the University of Sydney colleagues of Chambers, including Murray Wells, Peter Wolnizer, Robert Walker and John Staunton, along with fellow travellers from overseas like Robert Sterling, Tom Lee, Leonard Spacek (of Andersen fame) and Abe Briloff, Tony Tinker and Prem Sikkha) who have written on how reforms to the law of company accounts and audit ought to proceed. But, as we show in chapter 6, the professional and regulatory response has been to emphasise generally changes to the *processes* of corporate governance, especially audit. And the latest institutional reports, like IFAC's proposed Ethics Code ('Independence – audit and review engagements; independence – other assurance engagements', 2006) covering independence issues,[21] and the 2006 Australian Treasury review paper on *Australian Auditor Independence Requirements*,[22] show that this persists. The Treasury paper aptly illustrates since, for the most part, the discussion is directed towards auditors' personal characteristics, financial and professional relationships, rather than what auditors are doing when they are supposed to be independent. Accounting and the true and fair criterion barely receive a mention in the Treasury paper. The section heads identifying the core elements of the review of auditor independence are indicative of its focus: 'General standard of auditor independence; Specific restrictions applying to employment, financial and business relationships; Provision of non-audit services; Employment restrictions applying to former audit partners and senior audit personnel; Auditor rotation.'

Another reform in many jurisdictions has been to implement recommendations for audit quality oversight bodies. Again there is a 'process-driven' focus. In the US the audit supervisory board, the PCAOB, was legislated through *SOX*, while in Australia it is the self-regulatory Audit Quality Review Board, and in the UK the Public Oversight Board of the Financial Reporting Council. As the next chapter illustrates, while opportunities have arisen for professional bodies (at least in Australia) to undertake a major rethink of the function of accounting and auditing, there has been little attempt to redress the fundamental flaws in the audited financial reporting system. The need to revisit the function of accounting and audit remains – considering the outputs of the audited financial reporting system needs to be in focus.

## Auditing in review – 1844 to present[23]

Whether the function of the audit should be to detect material fraud or misstatement has been a recurring audit issue for over 160 years.[24] Table 4.2 implies that investors are seemingly of the view that unexpected failures should not occur, even if they are associated with material accounting misstatement caused by fraudulent intent.

Misleading, *creative* accounting is shown in chapter 4[25] to be more the consequence of compliance with the Accounting Standards than deviation from them. That has been said by us in the context of the national Standards prior to their debunking and the adoption of the AIFRS in Australia and EU IFRSs by the European Union. It applies equally to the contemporary IFRSs. And bearing in mind the reliance auditors have to place upon the integrity and honesty of senior managers – to not engage in *feral* accounting, not exploit the additional scope for creativity in the IFRSs – corporate auditors are arguably at greater risk than before. Public expectations of a better audit performance have been fuelled by the rhetoric from the accounting profession, the regulators and the ASX of how the AIFRSs are such an improvement on what emerged from using the AASBs.

Court judgments and professional pronouncements reveal that corporate auditors are portrayed as reasonably careful, skilful and cautious individuals responsible for an attest function with limitations. Corporate audits are paradoxical. Auditors are expected to presume the honesty of senior managers when relying on their representations. This is especially so, bearing in mind that many of the data set out in companies' financials are the products of estimates and other calculations that are entirely the required fabrications of management. Consider the reliance on management's views on the application of consolidation adjustments, on determining *revenue generating units* and the estimates of their future revenue flows and the rate at which to discount them, in the impairment calculations under the new AIFRSs, estimate of future lives for asset amortisations, how much expenditure to capitalise. Auditors are thus as much at the mercy of managers' honesty as they are at the risk of their own inadequacy regarding those matters bringing them unstuck. Yet, dominant senior managers can use their position and authority to override internal controls, coerce junior managers and employees, and induce compliant external service providers in order to create the necessary conditions for material accounting misstatements. Public expectations about corporate auditor responsibility, on the other hand, assume an unequivocal duty to detect error irrespective of cost.

The history of this complex and potentially damaging situation has its genesis in mid- to late nineteenth-century prosecutions of fraudulent reporting in the UK. At the time, the institutions of public accountancy were reluctant to set viable parameters for corporate audit responsibility and much was therefore left to the opinions of individual legal counsel and judges. An informal model of responsibility appeared fair to all concerned and yet was presumably viable enough to manage from a judicial point of view. Almost inevitably, the model involved ambiguous and undefined legal terminology such as 'reasonable care and skill', used later by public accountants to create their image of a reasonably careful, skilful and cautious corporate auditor.

Various excuses with regard to the corporate auditor's responsibility for fraud and therefore material misstatement emerged from an unstructured combination of legal judgments and individual accountancy practitioner comments. Eventually they drifted into being formal institutional audit guidance and standards.

Students in audit teaching programs are instructed to be *careful* and *cautious*, but not to insist that their clients' financials *tell it how it is*. As a consequence the expectations gap persists as a tolerated *professional oddity*. Most audit-related governance proscriptions are to limit the 'appearance' of dominant managers influencing auditors' professional judgments, threatening their independence. Few are directed towards the fundamental cause of material misstatements, or the failure to detect them. Underpinning the approach is the impression of greater control and regulation when, in reality, there has always been an acceptance by public accountants (sanctioned by legal judgments) of a limited duty to detect material misstatements.

Deliberate accounting misstatements with the intent to mislead cannot occur without senior executives' involvement, intent, incompetence, or virtuous compliance, as the case may be. Yet the creative consequences of 'proper' behaviour by executives who comply with the accounting standards is potentially an uncontrollable hazard. Historical evidence suggests dominant management is a sign of potential reporting problems. Whether this is always the case is a matter of conjecture. Headstrong accounting by Samuel Insull and John Spalvins at Adsteam, for example, has been shown to have been more on the mark than the accounting the profession was prescribing. In the 1970s the UK analyst John Argenti had perceived a dominant CEO as a weakness when calibrating his corporate failure-predicting A-score, and twenty years on Heimann-Hoffman *et al.*'s warning signs of fraud primarily concern dominant managers.[26] The problem for the corporate auditor is that, frequently, highly successful companies have dominant personalities at their helm. But the need to apply judgment and accumulated wisdom is what differentiates the professional from the journeyman.

What is most obvious is that individual public accountants and their institutions over many decades have preferred to focus on the symptoms of a disease (for example, technical auditing weaknesses such as poor internal controls or the manipulation of accounting standards) rather than the disease itself. The disease is inherently creative accounting in the hands of managers utilising complex organisational structures and financial engineering and a willingness to tolerate weak controls and a propensity to press employees. In fact, public accountants have consistently placed the major responsibility for detecting and preventing accounting misstatements on senior managers – the very individuals they are expected to rely on for honesty. Pertinently, Waddock concludes that: 'The accounting profession seems to have failed to acknowledge that accounting is fundamentally an ethical, rather than a technical, discourse' (2005, p. 147).

In denying or limiting their responsibility public accountants appear to have made this failure explicit. They have failed to recognise the need for corporate auditors to plan for and act against accounting misstatements and the causes of it. Lee *et al.* (2007) note:

> They admit they can do so – but, hypocritically, only as a management advisory service. They claim to do so in a limited way by assessing audit risk in relation to material accounting misstatement. But they have never accepted full and direct responsibility for dealing with the disease.
>
> If public accountancy education is to change to permit auditors to assume responsibility, instruction is required in the thinking and procedures necessary to identify and assess the red flags signalling managerial characteristics and traits, contractual opportunities and incentives, complex organisational and financial forms, as well as economic and operational conditions. To deal with these matters, more curriculum time needs to be available for relevant

aspects of economics, finance, law, management, and psychology – perhaps at the expense of technical accounting and auditing matters.

## 'True and fair' – more common sense than a will-o'-the-wisp

In the British idiom of financial reporting, the 'true and fair' quality criterion has been a fundamental principle – the cornerstone – of Commonwealth countries' corporate reporting regimes. Australia's 2005 Report of the Joint Committee on Corporations and Financial Services, *Accounting Standards Tabled in Compliance with the Corporations Act, 2001 on 30 August 2004 and 16 November 2004,* examined the meaning[27] and current applicability of the phrase in Australia within an IFRS regime. A previous Australian parliamentary inquiry by the JCPAA produced *Report 391, Review of Independent Auditing by Registered Company Auditors* (2002). It had dealt in more depth with the phrase's history, as have many accounting and legal historians.[28]

Over time, the 'full and fair' phrase has undergone minor changes – from 'full and correct', 'true and correct' in the NSW *Companies Act 1936,* to true and fair in the UK *Companies Act 1948* and Australia's *Uniform Companies Acts, 1961,* and similar phrases elsewhere, such as 'fairly presents'. But there has never been compelling argument that the original ethos was no longer the pervading essence, despite lengthy debate in the literature as to precisely what the phrase meant; whether, for example, the words should be read separately or as one. Accordingly, there have been countless changes in recommended accounting practices since the 1960s, then promulgation of prescribed rules-based standards. But the overriding ethos has, or should always have been, that a company's published accounting data show a true and fair view of its state of affairs at a stipulated date and its financial performance up to that date.

Up to the relatively recent past the true and fair criterion was considered to override the general practitioner rubric that the accounting standards be complied with. Chapter 4 noted that acknowledging confusion over whether the phrase was effectively an overriding quality criterion, the JCPAA *Report 391* (2002) concluded by construing that in Australia there were two contiguous separate tests to be satisfied by directors. In the first they are to comply with the relevant accounting standards (now presumably the AIFRSs), but, second, there also has to be an assurance that such compliance produces financial statements that depict a true and fair view of an entity's financial position and financial performance. The 2005 JCCFS Report (pp. 17–20) was less sanguine about the phrase being an override, well captured by the following extract under the heading: 'Are the proposed standards genuinely principles-based?':

3.28 ... No general principle or principles have been specified, no explanation of how the data to emerge from the [standards] will contribute to a true and fair view of an entity's financial position and performance has been made. Indeed no explanation of the dimensions of what a *true and fair view* entails has been forthcoming. For a successful transition [to an IFRSs regime] such a specification is a prius. [*Submission 7*, Professors Dean and Clarke, p. 4] ...

3.30 The committee noted standard AASB 101, *Framework for the Preparation and Presentation of Financial Statements*, which acknowledges that there is no 'true and fair view override' but which argues that the adoption of accounting standards will result in the production of true and fair reports.

Financial reports are frequently described as showing a true and fair view of, or as presenting fairly, the financial position, financial performance and cash flows of an entity. Although this Framework does not deal directly with such concepts, the application of principal qualitative characteristics and of appropriate accounting standards normally results in financial reports that convey what is generally understood as a true and fair view of, or as presenting fairly, such information.

3.31 The international equivalent of AASB 101, known as ISB 1, does however, contain a 'true and fair view' override in the following terms:

'In the extremely rare circumstances in which management concludes that compliance with a requirement in a Standard or an Interpretation would be so misleading that it would conflict with the objective of financial statements set out in the Framework, the entity shall depart from that requirement ... if the relevant regulatory framework requires, or otherwise does not prohibit, such a departure.'

3.32 The AASB explained this departure from the international standard as follows:

'Our local legislation at the present time has what you might call twin requirements, but I would say they do not relate to an override. The twin requirements ... are to both comply with the accounting standards and give a true and fair view. The Corporations Law says you must comply with the accounting standards as the first initial requirement. If the directors believe that complying with the standards does not produce a true and fair view, then the directors must give as much additional information as is required in order that a true and fair view is also given. ... it is not an override.'

I am afraid I cannot tell you exactly when [Authors: prior to 1992] but in previous Corporations Law in Australia we did have a true and fair view

103

override. The law said something like, 'You must comply with the accounting standards unless this does not give a true and fair view, at which time you do not have to comply with the standards.' The companies made improper use of that blatantly saying, 'We're not going to comply with the accounting standard because it does not give a true and fair view.' They really were not even giving good reasons; they were just saying: 'that's our view. There you are.' The law was changed to prevent that from happening, and I would fear that, if consideration were given again to a true and fair view override, we would suffer the same problems again.

3.33  The committee agrees that the presentation of a true and fair statement of a company's financial position and performance should underpin any system of accounting standards. However, the committee considers that this should be accomplished in the manner proposed by the AASB – by the presentation of additional explanatory material as necessary – to provide a clear view where the accounting standards do not. In the first instance, entities must comply with the Standards.

This vacillation in Australia's and the IASB's contemplation of an override quality criterion contrasts with the position in the US, where it has been claimed categorically that it does not operate. Different legal reporting regimes emerge to be factors preventing the immediate achievement of financial reporting comparability across countries. This is unlikely to change.

Adding to this apparent confusion, the two Australian parliamentary inquiries referred to above, contain legal opinions (or references thereto) suggesting that the claims in 3.32 and 3.33 are contestable and eventually likely to require judicial interpretation. Some commentators have suggested that the discussion is of little practical import, for under the new AIFRSs (and its equivalent UK) regime it is unlikely that any of the large accounting firms will allow their clients to utilise the override option.[29] But there is evidence that some public companies have been and are likely in the future to be prepared to do so.[30]

Perhaps the common sense by which quality is determined outside of accounting is expected to be applied in respect of it also – that the data in a company's financials are true and fair 'if and only if' they are serviceable for determining its financial performance and financial position, and for deriving the financial indicators invariably calculated with them. In the previous chapter we showed how far short of that audited financials complying with the AIFRSs are likely to be, notwithstanding the best of intentions. This is a state of affairs in respect of which government, regulators and the accountancy professions in various jurisdictions appear to be in complete denial.

*Auditors are on a hiding to nothing.* They are on a near impossible mission, trying to satisfy the joint criteria of the companies legislation – of companies complying with the accounting standards and attesting to the truth and fairness of their financial statements because they did so. It is mission impossible as, were auditors to acknowledge any reasonable English language usage of the true and fair criterion as an override, as the *cornerstone of accounting* (as the British Financial Reporting Council described it in its PN 1119, 2005),[31] the financials of virtually every company would have to be qualified. That is an inevitable outcome. Eventually the day will arrive when someone puts the companies' criteria together in a sensible manner and challenges assertions that AIFRS-compliant (or any IFRS-type) financials fit the bill.

There is evidence of an underlying current of discontent with the product of the rules-based standards. Frequent contrasts between rules-based and principles-based accounting attest to that. 'Box ticking' encouraged by the rules-based approach exposes the awareness that compliance with the accounting rules doesn't necessarily result in true and fair financials, or financials that 'present fairly' or 'faithfully represent' a company's wealth and progress.

Inklings of that awareness emerge in unexpected places. The 2006 published vision from the CEOs of the six global audit networks, *Global Capital Markets and the Global Economy* (2006), brings together the consensus of the major accounting firms – PricewaterhouseCoopers, Deloitte, Grant Thornton, Ernst & Young, KPMG, and BDO. And whereas they press for 'public reporting and public company auditing procedures' – not the content of the financials we might note – to better serve the global capital markets, they are at pains to declare that 'Today's rules produce financial statements that virtually no one understands' (p. 3). That begs the question – in what sense can such statements be fair or present fairly, if 'virtually no one understands' them? And if they fail on that count, in what workable sense can they be 'true and fair'? How can it be that auditors, including auditors from those leading auditing firms, have issued clean audit reports to rules-compliant companies whose financials they are incapable of understanding? Of course, a considerable part of that rhetoric is being presented as a case for the national IFRSs variants, and to issue a veiled condemnation of the US holding out on dropping their FASBs. The problem is that the IFRSs are no more principles-based than the standards they replace.

Having acknowledged the problem, unable to plead ignorance, auditors are at greater risk than ever.

# 6
# The Sound of One Hand Clapping

Previous chapters demonstrate that virtually nothing in the public domain is as misleading as companies' financial statements. Not because accountants or the others preparing them are dishonest, but by virtue of the rules with which they must comply. Accountants are victims rather than villains. With the best of intentions, companies' financials complying with the prescribed rules, now contained in the IFRSs, are almost certain to be *misleading*.

Yet companies' financial statements are the primary means by which information on how companies are faring is communicated to the commercial community at large. They are the medium through which the basic information supporting decisions regarding the investments of the populace's superannuation funds are made, government trade and taxation and other fiscal policy is determined, and general investments are made. Nonetheless, companies' financials are, by the norms of ordinary financial calculation, grossly misleading, tantamount to fraud. They are a fraud, insofar as everyone who has dealt with money, calculated in its terms, estimated and assessed their own wealth, or mused over how much they have earned, almost certainly would not calculate in the manner that is compulsory when they do like things in respect of companies.

Indeed, the products of this form of compulsory accounting are a farrago of falsehoods. Accounting is possibly the only human endeavour in which what is known to be utterly false is habitually declared to be true, the known financial characteristics of money for the most part are denied, and the conventional manner of calibrating in money abandoned. The *ordinary* meanings of words used in everyday discourse are willingly supplanted by *extraordinary* and mostly misleading usages. In conventional accounting money spent is treated as if it is still possessed, even though bank balances show that it isn't. Audited accounting is a very peculiar practice – truly legerdemain – utter jiggery-pokery.

Contemporary examples reveal accounting to entertain notions outside ordinary experience of commercial matters, beyond everyday experiences in dealing with money and undertaking monetary calculations.[1] Importantly, they emerge as much the likely result of diligent and well-intended compliance with 'the rules' as from deliberate intent to mislead. They confirm the distinction we drew between feral and creative accounting in *Corporate Collapse*, the *feral* being the misleading product of deliberate manipulation to mislead, and the *creative* the almost inevitable result of complying with the prescribed Accounting Standards.

Whereas there are all kinds of fancy explanations of the function of companies' financial statements, unquestionably the primary objective is to provide a true and fair view of their wealth and progress. *Wealth* in the sense of the nature, composition and money's worth of their assets and the nature and amount of their liabilities, and *progress* in the sense of periodic increase or decrease in net wealth over time. That has always been unequivocal since companies were capable of being created (under the British system) by mere registration under the UK *Companies Act of 1844*. That function underpinned the 1841 Gladstone Committee's specification that each company prepare an annual balance sheet disclosing its financial position and that it could be audited by 'a shareholder'. The Act did not require a formal profit and loss account be prepared. Also it was silent on the qualifications of the auditor.[2] Although through time the legislation has been expressed in different ways and within different perceptions of the imperatives, the general understanding of accounting's primary function has not changed.

As noted in chapter 5, significantly, the British Financial Reporting Council recently confirmed the *true and fair* appellation. Athough the UK *Companies Act* has been changed (SI 2004/2947) to align the wording with the international standards which the EU adopted in 2005, and notwithstanding the IAS1 *fair presentation* prescription, 'the concept of "true and fair" remains the cornerstone of financial reporting and auditing in the UK'.[3] That declaration might be seen as a bitter blow for the accounting profession in Australia, for since the early 1990s the two professional bodies have been unanimous that 'true and fair' was out, and that the American 'presents fairly' was in; 'presents fairly' being a proxy for 'in accord with the accounting standards'.

While *financial position* has been the common legislative description of what the balance sheet was to show – a common expectation of what a genuine balance sheet would disclose – the Accounting Standards were injected with the term in only the early 1990s in Australia. What was previously a balance sheet and a profit and loss account became a *Statement of Financial Position* and a *Statement of Financial Performance* (virtually) overnight, and without any visible or perceptible changes in the accounting mechanisms by which they were prepared.

At best, the nomenclature change can only be seen as an attempt to improve perceptions of the financial importance of the statements, for 'financial position' and 'financial performance' are terms in everyday use. It is to be expected that individuals would ordinarily think of their financial position as the money's worth of their separate assets and the amount of their liabilities. At times the worth of the collection assets would be the focus, and at other times it would be about the amounts for which their assets could be exchanged separately in the most optimal manner. At different times the focus would be on which assets are the most readily saleable, which the most liquid, which the most easily replaceable, which they can do without the most, and the like. That's how individuals ordinarily think of the components of their wealth. We know that because it is common experience. Yet no matter the label placed upon them, that is not what corporate financial statements showed in respect of a company's wealth before the nomenclature change. Nor is it shown following the return to 'balance sheet and profit and loss account' under the Australian AASBs or now under the AIFRSs.

## Zany accounting

WorldCom's capitalisation practices would come under examination when it was placed in bankruptcy in June 2002, reportedly with debts of $US41 billion and book assets of $US107 billion, and yet it was the 'largest US bankruptcy'.[4] WorldCom's failure was attributed not only to some ill-advised expansion to corner the US bandwidth market with expectations of a level of demand that, in retrospect, bordered on the insane, but also to the greasing of the way by some devious, aggressive accounting. Particular criticism was levelled at World-Com capitalising expenditures. Allegations were that they ought to have been expensed though reference is made to this being part of the 'fraud' at World-Com. However, in the context of conventional FASB-endorsed accounting in the US, it raises some interesting issues that are not peculiar to the US.

US accounting is generally on an exclusively historical-cost basis.[5] That outcome was part of the SEC's self-regulatory deal with the US accounting profession in Roosevelt's New Deal in the early 1930s. It was something of a safety-first tactic to avoid the possibility that corporate assets would be valued at more than their current market prices, as many had been found to be in the balance sheets of companies that crashed in 1929. There were vivid memories of how Insull had exploited the attacks on the historical-cost dictum. The cost basis was the conventional asset valuation basis in accounting worldwide, in the wake of hyperinflation in continental Europe after World War I.

In the 1920s there was considerable debate regarding the serviceability of accounts being prepared under the historical-cost rule. Unwarranted inferences were drawn from the utilities' rate-making cases in the US to bolster the plea for assets to be valued at their current replacement prices and scaling accounting data with price index numbers to standardise them. Scaling had been mandated in Germany in 1923 in response to the hyperinflation, as an alternative 'solution'.[6] And, on an upper theoretical plane, new theories of

**Illustration 5:** 'WorldCom, Enron accounting standards figures from bum'
*Source:* 'WorldCom, Enron accounting standards figures from bum', *The Australian*,
27 June 2002. Courtesy of Peter Nicholson.

business economics entailing departures from the historical-cost rule were
being promoted through the German *Betriebswirtschaftlere*, and the Dutch
*Bedrijfseconomie* movements by their primary advocates, Fritz Schmidt and
Theodore Limperg. Those ideas had infiltrated the American accounting litera-
ture primarily through the advocacy of William Paton, Henry Sweeney and Rufus
Rorem.[7]

Roosevelt and his SEC weren't going to have any of that. Self-regulation of
accounting by the profession came at a cost. By the late 1930s strict *historical-cost*
was to be the US convention.[8]

Critical to the historical-cost system is the idea of 'matching' costs with
related expenses. It is essential to the workings of the accrual system. Partition-
ing expenditures to be matched with what are deemed the 'related revenues'
results in the expenditure being capitalised, ultimately to be 'matched' with the
revenues deemed related to them. It's a dodgy process, fraught with potential
error. Whereas the expenses incurred are more certain, the related revenues are
purely conjectural (as we saw also with Enron's mark-to-model's estimates). So,
while WorldCom may have deliberately manipulated the outcome, it could just
as easily have erred merely as a matter of management misjudgment. Mistakes

109

of that variety are endemic in the conventional system. Every reported profit and every reported loss on the 'sale of fixed assets' is an adjustment of erred judgments regarding previous incorrect capitalisation and depreciation judgments. For the most part they are buried in catch-ups and nobody is any the wiser. Of course, over the life of an enterprise the catch-ups even out. It is only when a halt is made to proceedings, as in the WorldCom case, that the magnitude of the necessary catch-ups is likely to be exposed.

WorldCom's alleged manipulation of the historical-cost rule is contestable, for whether historical-cost is essentially a capitalisation-based or an expense-based system is debatable. The practice of *valuing* assets on acquisition at what was paid for them and then deducting (and expensing) an assessed depreciation charge invites the inference that capitalisation is the norm in respect of amounts ordinarily expensed without question. Amounts capitalised and amounts expensed are matters of judgment under the historical-cost rule.

WorldCom-like misstatements are certainly everyday errors under conventional accounting, almost certainly present (to a greater or lesser extent) in every company's financials. They are in fact part of the financials' inevitable creativity, and when intent is present, the means of financials going feral.

Waste Management's problem with estimating asset lives for depreciation purposes is not uncommon. It could be presumed that virtually every company's financials are misleading by virtue of their depreciation charges. Yet, Waste Management was pilloried for, inter alia, alleged manipulation of the depreciation charges in respect of its fleet of garbage trucks. Its simple *modus operandi* was to lengthen the estimates of the trucks' useful lives and thereby lessen the yearly depreciation charges, increasing reported profit figures. And whereas Waste Management may well have been aware that it was deliberately overestimating the lives and underestimating those charges, equivalent outcomes could have arisen by virtue of genuine mistakes. Well-intentioned accountants' application of a faulty notion of depreciation and a zany means for calculating its amount could have produced a like result.

In conventional accounting depreciation is said to be 'the allocation of the cost of an asset over its useful life' – an allocation of costs. It is likely that to other than accountants, it is no such thing. Elsewhere depreciation is sensibly understood to be the 'decrease in price' experienced by an asset over time. Compliance with the conventional notion in accounting has placed asset valuation in a fantasyland in which physical assets are deemed a value equal to what was paid to acquire them. That is an amount of money an entity no longer has or currently owes the vendor. Accountants will allocate as the annual depreciation charge a proportion of that amount calculated on the basis of a guess, hope or expectation, of the asset's useful life. While that can and should be informed guesswork, it is incapable of independent corroboration and remains purely conjecture exposing management, accountants and auditors to error.

Waste Management's accounting, including the process of lengthening its assets' estimated lives, was, in principle, compliant with the prescribed conventional depreciation accounting practice. The point is that the alleged deliberate accounting manipulation of under-expensing for depreciation of which Waste Management was accused, could as easily arise from legitimate error in making the impossible estimates required in conventional practice.

In essence, Waste Management's capacity to lower its depreciation charges and increase its reported profits was facilitated by a system requiring accountants to make guesses that are almost bound to be incorrect, despite the greatest of integrity. Importantly it is a process producing data unrelated to the financial characteristic being sought. A reasonable expectation is that the audited financials of just about every listed company contain such genuine errors of that kind. They are endemic in the accounting for depreciation in the conventional system. Whereas the new IFRSs' impairment mechanism might put a brake on underestimates of asset lives, it puts none on overestimates that result in undervaluations of assets' worths.

Under that IFRSs regime, assets cannot be booked at more than their *recoverable amount*. That is, at more than the greater of their net realisable value and the net present value of their future income streams. This entails *estimating* the future income streams from using an asset separately, or as part of a *cash generating unit* (CGU) discounting the estimated net income stream with an *estimated* appropriate discount factor, comparing it with the asset's selling price or the aggregate of the selling prices of the assets comprising CGU-assets' net selling price to determine the recoverable amount, and comparing the latter with the *booked* value to determine any *estimated* impairment in book value. Most assets will be booked at their 'cost less depreciation'. In that exercise, only the current selling price of the asset (or of the CGU assets) is likely to exist. Assets' lives are estimates. Their separate or the CGU's future net income streams are both estimates, and the discount factor is an estimate. As such, an asset's selling price is the only item capable of independent corroboration.

Estimates of the kind built into that exercise are even more conducive to creativity and feral manipulations than those only being exposed when companies estimate an asset's life expectancy, as at Waste Management. Indeed, the book value of an asset under the impairment regime is likely to be the hypothetical estimated NPV of its future income stream – pure guesswork, even with the best of intentions. At worst, it is capable of wild abuse, as occurred with Enron's mark-to-model guesstimates.

HIH's goodwill calculations led Royal Commissioner Justice Neville Owen (and others) to describe HIH's acquisition of the FAI insurance group as one of the worst commercial decisions of 2000, and a major contributing factor to HIH's collapse.[9] HIH's payment of nearly $300 million for FAI might also be labelled the year's best example of just how creative conventional accounting can be. Consistent with the conventional wisdom, HIH booked the excess of the price over the estimated worth of the FAI net assets it acquired as $275 million-worth of goodwill. Later the amount was increased to $438 million when the ex-FAI net assets were found to be even less than originally used to calculate the $275 million goodwill on the FAI acquisition.[10] And whereas that attracted all kinds of criticism, arguably it complied in principle with the reporting wisdom of the time. Yet nowhere outside of conventional accounting would money spent, which is gone for ever, be considered to give rise to an asset worth equal to what was paid for it. Nowhere else is money that has been spent considered to be an asset, especially in the HIH-like circumstances. There, with the best of imagination, what was received in return was merely a misguided expectation of future superior returns. At worst, as it turned out, it was merely the loss on an imprudent deal.

Yet HIH's booking of goodwill in that fashion was in good company. AOL Time Warner is high on the list, having booked approximately $US100 billion goodwill on the AOL Time Warner merger in early 2000. Not surprisingly the financial reality eventually materialised in the group's $US54 billion goodwill write-off two years later. Likewise, in 2002 News Corp's 5.7 billion euros Gemstar write-down of goodwill further illustrates the point. Creativity of that kind is an everyday event in conventional accounting,[11] though how it bites depends upon which rules are being followed. Different rules, different accounting results.

David Waller's *Wheels on Fire*[12] details the negotiations of the Chrysler and Daimler-Benz merger. He explains how the deal would have nearly fallen through were the acquisition to be not treated as a *pooling of interests* in the US and had to be accounted for as a *purchase* (pp. 193–6). Waller explains how the pooling arrangement meant booking goodwill would be avoided, as would be annual charges to amortise *goodwill*. Pooling would return greater profits. He aptly explains that goodwill:

> has nothing to do with bonhomie or the milk of human kindness; rather it is *a number* used by accountants to *plug the gap* when one company buys another for more than the book value of the latter's assets. (emphasis added)

*A number* and *plug the gap* capture the artificiality of it all. All the more so when the fact that the annual amortisation of goodwill in the US was to be calculated over a period not exceeding 20 years, while elsewhere (say, in Australia), over a period not exceeding 40 years. The point is that the *pooling of interests* and *purchase* accounting report different financial outcomes for an identical transaction. The former amounts to combining the existing balance sheets of the parties. No goodwill arises by virtue of unequal financial considerations in the deal, and thus there is no subsequent amortisation of goodwill to reduce

112

**Illustration 6:** 'A history of accounting'
*Source:* 'A history of accounting', cartoon by R. Petty, appeared in the ASRC Report (1978), p. 54. State of New South Wales through the Attorney-General's Department, 1978.

the 'accounting profits'. By contrast, in purchase accounting, which HIH had to pursue and Chrysler Daimler-Benz was able to avoid, 'goodwill' reflects the consideration difference relative to the fair values of the acquired net assets and has to be amortised thereafter, reducing reported annual profits. Rafferty's rules for sure – different place, different rules.

But it is also a case of different *time*, different rules.

Now, under the IFRSs, goodwill accounting might be even more hazardous. Under the IFRSs' impairment rules goodwill cannot be shown at more than its recoverable amount, the product of the invention, imagination and guesswork noted above. First the purchased goodwill has to be allocated to a 'cash generating unit' – those assets in the purchase of which the amount arose; for example, HIH's initial $275 million on the FAI purchase. Then the expected income

113

streams from the cash generating unit have to be estimated, the period over which the stream will be enjoyed estimated, and discounted with an estimated appropriate interest rate. All might be undertaken with the greatest of care and honesty, be serious estimates. But they will nonetheless be, at best, good guesses. Any excess of the book value of the goodwill over the discounted estimated cash generating unit net income stream is to be deemed the *impairment* of the goodwill. Under such a rubric, the manner in which HIH's $275 million goodwill on the acquisition of FAI might have been reported is anyone's best guess. And, at HIH even more difficult to interpret when a year after FAI's acquisition the goodwill 'number' was increased. In such a scenario contemplate the auditor's task of corroborating such a 'number'.

*BHP's 1996–98 write-downs* totalling nearly $A4.4 billion in the booked values of its assets further illustrate the consequences of compliance with conventional accounting. It is to be noted that those write-downs which related to the capitalised costs of investments were all against a background of failure to meet targeted divisional returns. Whether it makes managerial sense to benchmark business divisions' profitability against the top 20 all-comers in the securities market is clearly debatable. CEO Prescott's mid-1990s dictum was that each division had to earn 15 per cent on capital employed, without the availability of financial data serviceable for the public to make the necessary calculations. Regarding the non-performing investments, the losses prompting the write-downs did not occur, or occur solely, in the years they were charged. Almost certainly they would have accumulated over time. Most likely the write-downs have been made in the wrong years. Accordingly profits and losses would be misstated, all with the best of intentions. It follows that the numerators and denominators in any 'rate of return' calculations managers and analysts might have made would have been incorrect, and the calculations at best problematic.

To illustrate the impact of the accounting effects of allocating gains and losses to the wrong years imagine that those losses actually existed by the end of 1996. That is a reasonable assumption for the large portion of the 1998 write-down relates to the overvaluation of the Magna Copper investment in 1996. For example, were it that the $4 billion (after tax) written off by the end of 1998 had already accumulated by the end of 1996, according to BHP's financials the 1997 year would have started with a total shareholders' equity of $11.75 billion rather than the $15.75 billion reported. The 1997 and 1998 profits would have been $1.39 billion and $1.3 billion (rather than the reported $410 million and $1.47 billion (loss)); and the rates of return for 1997 and 1998 would have been more like 10 per cent and 13 per cent respectively (on a comparable basis)[13] rather than the 3.3 per cent and 12.7 per cent (loss) reported. Of course, by the end of 1998 all would have been square in the aggregate on that account, but the in-between indicators would have to have been misleading in both absolute and relative terms. Most importantly, every financial indicator relating to BHP for 1996, 1997 and 1998 would have been incorrect, the numerator and denominator of the conventionally calculated ratios incorrect, some understated, others overstated, most importantly without any intent to misinform or mislead. But the implications are clouded by the extent to which investments may have been grossly undervalued. The financial press noted[14] in 1997, for example, that the company's Escondida investment was undervalued on the basis of having earned $523 million on an investment booked at $1.4 billion. Point is, sensible analysis of companies' results with the kind of asset valuation practices presently in vogue is hazardous.

## A focus on uses rather than users

An idea that the primary focus of companies' published financial statements was to be their usefulness for users' decisions is built into the conceptual framework underpinning conventional accounting. Accountants are taught in virtually every accounting program that they must have a focus on the needs of the myriad financial statement users. Those statements are prepared, according to Australia's conceptual framework (SAC 2), to facilitate 'the making of economic decisions about the allocation of scarce resources'. That is an open-ended and, for the most part, indecipherable notion. But the decision usefulness focus is a meta dictum, addressing the uses of accounting data at a higher level than the fundamental level at which published statement data are more frequently and readily observed being used.

Casual observation shows how those data are used at a more basic level as part of the ordinary, everyday business of commerce. Financial statement data are used, for example, in the determination of the financial characteristics of companies' wealth and progress: short-term and longer term solvency, assessing companies' likely capacity to continue, and their overall financial viability, their leverage and other gearing indicators, rate of return on different bases, earnings per share, and asset backing. Interestingly those observations can be made without anything other than the broadest of an understanding of the decisions into which the determinations might be plugged. It is a matter of fact that such financial indicators are calculated. And while many decisions for which they might be input can be imagined, none is necessary to specifying the features of the financial qualities they are taken to indicate, or the qualities financial statement data must possess, to be useful in that fashion.

Few who know the minimum of things corporate would dispute that a company's *solvency* refers to its capacity to pay debts, or that its *rate of return* refers to the percentage increase in its wealth earned on its capital, that *asset backing* refers to the worth of its assets per issued share (net or otherwise). It is common knowledge that *leverage* and *gearing* are similar concepts reflecting the relative proportion of the internal and external borrowings and equity used to fund assets or, for example, that *working capital* is understood to reflect the relationship between the amount of the current assets to the current liabilities as an indication of capacity to pay debts in the immediate future. Those are commonly understood to be references to *financial* characteristics of companies. Reference is made to them habitually in evaluations and assessments of companies' financial states in the daily press, in financial and business magazines, radio and television. And everyone seems to understand broadly what is meant by the references. Few seem to misunderstand when the reference implies good news for interested parties, and when it is bad. But, more to the point, whereas there might be haggling in some circles as to how they are best calculated, they are known to be indicators of the financial characteristics of companies. That is the primary matter of interest, without any particular action or proposed decision contemplated. They and their like are indicators whose financial meaning, though perhaps neither their significance nor consequences, is neutral of the circumstances they depict.

Indeed, the focus on *users* and their unknown myriad decisions sounds profound. But basically it is humbug. For part of the problem with company disclosure lies in the dispute about what information is needed for the decisions the conceptual framework alludes to. For the most part they are undefined, unexplained. Specifying the financial data required is thus impossible. And, in any event, as likely as not the way they would mesh into the decision-making processes is itself unknown. Those processes are black boxes. Whereas we might know, or reasonably anticipate, the range of information that might be brought into commercial calculations, the exact process by which they are commingled, modelled, clearly is not.

In contrast with the mystery regarding the processing of data in all but the broadest of business decisions, the manner in which the data are used in the calculation of the financial indicators mentioned above is unequivocal. It is readily observable. *Readily observable* insofar as those indicators appear daily in the financial press, business magazines, the company analyses by the stock exchanges' research departments, and by brokerage houses, and in the broadsheets of the mercantile agencies such as Moody's, Standard & Poor's, Dun and Bradstreet and the like, much of which information has to be purchased. A more fundamental focus on the *uses* habitually made of companies' financial data might be far more fruitful to pursue, and thus the *usefulness* for use in constructing those indicators is a worthwhile quality criterion for companies' financial data to satisfy.

There is nothing novel in that. But it is not descriptive of a common view on the quality criterion to be met by the data comprising companies' financial statements. Underlying that minimum prescription is the prerequisite that, through aggregation, the components of those indicators produce financial statements that are serviceable in disclosing a company's overall wealth and progress, its financial position and financial performance. And that through dis-aggregation it is possible to produce, separately, serviceable financial measures of what the financial statements held out to represent – the nature, composition and amounts of its assets, liabilities, revenues and expenses.

## Frustrating the agenda for reform

*Usefulness* of that variety underpinned the campaign that the iconoclastic reformer Ray Chambers waged for over forty years to inject company financial disclosure with common sense and reality. Possibly the first international salvo was at a Symposium on the Foundations of Financial Accounting[15] at Berkeley in 1965. He recalled how alone in his hotel room he mused over a session at which the leading academics of the time had argued inconclusively about which of a range of asset valuation methods best 'accounted for inflation'. It struck him that inflation, though 'the issue of the moment,'[16] was in fact only symp-tomatic of the problem. It was not inflation *per se*, but that the data in financial statements complying with convention were never serviceable for deriving the usual financial indicators, neither in inflationary nor deflationary conditions, or even when prices were stable. So he set about listing all the financial indicators usually derived from the data in financial statements and rated them against the competing valuation systems discussed during the earlier session, including his own preferred Continuously Contemporary Accounting (known as CCA at the time). Predictably, none of its competitors measured up for any, whereas CCA did for each.

Presenting the analysis the next morning, he recounted how he was howled down that it was rigged. He was accused of only comparing the competing systems according to whether they were serviceable for indicating the finan-cial characteristics he nominated, on criteria that suited his CCA. A reasonable charge, but then, as now, those were and are the financial characteristics habitu-ally sought, those that analysts calculate and that the financial press comments on. His challenge for explanations of what had been included that ought not to have been, or things excluded that should have been included, went unanswered. Forty years later and after several repeats of similar exercises, the critics remain silent and Chambers' challenge remains unanswered.

Much the same message coursed through Chambers' critical examination of Australian Accounting Standards at a meeting of members of the ICAA in 1975: that, contrary to how the profession's Standards malfunctioned, the necessity that the Standards produce data that mesh with one another (analogous to how the components of serviceable machinery must mesh), the amounts reported for revenues and expenses, assets and liabilities, are sub-assemblies of the financial statements disclosing wealth and progress. Faced with a miffed profession unwilling to publish the paper, he published it in the international accounting journal that he had founded, *Abacus*.[17] There was growing heat entering the Standards debate, and Chambers was a central figure in the academic community. But his relationship with the practising arm of the profession was strained.

'Life on the fringe' was how Chambers explained his position in 1992 regarding the profession's deliberations on reform. For the most part his ideas were continuously sidelined, his proposals filleted.[18] Nothing illustrates that more than the inflation accounting debate in the 1960s and 1970s. It gives the flavour of the professional bodies' reluctance to listen to suggestions from outside the ranks of the practitioners.

High inflation through the late 1960s and early 1970s had the western countries' Accounting Standards setters scurrying to produce a method of *incorporating the effects of inflation* in accounts. Though the focus on inflation was understandable, it was nonetheless misguided. The issue was more properly a matter of injecting the accounts with the effects of *price and price level changes*. Sensitive to the political implications of inflation in the UK distorting the financial statements of British companies, and that income tax was being levied improperly on *inflationary profits*, in 1975 the British Government set up the Committee of Inquiry into Inflation Accounting under the chairmanship of Sir Francis Sandilands. It was to come up with a method of accounting for inflation, which in the immediate years prior had approached 25 per cent p.a. in Britain and Australia and higher in some other countries.[19] In particular, the committee was to explore the competing methods of indexing accounting data with price level indexes that were proposed. These included valuing assets at: their current replacement price or some other notion of current value; on the basis of their estimated net present values; or as Chambers had been advocating for a considerable time, on the basis of assets stated at their current selling prices with an adjustment to incorporate increases or decreases in general price levels.

Of course, whereas the Sandilands Committee was one of the first governmental committees to address the problem, the national professional bodies had been nibbling at the issue for some time.[20] Australia had issued several exposure drafts on indexing accounts in December 1974 and replacement price accounting in June 1975, before the Sandilands Committee reported.[21] Again, snubbed by the profession by its refusal to issue a draft on his CCA, to its chagrin Chambers privately published, and circulated nationally and internationally to 3000 interested parties, his proposal as an exposure draft, *Accounting for Inflation*. It took the same format and style as those drafts issued by the professional bodies. Though obviously miffed, the Australian professional accountancy bodies remained silent. With an ounce of luck it, and Chambers, would go away.

Sandilands reported to parliament in September 1975. The recommendation was for a form of replacement price accounting that he labelled *Current Cost Accounting*, acknowledging but rejecting Chambers' selling price proposal and hijacking the CCA initialism. Bruised, but not beaten by Sandilands' snub and label hijacking, Chambers' Continuously Contemporary Accounting was rebadged with the acronymn COCOA (later written as CoCoA). All of this was more the consequence of the professional bodies' paranoia than the Sydney School's tilt at the profession.[22]

To digress: for mischief, Chambers had two dozen matchbox folders printed with the motto 'Try CoCoA'[23] and placed at the table of a luncheon with several senior members of the Institute of Chartered Accountants in Australia. The joke was not appreciated. For some unknown reason the idea formed that thousands of the folders had been circulated around the world. That hadn't even been contemplated. But it was a good idea, and they soon were. A few are still around and with other mementos provoked by the episode are now collectors' items.[24]

Returning to our argument it is not surprising to many with a knowledge of economic history, that once inflation had subsided in the early 1980s the firefighting approach that has underscored disclosure for 160-odd years ensured that professional interest in inflation accounting waned. And like so many of accounting's endemic problems, it remains unresolved. It awaits revisiting when inflation will likely again get out of control internationally.

Against that background it was not surprising that Chambers pursued a serious Australian inquiry into the state of companies' financial disclosures generally. He was regarded as conventional accounting's most trenchant critic. That work caught the attention in the mid-1970s of a leading Australian politician, NSW Attorney-General Frank Walker, who appointed Chambers to chair a committee to review the existing accounting standards. Walker acted as he felt that the profession and indeed the federal government were dragging their feet. While there was a lot of talk, little action had eventuated. This prompted the NSW state government to go it alone, setting up the Accounting Standards Review Committee, 'to examine the accounting standards . . . promulgated . . . or at the exposure draft stage . . . and to consider any other standards . . . which should be considered in the interest of parties who use published accounting information'.[25]

## The 1978 NSW Accounting Standards Review Committee

Attorney-General Walker's Committee was a maverick attempt to reform. While there was at last an apparent regulatory response in the late 1970s, it would prove to be an opportunity lost.

Walker's Committee came against a background of collapses by notable Australian companies during the mining boom of the 1960s, and as the property push in early 1970s had prompted extensive public concern.[26] Collapses included: investment traders Mineral Securities Australia Ltd and Patrick Partners; construction group Mainline; property-cum-financier Cambridge Credit Corporation Ltd; the conglomerate Gollins Holdings Ltd; and the finance-cum-property development company Associated Securities Ltd. Like their counterparts in the 1960s, these unexpected 1970s collapses created public pressure on the regulators to reassess the utility of existing regulatory mechanisms – in particular, the utility of existing professional accounting and auditing practices. Gollins had collapsed in 1975 shortly after an interim six-monthly report had revealed a reported profit of $835 192. An official inspector's inquiries recalculated this published profit to really be a loss of $10 776 606.[27] Construction heavyweight Mainline had also suddenly gone belly-up a year earlier. Telling analyses of the 1970s collapses at Minsec, Mainline, Cambridge Credit, Gollins, Ariadne and ASL[28] are apt examples of the state of affairs.

Pervading public focus of the regulators, the government and the accounting profession, was the extent of non-compliance with practices prescribed by the profession. Non-compliance with the 'approved standards' was seen in all cases to be deviant professional behviour. The underlying cost-based accounting practices were not deemed to be the major problem.

Between 1975 and 1977 the NSW Corporate Affairs Commission had reviewed annually 249, 535 and 250 accounts of companies. This revealed 62, 253 and 211 instances of non-compliance, respectively. Monitoring continued after the release of the Accounting Standards Review Committee Report, with an analysis of 8699 companies between 1978 and 1982. It revealed non-compliance with one or more Accounting Standards occurring in 3428 (41 per cent) of companies. And whereas that result was presented as a serious threat to the disclosure of necessary financial information, it is argued here that just the opposite was equally likely.

Curiously, despite the ASRC Report the issue of non-compliance then, as now, was perceived to be a major problem. A dominant theme in this book is that compliance with the general run of the prescribed standards is more the cause of misleading, creative accounting than of deviations from them. Yet, the push for compliance by the regulatory bodies of a voluminous set of rules continues.[29] Critically, so many of the non-compliances related to prescribed practices that persist in being based on the counterfactual. These included: providing for depreciation on buildings when the overall market price of property (including the buildings) was increasing; providing for future income tax and booking future income tax benefits without the immediate existence of or any definite prospect that the supposed liabilities or assets would materialise, for example.

Of course, any subsequent change in tax rates will affect, often materially, the amount of reported asset or liability balances.

Whereas the ultimate response to the NSW Government's Report would be low-key and rather secretive (see below), the profession's early involvement was more supportive. A-G Walker had signalled a desire to address company law and accounting reform at the June 1977 National Congress of the Australian Society of Accountants. Stung by those major 1970s failures it came as little surprise in November when he announced his Accounting Standards Review Committee (ASRC). A five-member committee under the chairmanship of Professor Ray Chambers from the University of Sydney and then current president of the Australian Society of Accountants was proposed. He was to be accompanied by T. Sri Ramanatham and Harry Rappaport, law and accounting academics respectively in Chambers' Sydney University Accounting Department, and a member each nominated by the Society and the Institute of Chartered Accountants in Australia.[30]

Correspondence between the NSW President of the Society and the National President of the ICAA indicates that neither was pleased with the committee's composition. They had met with the Attorney-General on 18 November 1977, the day following the announcement of the committee's structure, and their understanding of the committee and how it was to function differed from what they considered to be implied from the public announcement accompanying its formalisation, and advertisements inviting submissions. Nonetheless, the Society nominated its appointee but the ICAA held off such action.

Correspondence from the Chambers Collection reveals that Waldron for the Society and Cox for the ICAA explained their misgivings regarding the committee, that it had been referred to previously as a 'steering committee' and not the 'review board' of which the Attorney-General was also talking of establishing; that it did not comprise the cross-section of people 'concerned with accounting standards and their practical application as to give [it] an acceptance in the professional and commercial community', and that its membership ought to include representatives of the Institute of Directors, stock exchange and small business. Nonetheless, they expressed the desire to 'maintain continuing discussion'.[31]

Three matters of particular importance are worth noting. First, the underlying tenor that the accounting problems could best be resolved by practical persons who practised it, rather than those who observe it and its consequences. Yet the complaints levelled at accounting and presumably conveyed to A-G Walker were that accounting did not produce practical, useful, serviceable data. Second, there was concern about the misconception that the committee sought the imprimatur of acceptance. General agreement has been a longstanding criterion for accounting practices dating at least back to the 1930s, rather than the means of achieving better practice and serviceable outcomes. And third, a further concern was that the members of the committee were to have constituencies for whom they might be mouthpieces; that they were to be on the committee as representatives of the Society and the Institute, not in their own right.

In January 1978 the Society appointee, Trevor Russell, resigned from the committee.[32] Two reasons were given by him. First, the committee was considering joint standards, and yet the ICAA was not participating in the work. So the outcome could not be considered the product of joint deliberations. This view was consistent with the stance that members were representatives. The ICAA had not offered a nomination to the committee. Second, in his view the work was not proceeding according to what he understood to be its 'proposed activities' in Chambers' letter of appointment to him, and by Waldron on his understanding of the matters along the lines of the 21 November 1977 letter (with Cox) to the Attorney-General.

Withdrawal by both the professional bodies was now effective. Committee members functioning independently rather than as representatives was something foreign to the profession's way of doing things. Further, frequent mention of the possibility of the creation of a new body, the Accounting Standards Review Board, appears to have influenced the professional bodies, particularly the ICAA. Having lost out on the composition of the current committee, the strategy adopted appears to have been to ignore it and play a neater game with the Board in prospect.

But behind the scenes there was action. On the eve of Russell's resignation Geoff Vincent, National Director of the ASA, authored a paper 'Current position of the NSW Standards Review Board'. In it he observes that 'the total scene has become somewhat political'. A question was raised whether Chambers had placed the ASA in an 'embarrassing position' by virtue of his having been a party to the profession's approval of the standards he was now evaluating. The paper noted that the other members of the committee were 'considered to be pro-Ray Chambers in outlook', further commented that there was concern 'about the technical capability of certain members', and that the 'present representation was ... unbalanced'. Of note, the idea of 'representation' prevailed. Curiously, though dated on the eve of Russell's resignation from the committee, the paper made no mention of his pending resignation. Likewise of interest is the explanation that the 'ICA have to date *selected* a nominee but have refrained from allowing ICA participation to date preferring to discuss first "certain points" with Attorney-General Frank Walker'. That indicated that the ICAA had seriously contemplated participating at one point in the proceedings. A complete misunderstanding of the situation is betrayed by expression of a fear in the paper that since Chambers was the president of the ASA and Chair of the Review Committee, that the ASA would be giving 'de facto' approval to the committee's recommendations.

With that in mind it might have been a smart move for the professional bodies, certainly the ASA, to participate and have their say. Significantly, although both obviously felt their professionalism was at risk – the paper by the Society's representative, Geoff Vincent, having expressed the expectation that the Report would be 'derogatory'. Significantly, neither the ASA nor the ICAA made submissions to the ASRC.

Were the intention that placing the committee without input from the profession would scuttle it, this was wrong. A-G Walker owned the bat and ball. Unmoved by events, he decided to persist and see what the committee came up with.

*A contemptuous silence* captures the response when the ASRC Report, *Company Accounting Standards*, appeared in May 1978. It recommended that the current batch of standards be scrapped and that a General Accounting Standard (GAS) – which in today's vernacular was a principles-based standard – be introduced through the *Companies Act*. Chambers was well positioned to prescribe his 'reform of the law of company accounts' which he had detailed initially in his 1973 monograph, *Securities and Obscurities* (1973b).

Predictably, Chambers' CoCoA was the blueprint for the GAS, in which all price and price level changes would be brought into account ensuring that income was all-inclusive, that the balance sheet disclose financial position, that physical assets be stated at their current money's worth (best indicated by their current net selling prices), and that consolidated financial statements be replaced by a format better indicating the financial implications of the related companies operating across the capital boundary as if they were one enterprise, and the nonsensical recourse to tax effect assets and liabilities be scrapped. In short, the GAS prescribed that data produced in the income statement and balance sheet would be serviceable along the lines we have pursued here and elsewhere.

We say predictably because Chambers had worked on developing CoCoA over the previous forty years. His dissatisfaction with data from the current systems over time was evidenced by the misleading financial statements of the companies that had failed, and in his analyses of the financials produced by those that had not. Chambers' CoCoA had had a long gestation period. And although it had its strong detractors, as at the 1965 Berkeley conference and as expressed in the 1975 UK Sandilands Committee Report, no one had answered his challenges to disprove his claims regarding the defects in the current system, or had shown how their alternatives would provide data as serviceable as those from his CoCoA.

Knowing the most likely outcome, both the opportunity to make submissions and to critique the Report presented those who expected CoCoA to emerge as the committee's recommendation with a unique public platform from which to launch their objections, promote their alternatives. In the worst light, perhaps the inaction of professional bodies not making submissions is indicative of their incapacity to do so. That they did not post their favoured alternatives to the committee's recommendations is perhaps indicative that they at least lacked the confidence to debate the matter.

Overall, the press seemed to be of the view that the committee had made a brave attempt to move towards more effective accounting, better disclosure by companies, and indeed it tended to suggest that historical-cost accounting had been dealt a blow. Despite this reception by the financial press on the release of the Report and its findings,[33] the profession met the Report with, arguably, the silence of contempt.[34] But this public silence may have been their safest tactic, for, in private, the professional bodies were busy.

Throughout the rest of 1978 and most of 1979, behind the scenes the ASA and the ICAA set to work devising a response to be communicated to the Attorney-General. Interestingly Chambers was not brought into the circle, but he had friends inside the tent. Now out of the ASA presidency, he was otherwise cut off from information regarding what was going on. Chambers privately received a copy of a draft of the joint response and information explaining that the ICAA was unhappy with the ASRC Report, as they thought it was 'too much ASA'. The general drift of the document was that historical-cost accounting ought not be replaced, that CoCoA was not a viable alternative, and more or less that the Report was hardly worth commenting on. Indeed, the profession's communication to the Attorney-General on 25 January 1980 offered general criticism and noted that 'we believe that detailed comments on various aspects of the report of the committee would serve no useful purpose'.

This was curious and inconsistent, given that in Australia over a decade earlier the ASA had seen fit to respond to public criticism of accounting by inspectors into company failures. Its White Paper, *Accounting Principles and Practices Discussed in Reports on Company Failures* (1966),[35] while virtually exonerationg accounting and blaming 'management' for the failures, had nevertheless recommended remedial actions embracing a general questioning of the form and content of published financial statements. And contiguous with the Review Committee's tenure, professional bodies around the world were seriously contemplating Exposure Drafts as part of the lengthy professional deliberations to consider reforms to account for inflation. Current market prices were being proposed to supplement historic-costs data (and ultimately by the end of the decade to supplant them). But the 25 January 1980 communication to the Attorney-General gave space to declaring that selling price valuations for physical assets would 'not give a true and fair view of the organisation as a going concern', though without an explanation as to why. And it trotted out the proposition that companies 'such as the BHP with substantial fixed assets ... could have no reasonable market value upon which to base its valuation, and hence would be reduced to scrap values – clearly an absurd situation'. That was a common argument at the time against selling price valuations. For the argument, however, it was 'an own goal', since 15 years later the BHP was writing down its steel plant at Newcastle to the market value. The committee's recommendation would in fact have been more likely far closer to the truth of the matter.

As part of gathering its ideas in late 1978 the NSW branch of the ASA had arranged for the NSW Group of 100 to survey its members' opinions on the committee's recommendations. Only 47 responded. A summary of the Group of 100 Task Force set up to review the Chambers Report was sent to NSW ASA Divisional councillors in May 1978. Again, there was no communication to Chambers or the other committee members, but friends apparently were leaking documents. Chambers received a copy of the Task Force Report via one of the ASA councillors in about September 1979, and wrote to the ASA Executive Director asking what was to happen to it. His letter contained a stinging criticism of the survey: it was 'vague . . . touches only on very few of the many features of the C.R. . . . [is] assertive rather than reasoned . . . makes no attempt to rebut the reasoning and evidence . . . [and] as a professional response . . . it is light weight indeed'. The ASA's President was formally sent the Task Force Report on 3 September 1979, explaining that the summary of the 47 replies included only those in respect of which there was a 'clear consensus (70%)'. It was a curious move bearing in mind that less than half the population canvassed had replied. Thus a clear consensus was being claimed for something approximating 33 per cent of the total Group of 100 members!

On 16 February 1981 Chambers wrote privately to the ASA President who succeeded him, Pat Lannigan, expressing his awareness of the profession's tactics:

I have since [the issue of the Report] thought it almost pusillanimous, that through the whole course of 1979, during which the response of the profession to the Report was under notice, not once was I asked to explain or justify any position taken in the Report; at no time before or since 25 January 1980 was I extended the courtesy of being informed what was to be, or was, communicated to the Attorney-General. What was an openly published statement which the committee had prepared with great care and was prepared to defend openly, was, in fact, attacked secretly, covertly. It was as if the executive committees were unprepared and unwilling to have their stance exposed to the general membership, or to the possibility of retort from the committee that produced the Report.[36]

Four days earlier Lannigan had given Chambers a copy of the 25 January 1980 letter (Chambers had already received a copy from friends in July 1980). But the files suggest that nothing came to him from the profession via official correspondence. After sidestepping detailed discussion of the Report with the 'serves

125

no purpose' comment, the letter reiterated that the 'prime responsibility for the development of accounting standards which result in the presentation of a true and fair view of the accounts of a business entity rests with the accounting profession'. It assured the Attorney-General that the professional bodies were 'giving consideration to a revised accounting standards setting procedure'.

This tale mirrors the reactions of the US accounting profession in the 1930s when it appeared that the setting of accounting standards/rules would be usurped by a government body, the Federal Trade Commission (chapter 1).[37]

Of course, as recent revelations about accounting misstatements confirm, the US profession's promises in the 1930s have not been fulfilled. Accounting bodies universally can hardly claim to have honoured the promise to settle accounting issues effectively in the implied short-run. Back to the ASRC saga: 25 years after the Pat Lannigan letter the latest of the successive standards the Australian profession developed in the interregnum have been set aside by it, and the AIFRSs adopted. This is not surprising. A misunderstanding by the professional bodies of the function of financial statements that was the focus of the Chambers Committee is evident in the 25 January 1980 letter. The Chambers Committee was pursuing the (one would think) widely held and likely incontestable understanding that the *Companies Act* provisions required financial statements to show a true and fair view of a company's state of affairs. That is, show a true and fair view of its financial performance and financial position. In contrast the executives of both the ASA and ICAA clearly stated their understanding to be that the application of the standards will result in a *true and fair view of accounts*. No wonder that more than a quarter of a century later the chaos continues.

A significant response by the Group of 100 was overwhelming agreement that the accounting bodies should have a 'hardline' reply to the Report and should 'offer an alternative to the Chambers Report'. But in their 25 January 1980 letter to the Attorney-General they declined to do the former, opting instead for silence. And to this date no alternative has been forthcoming.

The ASRC's May 1978 Report was extremely critical of the existing system of accounting. As noted, the NSW Attorney-General had, prior to its release, threatened state intervention in the Accounting Standards-setting process unless the accountancy profession issued sensible and enforceable directives. For whatever reason, little direct action resulted from this committee's Report and those threats.[38] By the early 1980s the NSW Labor Government had been voted out. Chambers' Report appears to have gone with it. The *silence of contempt* seemed to win through.

Yet the Zen riddle of the 'sound of one hand clapping' may well be interpreted to indicate that the Chambers Report was not a futile exercise. Just as the riddle might mean that sound is not an essential part of clapping, the silence from the profession does not invalidate the principles underpinning the committee's CoCoA recommendation. Indeed, the profession's responses to events surrounding the company failures, asset stripping and asset pricing concerns over the past thirty years have merely reinforced the criticism of accounting as it was, and what has become of it through successive modifications since.

Whereas the profession lampooned the prospect of obtaining reliable selling prices for physical assets, doing so is an essential part of the compulsory AIFRS 'asset impairment' regime. A major recurring complaint about CoCoA is no longer an incorrigible constraint.[39] The backfire of the BHP example illustrates how the 'impossible' can indeed occur, and how the 'ridiculous' is frequently the product of short-sightedness rather than reason. In principle, the all-inclusive income that the ASRC recommended is for the most part the order of the day under the AIFRSs. And despite the professional bodies' misunderstanding of the focus of 'true and fair' in its letter to the Attorney-General in January 1980 reflecting possibly the growing disregard for the quality criterion, we noted that the British Financial Reporting Council in 2005 stated unequivocally that true and fair is the cornerstone of accounting in the British system.

Setting up the Chambers Committee was a 'politically' shrewd response by the NSW Government to the prevailing public outcry at the circumstances in which companies with clean audit reports collapsed suddenly. Ignoring its recommendations was 'politically strategic' by the profession, given its public opposition to the committee's composition, its eventual refusal to participate on the committee, to make submissions to it, and its silence regarding its recommendations. That nothing official came of the Report is indicative of the gap between public rhetoric and the private and professional intransigence. That intransigence was inexcusable against the background of the collapses and 'accounting irregularities' that prompted the Report.

But the way in which that intransigence was manifested, the professional accountancy bodies' deafening silence on the NSW committee's work, raises questions as to how well the profession and the regulators at the time understood the serious technical nature of the problem.

# 7

# Commerce without Conscience: Group Enterprise or Separate Legal Entity?[1]

> English Company Law possesses some curious features which may generate curious results. A parent company may spawn a number of subsidiary companies, all controlled directly or indirectly by the shareholders of the parent company. If one of the subsidiary companies, to change the metaphor, turns out to be the runt of the litter and declines into insolvency to the dismay of its creditors, the parent company and the other subsidiary companies may prosper to the joy of the shareholders without any liability for the debts of the insolvent subsidiary.
>
> (Templeman J., *In re Southard & Co.* [1979] 1 WLR 1198)

## Shredding the corporate veil

A cavalier take-it-or-leave-it option appears to be the approach by some to the separate legal entity principle undergirding British corporate law. What was created for the benefit of the participants in corporate activity is turned against them on many occasions. Disclosure relating to corporate groups' financial status and performance is at best equivocal, generally misleading and, sometimes, completely meaningless. Protection offered by the corporate veil to shareholders in respect of claims on their capital, and to creditors by quarantining a company's assets to satisfy their claims, has frequently been misappropriated to their collective detriment but to the betterment of others.

For decades corporate groups have played a significant role in modern commerce, and featured prominently in the financial circumstances of notable collapses.[2] In particular, the asset quarantining impact of the corporate veil has dismayed both creditors and public alike. It is consistent with Sir Robert Chiltern's lament in Oscar Wilde's *An Ideal Husband* that modern corporate activity is often 'commerce without conscience'. In more recent times, a jury in Melbourne handed down a verdict related to corporate group actions that entailed what was described as a 'continuous conscious and contumelious disregard for the plaintiff's safety'.[3]

For over a century the law (on trusts, corporations, in equity, statute and taxation laws) in Anglo-Saxon countries has grappled with the conflict between the recognition of a company as a separate legal entity and the contiguous tendency (especially by accountants) to give some legitimacy to a group entity comprising a parent company and its subsidiaries. *Salomon v Salomon & Co Ltd* [1897] AC 22 was, for some, the apparent legal breakthrough (though for others it confirmed a long-held view about the corporation), with its ruling that there is a break between the assets and liabilities of the company and the assets and liabilities of the members of the company.[4] The corporate veil between the various interested parties was firmly drawn. A precedent in liquidation, it would be of interest to see how parties would view the actions (contracts, risk assessments) of groups of companies for ongoing transaction purposes over the next century.

But until recently in both settings in Australia at least, the group or economic entity boundary was generally a figment of accountants' imaginations and the product of technical looseness in everyday commercial talk. It lacked any general legal foundation.[5]

As corporate groups entailing parents and multiple subsidiary companies grew in popularity in the twentieth century,[6] the *Salomon* judgment was the subject of reassessment in many cases. Through asset shuffling creditors have found themselves left in companies without the assets to meet their claims, and the asset-rich companies have few liabilities. Such shuffling manipulates the veil, presumably with the opposite effect to what was originally intended. Robert Baxt, one-time academic, Australian Trade Practices Commissioner, and now leading commercial practitioner, recently observed the significance of the corporate veil in matters germane to the circumstances of, for example, the Bond, Patrick/MUA, Ansett/Air New Zealand and (say) the James Hardie and Wespoint affairs:

> In 1975 when Anthony Mason was a judge of the High Court of Australia, he appeared to be flirting with the idea of broadening directors' duties to shareholders when he suggested in *Walker v Winborne* that directors who disregarded the interests of creditors in a company [a separate entity but part of a corporate group] close to insolvency did so at their peril. But the High Court decision in *Spie v Ries* has dispelled that notion.[7]

Although Baxt was addressing specifically the Australian corporate setting, his comments could be taken to apply, in general, to the circumstances of the likes of Enron, Maxwell Communications, Parmalat and the myriad other corporate groups whose accounting manipulations shrouding their true financial states misled creditors and investors. Critical to the issue is the fundamental protective role that the corporate veil is expected to play. It is almost, as one commentator observed, 'impermeable'.[8] While recent commercial events and proposed reforms in Australia's 2007 *Corporations (Insolvency) Amendment Bill* recommending pooling are relevant to the capital boundary conundrum, refocusing attention on corporations operating within complex group structures, the issues clearly are not new.[9]

Several industrial and creditor disputes aptly illustrate the complexities emerging in the recourse to the *group* and *separate legal entity* notions. First, take the attempted retrenchment of Patrick Stevedores' Maritime Union of Australia employees following the alleged intra-group shuffling of funds, other assets and capital in the late 1990s. And, similarly, the redundancies after Air New Zealand jettisoned its owned subsidiary, Ansett in 2001. Also allegations regarding Australian employee dismissals were made when the contemporaneous Cobar and Woodlawn mines closed, and when redundancies occurred following the Nardell, Steel Tank and Pipes, and Newcastle's Bay Group collapses. Those and similar examples illustrated below highlight the inevitable entanglements arising from selective use of the separate legal entity notion *within* a corporate group setting.[10] And, while the focus in those matters was mainly on the plight of employees being left short of their redundancy and retrenchment entitlements, they serve to highlight the *modus operandi* of exploiting the group structure to frustrate creditors of all types, as is evident with James Hardie, HIH, Enron and Parmalat. In previous decades in other notable instances of financially stressed corporate groups other classes of unsecured creditors (including financiers) have found themselves caught up in financial hassles exacerbated by the group structure: for example, at Adsteam, Tricontinental, Qintex, Bond Corporation, Westmex, and in the Linter and Burns Philp financial affairs in Australia[11]; and overseas at: Maxwell Communications, Olympia and York.

It is interesting to note the frequency with which the losses appear to be borne substantially by the public companies when a group crashes, while the private companies of the major activist in the group fare much better. Whether by good luck or by arrangement, often the group structure facilitates an unfair outcome.

The separate legal entity impediment to accessing the total pool of group assets to satisfy the creditors of specific companies often is the nub of the problem. It is endemic in the holding company/subsidiary companies' structure. Outcomes from some of the cases below have not gone unnoticed by the legislature. Consider the Patrick/MUA affair, which resulted in the Australian Labor Party (supported by the Australian Democrats) introducing the Employment Security Bill into the Australian upper house, the Senate. It sought to impose new limits on companies that strip assets or manipulate their corporate structures to avoid obligations[12] to employees or other unsecured creditors. The federal parliament's mid-1998 inquiry into Corporate Restructuring and Employees Rights by the Joint Committee on Corporations and Financial Services, was a direct result. As were the 2004 parliamentary inquiries and reports, *Corporate Insolvency Laws – A Stocktake, Rehabilitating Large and Complex Enterprises in Financial Difficulties* and the 2006 *Corporations (Insolvency) Amendments Bill, 2007*.[13]

Consider in 2001 when Ansett employees were left alone, out on a limb, arguing for their entitlements after Air New Zealand cut loose its wholly owned subsidiary, Ansett Australia Pty Ltd. Protracted arguments followed between employees, unions and Air New Zealand about the company's alleged legal and moral responsibilities as a parent company in respect of any of the debts of its wholly owned subsidiaries.[14] Following significant press fallout from this and other cases that preceded it, the Australian Government established the Special Employment Entitlement Scheme for Ansett employees (SEESA) for the purpose of making these safety net payments to Ansett employees if there was found to be a shortfall in asset realisations. It has been subsequently amended and is now referred to as its employee GEERS (General Employee Entitlements Redundancy Scheme) 'safety net' – albeit a partial solution to a much bigger capital boundary problem.

The administrators of Ansett appositely describe what followed. The federal government announced its intention to guarantee that Ansett's employees would receive their entitlements to wages, annual leave, payment in lieu of notice and redundancies up to the community standard of eight weeks. This was not an unproblematic exercise, as the administrators observed:

> we believed it could take several years to complete the realisation of Ansett's assets . . . the Government maintained that SEESA was established for the benefit of employees and insisted it be given priority for the repayments of any advances made by it to the Administrators as if the Government 'stood in the shoes' of the employees and be repaid ahead of ordinary unsecured creditors.
>
> *Court Application:* In early December 2001, we applied to the Court . . . In the absence of an order from the Court, if as Administrators we borrowed the money there would not be a right of indemnity over the assets of the companies to repay the borrowings. The Government and the unions supported our application to the Court.
>
> On 14 December 2001 the Court made orders pursuant to Section 447A of the Act to the effect that Part 5.3A of the Act was to operate in relation to the Ansett companies as if:
>
> - the SEESA payments to redundant employees would rank according to the priority provided for under Sections 556 and 560 of the Act; and

- the SEESA payments were debts incurred by the Administrators in the performance and exercise of their functions as Administrators and for which they would not be personally liable to repay (except to the extent that they had assets available for the Administration to do so).[15]

In the aftermath of the HIH collapse, in March 2003 the HIH Royal Commissioner observed that directors of one of the relevant insurance companies within the HIH Group appeared to have adopted a 'group enterprise perspective' when attesting to its regulatory solvency position. Contiguously (and perhaps accidentally), with a deed of cross guarantee in place, HIH had 'netted-off' related company assets and liabilities in several APRA Annual Returns, thus by implication treating its insurance subsidiaries as if they were part of a singular corporate group enterprise.[16]

From many other instances it appears that HIH was not alone in that regard. Selected vignettes illustrate how the capital boundary is blurred when the group notion takes hold.

## Vignettes – when the group fiction gains command

Though the corporate group is a fiction, the notion of the separate legal companies comprising an economic entity pervades not only corporate accounting but the corporate regulatory environment. Thus, there is the strange spectre of the financial positions and performances being disclosed for listed companies not relating to any specific legal entity, but to their aggregated data, all massaged by the mysteries of what accountants call consolidation accounting. The entire exercise is a reporting lie. The base data for the performances are aggregates of those (after taking into account indefensible intra-goup adjustments) for the separate companies; the consolidated assets' and liabilities' balances likewise are the aggregates of the separate companies' assets and liabilities, not referring to the financial position of any of them. Curiously, though there isn't any such thing legally as the group profit or loss, or group assets and group liabilities, nobody seems to object to the authorised disclosure of those data. They draw on the ultimate of creativity in their construction and entail the ultimate audacity for passing them off to be what clearly they are not.

Two closely related transactions – the Bond/Bell Resources 'cash-cow transactions' and, a short time later, the Bell Group/major banks 'secured lending' saga – arguably characterise the managers' schizophrenia regarding the separate legal entity principle. Both occurred in the late 1980s. Bond Corporation, one of Australia's leading companies in the 1980s with more than 600 subsidiaries, suffered financial problems circa the 1987 stock market crash and was placed in provisional liquidation in the early 1990s.[17] Bell Resources, a listed company, was a subsidiary of Bond Corporation Ltd. The Bell Resources Group itself comprised more than 80 companies. The liquidation of the Bond and Bell Resources groups revealed two questionable series of intertwined cash transactions that would later be the subject of scrutiny. Both involved uncertainties in assessing solvency due to the complex group structures and financial arrangements.

*Bond/Bell Resources (cash-cow) transactions*[18] were the *modus operandi* that led to Bond Corporation's founder, Alan Bond, being convicted of contestably Australia's largest corporate fraud.[19] It entailed Bond Group intermediaries being used to facilitate upstream transfers of approximately $1.2 billion of cash funds from subsidiary Bell Resources to other Bond Corporation subsidiaries and related parties. Importantly, both Bond Corporation and Bell Resources were listed holding companies and under the control of Alan Bond – Bond Corporation through direct holdings, and 53 per cent of Bell Resources by virtue of holdings of related parties. Though illustrating only part of the fraud, Clarke *et al.* (2003, p. 179) drew on Johnson (2000, p. 66) to reveal the complexity of the cash-cow transactions. Intermediaries to the transactions were smallish Bond Corp-related companies. Borrowers were Bond Corporation Finance, Bond Corporation Holdings (BCH) and Alan Bond's family company, Dallhold Investments.

The Statement of Facts in *The Queen v Alan Bond* (1997: 18) exposes the motivation for the transactions: Early in 1988 Bond Corporation Holdings was having cash-flow difficulties and found it difficult to borrow from external financial institutions.[20] External financial institutions lent money to individual companies in the Bond Corporation or Bell groups using negative pledges, avoidance of which entailed related parties moving funds between group companies as if they comprised one enterprise. As we note, in such a fluid group arrangement assessing any individual company's solvency is problematic.

*Bell Group/major banks* lending using secured liens provides another setting to explore capital boundary issues. *The Bell Group Limited (In Liquidation) & Ors v Westpac Banking Corporation & Ors*[21] litigation began in 1995 when the Bell Group liquidator, with financial backing from the WA Insurance Commission, sought damages to the tune of up to $1.5 billion (which includes interest on the amount being sought over more than 15 years) regarding the allegation 'that when the [six major – three Australian and three overseas] banks took security for [the $250 million] loans [refinancing arranged by the Bell Group Board on Australia Day 1990] . . . they knew the companies were close to insolvency'.[22] It reportedly is the longest running court case in Australia's history. A judgment is expected to be handed down in 2007. In essence, the liquidator has argued that the banks agreed to extend (restructure) loans to the Bell Group of companies, provided they obtained security over assets relative to other unsecured creditors.

**Table 7.1:** Details of back-to-back loans used in Bond Corporation Group

| Dates | Lender | Intermediaries | Borrower | Amount ($ millions) |
|---|---|---|---|---|
| Early 1988 | Bond Brewing Holding Group | Subsidiary of Markland House | Bond Corporation Holdings Limited | Not stated |
| *Reason for transactions*: Syndicate of banks imposed a condition that revenues generated by Brewing Group were retained in Brewing Group. Bond Corporation Holdings Limited had difficulties in obtaining funds from external financial institutions. | | | | |
| Between 29 August and 3 November 1988 | Bell Resources Limited | Companies in Markland House group <br> One or two intermediaries were used | Bond Corporation Holdings Limited <br> Dallhold | 447.5 <br><br> 55.0 |
| *Reason for transactions*: Bell Group had given undertaking to bankers that it would not lend more than $25 million to companies outside the Bell Group. Bond Corporation agreed with Bell's financiers only to borrow from Bell Resources and J.N. Taylor for short-term accommodation needs. | | | | |
| At 15 November 1988 these loans existed | J.N. Taylor Finance | Merchant Capital Limited <br> Winnington Securities Limited and Markland Investments Limited | Bond Corporation Finance <br> Bond Corporation Finance | 101.0 <br> 25.8 |
| *Reason for transaction*: Not stated. | | | | |
| 24 November | Pascoe Limited | DFC Overseas Limited and Catton Finance Limited <br> European Pacific Banking Company and Catton Finance Limited | Bond Corporation Finance <br><br> Bond Corporation Finance | 50.0 <br><br> 50.0 |
| *Reason for transaction*: Rewind back-to-back loans existing at 15 November 1988 and to comply with NCSC requirement and borrowing requirements. | | | | |
| After 13 December 1988 | Bell Resources Finance | Markland House Group Companies | Bond Corporation Finance | 170.2 |
| *Reason for transaction*: Not stated. | | | | |

*Sources*: Statement of Facts included as a schedule in the case *The Queen v Alan Bond 1997* (unreported), *Pascoe Limited (in Liquidation) v Lucas 1997* and Sykes (1994), pp. 224–5. This table is reproduced from Johnson, 'Back-to-back loans: A fraud in transition', *Australian Accounting Review* (2000), p. 66.

It needs to be understood that, previously, nearly all Bond Group debt had been arranged primarily on a negative pledge basis.[23] At issue here is how to assess solvency or insolvency from internal and reported financial information within a group setting – a matter discussed in chapter 9.

Implications for accounting and auditing from both the Bond/Bell Resources transactions are important. Because of the dominance of Alan Bond and other top-level Bond Corporation executives, information about Bond Corporation reportedly was released to shareholders and lower level operational managers on a need-to-know basis. Regarding an earlier Bond transaction Mr Justice Sir Nicholas Browne-Wilkinson observed Alan Bond's 1980s failure to take over Lonrho 'is a very remarkable phenomenon when you think that you have a company that had by that stage invested 360 million [in acquiring a stake in Lonrho] – odd that not a single piece of paper is available supporting that fact'.[24] The audit and wider governance implications can only be speculated. Back to the Bond/Bell cash-cow transaction: in 1995 criminal fraud charges were laid against Bond and two other Bond Corporation directors over the cash-cow transaction and all were eventually found guilty, Bond and Mitchell in 1997, and Oates in 2005.[25]

Fund movements in the manner described above arguably are contrary to a fundamental principle of English law which holds that each entity within a corporate group is a separate legal entity. But practice often flies in the face of theory. Alan Bond admitted actions consistent with the erroneous but prevailing view that the group is, for all managerial intents and purposes, a dominance-friendly single entity. Notwithstanding that view being so strongly embedded in conventional consolidation accounting thought and practice and seemingly underpinning many directors' operational actions related to group activities (see also chapter 8), it is inconsistent with the legal framework in which companies generally operate. Special contractual instruments, like class order deeds of cross guarantee, mitigate that general proposition.

Conventional consolidation accounting is a piece of accounting sophistry that lies at the root of much commercial mischief, especially involving dominant senior management (such as Bond) when they engage in dubious financial transactions. A major difficulty for the creditors, auditors and even for directors of the separate companies in such cases is to determine the relevant entity.

## Employee victims of group-spin

### Patrick Stevedores/MUA

Frequently employees have found themselves on the wrong end of shortfalls when related companies go under. In 1997/98 the Patrick Stevedores/MUA waterfront dispute captured press headlines around Australia.[26] Although it was the plight of the waterfront workers who had potentially been left high and dry waiting for their severance entitlements that caught the eye, underpinning their situation was group-spin. Through an entanglement of intra-group trans-actions – the so-called September Transactions – Patrick's stevedoring compa-nies operating within the Lang Corporation Group affected workers' employ-ment contracts (and the consequential employee entitlements). Initially four employee subsidiaries were left bereft of sufficient assets to meet employee enti-tlements, whereas other creditors' obligations within the group were satisfied. The September Transactions reinforced the corporate veil between the employee companies' obligations and the assets of the other companies comprising the Lang Corporation economic group.[27] Earlier, companies within the Lang Group had revoked some cross-guarantee deeds that had been in place for several years.

Against that backdrop it is instructive to consider some brief particulars of the waterfront dispute between Patrick Stevedores group of companies (wholly owned by Lang Corporation Limited) and its MUA workforce.[28] They illustrate creditor exposure (at the end of the day) to the primacy of the separate legal entity principle in the financial management of corporate groups. They especially illustrate the potential for regulatory mayhem inherent in unfettered slippage between recourse to the group and separate legal entity principles.

Corporate restructuring selectively using an *employer subsidiary* with limited assets but the liability for employee entitlements, where other group companies are relatively asset-rich, is open to criticism. It can produce a scenario in which an employer subsidiary arguably is guided into insolvency and its employees dismissed in circumstances likely to deny them financial satisfaction of their holiday, superannuation and leave entitlements. The potential for selective and deliberate recourse to the separate legal entity principle to engineer outcomes is clear. And it is the relative free rein to vacillate between the group and separate legal entity principle, draw on legal authority for the former, and business practices for the latter, that causes the inequities. Such outcomes would be far more difficult to achieve were the corporate group entity and corporate group responsibility concepts to have legal substance,[29] or be clearly defined in the law to be absolutely without it.

It has been suggested[30] that selective recourse to the separate legal entity prin-ciple could become a pervasive corporate mechanism. That has the potential to affect a substantial number of Australia's workers, creating increased uncertainty about the continuation of their employment and the protection of their rights and obligations in the event of their employment terminating. A more structural focus exposes inevitable financial conflicts spawned by the dual functioning of the separate legal entity and group entity principles currently embedded in British corporate law. While the industrial relations aspects of these scenarios have attracted considerable attention, by virtue of the Patricks/MUA waterfront affair, their genesis in the structure of Australian corporate law has been out of focus.

Indeed, the difficulties in unravelling the financial implications of using the separate legal entity principle to resolve corporate group problems underpinned CAMAC's 'opting-in' suggestion in the late 1990s (which we shall return to later) and even prior to that in the 1980s developing the forerunner to the guarantee covenant of the ASC-administered class order deed of cross guarantee.

Although the deed was proposed to facilitate creditor protection against capital boundary hopping within a closed group (as a *quid pro quo* for granting groups various reporting relief benefits), the separate legal entity principle retains its sovereignty within the wider group structure, especially for ongoing activities. But the deed was another chink in the armour of that principle.

When introduced in 1991 (as part of the ASC class order administrative regime),[31] the ASC stated that the deed's guarantee covenant effectively meant that various wholly owned subsidiaries within a corporate group are to be regarded as part of the one entity (the closed group).[32] These covenants, if strictly applied, would have circumvented the oft-attributed *Salomon v Salomon*[33] separate legal entity principle enshrined in British-based corporate law. But deed usage indicates the closed groups within which companies undertake cross guarantees are usually only a part (sometimes a minor part) of the larger set of related entities. Selectivity in structuring the closed groups is a reasonable suspicion. Thus, where directors are allowed discretion as to which companies are included in the closed group, selective exposure to creditors' claims can defeat the intended regulatory outcomes. Class order deeds currently affect only the appearance of a potential equitable outcome for creditors.

Recourse to the primacy of the separate legal entity principle reducing the rights of unsecured employee creditors, relative to those of shareholders, has been the cause of many industrial relations anxieties. The interface of corporations and industrial relations laws has proven a conundrum. With limited opportunities for entity boundary hopping, employees generally have little or no access to the wider group assets.

Deliberate transference of assets, capital reduction, was the alleged *modus operandi* of the Patrick Stevedoring group to quarantine its employer subsidiaries from funds and then seek to retrench its MUA employees in early April 1998. Figure 7.1 depicts a part of the Lang Corporation group in 1997/98. Several companies comprising the group became entangled in the waterfront dispute through the complex web of transactions in September 1997. Those transactions are said to have involved the movement of $314.9 million of funds and related assets between wholly owned Patrick's group and other Lang group companies. The High Court noted that these transactions 'affected the capital structure, business, debts and inter-company accounts of the employer companies... [They] were not then known to the employees.'[34] Financial statements of the parent company (Lang Corporation Limited) and related group companies reveal that at the 30 September 1996 balance date, companies within Lang Corporation held investments in Lang group companies of around $131 million (with only around $9 million at the 1997 balance date). At the 1997 balance date Lang Corporation Limited held receivables (approximately $186 million) owed by group companies (excluding monies totalling in excess of $50 million owed Lang Corporation by the wholly owned TDG Group of companies, which were paid on 23 October 1997). These data form the backdrop for the September Transactions involving:

1) cash and cash equivalents amounting to $314.9 million paid by Company D to acquire assets (namely the stevedoring equipment, the rights to engage in stevedoring and all contractual interests other than those related to their employees) from the four employer subsidiaries (Companies F, G, H, I). Those assets were then on-sold to Company E.
2) cash and cash equivalents now held by the four employer companies were used to discharge loan obligations to other Lang Corporation group companies (the set of group companies designated C) as well as to the Parent (A); and
3) nearly all of the remaining funds of between $60 and $70 million in the four employer subsidiaries were used to buy back the four employer companies' shares (this effected what amounts to a capital reduction) from other Lang Corporation group companies (designated C), excluding the Parent.

The High Court's summary of these transactions is apposite:

Although the level of shareholders' funds would have been unchanged by the disposition of the employer companies' businesses at full commercial value [the value of $314.9 million being based on a Price Waterhouse Corporate Finance valuation in late 1996], the businesses were exchanged for a receivable not all of which was received [nor] retained by the businesses ... But, after applying so much of the purchase price as was needed to discharge intra-Group loans and other debts owing by the employer companies, a significant amount – counsel variously stated the amount as $60 and $70 million – was expended in buying back shares in the employer companies ... The issued capital and shareholders' funds of the employer companies were reduced accordingly. The result of the restructuring was that somewhere between $60 and $70 million of the capital of the employer companies, which would have been available to finance their business operations, was returned to the shareholders [except for 17% of the shares in Stevedores Tasmania] of other members of the Group. The $60 million to $70 million transferred to these shareholders was no longer available to employees or other creditors or potential creditors of the employer companies in the event of loss of [*sic*] or significant downturn in the business of the employers. The shareholders' funds of the employer companies were reduced to approximately $2.5 million. It seems that those funds might have been exhausted by April 1998 when the employer companies were placed under liquidation.[35]

Drawing upon that summary and the information in Lang Corporation's 1997 annual financial statements, figure 7.1 reconstructs one possible interpretation of the financial effect of the September Transactions. Because of data limitations this depiction is partial. Yet it is apparent that the four employer companies were left with reduced (almost zero) capital, but retained substantial financial obligations to creditors, including the aggrieved MUA employees seeking payment of outstanding leave and long-service entitlements. Intra-group loans owed by the four employer companies to other Lang Corporation Limited subsidiaries had been repaid. A Lang wholly owned subsidiary, Patrick Stevedores Operations Pty Ltd, by then owned the stevedoring assets including the stevedoring rights previously held by the four employer companies. Subsequently, the four employer companies were deemed insolvent and placed in the hands of a voluntary administrator with Patrick's MUA employees first being retrenched and then re-employed by the administrator, following Justice North's 8 April instructions.

Interestingly, it has been suggested that this type of restructuring could not have occurred in earlier periods when stricter checks and balances on buy-backs required all creditors to approve such capital reductions.[36]

Voluntary administration was the inevitable outcome of the two events just described. The September Transactions presented the four companies with immediate liquidity problems. This was exacerbated by the lack of expected stevedoring work contracts from Patrick Stevedores Operations Pty Ltd because of the violation of non-strike covenants in the September 1997 Labour Service Agreements between the employer companies and other Lang Corporation Group companies. Placing the four companies in voluntary administration by Lang breached one of the conditions of the labour supply contract. The contract was terminated leaving the administrators no option but to sack the waterside workers.[37]

Notwithstanding the apparent financially solvent states of other group companies which remained operating,[38] the employer subsidiaries were left unable to generate sufficient ongoing working funds. This raises the question of what the outcome would have been had a deed of cross guarantee been in place covering *all* the subsidiaries of Lang Corporation.

Of particular note is the ease and legitimacy in the current corporate environment in which assets can be relocated – how approximately $230 million of

139

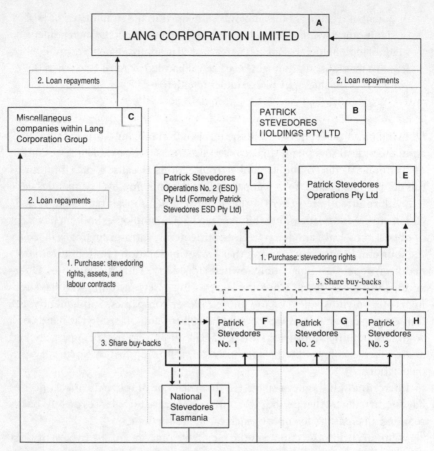

**Figure 7.1:** Preliminary analysis of the 'September Transactions'

*Sources:* HCA judgment, May 1998; Lang Corporation Annual Report, for the financial year ended 30 September 1997.

Notes:

(a) Each company is 100% owned by companies on a higher echelon in the same sector, except company I.

(b) The arrows represent cash and cash-equivalent flows between the companies for the following purposes:

⋯⋯⋯ Loan repayments; ----- share buy-backs; ▬▬▬ purchases including stevedoring rights.

(c) Companies B, D, E, F, G, H and I are part of the Patrick Stevedores Group.

(d) At the time of the waterfront dispute $228 million (approx.) was owed to external financiers by various Lang Corporation companies, excluding the parent.

bank finance raised by one or more subsidiary companies within the Patrick and Lang groups initially was moved in apparently normal group transactions to other group companies. It is symptomatic of common activity facilitated by the current parent and controlled entity structure with apparent selectivity in focus. Also, in accord with the group convention, security for the externally raised finance included charges over tangible and other assets of the separate subsidiaries within the related Lang Corporation/Patrick Stevedores groups and sub-groups. This arrangement further demonstrates the ongoing potential for and practice of commercially motivated selective balancing of the separate and group entity principles.[39]

Particulars of the Patrick's case also evoke a questioning of the efficacy of consolidated accounting data disclosed in the Annual Accounts of the Lang Corporation Limited and the Lang Corporation Group. Consistent with legislatively and professionally endorsed consolidation practices they neither revealed which companies within the larger economic group or the smaller Patrick's Stevedoring sub-group owed monies to one another, nor which subsidiary companies were in debt to external financiers. Although in accord with the professional Accounting Standards of the time, legislation and the ASX's continuous disclosure requirements, it is contestable of what financial characteristics the market is continuously informed with that variety of disclosure.

It is virtually impossible to isolate the separate commercial trading and financing activities of the individual operating subsidiaries from the aggregate of those of the other companies comprising a group reported in the consolidated data. But consolidation is undertaken with the avowed objective of providing greater financial insights. Its processes contradict the everyday experience that (subject to cost) disaggregation of data produces information about components of the whole – a disconnect with the common claim that for practical day-to-day commercial purposes aggregation of the separate companies' affairs effectively quantifies the affairs of *one entity*.[40] For instance, Justice Rogers noted: 'As I see it, there is today a tension between the realities of the commercial life and the applicable law . . . In the everyday rush and bustle of commercial life in the last decade [1980s] it was seldom that participants to transactions involving conglomerates with a large number of subsidiaries paused to consider which of the subsidiaries should become the contracting party'.[41]

Perhaps so, but ultimately, the law becomes the reality for the creditors. Generally, as the chapter-header quote of this chapter by Templeman J., *In re Southard & Co.* [1979] 1WLR 1198 suggests, the separate legal entity principle prevails for them. Justice Young similarly remarked that in reality: 'one gets a situation where there are a group of companies in which funds are moved from one to the other at the will of those controlling them and at any particular time most of the companies within the group will have a deficiency of current assets over current liabilities'.[42]

Through the September Transactions, the MUA stevedores for all *practical* purposes became employees of financially stressed companies within the Patrick Stevedores sub-group,[43] their employment transported to where the group's assets were not. To the point is that asset shuffling of the kind described is facilitated by the current arrangements.

## James Hardie – Amaca, Amaba or Abracadabra?[44]

The lengthy and ongoing James Hardie asbestos compensation imbroglio illustrates the schemozzle when accounting data for corporate groups are expected to reflect the *economic*, the *legal* and the *moral*, realities pertinent to the resolution of a social problem. In respect to James Hardie's asbestos problems they failed on each count. Here, the salient point to emerge is the mischief caused by the way groups are spoken of and accounted for, encouraging the misleading idea that parent companies have enforceable *legal* obligations to the shareholders and the creditors of their subsidiaries.

As at Patricks, the events prior to the formal commitment by James Hardie NV (the Company) Directors to fund asbestos-related claims against subsidiaries of the former parent company provide an apt setting for power plays regarding the separate legal enterprise principle in a group context.

On 1 December 2005 the NSW Government and a wholly owned Australian subsidiary, LGTDD Pty Ltd, had entered into what officially is described as a conditional Final Funding Agreement (FFA) to provide long-term funding to a Special Purpose Fund (SPF) that will provide compensation for Australian asbestos-related personal injury claims against the former James Hardie companies (Amaca Pty Ltd, Amaba Pty Ltd and ABN 60 Pty Ltd; ABN 60 being the former James Hardie Industries Limited [JHIL]). A variant of that agreement was approved by the shareholders of James Hardie NV in general meeting in February 2007.

Prior to 1987 Amaca and Amaba had been Hardie's asbestos manufacturers in NSW, and hence carried the primary (some argued the total legal) liability for the damage done by their products. The other James Hardie companies, now wrapped into ABN 60, were represented to have a moral liability by virtue of the prior relationship with Amaca and Amaba.

In February 2001, ABN 60 entered into a major corporate restructure whereby a charitable trust was formed to administer the affairs of Amaca and Amaba. After court approval this arrangement was completed in October 2001. In a report of court filings in February 2001 before Justice Kim Santow it was noted that JHIL would 'not disadvantage any creditors of the former Australian parent company [JHIL] including asbestos victims'.[45] Gideon Haigh's account *Asbestos House* shows that on several previous occasions other restructure options had been canvassed. Reasons for the movement of the parent company to the Netherlands (around late 1998) have been contested. Whether it was because the major part of James Hardie's business operations were now offshore or that there were tax advantages in moving domicile have been mooted, along with the view that it suited the company to quarantine its asbestos claims.[46]

The corporate group after the February 2001 restructure is illustrated in figure 7.2 taken from Annexure I of the 2004 Jackson Report:

The 2001 restructure established the Medical Research and Compensation Foundation (the 'Foundation' or MRCF) by gifting $A3 million ($US1.7 million) in cash and transferring ownership of Amaca and Amaba to the Foundation. Initially the stated goal of the MRCF was to fund medical and scientific research into asbestos-related diseases. Whether the funding set aside would be sufficient to fund the necessary research or to compensate sufferers of asbestos-related diseases was always going to be problematic. Perhaps it was thought that Hardie's restructuring could provide magical assistance. Long tail insurance claims like those that would be made by the time this book goes to press (and will be made over many years in the future by the asbestos claimants) were always going to be difficult to estimate.

Importantly James Hardie claims that the MRCF is managed by independent trustees and operates entirely independently of the Company and its current subsidiaries. ABN 60 does not directly or indirectly control the activities of the Foundation in any way; and, effective from 16 February 2001, has not owned or directly or indirectly controlled the activities of Amaca or Amaba. In particular, the Foundation's trustees are responsible for the effective management of claims against Amaca and Amaba, and for the investment of Amaca's and Amaba's assets.

Other than the offers to provide interim funding to the Foundation and the indemnity to the directors, evidence in the financials, and in the Jackson Report of the Special Commission of Inquiry confirm the view of the board of ABN 60 'that it has no direct legally binding commitment to or interest in the Foundation [MRCF], Amaca or Amaba, and it has no right to dividends or capital distributions made by the Foundation. None of the Foundation, Amaca, Amaba or ABN 60 are parties to the FFA described above, and none of those entities has obtained any directly enforceable rights or the related agreements contemplated under that agreement.'[47]

Corporate restructuring continued into 2003. On 31 March 2003 control of ABN 60 was transferred to a newly established company named ABN 60 Foundation Pty Ltd, now the sole shareholder of ABN 60. This was purportedly to ensure that ABN 60 was financially capable of meeting the payment obligations owed to the Foundation under the terms of a deed of covenant and indemnity. As a result of a series of transactions the MRCF could no longer access James

143

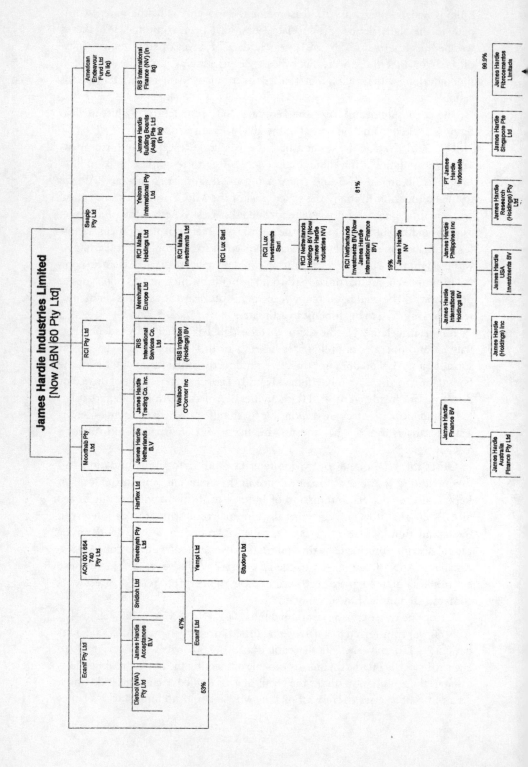

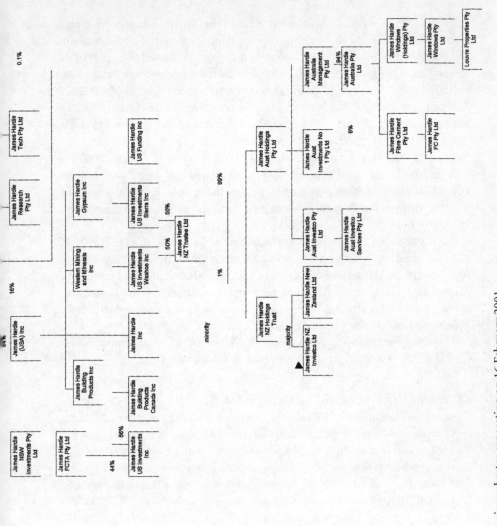

**Figure 7.2:** James Hardie Group following asbestos separation on 16 February 2001

Hardie shares as a form of indemnity or security for the asbestos claimants. Another major change flowing from the creation of the ABN 60 Foundation, was that Amaca, Amaba and ABN 60 were no longer perceived to be part of the James Hardie NV group, and hence no provision for asbestos-related claims had appeared in its consolidated financial statements from 2003 till 31 March 2005. A contingent liability had been identified previously in the Notes. The 2006 Directors' Report (*Financial Statements*, p. 10) revealed that its 2006 Q4 results 'were substantially affected by the recording of a net provision for estimated future asbestos-related payments of US$715.6 million at 31 March 2006'. The provision had been raised because the Directors stated that it was 'in accordance with US accounting standards, on the basis of the approach that it is probable that the company will make payments to fund asbestos-related claims on a long-term basis'.

Consistent with the interpretation of *Salomon v Salomon & Co Ltd* [1897] AC 22 the claimed legally defensible view in 2003 of the Directors of the Netherlands-registered James Hardie Limited NV was clearly stated in its 2003 and subsequent Annual Reports. That position was seemingly confirmed by the conclusions of the specially constituted NSW Government Jackson Commission Inquiry which, after examining various legal issues, reported in 2004.[48]

Consider the following from the James Hardie NV 2003 Annual Report (p. 74) which essentially has been repeated in subsequent years:

With the establishment and funding of the Medical Research and Compensation Foundation (the 'Foundation') in February 2001 (see Note 17), the Company no longer owned or controlled two Australian companies [Amaca Pty Ltd and Amaba Pty Ltd] which manufactured and marketed asbestos-related products prior to 1987. Those companies were former subsidiaries of ABN 60 Pty Limited ('ABN 60', formerly known as [James Hardie Industries Limited] JHIL). On 31 March 2003, James Hardie transferred control of ABN 60 to a newly established company, named ABN 60 Foundation Pty Ltd ('ABN 60 Foundation').

In prior years and up to the date of the establishment of the Foundation, these two former subsidiaries incurred costs of asbestos-related litigation and settlements. From time to time ABN 60 was joined as a party to asbestos suits which were primarily directed at the two former [wholly owned] subsidiaries which are now controlled by the Foundation . . . While it is difficult to predict the incidence or outcome of future litigation, the Company believes it is remote that any significant personal injury suits for damages in connection with the former manufacture and sale of asbestos containing products that are or may be filed against ABN 60 or its former subsidiaries would have material adverse effect on its business, results of operations or financial condition. This belief is based in part on the separateness of corporate entities under Australian law, the limited circumstances where 'piercing the corporate veil' might occur under Australian law, and there being no equivalent under Australian law of the US legal doctrine of 'successor liability'. The courts in Australia have confirmed the primacy of separate corporate entities and have generally refused to hold parent entities responsible for the liabilities of their subsidiaries absent any finding of fraud, agency, direct operational responsibility or the like.

From the brief summary of those James Hardie particulars, many issues emerge.

First, there is a need to distinguish the *moral* from the *legal* issues related to any asbestos-related litigation. Whereas the stated Directors' position may be considered contestable, at least the related debate has broadened the scope of concern to a consideration of whether the law should be changed to expand Directors' responsibilities to include social as well as legal obligations to parties other than shareholders, viz. employees and customers.[49]

Second, there is the need to reconsider the appropriateness of companies being able to use the separate legal entity notion, at will. It is questionable whether it is equitable for them to be able to say it applies or does not apply, according to whether the circumstances suit – 'yes', when they are subject to financial or other stress as were Amaca and Amaba, but 'no' when the James Hardie group is engaged in normal ongoing commercial affairs.[50]

Another issue is how to account for the asbestos liabilities in principle, and then within a group context. Prior to 2006 the James Hardie parent had stuck to an arguable legal position (reasoned as in the above extract from the 2003 Annual Report Note). The 2006 James Hardie NV Annual Report Notes to the Accounts confirms this position in its 'Note 12 – Commitments and contingencies'. Under that reasoning it did not show any liability in the parent accounts for the liabilities attaching to the ABN 60 subsidiaries, Amaca and Amaba. After 2001 and the formation of the Medical Research and Compensation Foundation the parent company, James Hardie, took the view that it was neither morally nor legally liable for the current or prospective asbestos-related obligations incurred by the ABN 60 subsidiaries, Amaca and Amaba. Those liabilities had been transferred to the MRCF.

Following the Jackson Report, the public outcry, and proposed 2006 NSW legislation, the directors of James Hardie have acted, in accord with US accounting standards, as if James Hardie NV is liable for an amount approaching $A1.5 billion, but there is uncertainty as to whether there is such a liability of this amount. As this book goes to press in mid-February 2007 the shareholders of James Hardie NV have voted in favour of recognising the asbestos compensation as a liability of their company, agreeing as a consequence to set aside funding annually to meet it.

147

**Illustration 7:** 'Ansett bales [sic] out of ASL'
*Source:* 'Ansett bales out of ASL', *The Australian*, 12 February 1979, p. 8. Courtesy of Larry Pickering.

## Ansett jettisoned by Air New Zealand

With similar effect, in 2001 Ansett employees were left alone, arguing for their entitlements, when Air New Zealand jettisoned its wholly owned subsidiary, Ansett Australia Pty Ltd. Protracted arguments followed between employees, unions and Air New Zealand about the company's alleged legal and moral responsibilities as a parent company in respect of any of the debts of its wholly owned subsidiaries.[51]

KordaMentha (Ansett administrator) observed upon its appointment that it faced a number of significant hurdles in handling Australia's largest voluntary administration to date with over $A1 billion in assets under administration:[52]

- it had no available cash to trade the business;
- Ansett's senior management and financial records were in New Zealand, leaving a management and information vacuum in Australia;
- the terrorist attacks on 11 September 2001 had decimated the aviation industry, destroying the market for assets and reducing Ansett's ability to compete in a fiercely competitive market (the Ansett Administration began on 12 September 2001);

- the Ansett fleet consisted of 134 aircraft, 53 of which were subject to lease and finance arrangements;
- Ansett had leased about 350 properties;
- Ansett employed 15 000 workers, most of whom were members of unions;
- it faced a serious backlash from Global Rewards (i.e. frequent flyer) creditors; and
- a federal election was imminent.

It was clear to KordaMentha that the sale of the Ansett mainline business in accord with the object of Part 5.3A (Voluntary Administration) of the *Corporations Act 2001* (Cth) would be highly unlikely unless Ansett was able to resume flight operations quickly. The object of a Part 5.3A administration is effectively to maximise the chances of the company, or as much as possible of its business, continuing. To do this, KordaMentha felt that Ansett needed an injection of capital and, the administrators believed, to change its outdated work practices. Due to the operations, records and assets of Ansett and Air New Zealand being intermingled, it was necessary to disentangle Ansett from Air New Zealand. This was achieved through negotiation of a compromise with Air New Zealand. This prospect raises the grouping issue – that corporate groups are entirely artificial, and can be bundled (grouped) and unbundled (de-grouped) virtually at an administrative will, in stark contrast with the import of the *Salomon v Salomon* separate legal entity principle in that individual companies' limited liability characteristic is not violated, breached or bundled by mere administrative arrangements.

On 8 August 2001 Air New Zealand wrote a Letter of Comfort to three Ansett companies confirming its policy to take such steps as were necessary to ensure that its wholly owned subsidiaries could meet their debts as and when they fell due. It amounted to a solvency declaration. Importantly, the Letter of Comfort also provided that Air New Zealand would make available, on request in writing from time to time, advances for the sole purpose of enabling the three Ansett companies to pay working capital liabilities incurred by them in the ordinary course of business. The maximum aggregate of all such advances was not to exceed $A400 million.

Had the administrators been able to negotiate a prompt commercial settlement of any claims (including the Letter of Comfort) the Ansett Group may have had against Air New Zealand, Ansett arguably had the best chance of receiving cash for its claims and survival. KordaMentha felt (as did others) that were legal proceedings to have commenced for recovery, Air New Zealand may itself have been forced into administration (statutory management in NZ) precluding any recovery by the administrators. After intense negotiations, Air New Zealand

agreed to pay $A150 million, to waive its right to prove in the Ansett adminis-
tration and its right to $A32 million in priority payments advanced to Ansett for
wages; a total of $A182 million. In return, Ansett and the administrators agreed
to release Air New Zealand and its directors from certain notional legal claims.
The terms of the agreement were set out in a Memorandum of Understanding
which was signed on 4 October 2001.

Prior to this it has been reported that the KordaMentha Research Unit exten-
sively researched Chapter 11 procedures as they applied to airlines to determine
whether a US Chapter 11-type arrangement would likely have saved Ansett,
which badly needed cash.[53] It identified that the US Government had provided
billions of dollars to US airlines via Chapter 11, and concluded that there was
a lack of evidence to convince that the Chapter 11 process in the US would not
have saved Ansett. In its paper number 305 the Research Unit state that the New
Zealand Government saved Air New Zealand by an injection of cash in excess
of $A800 million. However, the Australian Government, as well as many other
governments throughout the world, decided not to inject cash into faltering
airlines such as Ansett. The Report (p. 5) observes:

> Companies in Chapter 11, just like under voluntary administration, need
> cash and capital to trade during, and emerge from, Chapter 11. US Air-
> ways reorganised under Chapter 11 protection. US Airways' exit from
> Chapter 11 was facilitated by a $US900 million US government loan, the
> cancellation of all equity, 2¢ in the dollar to unsecured creditors, $US240
> million of fresh equity, an injection of $US100 million of at-risk debt as well
> as annual wage and benefits concessions from employees of approximately
> $US1.9 billion a year. Additionally, priority for employee claims under Chap-
> ter 11 is limited to $US4650. With access to these concessions and addi-
> tional capital, especially $US900 million of government funds, US Airways
> (or Ansett) could have reorganised under Australia's voluntary administration
> regulations.

> Ansett traded for five months under administration. Ansett's trade-on was
> made possible by, amongst other things, significant EBA concessions, a
> $150 million settlement with Air New Zealand, federal government under-
> writing of passenger tickets, the continuing involvement of relevant manage-
> ment, significant cost-cutting and fleet rationalisation. Singapore Airlines and
> Patrick Corporation both considered recapitalising Ansett. The 'Tesna' con-
> sortium committed to recapitalising Ansett. However, Tesna eventually chose
> not to proceed. It is also worth noting, many Ansett businesses were sold and
> continue to operate. Kendell & Hazelton (now Rex), SkyWest, Aeropelican,
> Show Group and Ansett Cargo were all recapitalised and sold during the Ansett

voluntary administration. The engine shop, simulator centre and engineering continue to operate and will also be sold.

Under the heading 'Grouping of Complex Entities',[54] based on their experiences the administrators observe 'that large and complex enterprises such as Ansett, Newmont Yandal and Stockford typically have complicated group structures that may or may not incorporate cross-guarantees which may be ASIC approved'. Interestingly, the Research Unit note that CASAC's *Corporate Groups: Final Report* (2000) had recommended that administrators have the ability to pool the administration of group companies in the absence of creditor or court opposition. Particularly noteworthy was KordaMentha's experience that:

- usually groups are run by management with little regard to them as separate legal entities, with unexpected and certainly unintended outcomes on insolvency;
- centralised treasury function results in no cash in operating entities;
- employees in companies but operations in different companies making the administration much more complex, difficult and expensive;
- holding companies (for example, Air New Zealand) that remove wholly owned subsidiaries; and
- difficulty in apportioning assets sold that have been viewed as group assets, for example, intellectual property.

Following an idea mooted in the 1982 UK Cork Report, but in contrast with CASAC's suggested 'opting-in' proposal, KordaMentha promoted an 'opting-out' mechanism, observing (in its Ansett Report number 305) that all 'related wholly owned companies should automatically be grouped unless they apply to ASIC not to be – effectively to opt-out'.[55] Currently Australian companies can only indirectly opt in to grouping via cross deeds of guarantee. Further, they noted in their report that in recent changes to company consolidations laws for taxation purposes, the tax liability is joint and several for all group companies, unless a company opts out. Thus, in its Report number 305 KordaMentha recommended a symmetry between taxation and corporate laws. But the 2005 *CLERP 9* Corporations Law reforms did not accept the general CAMAC opting-in, and by implication we might assume any opting-out mechanism. Yet, the more selective grouping effect through a class order deed of cross guarantee is still permitted. And the latest proposed Australian law reforms, the November 2006 *Corporations Amendment (Insolvency) Bill 2007*, allow for pooling but do not mandate it – an approach that is in place in jurisdictions like New Zealand and Ireland and applies in current case precedents in Australia.[56] Significantly,

151

all creditors have to be satisfied with this approach. Any dissenting creditor can cause the pooled option to be scuttled.

Under the 'schizophrenia' approach, the Air New Zealand parent company fortuitously found itself outside of the capital boundary rope – safe from creditor demands. Baxt and Lane's (1998) reference to 'directors' schizophrenia' appears apt. The illusory impression of group security evident on an Air New Zealand group consolidated accounting net assets basis was illusory. Clarke *et al.* (2003) provide many other instances where consolidated accounting is shown to be accounting's greatest conjurer.

Summarising, these three employee cases capture the essence of the impact on employees (and other unsecured creditors) of the information quagmire created by the group structure coupled to uncommercial conventional consolidation accounting. It is not merely that the legal position is unknown by the public at large, the group structure is as amenable to manipulation as it is to misinterpretation and misinformation.

It seems reasonable to suggest that the general public (and employees) ought to be able to assess the wealth and progress of companies from their financial statements. Australian Workplace Agreements seem to enhance the general case that companies' financial data are critical inputs to any wage inquiry. But a noticeable feature of company collapses is, on the basis of public information, the surprise, the suddenness, of them, following the opposite impression to be gleaned from their annual reported audited financial performances and financial positions. In the fallout following collapses invariably there are victims of unsuspected consequences. Frequently, as shown, these victims include workers who lose employee entitlements or have had to wait so long before receiving them (or for government intervention as in the cases of Patrick, Nardell and others) and those who couldn't undertake work because they were unable to get trade indemnity insurance following the collapse of HIH.

## More group games and their impacts on other market participants

### HIH collapse and aftermath

HIH was reportedly the second largest insurance company in Australia and 'one of the largest corporate collapses' in Australia, with an estimated deficiency of \$A5.3 billion[57] With more than 240 companies, HIH had been operating in sixteen countries over five continents. The group comprised several Australian insurance companies maintaining ubiquitous insurance cover for a variety of purposes. Incurring significant amounts of obligations that had been purportedly reinsured (rather than provided for) proved a major factor in the collapse of

HIH. Reinsurance was shown to consist of certain sham transactions that were actually loans. Overseas expansions in the UK and the US evidenced group enterprise action that was claimed by many appearing before the HIH Royal Commission (HIHRC) to have been a significant factor in the HIH collapse.

The proposed statements of claim lodged by the HIH administrator threatened a $A5.3 billion lawsuit against many, including the federal government and Australia's national insurance industry watchdog APRA, its prudential regulator, suggesting they were negligent in allowing HIH to collapse in 2001. Indeed, the HIH Royal Commission Report (HIHRC, 2003, Vol. I, p. xiii) concluded that 'despite (myriad governance) mechanisms the corporate officers, auditors and regulators of HIH failed to see, remedy or report . . . [the] obvious'. This was a situation arguably not assisted by the dominance of HIH CEO and founder Ray Williams.

*Acquisition of FAI and the Allianz sale* proved to be two of the worst deals imaginable as Williams allegedly pushed them through with little HIH Board resistance. In the HIHRC it was claimed that Ray Williams played a dominant CEO role at HIH at all times, with its Board proving to be an ineffective monitor of his activities. The HIHRC report (2003, Vol. III, paras. 273–7) details how two major and ultimately fatal transactions were allegedly driven by Williams – the FAI acquisition by HIH and Allianz's purchase of a major part of HIH's cash-flow base just before its ultimate collapse.[58] The FAI acquisition was claimed by some to be HIH's Achilles' heel and as bad a commercial decision as was possible. Williams, either with the absolute trust and confidence of his Board, or too much strength for them to contain, was able to ensnare HIH in the FAI takeover without presenting any appropriate *due diligence* report.[59] According to the HIHRC (2003, Vol. III, para. 273) report:

> Decisions . . . were often made by the Board on short notice with insufficient information and without adequate analysis . . . [The Board accepted] views of management uncritically . . . the opening of the UK branch, the reacquisition of Care America, the FAI acquisition and the Allianz transaction.

Williams might be considered the epitome of the dominant senior manager. However, whereas Arthur Andersen was subjected to some criticism in respect of its audit of HIH (primarily for what it did not detect), no charges were laid against the firm of Arthur Andersen.

When dominance dazzles commercial reality one wonders whether it is possible for a board to be an effective monitor, especially with accounting being such a malleable mechanism for reporting on the financial affairs of corporate groups. According to the HIHRC (2003) Report, for the most part the HIH Board, and perhaps the auditor, accepted much that Williams put to them. His dominance presumably overrode his sensitivity to the commercial reality

**Table 7.2:** HIH – actions against officers

| Name | Position | Possible breaches noted by HIHRC Report | Subsequent actions |
|---|---|---|---|
| Rodney Adler | FAI CEO and HIH non-executive director | Might have breached four sections of the Corporations Law relating to use of his directorship to benefit himself, HSI and Cooper. Might have breached two sections of the *Crimes Act*. Eleven possible breaches of the Corporations Law relating to share trading. Eight possible breaches relating to improper use of position and information. | Convicted and sentenced on 14 April 2005 on four criminal charges; two of disseminating false information likely to induce people to buy HIH shares; one of making and publishing false statements; and one of being intentionally dishonest and failing to discharge duties in good faith. Sentenced to 4.5 years' gaol with a non-parole period of 2.5 years. |
| Ray Williams | HIH founder and CEO | Might have breached 16 sections of the Corporations Law relating to dealings with the board and accounts. Twenty possible breaches related to HSI, dealings with the board, FFC transaction and the Ness transaction. Six possible breaches relating to the Allianz deal, the Hannover deal and loans to Frank Holland. | Convicted and sentenced on 15 April 2005 on three criminal charges arising from the management of the HIH group of companies in the three-year period 1998–2000. Sentenced to 4.5 years' gaol, 2 years 9 months non-parole period. |
| Brad Cooper | Entrepreneur | Might have breached 10 sections of the Corporations Law and seven possible breaches of the *Crimes Act* relating to HSI. | Convicted and sentenced on 3 June 2006 on six charges of corruptly giving a series of cash benefits to influence an agent of HIH; and on seven charges of publishing false or misleading statements with intent to obtain a financial advantage. Sentenced to 8 years' gaol, minimum five. |

| | | | |
|---|---|---|---|
| Dominic Fodera | HIH Chief Financial Officer | Might have breached up to 19 sections of Corporations Law relating to failing to ensure accounts were accurate, failing to inform board and auditors. Twelve possible breaches relating to deals with Hannover, Société Générale, General Cologne Re and National Indemnity. | Committed on 9 August 2006 to stand trial on six criminal charges; was convicted on 4 April 2007 on a criminal charge of authorising the issuing of a prospectus from which there was a material omission. He is expected to be sentenced on 10 May 2007. |
| Tim Mainprize | FAI Finance Director | Might have breached two sections of Corporations Law relating to Project Firelight. Four possible breaches relating to FAI's Part B statement. Three possible breaches relating to duties. | Acquitted on 14 November 2005 on two counts of failing to act honestly in the exercise of his powers and discharge of his duties as an officer of FAI General and one count of providing false and misleading information. |
| Charles Abbott | HIH non-executive director | Might have breached two sections of Corporations Law relating to payment of $1 million to Blake Dawson Waldron. Might have breached two sections of Corporations Law relating to consultancy payments to his private company. One possible breach relating to a Brad Cooper introductory fee. | Charged with dishonestly misusing his position as a company director under s.184(2) (a) of the *Corporations Act*. Criminal charges dismissed on 7 June 2005. |
| Bill Howard | Head of HIH Financial Services and Investment Manager | Might have breached five sections of Corporations Law relating to failing to inform auditors. Two possible breaches of Corporations Law relating to Blake Dawson Waldron. Eight possible breaches of Corporations Law if deemed an 'officer' and one possible criminal charge in relation to HSI. | Convicted on 23 December 2003 and sentenced to 3 years' gaol – sentence fully suspended. |

*Sources*: Columns 1–3 are based on the HIHRC Report (2003); column 4 is based on ASIC media releases at <www.asic.gov.au>.

of HIH's circumstances. In the years since the collapse the industry regulator, APRA, has adjudged several of HIH's directors and other corporate officers unfit to work in the insurance industry. Also the Director of Public Prosecutions has charged and had several officers in the courts on behalf of ASIC, including those listed in table 7.2.

The importance of the collapse for corporate operational purposes discussed here is that the HIH Royal Commissioner observed that directors of one of the relevant insurance companies within the HIH Group appeared to have adopted a group enterprise perspective when attesting to its regulatory solvency position. Contiguously (and perhaps accidentally) with a deed of cross guarantee in place, HIH had netted-off related company assets and liabilities in several APRA Annual Returns, thus by implication treating its insurance subsidiaries as if they were part of a singular corporate group enterprise.[60]

## Overseas Group Shenanigans

### Enron – the 'Crooked E'[61]

Many are now asserting their earlier prescient observations of the faltering state of the 'crooked E'. Yet, at the time, it was generally a shocked financial press and public that greeted announcement by CFO Andrew Fastow in late 2001 that the Enron Corporation, seventh largest US company, announced a third-quarter loss – a $600 million operating loss and a $1 billion write-down of impaired assets connected to its off-balance sheet special purpose entities (SPEs) partnerships. An SEC investigation immediately commenced into conflicts of interest resulting from the SPEs. Enron disclosed a downwards restatement of its published earnings from 1997 to 2001 inclusive and entered bankruptcy protection. A criminal investigation took place and Enron's auditors, Arthur Andersen (AA), and its engagement partner were found guilty of obstruction of justice for shredding Enron-related working papers – something they admitted but denied wrongdoing. AA would suffer enormous reputation and client loss and would be liquidated in 2003. Ironically the 'obstruction of justice' conviction would be subsequently squashed on appeal in 2004 – but the damage was done.

Enron was adept in its use of the group structure to dolly up its financials. Its use of SPEs to shift non-performing assets and debt off its balance sheet, and to pyramid asset values, is well established. Its use of SPEs is generally characterised to have been a deviant misuse of a perfectly good commercial structure. Two issues are important regarding Enron's SPEs. First, the idea that the SPEs are a sound financial structure; second, that not including the SPEs' earnings, assets

**Illustration 8:** 'WorldCom, Enron Accountancy Standards cooked books'
*Source:* 'WorldCom, Enron Accountancy Standards cooked books', *The Australian*,
28 June 2002. Courtesy of Peter Nicholson, www.nicholosoncartoons.com.au

and liabilities in its consolidated financials is a major disclosure problem. Both
are contestable.

SPEs emerged as special commercial vehicles as part of the structured financing schemes that developed in the US during the 1970s. There they served as
separate entities to house pools of assets for 'securitization or self-insurance,
as special subsidiaries, for risk management, capital allocation, other strategic
reasons'.[62] Culp and Niskanen present that as not only commercially prudent,
but also as financially sound in respect of the consequential accounting for the
financial outcomes of the SPEs' activities. SPE data were not to be included in a
partner's consolidated statements if the arrangement satisfied the SPE qualifying
criteria:

- it had an equity base contributed by other than the project's sponsor of at
  least 3 per cent of the value of the assets conveyed to it;
- the SPE was not to be controlled by the sponsor or its management; and
- risks and economic rewards were conveyed to the SPE.

An immediate accounting implication of an entity meeting the SPE criteria
is that identical transactions undertaken alternatively by either an SPE or a

157

'subsidiary' are to be accounted for differently, though the financial implications of them must be the same. For example, the sale of an asset by a company to a criteria-satisfying SPE in which it is a partner would be deemed a genuine arm's-length transaction. The vendor would book the sale and disclose a profit or loss on the sale in accord with the accounting rules in force. If the partnership did not qualify as an SPE and was deemed an entity controlled by the vendor, the same transaction would be eliminated in the consolidation of the financial statements of the vendor and the purchaser. Depending upon whether the entity is a controlled partnership or company, or a legitimate SPE, the same transaction would be disclosed as having different financial outcomes. While SPE-type arrangements might be considered as useful structured finance vehicles, they must equally be considered to have features that are not user-friendly (nor socially acceptable) if their structure triggers alternative accounting disclosures for identical transactions. Of those disclosures only one or the other can be true and fair or they both could be misleading. That they are both true and fair depending upon the SPE status of one of the parties is financial humbug, utter nonsense.

In some ways the background to the SPEs is murkier than it might at first appear. Culp and Niskanen (2003, pp. 157–8) explain that the early structured financing through securitisation led to alternative *on* and *off-balance sheet* financing arrangements. In the US, corporate separateness, asset divestiture, and off-balance sheet financing are facilitated by SPEs. It is only a matter of arranging to satisfy the qualifying criteria. Post-Enron moves to increase the 3 per cent *de minimus* equity rule to 10 per cent illustrates that nothing in the Enron experience has suggested that the SPE arrangement is fundamentally flawed. The perception appears to betray an understanding that the implementation is too easy. By the mid-1990s using SPEs to 'manage liabilities', get them off the balance sheet, appears to have been a common practice. In that setting it is strange that Enron has been singled out as having misused the SPE structure in an unusual way to hide debt, divest itself of poorly performing assets and manipulate revenue streams. Enron seems to have done with the SPEs what they were set up for and what the weak qualifying criteria encourage – achieve 'corporate separateness' on the cheap.

Enron's SPEs, of course, appear to have been the epitome of what Partnoy[63] labelled 'infectious greed'. Notwithstanding that the SPE qualifying criteria are weak, Enron set out from the start to circumvent them, to control the SPEs it sponsored contrary to the criteria, exploit the consolidation accounting relief to avoid the impact of the poor investments it could slop off to the SPEs, and massage its balance sheet by sending debt to the SPEs' balance sheets rather than report it in its own.

The major issue, however, is not whether Enron misused the SPEs. Its breach of the SPE rules is not in doubt. Indeed it admitted to as much. And in respect of that it is interesting to note that Arthur Andersen forced the consolidation of its Chewco SPE in 2001 precisely because Chewco was unable to satisfy the corporate separateness criterion. The real issue is that the SPE episode illustrates once again the penchant for rearranging business structures to make them appear different from what they are, and the inventiveness of accounting disclosures to give the financial outcomes a preferred slant.

Enron's alleged abuse of the SPE structure has also exposed a common misunderstanding of the techniques of consolidation accounting and the nature of the information disclosed in consolidated financial statements. In the wake of Enron's SPE affair it was generally argued that consolidation of the SPE's data would have better disclosed Enron's debt. That seems to ignore that all internal indebtedness (debt between the related entities) is routinely eliminated in the consolidation process, and the remaining (external) debt aggregated in the idiosyncratic consolidation manner. This is undertaken in such a way (as explained in chapter 9) that it is impossible to establish which of the group companies are indebted to whom, which are net internal and which are net external borrowers or lenders as the case may be. Rather than give insight into company debt, consolidation processes obscure it.

Enron's demise has had major ramifications for the US and other major capitalist economies. It spawned a new financial condition 'Enronitis', referring to the securities market's loss of confidence due to concerns that accounting and auditing practices were being abused. It was claimed, seemingly with justification, that the market was not being properly informed. We do not disagree with that.

# 8

# Groupthink: Fact or Fiction?

Regulating corporate groups is well captured by Alfred North Whitehead's 'misplaced concreteness' – especially that recourse to the fictional corporate group notion that persists in the community.

*Counterfactual beliefs* regarding corporate groups prevail. The idea that holding companies and their subsidiaries comprise an entity with the characteristics of a separate company, earn profits and have assets, incur liabilities, and suffer losses, is firmly entrenched in commercial folklore. That perception of a single group entity is a consequence of the extent to which such fictions are embedded in corporate language. It's the way companies are talked about. This was alluded to in chapters 2, 4 and 7. So it is no surprise that corporate groups have been perceived to have played a significant and deleterious role in notable Australian unexpected corporate collapses for decades.[1] References to listed companies' wealth and progress, analyses of their supposed financial characteristics, are almost always references drawn from what the consolidated data show – to data not relating to any actual legal entity, but to a fictional agglomeration of related companies. If the nature of corporate groups is so misunderstood and *groupthink* so firmly entrenched,[2] it is inevitable that the regulating of groups will be based upon false premises.

And the fiction of corporate groups is thoroughly entrenched. The evidence is that corporate officers' perceptions of the nature of a corporate group are based on unusual, mostly one-off, settings. Notions such as 'group solvency' and the means of assessing it, administrators' penchant for asset and liability pooling arrangements, proposed regulatory opting-in and opting-out arrangements, the ASIC class order deed of cross guarantee, and the late 2006 announcement by the Australian Government of its desire to have pooling formally incorporated as part of the administration process in certain circumstances,[3] have a spin-off effect in directors' and officers' thinking when ongoing day-to-day activities of firms are being undertaken. Understanding the way society, particularly the *corporate* society, views the activities and financing of corporate groups is shown to be critical in any exercise aimed at achieving an orderly commercial environment.

It is not a uniquely Australian problem, but chapter 7 revealed that the asset quarantining impact of the corporate veil and groupthink has been shown frequently to have dismayed both Australian creditors (sometimes employees) and public onlookers alike. Against that background several uniquely Australian Government regulatory initiatives in recent decades have been introduced to mitigate the effects of groupthink. Particularly significant is the implementation of a voluntary, regulatory-approved ASIC deed by which group companies guarantee the debts of one another, as well as attempts to lift the veil such as – *ex ante* 'opting-in' and 'opting-out' arrangements and *ex post* judicial and legislative pooling facilities.[4]

## Deeds of cross-guarantee

Henry Bosch initiated an early variant of the deed, a Deed of Indemnity, in 1985 when he was Chairman of the NCSC. The general drift was that the companies party to the deed guaranteed one another's debts. It appeared to be a back-door way of lifting the corporate veil. And perhaps it would have been were the deed compulsory for all parent companies and their subsidiaries. Purportedly, his objective was to reduce the regulatory burden on companies by bestowing accounting and auditing relief on companies party to a deed.[5] Being a party to the deed is voluntary, so even where there is a deed not all group companies will necessarily be party to it. Figure 4.1 related to an indicative ASX listed company with over 200 subsidiaries of which at 30 June 2006 less than twenty were party to a Deed of Cross-Guarantee, five less at the end of the year than at its beginning. Deed groupings persistently have shown this to be common. Those that execute the deed form what is referred to as a *closed group*. The motivational *quid pro quo* (in the public favour) took the form of cross-guarantee covenants that would crystallise upon liquidation of any of the parties, require directors of each of the companies involved in the deed to provide annually a solvency declaration, and that it was in the company's interests to be a party to the deed.[6]

In closed-group liquidations the debts of closed-group companies are pooled and their assets are in effect pooled to contribute to discharging them. Thus, deeds effectively 'lift' the *Salomon and Salomon* corporate veil to mitigate the 'limited liability within limited liability' effect otherwise a feature of group activities. Another *ex ante* reform is the 'opting-in' arrangement proposed by CASAC by which directors would identify at the beginning of a reporting period which companies were to be regarded as integral to the group – hence comprising the group enterprise – for all contractual and other legal purposes. Such proposals are indicative of a regulatory awareness of the potential to manipulate group structures for the benefit of particular companies in them.

161

Interestingly, the ASIC deed effectively creates a new reporting entity. Directors of the ultimate holding company of the economic group must prepare a set of consolidated financial statements for each closed (and extended) group and report it in the Notes to the Accounts of the ultimate parent or chief entity. Evidence reveals myriad ways in which this information is reported, from a full set of financials to summary financial data about the closed group.

Notwithstanding its euphoric origins, some deed usage appears to have been selective, and, in the limited instances where a deed has been operationalised, it has not enhanced creditor protection. Corporate officers' perceptions of the effectiveness, efficiency, or equity of such proposals are expected to be potential drivers of that selectivity. Commentators have expressed the general view that directors are 'schizophrenic' when it comes to managing and administering entities,[7] vacillating between alternative corporate structures and modes of disclosure according to what suits the occasion. Companies' dominant motivations for participating in the deeds, and the financial and social costs and benefits associated with their usage,[8] are clearly critical issues. For unless the deeds satisfy their avowed regulatory objectives for the benefit of the commercial community at large, their continued existence cannot be justified.

Closed groups frequently appear to have the inequitable potential to quarantine assets from some creditors, as shown in chapter 7 and earlier. Moreover, when need and opportunity arise apparent obligations under the deeds have not been called in – deed covenants have only been crystallised in a few cases.[9] Financial benefits accruing from the deeds look to have flowed primarily to selected members of the corporate groups, without commensurate benefits to all creditors. And those benefits appear to be wider than previously acknowledged in the rhetoric promoting them.

Deed covenants require a holding company (though not necessarily the ultimate parent company) and a set of nominated subsidiaries to guarantee the unsatisfied debts of one another, extending the *capital boundary* of each of the separate companies comprising a closed group, none of which is required to prepare annual accounts or, as a consequence, to have annual accounts audited. Direct reporting costs savings and the increased ability to withhold data from the market, information normally elicited from disclosures in audited annual accounts of the subsidiaries – information sensitive to competitors, such as margins on differing subsidiaries' specialised operations – are a potential significant benefit of deed participation, though equally a potential loss of disclosure of important information to the market. Withholding certain *proprietary* information from the market has been a less cited and perhaps not well-known benefit flowing to the closed-group companies. This suggests, that contrary to the promises underpinning their original promotion, the market stands to incur unintended costs when a deed exists, in the sense that it is deprived of information, and conversely the closed group potentially enjoys an unintended financial benefit. Reduced financing costs are another, albeit problematic, purported benefit for deed participants. Cross-guarantees would allow lenders in effect to deal with only one company in a closed group (the group banker), thereby reducing the financing negotiation costs.

Despite deeds being promoted by Bosch and others as a boon to creditor protection, it seems that the potential benefits from the deeds are heavily weighted in favour of the participating companies. For a variety of reasons, to date the courts have not had to adjudicate on an ASIC deed dispute. One factor has been the advent and general popularity of voluntary administration legislation in common law jurisdictions as formal liquidation has emerged to be a less common practice than previously. Second, even in those cases in which a closed group has been liquidated, the earlier NCSC deeds did not appear to have provided substantial benefits to creditors, partly because the judiciary/administrators have set them aside due to the perceived difficulties of implementation.[10] This is also a feature of the ASC and ASIC deeds.

An impediment to creditors benefiting from the deed's cross-guarantee covenants has been the perceived 'cross-claim dilemma' – how the cross-guarantees function relative to one another through the closed group. One judge referred to it as an 'infinite regress problem',[11] and was particularly cited in the J. N. Taylor, Hooker Corporation and Equiticorp administrations of the late 1980s and early 1990s, albeit involving applications of the NCSC Deed of Indemnity with its less encompassing, unidirectional indemnity covenants.[12] Failure to enforce the guarantee covenants caused one commentator to observe that ASIC-approved cross-guarantees are being 'drowned' in the 'pooling' and other ad hoc miscellaneous solutions adopted by the various administrators.[13]

Recourse to pooling was proposed more recently by the Ansett administrators, KordaMentha.[14] Such a move to cut the Gordian knot of complexity is understandable in the somewhat chaotic, uncertain environment when a large corporate unexpectedly implodes. There is precedent for it in international practice. It conforms, for example, to the US remedy described as 'substantive consolidation', specified under s.105 of the US Bankruptcy Code (11 USC), and with a similar *ex post* judicial arrangement available under the New Zealand and Irish companies legislations.[15] With this international precedent it came as no surprise that the 2006 Australian-proposed corporation insolvency amendments have included a pooling option for administrators.

## Deed usage

Though rarely talked about and generally out of sight and out of mind, the deeds effected since 1991 are indicative of their perceived corporate usefulness and the commercial reality that significant corporate business is undertaken

163

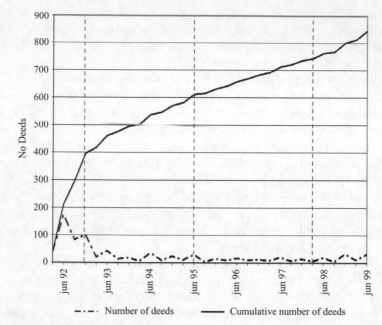

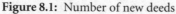

‑ ‑ ‑ Number of deeds        ──── Cumulative number of deeds

**Figure 8.1:** Number of new deeds
*Source:* Dean *et al.*, 'Corporate restructuring, creditors' rights, cross guarantees and group behaviour', *Company and Securities Law Journal* (1999).

through intertwined corporate group activity.[16] Earlier commentaries[17] on the projected role of the deeds predicted a falling popularity, due to the extent that the burden of the legal obligation on directors to certify the financial integrity of the closed-group members became more apparent. But there is evidence of persistence in deed popularity.

The extended shelf-life of deeds, and the incidence of the adjustments made to those already in existence through assumption (entering into) and revocation (withdrawing from), invites the inference that the changes are made by boards driven by explicit strategies. As a proportion of all Australian listed companies, approximately 15 per cent of all listed companies have executed a Deed of Cross-Guarantee – of the Top 50 (more than 55 per cent) and of the Top 200 approximately 45 per cent. Further, our deed database reveals that as at 30 June 1999, the number of operating closed groups exceeded 800, and was growing at around 10 per cent per annum.[18] The time path to that point is shown in figure 8.1.

The linear growth of around 23 deeds per quarter for 1.5 years until June 1994 followed the changeover to the ASC deed from its NCSC antecedent that was virtually completed by 31 December 1992. Quarterly growth rate steadied to 14 for four years until the June quarter 1998, and has since grown at around 20. Surprisingly, the first *Simplification Act* (September 1995) distinguishing large and small firms and changing their reporting obligations, appears to have had little impact on deed uptake. In contrast there is some evidence of an increase in the deed's popularity following the second *Simplification Act* (September 1998). However, in late 1998 other contiguous changes – specifically the notion of an extended closed group – allowing controlled and foreign-owned to participate alongside wholly owned Australian subsidiaries may also have proved significant. Extension of the ambit is likely to have enhanced the value of most deed drivers. The selectivity advantage may have been increased. For the greater the number of companies enclosed in closed groups, the greater the potential accounting and auditing cost savings as well as the potential financial benefits from the secrecy of withheld proprietary information afforded under the deed.[19]

Against that background, the composition patterns of closed groups is important to any understanding of how, and the purposes for which, the deeds are being used – and overall who are the greater recipients of their benefits. Over the deed's history the closed-group size distribution is positively skewed, with an average of around 10 companies per deed. At the top end of the distribution as at 30 June 1999, the four largest guarantee groups are controlled by Harvey Norman Holdings Ltd, Boral Ltd, Pioneer International Limited, and the News Corporation Ltd, with 162, 126, 104 and 95 members, respectively.[20] At the other end of the distribution there is a high frequency of deeds with two companies; the mode is three companies. This may be influenced by secondary holding companies (within a group) executing a deed.

To put that in perspective, Ramsay and Stapledon[21] observe that at the end of 2000 the overall average of 'controlled' entities (*subsidiaries*) of a sample of Australian listed groups was 28 (with the largest being News Corporation with 776). Ninety per cent were wholly owned. In nine of the remaining 10 percentage points ownership related to companies that were 50 per cent to 90 per cent owned, and the remainder to companies that were less than 50 per cent owned; the number of vertical subsidiary levels in a corporate group chain ranged from one to 11, with an overall average in the two largest market capitalisation quartiles of three to four subsidiary levels.

Our verified closed-group database (up to 2000) shows that there also is a significant continuing adjustment of deed composition – with revocations and assumptions largely offsetting each other annually with respect to the size distribution, with around 50 per cent of parent companies implementing revocation and/or assumption deeds annually. Interestingly, this deed activity is evident within several well-known Australian listed companies. For instance, at James Hardie Group, since its first deed in March 1992 until 1999 there was nearly yearly activity in revocation and assumption deeds between one of the two chief entities (James Hardie Industries Limited and James Hardie Australia Holdings Pty Ltd) and several controlled entities. Similar deed activity occurred in the periods prior to the Patrick/MUA September Transactions (discussed above in chapter 7).

165

Prior work has questioned the capacity of directors to make effective evaluations of solvency and other financial indicators from the data in conventional financial statements (on either an individual or consolidated basis) prepared in compliance with the current suite of Accounting Standards.[22] In view of the sanguine approach of the courts to the lack of serviceability of accounting data, it may be that directors know their solvency statements are as unlikely to be proven wrong as they are to be helpful. Whether closed-group data assist in those solvency assessments is contestable.

*Querying the motivation for deed usage* is a natural response to their proven resilience in companies persisting with those that have been in place for some time, and with revocations and assumptions being common. Whether they are a matter of convenience, attracted by the cost savings (reporting or otherwise) they promise, or the potential usefulness of the closed-group structure in the event of a company outside the group becoming insolvent, is questionable. An understanding of whether the deeds are meeting their objective of enhancing creditor protection and providing cost savings is necessary to justify their regulatory support.

*Prima facie*, accounting and auditing cost savings are contestable. On the assumption that accountants and auditors are each doing their job, the preparation of audited consolidated financial statements for the overall group (of which the closed groups are merely parts) necessitates a comprehensive audit of all group companies if the auditor is to form and report an opinion in accord with the *Corporations Act 2001* (Cth). And, of course, there cannot be a proper audit without the compliant financials of each of the subsidiaries. However, it is claimed that creating a closed group through the means of a deed changes the basis of the auditing 'materiality test' for related party transactions. Many argue that this has the effect of reducing auditing costs for some economic groups. But as it currently stands, either auditors are offering their statutory audit opinions on consolidated financials containing closed-group data that are not compiled in accordance with the prevailing Accounting and Auditing Standards and are not fully audited, or those data do accord, are audited, and accounting and auditing cost savings are a non-event. It is difficult to imagine that auditors would risk their professional reputation by issuing unqualified opinions on financials of whose content they cannot be sure. Our priors have always been that something other than accounting and auditing cost savings is a likely co-motivator for some of the new deeds being entered into. That 'something else' is perhaps the primary driver for some.

Given the above, the Top 225 of the largest Australian (stock exchange) listed companies as at 31 December 2002 were sampled. Of these companies approximately 40 per cent of the manufacturing companies had a deed in place. Those deed companies were approached to provide insight into the following questions:[23]

a) What do managers perceive to be the functions and advantages of the deeds existing within their group?
b) Are the deeds used in a strategically selective or in a perfunctory fashion; and on balance?
c) How are solvency assessments undertaken when groups are involved – what entity is the focus of the assessment?
d) What are officers' views regarding the *ex ante* mechanisms such as pooling?, CASAC's opting-in and opting-out arrangements?
e) Do the deeds deliver a net benefit to society justifying their continuation?[24]

Adopting the Ramsay and Stapledon[25] approach, 30 unit property trusts and overseas registered companies were excluded as their activities and financing patterns differ greatly from the rest of the population.[26] Descriptive statistics of the population and sample of deed users reveal the 'Consumer' and the 'Health Care' industries with a greater preponderance of deeds in place relative to other industries.[27] 'Financial Services' has a substantially lower proportion of deeds in place; annual reports reveal deed companies having, on average, higher market capitalisation ($3 341 279 000) relative to non-deed companies ($3 177 243 000); and having on average, higher audit firm fees (audit and non-audit services costs) – $1 104 000 and $1 608 000 to $714 000 and $926 000.

Table 8.1 responses reveal the decision to execute the deed is strategic.

Officers perceived several advantages in executing a deed, accounting and audit relief in particular. Seventy-five per cent indicated it being either 'Important' or 'Very Important'. This is confirmed indirectly by evidence of deed executions occurring immediately prior to the four main reporting dates – 31 December, 31 March, 31 July or 30 September. Further confirmation was 75 per cent identifying the impending reporting date to be a 'Moderate' to 'Great' influence on the deed adoption, and the sample comments that audit relief: was '[A] Very High priority as a deed driver. Reducing auditing and accounting costs is very important to us', 'It saves us trouble in terms of filing separate financial statements. Compliance time is cut down'; and 'Accounting and audit relief was the key driver'.

Those insights invite speculation regarding the manner in which interim and final results and positions are determined without the everyday accounting and subsequent preparation of financials for the closed-group companies being undertaken with the same degree of professional diligence and compliance as for those without the deed in place. To the extent that the inquiry justifies generalisations, and the statistical dimensions suggest that it does, the implication to be drawn is that the financials of the approximately 55 per cent of the top 100 companies with a deed in place possibly have been signed-off with clean opinions by auditors who are in no fully informed position to do so. The prospect of cost savings is difficult to reconcile, and especially so when the necessity for the preparation and audit of consolidated statements and the directors' solvency statements regarding each closed group are added to the tasks.

An ability to withhold proprietary information appeared to be a major deed driver for several companies. Deeds facilitating confidentiality are a much more

**Table 8.1:** Officers' perceptions of deed functions

| Question 9: How important was the opportunity to gain accounting/auditing relief? | | | | | | | |
|---|---|---|---|---|---|---|---|
| Company Officer Responses | None 1 | Little 2 | Some 3 | Important 4 | Very 5 | N/A 6 | Unanswered 7 |
| Total | 0/28 | 1/28 | 4/28 | 10/28 | 11/28 | 1/28 | 1/28 |

| Question 8: How important was the opportunity for greater confidentiality? | | | | | | | |
|---|---|---|---|---|---|---|---|
| Company Officer Responses | None 1 | Little 2 | Some 3 | Important 4 | Very 5 | N/A 6 | Unanswered 7 |
| Total | 3/28 | 8/28 | 8/28 | 5/28 | 4/28 | 0/28 | 0/28 |

| Question 1: Did your company use a regulatory-approved [NCSC] cross-guarantee financing instrument before reporting relief became available in 1991 through the use of the ASIC-type deed? | | | | | |
|---|---|---|---|---|---|
| Company Officer Responses | Yes | No | Don't know | N/A | Unanswered |
| Total | 5/28 | 23/28 | 0/28 | 0/28 | 0/28 |

| Question 2: Do you have any other cross-guarantee financing instruments currently in place? | | | | | |
|---|---|---|---|---|---|
| Company Officer Responses | Yes | No | Don't know | N/A | Unanswered |
| Total | 13/28 | 15/28 | 0/28 | 0/28 | 0/28 |

| Question 7: Did you have any concerns you might be liable for debts incurred by a rogue subsidiary? | | | | | |
|---|---|---|---|---|---|
| Company Officer Responses | Yes | No | Don't know | N/A | Unanswered |
| Total | 4/28 | 24/28 | 0/28 | 0/28 | 0/28 |

| Question 23: How much influence would the following factors have on the timing of your corporation's implementation of a deed or any change to a deed?: (a) The impending reporting date; (b) A new venture; (c) A proposed loan application? | | | | | | | |
|---|---|---|---|---|---|---|---|
| TOTALS* | | | | | | | |
| Company Officer Responses | (a) | (b) | (c) | (a) & (b) | (a) & (b) & c) | (a) & (c) | (b) & (c) |
| 1. None | 0 | 3 | 4 | | | | 3 |
| 2. Litle | 2 | 5 | 7 | | 1 | 2 | 2 |
| 3. Average | 3 | 3 | 4 | | 1 | | |
| 4. Moderate | 7 | 7 | 3 | 3 | 1 | | 1 |
| 4.5 Moderate/ Great | 1 | | 1 | | | | |
| 5. Great | 10 | 6 | 1 | 3 | 1 | | |
| 6. N/A | | | | | | | |
| 7. Unanswered | 2 | 1 | 3 | | 2 | 1 | |

| Question 22: Given your experience would your company use an Assumption Deed in order to: (a) add a subsidiary to an existing closed group after the subsidiary had moved into a different risk category due to altered circumstances?; (b) integrate a newly acquired company into the existing closed group?; (c) Other reasons? | | | | | |
|---|---|---|---|---|---|
| Company Officer Responses* | Yes | No | Don't know | N/A | Unanswered |
| (a) | 11 | 9 | 1 | | 5 |
| (b) | 21 | 2 | | | 3 |
| (c) | 3 | | | | 24 |
| (a) & (b) | 9 | 1 | | | 1 |
| (a) & (c) | | | | | 1 |
| (a) & (b) & (c) | 1 | | | | 2 |
| (b) & (c) | 1 | | | | |

* Note: not all deed-user companies responded to every question.

significant factor influencing deed usage than previously recognised (or at least identified in the literature). 'We might have saved $50 000 from the auditors. But, more importantly we saw a loss of competitive advantage if we did not execute the deed – we didn't want our competitors to know what we were doing,' notes one company officer; and another that: '[Accounting and auditing relief is] Not very [important]. In terms of what was disclosed (balance sheet and earnings) there could be grounds for saying that we weren't disclosing margins, but there is some confidentiality element underpinning the deed use. When our Company staff search other companies' financial affairs, some of them have class order guarantees and this means that we can't get at information.'

It would appear that the reporting relief for subsidiary companies having to prepare financial reports is significantly augmented by the benefits to corporate groups of not being required to convey potentially market-sensitive information as well as being relieved of disclosing and auditing certain related party trans-action data. As an aside, this observation invites caution about the usefulness of Segmental Reporting Disclosures required by existing Accounting Standards. Importantly, employing the deeds as the means of withholding information from the market was not part of the declared purpose of their introduction and contradicts the impression that they were primarily for creditor protection.

And, as the option to withhold segment data through taking up the deed is only available in Australia this makes highly contestable the claim that a drive for comparability underpins the adoption of IFRSs.

Table 8.1 fails to show any evidence to support a proposition that capital rais-ing benefits are a major deed driver. Generally, internal officers of the group – the company auditors or its solicitors – had been most influential in the decision to execute the deed. Follow-up questioning revealed another notable observation. Several respondents were unaware that few deeds had been operationalised as the cross-guaranteeing covenants require a closed-group company to be placed formally in liquidation before the cross guaranteeing crystallises.

Somewhat counterintuitively, there is only limited concern over possible actions of a rogue subsidiary, highlighting an awareness by deed users of having tight managerial controls over a closed group: 'Mitigating this possibility [of actions of a rogue subsidiary] we are aware of all operations. We have divisions rather than legal entities. We get monthly reports from our divisions.' 'We're exposed to debts of subsidiaries, but [at any time] can cut them loose. We manage the exercise so tightly that we are not concerned. We would hope that we didn't have rogues, but if this liability occurred then we would be liable under the guarantee.'

Inclusion of some but not other companies in a closed group, and subsequent assumptions and revocations, evokes questions regarding selectivity. Table 8.2. provides some insights to the matter.

**Table 8.2:** Deed structure – strategically selective or perfunctory?

| Question 2: Do you have any other cross-guarantee financing instruments currently in place? | | | | | |
|---|---|---|---|---|---|
| Company Officer Responses | Yes | No | Don't know | N/A | Unanswered |
| Total | 13/28 | 15/28 | 0/28 | 0/28 | 0/28 |

| Question 4: Are all Australian-registered companies in your corporate group signatories to a deed? | | | | | |
|---|---|---|---|---|---|
| Company Officer Responses | Yes | No | Don't know | N/A | Unanswered |
| Total | 11/28 | 16/28 | 0/28 | 1/28 | 0/28 |

| Question 6: Are any of the signatory companies to a deed ineligible for class order accounting and auditing relief benefits? | | | | | |
|---|---|---|---|---|---|
| Company Officer Responses | Yes | No | Don't know | N/A | Unanswered |
| Total | 8/28 | 19/28 | 0/28 | 1/28 | 0/28 |

| Question 8: How important was the opportunity for greater confidentiality? | | | | | | | |
|---|---|---|---|---|---|---|---|
| Company Officer Responses | None *1* | Little *2* | Some *3* | Important *4* | Very *5* | N/A *6* | Unanswered *7* |
| Total | 3/28 | 8/28 | 8/28 | 5/28 | 4/28 | 0/28 | 0/28 |

| Question 14: Underpinning the commercial activities of many groups of companies is the notion that they operate as a 'group enterprise'. Do you manage your group of companies: (a) as a group enterprise?; (b) as a group of related, but separate, legal entities (the intention being that no company's performance would suffer in order to promote the performance of the group as a whole)? | | | | | |
|---|---|---|---|---|---|
| Company Officer Responses* | Yes | No | N/A total | Unanswered total | Other total |
| (a) | 16 | 8 | | 3 | 1 |
| (b) | 10 | 7 | | 9 | |
| (a) & (b) | 3 | 1 | | | |

Question 15: If your corporate group suffered financial distress, would you expect the liquidator to: (a) implement cross guarantees in respect of the related companies?; (b) adopt a grouping approach (pooling) in respect of the separate companies?

| Company Officer Responses* | Yes | No | Unanswered total | Don't know total |
|---|---|---|---|---|
| (a) | 20/28 | 2/28 | 4/28 | 2/28 |
| (b) | 11/28 | 7/28 | 8/28 | |
| (a) & (b) | 6/28 | 0/28 | 0/28 | |

Question 13: Does your corporate group use more than one deed within the larger economic entity?

| Company Officer responses | Yes | No | N/A | Unanswered |
|---|---|---|---|---|
| Total | 4/28 | 23/28 | 1/28 | 0/28 |

Question 20: Given your experience would your company use a Revocation Deed to: (a) remove a subsidiary that has moved into a different risk category due to altered circumstances?; (b) prepare for a closed-group restructuring which will reincorporate the company into a new deed?; (c) isolate a company that might financially jeopardise the closed group?

| Company Officer Responses* | Yes | No | N/A | Unanswered total | Other total |
|---|---|---|---|---|---|
| (a) | 11 | 10 | | | 4 |
| (b) | 10 | 7 | 1 | | 6 |
| (c) | 10 | 10 | | | 5 |
| (a) & (b) | 1 | | | | |
| (a) & (b) & (c) | 7 | 6 | | | 5 |
| (a) & (c) | 3 | 3 | | | |
| (b) & (c) | | | | | 1 |

* Note: not all companies responded to every question.

Those data generally confirm that company officers look positively on the potential managerial flexibility inherent in the deeds. In particular, nearly half of the Question 2 responses reveal a lack of any other cross-guarantee financing instruments in place prior to executing their deed (resulting mainly from requests by lenders – primarily banks). Supporting data in table 8.1 suggest that there are other non-finance related strategic reasons for executing an ASIC deed. Answers to Question 8 provide more clues: '[For a variety of reasons] ... saving on the class order – audit costs – therefore doesn't apply in the first few years. The savings would be on confidentiality'.

Circumstantial evidence of operational reasons why certain Australian-registered group companies would be included as signatories to the deed is entailed in corporate officers' comments: 'All are Australian-based controlled entities, which have been subjected to at least one external audit, are not subject to group materiality but are included under the class order'; and, 'We undertake a number of acquisitions and have a rule of thumb that we do not include a newly acquired entity as a party to the deed until we have owned it for at least twelve months, ensuring that we have a better understanding of its corporate history. There are also a small number of entities that, for financial reporting requirements, still need to have separate financial statements prepared, and as such we do not include these as a party to the deed.' Nearly 30 per cent of respondents indicated companies included in a deed were otherwise ineligible for the class order relief (because they were generally small companies). Qualitative responses by several officers noting the inclusion in the deed of 'small' proprietary companies (not subject to the requirement to prepare audited accounts) add to the problematic nature of accounting and auditing relief being the sole driver for such companies.

Whereas approximately 85 per cent of respondents employed only one deed, the other 15 per cent confirmed earlier anecdotal evidence of companies having multiple deeds. While not surveyed here, Goodman Fielder (acquired as part of the Burns Philp group in 2004, only to be re-floated in 2006), for example, had between eleven and thirteen closed groups in the early 2000s. In respect of Goodman Fielder, a forthcoming view of a respondent explained that: 'Goodman Fielder was a fundamentally decentralised company, around acquired products. The management culture was decentralised where business units ran themselves.'

Deed take-up seems to depend on how management perceive a corporate *group*. Justice Rogers-type observations about the prevalence of a group enterprise approach to commercial activity noted previously (pp. 141) is confirmed by comments offered by several company officers reflecting the perceived complexity of group commercial operations and uncertainty of how a group is to be administered: 'The culture of our company is that it is group related, but each of the companies is a separate legal entity. For management purposes we

173

view things not necessarily along legal lines but along product classification (e.g. concretes, building products with a residential focus, bricks, tiles), then we move offshore to a US operation that is predominantly a brick business. So, the businesses are managed functionally along product lines. One subsidiary may have a number of products'; 'Each company's operations are managed as a separate business'; 'We operate them as divisions, not as separate legal entities. Some of those companies fall across different divisions. Divisional general managers are responsible for supermarkets, wholesaling, etc.'; and 'We operate as a group but are very conscious of individual entity responsibilities'. All comments indicate a degree of having two-bob-each-way – operating as a group enterprise but acknowledging the separateness of the companies.[28]

Whether Baxt and Lane's (1998) 'schizophrenia' phenomenon regarding group action exists in a significant way is contestable from the variability and uncertainty of views as to how a liquidator might implement deed covenants.[29] The following sample of qualitative responses indicates that:

> In effect we would anticipate pooling, even though each company is treated [for ongoing purposes] as a separate legal entity. There would be a minimal impact, because every deed we have is with 100% wholly owned subsidiaries. We have always thought that the purpose of the deeds is to make them as one. So if Company I went belly-up then we are in it together – all subsidiaries in the Group.

> Definitely not the pooling approach unless something has changed under the insolvency laws. The liquidator, from my experience, may well lodge a claim of debt, but if the only way to lodge it is via a deed then they will implement the deed.

> There are financial implications of the deeds. I would expect a liquidator to come in and expect Company O [the holding company] to pay for the deficit of the company in trouble.

Decisions to execute a deed appear to be strategic, selective, drawing upon perceptions of several advantages augmenting the conventional wisdom that accounting and auditing relief is the main deed driver. How those cost savings materialise is nonetheless still something of a mystery. Proprietary non-disclosure factors have emerged as a major deed driver, suggesting that a deed is more likely where managers adopt a tightly managed group enterprise approach to their ongoing operations.

Deeds obviously have the potential to generate savings in many forms to corporate groups, with associated potential costs due to the cross-guaranteeing covenants. For many large companies the deeds have the potential to determine whether certain related party transaction information is conveyed to the marketplace. It is a mechanism by which market-sensitive competitor information may be withheld. Anecdotal evidence (for example, in respect of the Patrick/MUA, Air New Zealand and James Hardie cases) and the general level of Assumption Deed and Revocation Deed activity (we noted approximately 50 per cent of deeds are active) are consistent with the proposition that corporate officers are aware of the potential for asset and liability quarantining, and deed execution adds to that potential.

Inquiry into the understanding of the corporate officers of deed-executing companies has side-benefits by virtue of the focus it places on directors' solvency statements.

*Respondents' views on solvency* are insightful when viewed within the framework of analyses of some recent Australian court revelations[30] in respect of the Bell Group, One.Tel, Westpoint and the earlier Water Wheel and HIH collapses.[31] They highlight the importance of corporate officers really understanding the concept of insolvency for an orderly regulation of companies' affairs, and for the disclosure of financial data from which stakeholders might assess it. Our evidence, however, supports previous case-based and analytical material suggesting that a pervading uncertainty exists with corporate officers as to the notion of solvency and how to assess it.

If company officers are uncertain as to what solvency means, how can they ensure the disclosure of data by which it might be assessed? How can solvency statements be made in accord with the considerations attending the exercise of deeds? Whither directors' capacities to ensure their companies are not trading while insolvent, a critical corporate governance check on unfettered corporate action and one requiring fundamental inputs from audited accounting information? Australia's Bell Resources and Bond Corporation, Adelaide Steamship, Patrick Corporation groups' solvency difficulties in the 1990s, and the more recent One.Tel, Ansett, HIH and Westpoint affairs, highlight problems when companies allegedly have continued to trade when in financial difficulties (Clarke *et al.*, *Corporate Collapse*, 2003).[32]

Solvency has been claimed to have become more critical in recent decades.[33] Australia's *Corporations Act 2001* (Cth) requires that directors assess continually whether their company is solvent before allowing it to continue trading, and to make a declaration of solvency s295(4)(c) in its published annual report. And, of course, auditors have the roving responsibility to monitor whether their clients are going concerns. Yet, as the following evidence implies, directors' and other officers' understanding of the solvency concept is at best equivocal, frequently contestable. This is especially so within the group settings that are characteristic of listed companies.

Were it that they had a better grasp of the elements of solvency, they might be more enthusiastic for ensuring that the data in their financials were serviceable for determining it. Table 8.3 provides data relating to individual corporate

**Table 8.3:** Perceptions about solvency

Question 16: Do you consider the solvency statement required by law to be prepared for each closed-group company as a serviceable trade-off for the reporting relief given pursuant to executing the deeds?

| Company | Yes | No | Don't know | N/A | Unanswered |
|---|---|---|---|---|---|
| Total | 23/28 | 5/28 | 0/10 | 0/28 | 0/28 |

Question 17.1: When preparing your solvency statement, what information do you draw on: a) the financial statements of individual companies within the group; b) financial statements of your company's closed group prepared in accordance with Accounting Standards; c) information other than company's closed-group financial statements?

| Answer Options | Yes total | No total | N/A total | Unanswered total |
|---|---|---|---|---|
| a) | 18/28 | 2/28 | One company | 6/28 |
| b) | 15/28 | 7/28 | said that c) was | 5/28 |
| c) | 10/28 | 7/28 | N/A for their | 8/28 |
| a) & b) | 6/28 | 1/28 | company. | 1/28 |
| a) & b) & c) | 4/28 | 0/28 | Another said | 0/28 |
| a) & c) | 3/28 | 1/28 | the Q didn't | 4/28 |
| b) & c) | 1/28 | 3/28 | apply at all | 3/28 |

Question 17.2: If you answered (b) in 17.1 then do you consider your company's closed-group financial statements prepared in accordance with Accounting Standards, alone, provide a sufficient basis for your solvency statement?

| Company | Yes | No | Unanswered | N/A |
|---|---|---|---|---|
| Total | 5/28 | 10/28 | 0/28 | 13/28 |

**Table 8.3:** (*Cont.*)

| | Yes | No | N/A | Unanswered total |
|---|---|---|---|---|
| Question 18: Which of the following financial characteristics of the closed group can be calculated from the closed-group consolidated assets, liabilities, and profits data disclosed as a Note to the Accounts: a) Solvency; b) Gearing; c) Asset backing? | | | | |
| a) | 19/26 | 5/26 | | 1/26 |
| b) | 19/26 | 1/26 | | 5/26 |
| c) | 20/26 | 1/26 | | 4/26 |
| a) & b) & c) | 16/26 | 2/26 | | 1/26 |
| b) & c) | 2/26 | | 1/26 | 3/26 |

officers' understanding of corporate solvency, and how their perceptions were affected by the existence of a deed.

*Management style* is critical in understanding how corporate groups operate. Officer responses here reinforce that view. At a general level the spread of the responses to Question 14 (table 8.2) reveals diverse perceptions by officers in respect of ongoing operational group activities. They suggest uncertainty as to what 'group activity' is perceived to entail legally, a matter exacerbated when officers were asked (Question 15) (table 8.2) to consider similar issues, but assuming entities are facing financial distress. But if the prevailing perception is that the set of group entities operate as a group enterprise, consistent with Justice Rogers' observations, the spread of responses suggests that there is uncertainty of the separate legal status of each group company:

Each country's operations are managed as a separate business.

We operate them as divisions, not as separate legal entities. Some of those companies fall across different divisions. Divisional general managers are responsible for supermarkets, wholesaling, etc.

This is not an easy question – the answer is a bit of both (e.g.: electricity trades as the trading entity). Overall we look at it as an enterprise. Over time our legal structure has moved more towards the management structure, but it was not and does not remain very clean. We increasingly manage as a group of entities.

The Company looks on individual companies as branches. E.g.: X Ltd is a wholesaler that has its own management structure and issues to deal with. We all move forward together. Y Ltd provided 70% of product to Company O businesses then sells 30% to other competitors.

We operate as a group but are very conscious of individual entity responsibilities.

This is tricky, because it could be halfway. Other bases – our core business is gambling and we have licences in different jurisdictions that are conducted out of separate companies. The CFO reports to the Board on a consolidated basis. It is a loose coupling of centralised and decentralised entities.

We recognise that each business unit needs to perform in its own right. That said, the legal structure need not mirror the management structure.

While aligned with Rogers J's observations in the 1980s and early 1990s, Baxt (2004) and Baxt and Lane (1998)[34] have claimed that the common law does prevail – that each company at law is (generally) regarded as a separate legal entity.[35] But that doesn't appear to resonate in corporate officers' equivocal responses on the matter. 'Would a liquidator implement cross guarantees in respect of the related companies?' 'Absolutely. Perhaps banks are now trying to be more pragmatic. But there is a huge amount of tension among the big bank groups who just want their money.'

Table 8.3 provides additional insights on how officers perceive what material is to underpin an assessment of solvency. There, 55 per cent of responses to Question 17.1 indicate that they would rely on data drawn from financial statements of a company's closed group prepared in accordance with consolidation Accounting Standards. But 64 per cent reported that they would draw on the data in the financial statements of the individual companies' financial statements. Surprisingly the overwhelming majority indicated that they would make only minimal recourse to 'other data', such as internal cash-flow projections and letters of comfort, when determining whether entities can meet debts as and when they fall due. But this was qualified in responses to follow-up questioning.

Company officers hold equivocal perceptions regarding solvency and entertain multiple factors in their determinations of it: 'We would rely on the management accounts that are system-generated'; 'Yes – we establish an understanding that the company is meeting its creditors' claims'; 'As a director you sign for the accounts of that particular company. There might be other information such as the letter of comfort [from another company – perhaps within the group]'; 'Assume our company has negative working capital. How can you, as a director, say that you can pay debts as they fall due, when liabilities exceed assets? You can point to the letter of comfort and also budget forecasts. But stepping back the split between current and non-current must be cash equivalent'; 'One of the business issues for corporates is how to treat commercial bills, which, by their nature, roll over after 280 days. We carry $15 million worth of bills at balance date. We plan to repay $3 million. Every year we have a different auditor who says they mature and therefore must be current. In effect we are saying we have the collateral to pay off debts, and can borrow against them'; 'Cash flow projections and availability of credit'.

Yet solvency and how to assess it and what reliance is placed upon directors' and corporate officials' and auditors' assurances regarding it, are possibly the most critical of corporate disclosures. An extract from an interlocutory judgment in *The Bell Group Limited (In Liquidation) & Ors v Westpac Banking Corporation & Ors*[36] is apt. It made reference to how financial intermediaries as part of their bond financial dealings may require their clients to prepare a certificate of compliance (*vis-à-vis* the relevant bond covenants) and a solvency certificate:

> 63. It is now necessary to go back to July 1989. On 13 July 1989, LDTC [Law Debenture Trust Corporation] made its first request of the Bell Group for certificates of solvency for each of the bond issues. Previously, LDTC had requested compliance certificates. The insolvency certificates were requested 'in light of concerns which have been expressed to us on behalf of certain holders of bonds convertible into shares of the guarantor and in the light of current press comments'.

> The form of certificate sought was refused by the Bell Group. In particular, LDTC had sought a certificate that BGNV [Bell Group NV], BGF [Bell Group Finance Pty Ltd] and TBGL [The Bell Group Ltd] were solvent. Ultimately, on 19 October 1989, LDTC was provided with certificates of solvency as follows:

>> The company certifies that it is able to pay its debts and meet its obligations in respect of the Trust Deed as and when they fall due and the *realisable value of the company's assets exceeds the amounts of its liabilities, including prospective and contingent liabilities.*

> 64. Further certificates of solvency were sent dated 11 December 1989. Certificates of solvency were requested again by LDTC as at 31 December 1989. On 22 January 1990, LDTC wrote to TBGL requesting certificates of compliance 'in the usual form in view of recent events'. Compliance certificates dated 24 January 1990 were sent by the Bell Group.

> 65. The plaintiffs allege that information was deliberately withheld from LDTC by the Bell Group companies contrary to their obligations under the trust deeds. It is also alleged that the Banks (or some of them) were aware that relevant information was not being given to LDTC.

> 66. After 3 July 1990, several attempts were made to restructure the Bell Group. None of the attempts came to fruition. Eventually the companies collapsed. (WASC 315, 2001, pp. 26–7 paras 62 *et. ff.*, emphasis added)

The important point to note is that ultimately recourse is had to determining what *is* the realisable values of assets and liabilities, not conventional book values following the Standards.

Those views recorded in table 8.3 justify skepticism regarding the service-ability of the data disclosed in conventional consolidated accounts, especially closed-group consolidated accounts provided as part of the parent company's Notes to Accounts in assisting officers prepare solvency statements or certificates. Specifically, whereas some officers indicated that the latter alone would not provide useful data for solvency reporting and assessments, around 75 per cent of responses to Question 18 perceived closed-group reporting data to be useful for calculating both solvency and gearing in respect of the closed group. Our inquiries of corporate officers confirm that, though there is an 'in principle' understanding of what is meant by the notion of solvency, the capacity to pay debts as and when they fall due, attempts to operationalise the concept in a group (particularly in a closed-group) setting are fraught with problems; there are: (i) uncertainties about which entity should be the focus of the solvency assessment; (ii) equivocal perceptions of the extent to which conventionally prepared standards-based financial statements provided useful insights into determinations of solvency; and (iii) differing perceptions as to the extent to which internal cash-flow projections were critical to such assessments.

That is consistent with the evidence in case-based examinations of company groups that have failed (over many decades in several countries). The main problem is that the Accounting Standards compulsory in the past were not geared to produce the data necessary to determine financial position as described above. But neither are the AIFRSs now in force.

Whereas the Accounting Standards contain some instances of specifying current market prices for certain assets, including for the investments of general insurance companies (AASB 1023, now compliant with IFRS 4 Insurance contracts, for example), this all changed to the fair-value option which applied after 1 January 2005. Although some financial assets and liabilities might not be included as they may now be considered not verifiable. In respect to general insurance companies it is to be noted that notwithstanding the specification of market prices for investments, operational assets are not required to be marked-to-market. While the distinction between investments and operating assets in conventional accounting has a long history, it is a curious one. Especially so as the different valuation rules applicable to them in AASB 1023 serve no useful purpose – something that may again change under Basel, Phase II.

Considering all these and other issues that emerged in his review of events at HIH, Justice Owen (HIHRC, Ch. 20, p. 61) observed: 'The assessment of the commercial insolvency of an insurance company under the Corporations Law can be complex and difficult for reasons that include the uncertain nature of an insurer's liabilities. These uncertainties may relate to future events and be subject to contingencies, including the outcome of future litigation.' Given also the grouping and pooling issues that Justice Owen observed at HIH, he made this assessment of what is involved in determining the state of insolvency: 'the first step would be to identify the corporate entity that has incurred the debt or debts in question. That entity is very likely to be a subsidiary rather than the holding company' (p. 62). That comment stresses the importance of understanding the separate legal entity principle enunciated in *Salomon v. Salomon*.

## Pooling and opting-in arrangements

Reviewing the activities, financing and related structures of corporate groups in Australia, CASAC[37] identified the need to provide more *ex ante* certainty to interested parties about which entity was engaging in commercial activities – or whether it was acting on behalf of a corporate group. It argued that leaving the courts and administrators to decide such questions, *ex post*, created an unnecessary level of uncertainty for an efficient operating economy to exist. Several reforms to the *Corporations Act* were proposed, loosely referred to as (i) 'pooling' (including set-off on intra-group debts), and (ii) so-called 'opting-in' proposals.

The first category, entailing *ex post* capital boundary adjudications, has been discussed above. The second, an *ex ante* solution to capital boundary problems, effectively gives directors an opportunity to nominate to the marketplace which of the subsidiary companies should comprise the 'group enterprise' for contractual purposes. Interestingly, this appears to mirror what is available to directors presently under the ASIC Class Order Deed.

Table 8.4 shows that company officers' opinions appear to vary in respect of 'opting-in'- and 'pooling'-type proposals.

Qualitative officer responses were obtained in follow-up questioning

*Company D*: 24(a): [Indicated it would be detrimental if we were to go back to the Adsteam situation in the early 1990s] 'Consider the effect if the assets of all the "public" companies had been pooled and sold off. Pooling suggests a fire-sale approach rather than working through asset sales in the normal course of business.'

[Citing the recent (then 2003) Pasminco example, where the group of companies is in voluntary administration, it was noted that the administrator is planning to float the company again with the aim of trading out.] 'These are great assets that can be worked out.'

24(b): 'Pooling is not all desirable. Separate legal entity is the glue of the capitalist system in the UK, USA and Australia. Pooling gives a poor outcome to the key stakeholders.'

181

**Table 8.4:** Perceptions about applicability of 'pooling'

| Question 24: Do you agree with CASAC's proposed reform to the *Corporations Act*, that: (a) 'Liquidators should be permitted to pool the unsecured assets of two or more related companies in liquidation with the prior approval of unsecured creditors of those companies.'; (b) 'Courts should be permitted to make pooling orders in the liquidation of two or more companies.' | | | |
|---|---|---|---|
| Totals* | | | |
| Company Officers' Responses | a | b | a, b |
| Yes | 15 | 14 | 14 |
| No | 7 | 8 | 7 |
| Circumstance specific | 2 | 2 | 2 |
| Unanswered | 3 | 3 | 3 |

*Note:* not all company officers responded to this question. Due to time constraints the interviews for two companies were finished before questions 24–6 could be answered.

*Company H*: 24(a) and (b). 'Not if those arrangements had not been agreed to by the groups concerned.'

*Company N*: 24(a): 'It's a twin-edged sword depending on how you run the group. It wouldn't interfere with the way we run our business. If you are a creditor then it could work against you. Consider two entities, one of which is solvent or has more assets. How do you get that approval? This would have to be in the scheme of arrangement. Would you get the approval of the creditors from both companies separately or together? All in principle. It removes inter-company creditors, so that in the past this triggered the deck of cards.'

24(b): *Interviewer*: 'There are real implications of doing this. Once you start to accept a pooling approach then your assessment of risk on an individual basis means nothing.'

*Officer*: 'How does it work with structural subordinations? – We are only talking about an unsecured lender. An unsecured lender could pull the whole entity down.'

*Company O*: 24(b): 'What's in the best interest of all of the creditors? Some situation may be where the creditors don't want it to take place. If the creditors don't want it then they shouldn't do it.'

*Company P*: 24(a): 'I would look at the credit quality of that particular company. The suggestion cuts across the view that you are dealing with a particular entity, which would interfere with the credit rating of companies. It would make it difficult to work out the actual credit rating of the company. Possibly it is an unworkable suggestion.'

24(b): 'Under New Zealand law there doesn't have to be a cross guarantee in place. This makes it difficult to judge what the credit quality of a company is. Ireland has similar legislation.'

*Company W*: 'It just seemed to be common sense that companies that had set themselves up with cross guarantees would then flow from the deed take-up'

The majority of responses stated a preference for some form of pooling arrangements in corporate administrations. But a substantial minority opposed them. The qualitative responses again reflect the diversity of views on this complex issue. Of course such responses have a particular currency given the Australian Federal Government's move to introduce pooling as an option for administrators, likely to be effective from 2007 onwards.

**Table 8.5:** Perceptions about 'set-off'

| Question 25: Do you agree with CASAC's suggestion that in respect of the *Corporations Act*: 'There should be no change regarding the priority of intra-group claims in the insolvency of a group company' (that is, no set-off). | | | | |
|---|---|---|---|---|
| Company Officer Responses | Yes | No | Unanswered | Circumstance specific |
| Total* | 13/26 | 7/26 | 1/26 | 6/26 |

* *Note*: not all company officers responded to this question. Due to time constraints the interviews for two companies were finished before questions 24–6 could be answered.

The responses suggest that the status quo (no set-off) should be retained. Interestingly, however, additional qualitative responses to table 8.5 answers suggest there is some confusion in respect of what set-off really entails.

Qualitative officer responses in follow-up questioning:

*Company D*: 'In some companies there is one particular client with a group of clients, with all types of equity. The capital structure is clearly designed to move funds outside that group of companies. So in some situations, yes, but it would depend on the circumstances. Out-and-out fraud is clear in terms of structuring, and then they should be set-off. By setting-off you could be corrupting by virtue of the 100% preference.'

*Company H*: 'If corporations have no class orders then they need to stand on their own, so therefore no set-off should be allowed.'

*Company N*: 'There is the risk of set-off and no priority treatment.'

*Company O*: 'What they are saying is that if you don't pool then the inter-group claims remain in there, which need to be satisfied. If that's the approach you are going to take then it would be logical if there were no pooling. Would creditors really understand this? People act out of self-interest. We have a problem in Company O in terms of getting financial transparency across and within the divisions. It would be great if there was some differentiation so that we can hold people more accountable. Divisionalisation would be an advantage.'

*Company P*: 'Offset is always a problem. Does Company P believe in setting-off? It depends which side of the fence you're on. If you look at entities within the group as separate legal entities, then their dealings with group entities should be treated in just the same way as you do with outside companies.'

*Company R*: 'Not having set-off makes things complicated because it inhibits us doing business that could be set-off. Logically a set-off makes sense. There are implications for parties.'

*Company V*: 'This has to do with insolvency laws and how the insolvency regime works.'

*Company W*: 'I hadn't thought it through but if pooling occurs then set-off would be irrelevant.'

*Interviewer*: 'The issue is, if you do offset then you must think of each company as a 100% legal entity.'

*Officer*: 'In a closed group we [contract to] pay [meet group] debts and obligations, and assume the judges will implement the deed.'

Whilst Australia's *CLERP 9* proposals did not pursue CASAC's opting-in proposal, table 8.6 shows there is substantial support for it.

Qualitative officer responses in follow-up questioning:

*Company D*: 'This is an alternative to the Deed of Cross-Guarantee. We're not sure. Do creditors care at the end of the day? They often don't know with whom they are trading. Banks are credit specific.'

*Company H*: 'We support separate legal entity; therefore we rejected the proposal.'

*Company N*: 'We could selectively opt in as if they were in the one group.'

**Table 8.6:** Perceptions about 'opting-in'

| Question 26: Do you agree with CASAC's proposed reform to the *Corporations Act* regarding the regulation of corporate groups that: 'a wholly owned corporate group should have the choice to be a consolidated corporate group for all or some of its group companies, and be governed by single enterprise principles?' | | | | |
|---|---|---|---|---|
| Company Officer Responses* | Yes | No | Maybe | Unanswered |
| Total | 16/26 | 5/26 | 2/26 | 3/26 |

\* *Note:* not all company officers responded to this question. Due to time constraints the interviews for two companies were finished before questions 24–6 could be answered.

'You can decide not to do this, but I don't think they (legislators) can get people to adopt them. We want to trade with companies with separate legal entities. This would drive more complexity in terms of accounting and auditing. Now one might ask why we are setting up a whole series of processes under the non-separate legal entity principle. This is quite fraught with problems.'

*Company O*: 'Opting-in – we could choose to treat companies in the closed group as a single separate entity. Once they're in no separate reports need to be prepared.'

*Company P*: 'There is the suggestion that you can nominate companies that would be in a Clayton's cross guarantee. This was put forward as part of the *CLERP* proposals. We would prefer to go the full way towards adopting the cross guarantee.'

*Officer*: 'Cost savings aren't everything. Our understanding is that the Group has always operated as an entity of viable legal entities on an autonomous basis. They are separate businesses in their own right that must stand up and be counted. For example, an asbestos claims company shouldn't bring down the whole Group. In this regard Company P is generally decentralised from an operational standpoint. It is decentralised into product areas that cut across legal entities.'

*Company R*: 'Yes, but once it's in it needs to be locked in, and can't move in and out. This one didn't get up in *CLERP 9* – a major issue in corporations law reform.'

It is revealing that the majority of corporate officers appeared to favour the opting-in idea, and by implication the similar outcomes that might be expected

185

to arise were deed covenants crystallised. Yet, curiously, the economic group notion is retained as the perceived dominant corporate form.

## Deeds, groups, equivocation and confusion

The structure of the deed has been modified on several occasions since its introduction in 1985, but the deed remains a uniquely Australian regulatory instrument underpinned by equally unique objectives. Little empirical information has been available previously about the deed. Data reported here reveal that deed usage has proven popular, with the number of closed groups growing at approximately 10 per cent per annum over the years 1991–99. Financial benefits have accrued annually to those corporate groups having a deed in place, with what appears to be minimal commensurate benefit to creditors flowing from the *quid pro quo* guarantee covenants.

On balance, there is good reason to doubt the deed has proven to be a net benefit to society. Indeed, there is compelling reason to doubt that creditors have benefited.

Views on CASAC's opting-in reforms provide evidence that might surprise some, including regulators. Officers are uncertain about the costs and benefits of the proposed opting-in changes to Australia's corporations legislation outlined in the CASAC[38] report. However, there is majority support for the general case of allowing companies' officers to determine, *ex ante*, which of their companies could be deemed effectively 'one enterprise', thereby lifting the corporate veil, giving the same effect as from the *ex ante* execution of an ASIC-approved Deed of Cross-Guarantee.

Yet equivocation persists on the issue. Governments, regulators, and their advisers whose observations about potential policy changes in the wake of events at James Hardie, Patrick/MUA, Air New Zealand/Ansett provide insights into rationales for not 'tinkering with what is already the quite fragile structure of our corporations law'.[39] The latest Australian Government recommendations to allow pooling in administrations is one such tinkering whose wider consequences for ongoing commercial activities do not appear to have been fully appreciated by the legislators.[40]

The data analysed above put in perspective proposals to bring the deeds directly under the *Corporations Act 2001* (Cth). Specific changes entail large proprietary companies within a closed group being required to replace the ASIC deed with a statutory deed of cross-guarantee. Those changes, which continue the benefits to companies from executing a deed with a holding company, are shown to be based on questionable experiences over the last two decades. They fail to incorporate the unintended costs to society and benefits to the companies that have emerged.

# 9

# An Alternative Group Therapy to Consolidation Accounting[1]

> It is . . . misleading to imply that a group can have a state of affairs or can earn profits . . . no set of consolidated accounts can give a true and fair view of anything.
>
> (Accounting Standards Review Committee, 1978, pp. 128–9)

Whether consolidation accounting practices should be tolerated is contestable. Accounting data are reasonably expected to reflect financial reality in its legal, social and economic contexts. And whereas reality might be less than transparent, consolidated financial data cannot by any stroke of the imagination be considered a realistic reflection of the aggregative wealth and progress of the related companies. For conventionally prepared, consolidated accounting data are pseudo aggregations of the related companies' separate conventional accounting data – some as they appear in the originals, some adjusted to accommodate presumed, often counterfactual, characteristics of the transactions between them.

Continued support for consolidation accounting proceeds more by default than design. Perhaps misunderstanding within both the accounting and legal professions of the nature and financial significance of the information in consolidated statements is the primary contributor to that default. Specifically, it is contestable whether the ASC's (as it was then) assertion that 'consolidated accounts . . . [provide] more meaningful information for users of the accounts' is sustainable. Equally contestable is the claim that enforcement of these 'new requirements' by the accounting profession will ensure 'most of the major and well-used opportunities for the manipulation . . . under the previous Companies Code will disappear'.[2] The underlying rationale for consolidated financial statements is that the related companies comprise an economic group and preparing financials as if it were provides useful information about the related companies. From the start, accounting consolidations are counterfactual – the group is not a legal entity. Accordingly, there is no such thing as group performance, group financial position, group solvency, group gearing, and the like. Such matters

187

relate to the financial characteristics of separate legal entities. Corporate groups are accounting fictions. At best, the group label is a convenient, though sloppy and misleading, shorthand way of referring to a metaphoric bundling of a parent company and its subsidiaries. Consolidated financial statements are the ultimate in misinformation.

In supporting a mandatory legislative requirement to prepare consolidated accounts, some of the judiciary and members of the accounting profession have claimed that consolidated data best reflect the aggregated operations of the related companies as if they comprised a single economic or business entity. That is claimed to be the substance of the transactions between the related companies. Though supported by critics who wish to reduce conformity with the separate legal entity principle,[3] consolidation might also be contested against a background of corporate strategies which have bestowed considerable advantage through exploiting it. Yet, despite the rhetoric, a 'group' of companies is neither a single entity under the present general interpretation of the law, nor (usually) reasonably identifiable as a separate economic unit. Thus aggregative representations of the outcome of the so-called group operations and their financial position are financial nonsense. Contrary to what is claimed, consolidated financial statements are the product of relying on the purported economic form, rather than the legal form and its consequential financial substance.

It is assumed (but not evidenced or well argued) that consolidated reporting gives interested persons information on the overall financial status and current financial performance of group companies 'as an economic unit'. Distinguished legal opinion, for instance from Professor Gower, explains that the UK legislature has: 'recognised at least since the *Companies Act 1948* . . . where there is a relationship between companies such that one, the parent or holding company, controls the others, the subsidiary or sub-subsidiary companies, then, for certain purposes, including especially presentation of financial statements, all must be treated as one . . . The most important of these [qualifications to the separate entity principle] relate to accounts . . .'[4] Judicial dicta support this view. Lord Denning MR declined to treat a wholly owned subsidiary, Fork Manufacturing Co. Ltd, as a separate legal entity.[5] And Denning's dicta in *D.H.N. Ltd v Tower Hamlets* explained: 'We all know that in many respects a group of companies are treated together for the purpose of general accounts, balance sheet and profit and loss account. They are treated as *one concern*.'[6] 'Treated as if', of course, doesn't make them so! And Mason J. in *Industrial Equity Ltd v Blackburn*, while rejecting Gower's proposition and championing the separate legal entity principle, noted (in *obiter*) that the purpose of consolidation is to: 'ensure that the members of, and for that matter persons dealing with, a holding company are provided with accurate information as to the profit and loss and state of affairs of that company and its subsidiaries within the group'.[7]

In the early 1990s the 'group' notion was endorsed in an ASC media release, 'Public hearing: accounting relief for wholly-owned subsidiaries'. On the basis of a presumed commonality of interests of all 'closed-group' companies (see chapter 8), it was suggested that 'consolidated accounts would more accurately reflect commercial realities'.[8] *How* was not disclosed, though from these observations it would be reasonable for laypersons to expect consolidated statements to contain an aggregation only of the data in the separate companies' accounts, perhaps adjusted to avoid double counting, but neither including data not sourced in those accounts nor excluding data which are. That is far from the reality. Consolidation accounting does both.

Groupthink remains virulent. Consolidated financial statements persist as the group therapy being prescribed by national professional bodies and in the relevant IFRSs. However, there is good reason for concern over the serviceability of consolidated financial statements. Consider the 1992 Royal Commission inquiry into the $2.2 billion bale-out of the State Bank of South Australia which alluded to its doubt on the matter when referring to 'the different accounting practices which can be applied to consolidated, group, equity and aggregated accounting'.[9] The CASAC (2000) Corporate Groups Report and the revelations at the HIH Royal Commission confirm the currency of those concerns.

It is not only a problem of variant accounting practices. More fundamentally, the proposition that group accounts are prepared to reflect accurately the operations of the group as a single economic or business unit runs contrary to the historical development of consolidated accounting. Allusions to consolidations being the product of an evolutionary refinement are in error. As just noted, equally questionable is the proposition outlined by Mason J. that consolidated or group accounts can ensure that the members of, and for that matter persons dealing with, a holding company are provided with accurate information as to the profit and loss and 'state of affairs' of that company and its subsidiaries within the group.[10]

In this book on several occasions we note that if the group is representative of neither a legal nor an economic entity, how can it be said to have a state of affairs?[11] Critical to that issue is what is meant by 'state of affairs', particularly as it applies to related companies, their members and their creditors. Money is the primary concern of all parties. Legally, one of the imports of the separate legal entity principle has been to isolate the fund that belongs to the company from the fund that belongs to its members. The company fund is liable for the company's debts and the members' fund is liable for the members' debts. In that setting, consolidated accounts are more likely to be a source of deception than illumination for the users of accounts in general, for the creditors and for those dealing with the separate companies in particular. Case vignettes in chapters 5 and 7 confirm this.

## Fuzzy financials

It is far from universally agreed what function consolidation or group accounting serves. In Australian consolidation prescriptions, AASB 1024 (now AASB 127 under the AIFRS regime)[12] and the relevant sections of the *Corporations Act*, it is presumed that the function is to 'depict the affairs of an economic entity or group' of companies. AASB 127 broadens the base of the consolidation process. However, Walker's comprehensive history of consolidated accounting exposes that numerous functions were posited initially, though few supported the current rationale being offered:

> [In the 1920s, UK] consolidated statements were not regarded as primary reports. Nor were they thought of as depicting the affairs of an 'economic entity' or of a 'group' of companies . . . In the 1920s, consolidated statements were regarded as supplementary remedial reports. (1976, p. 77)

> . . . U.K. accountants were concerned with amplifying the reports of holding companies and to *overcome the limitations* of conventional cost-based methods of accounting for inter corporate investments. (1976, p. 353, emphasis added)[13]

Consolidating the separate financial statements of the parent company and its subsidiaries in effect lifts the corporate veil as if the accounts of each were those of the mere branches of one. Aggregated data are thereby presented to be more informative than disaggregated data. This is a curious proposition, for virtually everywhere else in human endeavour, disaggregation and deconstruction are being proposed as the window on enlightenment. But the idiosyncratic consolidating mechanics make those aggregations even less capable of meaningful interpretation than their components are in the separate financial statements of the controlled entities.

Consider the general proposition driving consolidation techniques – the notion of a 'group' comprising the parent entity and its subsidiaries or controlled entities. So much of the debate underlying (and deemed to support) Australia's AASB 127 and the sections on consolidation accounting in the *Corporations Act 2001* (Cth) addresses superficial niceties regarding the artificial group entity to which the consolidated statements refer – how to identify a parent company, a subsidiary; how to eliminate the 'effect' of intra-group transactions and the like, rather than the inherent conflict between the 'group' notion and the separate legal entity principle.

Consolidated statements report on a fictitious structure, the group, which lacks legal capacity generally to exercise property rights, to own assets or incur liabilities, to sue or be sued, to incur physical or financial damage or impose it upon others. The statements contradict the legal, social and financial essence which their constituent corporations enjoy. By virtue of legal incapacity, *group* assets and *group* liabilities are an impossibility unless the legislature intervenes, for example, by introducing covenants such as apply under an ASIC class order deed, or through the courts' resolving liquidation disputes by ordering *ex post* a pooling of group assets or allowing advance 'opting in' arrangements (chapter 8). Recourse to the group notion does, however, facilitate the labyrinths that have proven so friendly to corporate finagling. Despite being paraded under the 'accounting politically correct' substance-over-form banner, consolidated data are neither informative nor user-friendly.

The substance-over-form safe banner is an accounting fetish, with a history dating from the 1920s. In essence, the objective is to prescribe that accounting captures the financial substance of transactions. But in the context of consolidated statements the substance-over-form criterion offers no shelter. While the legal and financial substance is that the assets and liabilities included in the consolidated balance sheet are those owned and owed by the separate constituent subsidiaries, the form is that they are presented to be assets and liabilities of the mythical group entity. Consolidated income or loss is the adjusted aggregate of the separate profits and losses of the parent company and its subsidiaries. Consolidated statements are a particular instance where, contrary to the profession's dictum, the form is forced upon accountants in preference to the legal substance.

Conformity with other Accounting Standards in the consolidation process exacerbates that effect by requiring specific adjustments of the data originating in the separate financial statements of the constituent companies. In the ordinary course of events, those Standards create artifacts of their own – compulsory impairment calculations of the price paid for fixed assets, creation of tax effect balances, and the carry-forwards of various types, are examples. Some data appearing in the accounts of the separate entities are expunged from the consolidated financial statements; others are modified in a variety of ways once the same Standards are applied to the aggregative data under the consolidation rubric. For example, compliance with tax effect accounting standards in relation to eliminated profits and losses on intra-group transactions (on the grounds that they are unrealised – from the economic entity point of view) injects consolidated financial statements with data that have not appeared in the accounts of any of the constituent companies. Superimposed is the impact of consolidation techniques, creating data exclusively the province of consolidated statements, goodwill on consolidation, discount (premium or capital reserve) on consolidation, adjustments to consolidated fair values, consolidated assets and equities, creation of future tax benefits, and provisions for deferred income tax not in, or opposite to, those in the constituent companies, and the like. These are mere artifacts of the consolidation process.

Through applying the standards and the relevant sections of the *Corporations Act 2001* (Cth) consolidated balance sheets have usually contained data for which no corresponding amount appears in the constituents' balance sheets. Using the lower of cost-or-net realisable value rule to book inventories may (in the aggregate) not correspond with the prevailing outcome of complying with the rule by the constituents. Many consolidated balances (assets and liabilities) do not have any counterpart elsewhere in the framework of conventional accounting. *Goodwill* and *discount on consolidation* (*profit* or *gain*) are purely consolidated accounting artifacts. Nor do they necessarily have any relevance to the financial assessments and evaluations habitually made in commerce. The genuine financial impact of transactions between companies within the group is eliminated irrespective of the validity of the data according to the evidence of the market. The outcome is curious – artifactual data only generated by the consolidation process are inserted in the consolidated statements, whereas genuine transaction data are excluded. Consolidation processes manage to nurture the worst of both sides of creative accounting. Elimination of the financial impact of legally binding transactions (for example, sales and purchases) between group members is a prescribed mechanism. Similarly, legally determined profits and losses made by the separate entities by virtue of transactions with other group subsidiaries are deemed to be fictitious, not at arm's length, *from the economic-entity point of view*. It is implicit in the claims made that under the new legislative prescriptions the consolidation process negates the possibility of assets being shuffled around group companies at ever-increasing prices.[14] This is debatable in principle, and evidenced to the contrary in practice. There is a long history of asset shuffling. The experiences discussed in chapter 7 of the Patrick Stevedores' employees finding their employer company in the Lang Group being asset-poor and initially unable to meet their termination entitlements during the 1998 *Patrick Stevedores v MUA* dispute are a case in point. Likewise was the lot of the STP, Woodlawn, Cobar Mines affairs, Nardell and Ansett employees as noted above. Arguably, the group structure facilitated this. It would seem also that Bond Corporation's milking of the Bell Resources (chapter 5) cash box was made all the easier because of the group structure. Other than artificially and selectively to lift the corporate veil when it suits and to exploit a corporate's limited liability when it suits, it is difficult to find a single legitimate reason for operating through a corporate group. And of course, none of those benefits flows to the community at large.

In consolidation accounting within a historical cost accounting framework, the 'group' purchasing company would report the asset at its cost (or deemed cost) and the 'group' selling company book its profit (or loss) on the sale; both are presumed fictitious in the group context and hence adjusted in the consolidation process. Of course, both the sale and consequently the purchase may be contracted on a genuine commercial basis. Assets are 'worth' what they can be sold for, not what they cost to purchase. A 'view from the market' would dispose of the arm's-length problem. A 'view from the group' cannot.

Counterfactual reasoning encourages corporate groupthink. Separate companies and related entities are deemed to be *de facto* branches of the parent company. Indeed, early consolidation procedures were labelled the 'branching of profits and losses . . . depicting the affairs of a holding company and its subsidiaries as if they were a single organisation or as if the subsidiaries were merely *branches* of the parent'.[15] But in accounting, what is declared or stated often enough becomes part of the received wisdom. Most analyses in the financial sector of major corporates are undertaken on the basis of the consolidated data – rates of return, solvency, gearing, asset backing, earnings per share, overall financial performance and financial position, even though none of those absolute or derived financial indicators is meaningful outside the context of the separate individual companies from whom the data were drawn.

Dispensing with the legal status of the constituent companies and other entities is mischievous and tampers with commercial and financial reality. The separate companies have an unquestionable separate legal status bestowed upon them by virtue of incorporation, and nothing short of liquidation can deprive them of it.

Consolidation techniques entail recourse to the counterfactual: notions of group profits and losses, group rate of return, group gearing and the like, imply that the profits and losses of the separate entities will filter ultimately (through dividend payments or liquidation distributions) into the ultimate parent entity; the notion of group solvency implies that the assets of the entities comprising the group are separately and collectively available for the discharge of the liabilities of one another. Reference to asset backing in respect of the group data implies that those with a shareholding in the ultimate parent are shareholders in the subsidiaries; and the idea of group liquidity implies that the cash boxes of each are there to be raided by the others. If all that were *really* the case, cross guarantees would be unnecessary. Expositions of consolidation techniques are presented as mathematical formulae, to be applied, without regard for the constituent companies' separate legal status, to achieve the level of aggregation required. Notions of a distributive flow of wealth through the subsidiaries to the ultimate parent entity, with leakages to the subsidiaries' shareholders with a non-controlling shareholding, are embedded in those formulae, though rarely

193

disclosed to be what they are. That evokes an obvious question: if the desire is to report the activities of the separate (especially wholly owned subsidiary) companies as if they were mere branches of the controlling company, why not make them so in the first place?

An answer is less obvious. Eisenberg has noted that economic grounds were not driving the formation of most, if any, corporate groups.[16] And there cannot be any accounting argument in favour of the holding/subsidiary company structure. For if a branch structure were to be employed the outcome would agree in broad objective – data aggregation. Idiosyncrasies of the legislatively prescribed reporting requirements of the *Corporations Act 2001* (Cth) and relevant accounting standards promote the substantial differences in the reported data that emerge. But while the defects of historical-cost accounting would remain, the aggregation of the branches' data would not require the fabrication of accounting artifacts as occurs in the professionally and legally prescribed consolidation process.

Consolidated data are accounting's fabrications *par excellence*. The aggregates for the assets, equities, revenues and expenses of the constituents are virtually certain to vary from those in the consolidated statements of financial position or financial performance. Consolidated income or loss will vary even further from the aggregate of the constituents' results by virtue of compliance with processing standards, requiring the amortisation of the excess of the cost of the investment over the proportionate amount of the subsidiaries' equities acquired. Supposed indications of the solvency of the group, debt-to-asset cover, asset backing and other ratios conventionally calculated, are almost certain not to correspond to the aggregation of those for the separate companies.

By virtue of the compulsory elimination technique, neither aggregate sales revenue nor aggregate expenses (by class or in total) necessarily equal the total of those of the separate companies. Combining the elimination of intra-group transactions and tax effect accounting exacerbates anomalies, frequently introducing data to the consolidated statements without counterparts in the separate accounts of the constituents – deferred tax asset balances appear as a consequence of applying the tax effect rules to the reduction of the supposed unrealised profit component in asset balances arising from the elimination of intra-group transactions. Deferred tax liability balances emerge from the combined effect in respect to the elimination of intra-group losses, and similar adjustments to tax effect any deficiency or excess amortisation and impairment adjustments attached to the unrealised profits in respect of non-current asset sales and purchases within the group. Yet neither deferred tax asset nor liability may appear in the accounts of any of the constituent business entities. And when they do appear, they may well be in the opposite direction to the aggregate of those represented in the consolidated balance sheet.

It is doubtful if anybody can make financial sense of such outcomes. Certainly they defy common sense. Unbundling them in a group comprising hundreds of related companies is nigh on impossible. Yet it all is done purportedly in the name of disclosure and clarification. It is a matter of chance rather than design if data so contrived, so removed from real-world referents, inform of the wealth and progress of the constituent companies, either individually or collectively. Yet, despite the financial obfuscation they facilitate, their counterfactual underpinnings and the resulting artifacts, surprisingly consolidated financial statements are perceived by legislative drafters, by many legal practitioners, by the courts and by many accountants, to be the means of providing greater financial insight, a legitimate means of lifting the corporate veil. To the contrary, they achieve precisely the opposite.

It is futile to expect progress by tinkering with a form of accounting based on the counterfactual. Radical solutions are called for.

## Alternatives to consolidation accounting

### *Proscribe wholly owned subsidiaries with recourse to branch operations and branch accounting*

One solution would be to proscribe wholly owned subsidiaries.[17] Manipulations of the kind already referred to through group structures have a long history. Lord Kylsant's shuffling of the Royal Mail's secret reserves in the 1920s was a seminal example. Samuel Insull's pyramiding of asset values is another. Fast-forwarding to Australia in the early 1990s, Bond's emptying of Bell Resources' cash box showed how it was done, as mentioned above. And of late, Enron's offshore SPE manipulations, and the James Hardie affair, were a variation on a common theme. Few seem to have noted that were there no group, no parents and subsidiaries, just companies with divisions or branches, none of the threats and pleas to lift the corporate veil would have been necessary and James Hardie would not have had its perceived separate legal entity protection. Endless debate, claim and counterclaim over unanswerable questions of ethical and moral obligations would have been unnecessary.

In the 1990s UK financial chicanery within Robert Maxwell's public/private entanglement provides an apt justification of the need for radical reform. His corporate monolith of over 400 public companies, intertwined with 400 Maxwell private companies, was further complicated by their incorporation across several national jurisdictions.[18] The structure shown in figure 9.1 effectively denied regulation.

Regulatory impossibility has not gone unnoticed – it has just not been acted upon. A joint report in 1995 by international regulators in the banking, securities

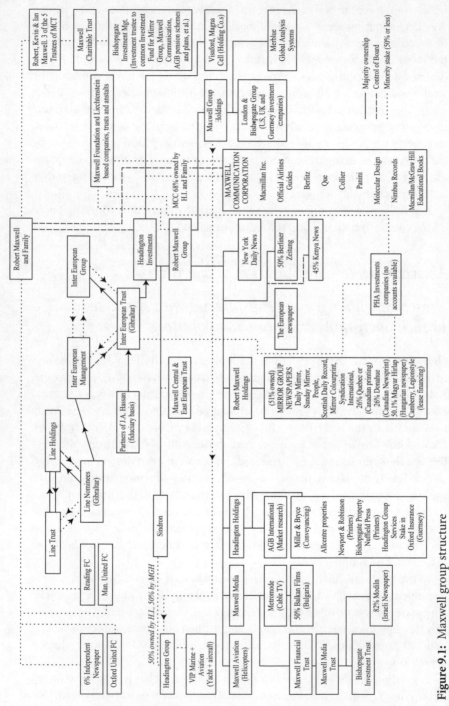

**Figure 9.1:** Maxwell group structure

*Source:* Bronwyn Maddox, 'A global web of connection following four decades of growth', *Financial Times*, 6 November 1991.

and insurance fields, 'Supervision of financial conglomerates', noted that where complex company entanglements impede effective supervision, power should be given to regulators to prohibit those structures. This response was similar to the revelations following the US utility holding/subsidiary company abuses in the 1920s and the perceived abuses in respect of the major Japanese *zaibatsus* resulting in their enforced break-up by US authorities after 1945. Such a response is long overdue in the general corporate arena. But little by way of real reform has emerged, nor is likely if the current frame of mind prevails.

In the 1990s amendments to Australia's corporations legislation sought to address abuses related to insolvent subsidiary trading, as do the November 2006 proposed pooling amendments and CASAC's 'May 2000 opting-in' proposals contained in its *Corporate groups: Final report*.[19] Sanctioning the bypassing of the fundamental principles of company law is a precedent likely to turn and bite the regulators. Lifting the corporate veil, stepping past the separate legal entity principle on occasions of financial stress, invites the inference that the holding company/wholly owned subsidiary structure is failing the 'net benefit to society' test. Compromising the principles of company law, a legislative lifting of the veil would be unnecessary were subsidiary companies to be prohibited. Corporate abuses through group structures are evident in the fallout from corporate failures and dilemmas repeated each decade in Australia since World War II.[20] Erosion of public confidence in the Australian capital markets resulting from the large group collapses in the 1960s and 1970s was repeated in the 1980s. Commenting on the collapses of the 1960s and early 1970s it was noted that 'inter-company shareholdings and transactions have given cover to fraudulent dealing and to legally less serious but financially no less deceptive misstatements of results and position'.[21] That observation equally describes events in the 1980s, 1990s and post-2000.

Many well-known Australian entrepreneurs of the 1980s reportedly used related party transactions, especially round robins. In particular, the reported deals prior to Rothwells' collapse and then in its ill-fated rescue; deals between a Spedley Holdings shelf company, P152 and a related public company, GPI Leisure Ltd;[22] and deals involving intermingled private and public companies within the Linter[23] and the APA/Unity groups. The holding/subsidiary company structure certainly appears to have facilitated more than hindered those deals. It also effectively shielded them from the public gaze and scrutiny.[24]

Similarities in the events at Stanhill Consolidated, Reid Murray Holdings and at Minsec and Cambridge Credit Corporation decades earlier are all too clear. Commercial practices such as these have a disorderly, sometimes chaotic effect on confidence in the securities market in particular and the capitalist system in general. In the UK, echoes of Prime Minister Heath's 1970s 'the unpleasant and unacceptable face of capitalism' lament can be heard clearly in the aftermath of reported shuffling of assets within the Maxwell empire prior to its collapse to the detriment of thousands of pensioners dependent on the Maxwell Pension Funds. Even more recently, the bewildering financial merry-go-rounds that, based on the HIH Royal Commission's revelations and initial inquiries into the Westpoint and Fincorp collapses, appear to have featured prominently gives the impression that the skill has not been lost. It is demonstrable that groups can be a mechanism for manipulation.[25]

If wholly owned subsidiaries are in effect *de facto* branches, and if consolidation accounting is intended to simulate branch accounting, the commonsense answer is to make them branches. Proscribe (at least) wholly owned subsidiaries and be done with it. This would avoid the confusion generated by the regulatory imposition of the *avant-garde* ASC class order deed, CASAC's proposed opting-in, Cork's opting-out and the proposed pooling arrangements under the 2007 Australian insolvency reforms.

Consistency and also common sense support a similar hard-line approach regarding partly owned subsidiaries. Now that *control* is the subsidiary criterion, partly owned companies are, in effect, no more than inter-entity investments. Possibly, the total deletion of subsidiaries, or at least any justification for a special accounting treatment regarding them, would be too radical for the corporate sector. But investments in the shares of other companies and unincorporated entities have the same nature, irrespective of the differential power of control or other privileges they might bestow.

Distinguishing between investments according to the degree of control exercised over them is no justification for differentiating the basis for their valuations, though it might well justify differences between their market prices. Whether there *is* control would have an impact on the prices the respective shareholdings would fetch in the market. The market might reasonably be expected to unravel that. Accordingly, investments in the shares of other companies should also be reported at their current market prices too. The financial affairs (assets, equities, revenues and expenses) of what are now known as wholly owned subsidiaries could be absorbed completely as the financial activities of branches or divisions of the primary company. Shares in what are now part-owned subsidiaries would be accounted for as investments in securities and stated at their current market prices. As such, the accounting for them would be identical with the accounting for all shareholdings in all other companies to which no controlling significance attaches. If the market does not accord the investment any market worth, then the accounts ought to report just that. It would seem reasonable to produce in addition schedules of assets and liabilities of the partly owned subsidiaries, as outlined in a later section discussing an alternative market-based system of accounting for wholly owned subsidiaries.

That contrasts with accountants' and the legislatures' attempts to restructure corporate relations to alleviate the effects of commercial abuses worked through holding/subsidiary company structures. Patching up reporting by groups has kept many busy for a long time – possibly at considerable cost – but ultimately the outcomes appear to have fostered (or at least left untouched) the precise irregularities they were intended to remove.

*Market price accounting for groups*[26] is a workable, more likely to be acceptable, solution. Consistent with the overall principles pursued above, the general mode of mark-to-market accounting can accommodate an effective accounting for related companies. A commonly declared overall objective of conventional consolidation is greater insight into the wealth and progress of related entities than provided by their acquisition cost. Conventional consolidation accounting sidesteps the *Salomon v Salomon* separate legal entity principle through the aggregation of the separate entities' assets and liabilities, revenues and expenses, injecting consolidation-specific data and adjusting legitimate transaction data, under the umbrella of a supposed group entity. In the wash-up, consolidated data fail miserably to achieve their stated objective.

In 1967 Chambers wrote complaining of that failure: 'Consolidated Statements were not really necessary', though the sort of information they sought to present had relevance for the evaluation of the financial outcome of inter-corporate investments. His proposal, outlined in the 1978 ASRC Report discussed in chapter 6 (and our version shown in this chapter's appendix), comprises: a statement of financial position of the parent company and a statistical summary detailing the nature, composition and aggregative money's worth of its related entities' assets and the amounts of their liabilities. Consistent with the key features of his CoCoA in which all assets would be stated at their current cash equivalents (for vendible physical assets generally best indicated by their market selling prices at the reporting date); income would be all-inclusive, including all gains and losses arising in the worth of assets during the period under review, and gains and losses in the general purchasing power of money are brought into the income calculation by means of an annual capital maintenance adjustment. Accordingly, all inter-corporate and other investments would be stated at their current cash equivalents – that is, they would be marked-to-market.

Markets are never perfect. Information is never complete. But the market prices of items are as objective an evaluation of their contemporary money's worth, of their current contribution to the wealth of their owners, as can be found. The better the information, the better the evaluation, the better the financial assessments, and the better should be decisions to invest and disinvest. A properly informed securities market requires accurate information of the current wealth and past financial progress of companies. Share prices might reasonably be expected to capture not only their companies' current financial position and an understanding of how it arose, but also impound all the expectations and fears for the future that the information might evoke. A rational economic perspective would suggest that.

199

Even if wholly owned subsidiaries were proscribed, as suggested in the previous section, the great problem of accounting for investments in shareholdings remains. If subsidiaries remain, the problem is exacerbated. Whatever the case, it seems critical for an orderly securities market that all shareholdings be accounted for on the same basis. Differences in circumstances attaching to the shares – giving or not giving control as the case may be – would be impounded in their prices. If that were so in properly informed markets, perceptions of the relative degree of control and other advantages or disadvantages attaching to a particular shareholding would be transparent.

A professional and legislative rethink of how to effect the capital boundary in relation to what are currently defined as related companies lends itself to the alternative presentation of the aggregative data. Aggregative data are 'relevant' to the interests of those who desire some aggregative financial overview of the related companies and other controlled entities; they are more 'reliable' than present consolidation information since no manipulation of the data is required to effect the aggregations; because of their contemporary and non-manipulated nature they are 'comparable' with the aggregations on both inter-firm and intra-firm bases; and readily 'understandable' by dint of the aggregated data being in the same general form and having the same financial significance they possessed in their separate financial statements[27] from which they were drawn. Importantly, aggregations of that kind provide corroborable (verifiable) base data common to all, irrespective of whatever adjustments or manipulations individuals choose to make privately.

Underpinning conventional consolidation calculations is a peculiar line of reasoning that contradicts the separate legal entity principle of company law. It implies mathematically that the investor company has immediate uninhibited access to the assets and responsibility for the discharge of the liabilities of the entities it is *deemed to control* – 'deemed to control', for it is a subjective matter of interpreting from the attendant circumstances whether control actually exists.

That determination is very important. For, in the Australian context, the group is to include controlling interests in incorporated and unincorporated enterprises. Yet we know that control, *per se*, is insufficient to facilitate legal access to the resources of a controlled entity. And we must presume that consolidated statements are intended to reflect legal compliance. Consider the example above, with its criticism of the back-to-back loans by a Bond Corporation related entity through which Bond Corporation is alleged to have siphoned Bell Resources' cash box into the Bond Corporation group. Not only was there 'actual' control, and the access it facilitated deemed insufficient to effect legally the transfer of assets via related group entities, it brought a custodial sentence for Alan Bond. That leaves no doubt that the cash of Bell Resources was not legally a resource of the Bond group.

A working assumption underpinning the alternative we present is that for the share price to be useful the market must be informed with accurate information of the wealth and financial progress of the companies in which the shares or ownership interests are held. Currently, the market is uninformed or misinformed to the extent that conventional income statement and balance sheet data are drawn on to assess financial performance and financial position. Periodic statements of financial performance and statements of financial position need, therefore, to simulate properly the only kind of calculation that can determine the financial outcome of a business venture over its entire life – a comparison between the net sum of money with which it commenced and (in like terms) the net sum of money or its equivalent with which it finishes – for that is all that periodic financial statements can reasonably achieve. It is the function that they properly can be expected to serve.

Financial impediments to having wholly owned entities liquidated and the assets transferred to the investor are accepted. Also accepted is the need for financial information in respect of what underlies substantial investments in other entities. The events at Enron, HIH, WorldCom, Ansett, Westpoint and the like evidence conventional consolidation exacerbating the inherent defects in conventional accounting prepared in compliance with the standards. Even were the group structure to be retained, there is a critical imperative that the accounting for it be improved. We propose a form of accounting for inter-corporate investments that removes the defects of consolidation but achieves the objectives attributed to it.

First, in accord with Chambers' CoCoA, all the assets would be stated at either their face cash amount (debtors and cash) or their cash equivalent, best represented by their current selling prices verified by the auditors (non-current assets, inventories).[28] Second, unlisted shares in subsidiaries would likewise be stated at the proportionate amount of the underlying money's worth (approximate selling prices) of the net assets in those entities. Third, had the controlled entities been listed companies, the investment in them would have been entered at the current selling price of the quoted shares – the proportionate equity in the net worth of the underlying net assets would be noted in parentheses at the balance sheet entry. This captures both the current selling price of the stock and the extent to which the listed price reflected *ex ante* assessments by the market of the company's future prospects in comparison with its current financial position. Fourth, all amounts in the statements would either be indicative of actual amounts of money or the equivalent thereof, as best indicated by the current selling prices of vendible assets. No amounts would, or could, be stated for non-vendible items. Thus, all the data would be denominated in monetary units of the same current general purchasing power dimension, contemporary as at the reporting date and therefore financially homogeneous, capable of having mathematical operations performed upon them to yield arithmetically valid and interpretable products.

There is no place in such a schema for any artifacts of the system, no place for data not indicative of actual amounts of current money or its equivalent. No place for making charges (such as for depreciation) unless they are substantiated by the observable financial implications (the declines in the assets' selling prices). There would be no necessity to concoct rationales that no sensible person would accept in respect of their own financial affairs.

Not only would those data then *tell it how it is*, as can best be determined at the time, they also would tell it in terms of the common and established understanding of financial matters outside of accounting. In that setting, accounting can be a financial instrument effectively meeting the reasonable information functions accorded it, and assisting in improving the corporate governance mechanisms. Enron's financial reporting shenanigans confirm the potential usefulness of our group accounting proposal. For whereas some commentators have contended that Enron's SPE capers highlight a need for a wider application of conventional consolidation accounting to all types of entities, the impotence of such a proposal was exposed earlier. Only disclosure of the market worth of the SPEs, or alternatively the market worth of their separate assets and the amount of their separate liabilities, would provide the financial information of the kind the critics seem to have sought in vain. In essence, in what is proposed here deleterious effects of the financial obligations of Enron's SPEs would be reflected in their assessed (and audited) market worth of the net assets and reported in our proposed group accounting mechanism, through both the statistical annexure and the inter-entity indebtedness matrix. Of course, where undetected ingenious-type fraud is involved in the manipulation of asset and liability balances, no accounting mechanism can be expected to provide reliable information.

The prescription described here and illustrated elsewhere is an accounting mechanism in which periodic statements of financial position contain data from which aggregations of the money and the money's worth (selling prices) of the physical assets and the amount of the liabilities can be determined, and articulated income statements produced. Adjusted for changes in the general purchasing power of money, income or loss automatically calculated as the change in the company's net wealth (stated in constant terms) then quite properly becomes the approximate increase or decrease for the period in the general purchasing power attributable to the company's net wealth. Conventional accounting complying with the Accounting Standards (AIFRSs) falls far short of that. Consolidation procedures inject their own fictions into the conventional accounting system, fuelling the information shortfall. In the end a necessary condition to reporting share prices data entails a restructuring of accounting.[29]

If that were to be so, the reporting for share investments in unlisted companies, for wholly owned subsidiaries, for other unlisted companies and unincorporated entities, falls into place. A reasonable surrogate for a company's non-existent share price or a proportionate share in an unincorporated entity's equity would be the proportion of its assets and liabilities (accounted for as above). At least those data are indicative of what underlies the shareholding, irrespective of whether it amounts to a controlling interest or to the merest of a minority interest. If subsidiaries were to remain, or if for substantial shareholdings disaggregated data were deemed necessary, they could easily be provided in supporting schedules of the various classes of assets and liabilities of the companies in which the investments were held. Indebtedness, inter-company sales and purchases, expenses and the like, and the double counting they may entail in bland aggregations of those data between related entities, can be disclosed in easily constructed schedules. The veil is drawn over such information by the elimination rule in conventional consolidation accounting; precisely the opposite of what is intended.

Our alternative group accounting approach partly accords with the view that: 'the larger and the more diverse the group, the greater is the need for the disaggregation of consolidated accounts to show the performance and worth of operating subsidiaries, entities or divisions within the group'.[30]

Reporting the selling prices for physical assets automatically corrects in the balance sheet of the purchaser, for the consequence of transactions that have not been at arm's length. Related businesses could trade assets at whatever prices they chose and, separately, properly report the consequential profits and losses; avoid the financial solecisms in consolidated financial statements. They could also avoid the counterfactual assumptions underlying consolidations' procedures, eliminate the complex and contradictory calculations endemic in the consolidation process as part of conventional accounting practice, and provide all the necessary aggregated and disaggregated data which it is said consolidated financial statements are to give – but which they fail to deliver. The general structure of the alternative proposed appears in the appendix to this chapter.

Perversely, this alternative achieves the information objectives claimed for consolidated financial statements, without their sophistry, without their make-believe. Some of the scope for the manipulations so evident in many unexpected corporate failures is removed. Consumers of the data can treat the related businesses as single entities if they choose. They can aggregate and disaggregate as they like. The data to do so would be there. They can group, sub-group and re-group, as they see fit, without artificially lifting the veil of incorporation. They can peep under the veil or peer through it if they wish without offending the separate legal entity principle, for so long the foundation of British-based company law.

To provide greater insight into the wealth and progress of related entities than that provided by their investment cost at the date of acquisition is the commonly declared overall objective of conventional consolidation accounting.

Conventional consolidated data cannot achieve the objectives attributed to them: specifically to show an aggregative financial position of the related entities, assess their overall solvency, determine their potential cash flows, or otherwise evaluate their overall or individual performances. Through the elimination rule conventional consolidation removes the capacity to determine the possible solvency of the separate subsidiaries, removes the capacity to determine which of the group companies are net borrowers and which are net lenders within and outside the group, their sales turnover with and outside the group, separate asset and liability structures and employee obligations. They obfuscate rather than illuminate performance and position.

A professional and legislative reassessment of how to effect the capital boundary in relation to what are currently defined as related companies is well overdue. The alternative aggregative data provide a workable solution. Overall its features remove most of the causes for the creative accounting in consolidations and the opportunity it affords for group manipulations as illustrated in the vignettes in chapters 5 and 7.

## Appendix: improved corporate group accountability

The commonly declared overall objective of conventional consolidation accounting is to provide greater insight into the wealth and progress of related entities than that provided by their investment cost at the date of acquisition. We have contested that conventional consolidated data can achieve the objectives attributed to them: show an aggregative financial position of the related entities, assess their overall solvency, determine their potential cash flows, or otherwise evaluate their overall or individual performances. We have suggested that were there to be a professional and legislative rethink of how to effect the capital boundary in relation to what are currently defined as related companies, Chambers' alternative presentation of the aggregative data provides a workable solution. The overall effect of the features of his CoCoA is to remove most of the causes for the creative accounting that we have identified elsewhere. His system is now illustrated by example.

Imagine statements of financial position drawn up along those lines (see table 9.1). Suppose that H Ltd has a 75 per cent interest in A Ltd and a 60 per cent interest in B Ltd, while A Ltd has a 20 per cent interest in B Ltd.

Not only do the data tell it how it is, as can best be determined at the time, they also do so in terms that draw on the common and established understanding of financial matters outside of accounting. In that setting, accounting can be a financial instrument that effectively meets the reasonable functions accorded to it. It will assist in improving the governance mechanisms related to the corporation.

**Table 9.1:** Hypothetical statements of financial position of H Ltd, A Ltd, and B Ltd, as at 30 June 2009

|  | H Ltd | A Ltd | B Ltd |
|---|---|---|---|
|  | $000 | $000 | $000 |
| Non-current assets | 251.00 | 157.20 | 310.00 |
| Inventories | 34.00 | 16.00 | 56.00 |
| Debtors | 26.80 | 28.00 | 31.00 |
| Cash | 15.00 | 15.00 | 14.00 |
| Investments: |  |  | 15.00 |
| Shares in A Ltd* | 177.75 |  |  |
| Shares in B Ltd* | 218.40 | 72.80 |  |
|  | 722.95 | 289.00 | 426.00 |
| Less liabilities | 35.00 | 52.00 | 62.00 |
|  | 687.95 | 237.00 | 364.00 |
| Less capital maintenance reserve | 163.95 | 72.00 | 48.00 |
|  | 524.00 | 165.00 | 316.00 |
| Less paid-up capital | 500.00 | 100.00 | 300.00 |
| Retained profits | 24.00 | 65.00 | 16.00 |

*Note:* \*The proportionate current money's worth of the underlying net assets valued at their current cash equivalents.

H Ltd's statement of financial position and the statistical annexure to which Chambers referred could appear as in table 9.2.

Comparing a conventional consolidated accounting financial statement with the H Ltd statement of financial position in Table 9.1, the accompanying statistical annexure and inter-entity indebtedness (cross-claims) matrix highlights several features of each:

1) With the proposed mode of reporting, the fictitious notion of a group entity, with rights and obligations similar to those attending incorporated bodies, is dispensed with; the group notion is unnecessary for disclosing the financial affairs of the related entities either separately or collectively.

2) The traditional 'elimination rule' has the equal potential to understate and overstate the current monetary worth of assets traded between related entities. For example, the application of the elimination rule in the circumstances posited would have moved the amount stated in the consolidated statement of financial position for non-current assets further away from their worth at (say) 30 June 2009 than would have been the case had the rule not been applied – were the selling price of the assets (say) $241,000,

**Table 9.2:** H Ltd statement of financial position

| H Ltd & Subsidiaries financial position | | | | Statistical summary | |
|---|---|---|---|---|---|
| | $000 | $000 | | $000 | $000 |
| Paid-up capital | 500.00 | | | 400.00 | |
| Capital maintenance reserve | 163.95 | 663.95 | | 120.00 | 520.00 |
| Retained profits | | 24.00 | | 81.00 | |
| Total residual equity | | 687.95 | H Ltd | 396.15 | |
| | | | Other | 204.85 | 601.00 |
| Debentures | | | | | 30.00 |
| Trade creditors | | 35.00 | | | 54.00 |
| Provision for dividends | | | | | 30.00 |
| | | 722.95 | | | 715.00 |
| Non-current assets | | 251.00[a] | | | 467.20 |
| Inventories | | 34.00[a] | | | 72.00[a] |
| Debtors | | 26.80 | | | 59.00[b] |
| Investments | | | | | 15.00 |
| Shares in A Ltd | | 177.75 | | | |
| Shares in B Ltd* | | 218.40 | | | 72.80[c] |
| Cash | | 15.00 | | | 29.00 |
| | | 722.95 | | | 715.00 |

*Notes:* [a] Purchased internally – non-current assets – profit net $9000; inventories – aggregate profit $6500.
[b] See figure 9.2 for a sample inter-entity indebtedness matrix (for Hooker Corporation).
[c] Held by another controlled entity, A Ltd.

the net $9000 eliminated from the H Ltd non-current assets (ex A Ltd) if left would have recorded the assets at $241,000, still short of their current worth, but in the right direction. At the same time, the elimination of the depreciation on those traded assets would have overstated the reported group profit. The tax effect adjustment would understate the tax expense and overstate the profit. The same is true regarding some of the amounts emerging from the trading in short-term inventories. The elimination of (say) $6500 unrealised profit would have reduced the inventory to $76,100, well short of its current worth of $106,000. In respect to other amounts, the movement would not have been sufficiently in the correct direction. Stating assets at approximations of their current selling prices avoids those anomalies. The elimination rule is unnecessary. It matters little under the proposed system whether the transactions are sham – not at so-called 'arm's length'. Ultimately it matters little at what price goods and services are traded between the related enterprises, whether it is equal to, above or below the prices otherwise prevailing in the market. It does not matter from whom or when the physical assets are purchased. At least no later than reporting date, each of the physical assets would be restated at the evidenced prevailing market prices as verified by the auditors. It is worth noting that this is a task that the auditors are required to do for many assets at present and possibly even more so in the future, pursuant to conventional accounting (with impairment) and other legislative strictures; clearly much more so than when Chambers first proposed his system in principle.

3) Under the proposed method, the amounts stated in the H Ltd statement for the investments held in A Ltd and B Ltd correspond with the proportionate share of the market worth of the underlying net assets of the companies in which the shares are held.

4) Investments in listed and unlisted companies would be stated on the same monetary basis. The expectations of the market embodied in share prices would be disclosed in a manner facilitating a comparison with the current financial state of the relevant company.

5) The 'outside equity interest' of minority shareholders in the subsidiaries is stated on the same basis, as is that of the parent company. It is not necessary to resort to the conventional consolidation rhetoric that the interests of the outside shareholders are supplementary data prepared from the group point of view, and that the amount of the minority interest is a balancing item. The usual arguments as to whether all or only the 'group share' of 'unrealised profits and losses on intra-group transactions' should be eliminated – 'whether the outside equity interest in unrealised profits and losses is earned or incurred' is completely avoided.

6) The proposed method automatically takes into account the 20 per cent interest of A Ltd in B Ltd, without resort to calculating 'indirect outside equity interests', as would be necessary in preparing the consolidated statement.

7) Were it desired, the data for all the related entities, or for collections of them, can be aggregated or otherwise arranged in whatever format is desired with complete mathematical propriety, for all the data are indicative of contemporary amounts of actual cash or its equivalent.

8) The parent company's statement of financial position continuously presents contemporary representation of the worth of the investments in the controlled entities. No additional statement is necessary. The statistical summary of the assets and liabilities of the subsidiaries is required only for the purposes of providing information of the nature, composition and current worth of their separate companies' assets and liabilities. In Australia, many of the companies deemed as 'large' would also be required to prepare separate accounts and have them audited.

9) The proposed statistical summary of assets and equities has the potential to provide more information regarding the individual subsidiaries and other controlled entities than consolidated financial statements, by virtue of its capacity to be arranged to present data about the controlled entities' separate assets and liabilities, or to provide aggregates and sub-aggregates as required. It is to be noted that controlled entities' investments in other entities would be accounted for on the same basis as their parent company has accounted for its investment in them.

10) Aggregate and net inter-company (entity) indebtedness are disclosed; as are the gross and net amounts owed to and by the related companies through the products of the supporting inter-company debt matrix. Such an N × N matrix would show the amounts owed to and by the related companies to one another and by the related companies to unrelated entities. Whereas the related companies' indebtedness will net out, it would be possible to identify to whom each is indebted (essential to determine their respective solvencies), the capacity of each related company to off-set mutual indebtedness with another related company, and the total indebtedness of each to both related and unrelated companies. Computer spreadsheet mechanisms make this a relatively easy task. It has been suggested to us that the matrix would become unduly messy where the number of subsidiaries is large. For example, consider News Corporation with its hundreds of subsidiaries. There the number of inter-company claims and cross-claims would be extensive. But knowledge of those claims and the need to 'eliminate' them is already required as part of conventional consolidated accounting techniques. Under our alternative, all that is being proposed is a listing of those claims via a formal spreadsheet, thereby enabling those legally binding claims and cross-claims to become *transparent* rather than be eliminated, as at present.

11) With corporate liquidations, administrators already need to prepare schedules of cross-claims and others within and outside the group when preparing a statement of affairs. This has been demonstrated in Houghton *et al.*'s (1999) analysis of one of Australia's largest administrations, involving the Hooker Corporation. The type of matrix proposed is illustrated in figure 9.2, drawing on Houghton *et al.*'s Hooker liquidation data. Similar cross-claim data would apply in ongoing firms. A feature of the way the data are presented is the ease of identifying possible cash-flow implications of the inter-company external asset/liability positions of the companies in the group. Similarly, N × N matrices could be prepared for other intra-group elements such as sales, expenses, profits and dividends.

12) Also, with today's technology there would be minimal trouble in having these inter-company receivables and payables updated and reported continuously to interested parties if necessary. These matrix data could even

| Lending Company | Borrowing Company | | | | | | | | ⋯ | | | Internal assets | External assets |
|---|---|---|---|---|---|---|---|---|---|---|---|---|---|
| | 1 | 2 | 3 | 4 | 5 | 6 | 7 | 8 | ⋯ | 26 | 27 | | |
| 1 | | 24,631,496 | 2,787,954 | | | | | 7,328,032 | ⋯ | 1,916,048 | | 109,879,061 | 76,337,335 |
| 2 | | | 75,321 | 336,704 | | | 311,857 | 350,017 | ⋯ | | 719,440 | 2,609,164 | 25,523,512 |
| 3 | | | | | | | | | ⋯ | | | 0 | 834,262 |
| 4 | 1,886,487 | | | | | | | | ⋯ | | | 1,886,487 | 1,001,833 |
| 5 | 67,792,306 | 440,846 | | | | 6,937 | | | ⋯ | | | 68,240,089 | 22,103,584 |
| 6 | 6,434,972 | 32,092 | | | | | | | ⋯ | | | 6,467,064 | 1,019,142 |
| 7 | 3,433,477 | | | | | | | | ⋯ | | | 3,433,477 | 3,533,127 |
| 8 | | | | | | 6,249,135 | | | ⋯ | | | 6,249,135 | 270,403 |
| 9 | | | | | | | | | ⋯ | | | 0 | 25,319 |
| 10 | | | | | | | | | ⋯ | | | 0 | 6,597,296 |
| 11 | | | | | | | | | ⋯ | | | 0 | 3,345,032 |
| 12 | 2,343,810 | 282 | | | | | | 13,451,000 | ⋯ | | | 15,795,092 | 2,745,765 |
| 13 | | | | | | | | | ⋯ | | | 0 | 519,351 |
| 14 | | | | | | | | | ⋯ | | | 6,375 | 28,169,567 |
| 15 | | | | | | | | | ⋯ | | | 0 | |
| 16 | 93,207,497 | | | | | | | | ⋯ | | | 93,207,497 | 612,840 |
| 17 | | | | | | | | | ⋯ | | | 2,166 | 10,036,065 |
| 18 | | | | | | | | | ⋯ | | | 12,700,551 | 22,821,537 |
| 19 | | | | | | | | | ⋯ | | | 1,043,415 | 1,742,448 |
| 20 | 41,512,071 | | | | | | | | ⋯ | | | 43,365,571 | 38,815,223 |
| 21 | | | | | | | | | ⋯ | | | 0 | 2,387,578 |
| 22 | | | | | | | | | ⋯ | | | 0 | 1,290,313 |
| 23 | | | | | | | | | ⋯ | | | 0 | 1,928,129 |
| 24 | 6,806,813 | | | | | | | | ⋯ | | | 6,806,813 | 19,377,359 |
| 25 | | | | | | | | | ⋯ | | | 0 | 895,583 |
| 26 | | | | | | | | | ⋯ | | | 0 | 976,143 |
| 27 | 3,244,227 | | | | | | | | ⋯ | | | 3,244,227 | 7,690,076 |
| Internal Liabilities | 226,661,660 | 25,104,716 | 2,863,275 | 336,704 | 0 | 6,256,072 | 311,857 | 21,129,049 | ⋯ | 1,916,048 | 719,440 | 374,936,184 | 296,933,648 |
| External Liabilities | 1,644,061,448 | 35,231 | 6,438 | 12,246 | 57,552,323 | 762,969 | 468,067 | 35,195 | ⋯ | | 891,482 | | 1,983,623,992 |

**Figure 9.2:** Inter-entity indebtedness matrix – Hooker Corporation

*Source:* F. Clarke, G. Dean and E. Houghton, 'Revitalising group accounting: Improving accountability', *Australian Accounting Review*, November 2002, pp. 58–72 at 69.

be placed on a company's website and downloaded by those who require it. Indeed, one would presume that the data in this proposed matrix must already exist for auditors to be able to do their job properly and for directors to be able to attest in an informed way to the respective solvencies of their companies.

13) Market prices for listed investments would be the primary basis for statement of financial position reporting. But, either when listed or not listed, there would always be a reporting of the proportionate share of the investee's underlying net assets on the basis of their cash value or approximations to it as evidenced by their current selling prices. The proportionate share in the underlying net assets of the investee would be stated in parentheses immediately below the market price of the investment. Thus all intercorporate investments – irrespective of whether they bestowed a controlling interest – would be accounted for on the same basis, disclosing where applicable both the market price of the shares and the proportionate underlying net assets of the investee.

# 10
# 'Patching': Past, Present, Prospect

We should speak ... of the immorality of accounting; for it has been quirks of accounting that have provided many of the opportunities for the misdemeanours of ... corporate officers ...

Piecemeal patching will not make a worm-eaten craft seaworthy; neither will piecemeal *tinkerings* of individuals, boards and committees make cost-based valuations trustworthy.

(Chambers 1991, pp. 16, 17, 18, emphasis added)

## Past 'tinkering'

Past tinkering with financial disclosure has exacerbated the situation rather than alleviated it. Matters aggravating and promoting indecent disclosure were outlined in the Prologue. First, financial disclosure in accord with conventional accounting generally fails to disclose the wealth and progress of companies, and the recently promoted IFRSs will do little to remedy that. Second, the corporate governance regimes currently in place are misplaced, and do not offer remedies for the corporate ills evident in history and repeated in the recent past. Third, in many cases auditors' near impossible quality control task is not alleviated by either the prospect of compliance with the IFRSs or by the implementation of the general features of the corporate governance regimes. Fourth, it may be that the prevailing corporate structure needs modification to cope with, and be governable in, the modern business environment. Accordingly, an important theme here is that existing regulatory and governance initiatives, while having many virtues, are unlikely to mitigate the recurring features that emerge in the autopsies of many large, essentially unexpected, corporate failures.

Whereas most of those failures over many decades have entailed some devious behaviour, for the most part their accounting complied generally with the Standards. That was our primary message in *Corporate Collapse* (2003). Nothing has changed. At the margin there is likely to be deviation. This is especially so as foozles become frauds. In some instances, deviations from the approved practices made more sense and possibly produced better data than did compliance with the Standards. A reasonable analysis of consolidated data in accord with the Standards (chapter 9) easily reveals them to be grossly misleading, based upon false premises, to employ senseless procedures, and to induce analyses that contradict both company law and financial fact.

## Present 'tinkering'

Through questionable group activities within an overheated market, the anomalies in conventional accounting persist. Enron's collapse is generally taken as having been the catalyst for worldwide corporate reform. It and the numerous contiguous earning restatements in the US fuelled support for the introduction of the IFRSs, though curiously virtually everywhere than in the US. Enron's supposed manipulations of SPEs were shown to be substantially in accord with the approved practices. Of course some particularly feral practices were not. But the important issue is that even the compliant produced misleading data. Enron's mark-to-model method of recording periodic gains on energy contracts is apposite – having been approved by the SEC in the early 1990s – so it was basically a compliant practice.

Commentators have questioned whether what occurred at Enron, World-Com or at HIH was worthy of the attention it received or of the regulatory reforms that emerged. A good illustration of this is the response of critics to explanations that the 'outrage at the devastating corporate scandals that have periodically roiled corporate America, including the collapse of baker Jay Cooke in 1873 and of the Chicago utility magnate Samuel Insull in 1932 [and that this] has been the lightning rod for nearly all of our [US] most important corporate regulation'.[1] That 'American investors aren't concerned about their excessive exposure to risk-taking', since the 'financial markets regulate themselves in this regard by pricing risk', is unconvincing. But nevertheless, there needs to be a recognition that 'there are serious limitations to the corporate social responsibility reforms'.[2]

Monitoring and enforcement have been beefed-up everywhere. Generally that is positive. But, whereas many governance, accounting and auditing-related reforms are potentially improvements, much better monitoring and enforcement mechanisms are needed by the corporate cops – ASIC and APRA in Australia and (say) the SEC in the US. In particular, it is essential that financial disclosure 'tells it how it is', delivering data serviceable for showing a company's wealth and progress, and from which its critical financial characteristics can be derived. ASIC's avowed monitoring of independence rules of the Big 4 in Australia and its setting up special units to 'crack down on [accounting/auditing] industry rorts', are wishful thinking without financial disclosure indicating the actual state of companies' affairs. This crackdown has resulted in some major company liquidators being suspended for periods up to a year by the Companies Auditors and Liquidators Disciplinary Board; one for failing to 'disclose a relationship with the group that referred business', and another for 'miss[ing] many indications its finances were not flash'.[3]

But there is a general question over such actions. Regarding the efficacy of toughening up on relationships, we have our doubts. While any monitoring and enforcement actions ensuring auditors are keeping their eye on what is being reported about a company's finances are to be applauded, they serve little purpose if the criteria by which they evaluate the disclosures are disconnected from legal, and hence financial, reality.

Enron's crash and the subsequent scandals at WorldCom and (say) Fannie Mae were said to have roiled Wall Street, stiffened white-collar penalties and upped regulatory scrutiny over publicly traded companies. Many regard such actions as the required panacea to mitigate group scandals and accounting irregularities. Undeniably, gaol sentences have increased – for example, in the US Bernie Ebbers (25 years), Jeffrey Skilling (24 years, 4 months), Rigas (15 years), Dennis Kozlowski (8 years), Andy Fastow (6 years), Richard Causey (5.5 years), and Walter Forbes (12 years, 7 months); in Australia, Ray Williams (4.5 years of which 2.5 years were non-parole) and Rodney Adler (4.5 years with 2.5 years non-parole).[4] But at issue is whether this will prove to be an effective long-term solution in mitigating unexpected collapses.

Corporate regulation has taken a curious turn in which internal mechanisms have been introduced to effect external control. Although the regulatory structures at ASIC, APRA, the SEC and the like are geared to effect external control of corporate affairs – how they function, what they report, what documents they file and what is disclosed in them, etc. – it has been patched up from time to time in response to company crises. The last wave of crises appears to have convinced governments that this form of 'control' has failed. This has been the catalyst for governments to switch their focus to imposing internal control mechanisms for corporate affairs in the form of corporate governance regimes that attempt to impact the internal workings and structures to discourage wrongdoing. Ensuring the 'right' governance boxes can be ticked is the new *modus operandi* for the regulatory agencies.

That likely ineffective switch from external to internal governance fails to recognise the importance of fundamental matters related to financial disclosure. As well as structural and other disclosures there needs to be a rethink of the financial data disclosed by corporate entities, especially when aggregated as a group.

We are told that with globalisation and the likelihood of universal compliance with IFRSs, the disclosure problems of the past will be solved. There is said to be a strong desire to move away from the mixed accounting system, entailing a coupling of capitalisation of expenditures and value-based data, to an impairment system based primarily on 'fair values'. But it remains constrained by the conventional historic-cost thinking, like matching. Whether any substantial benefit emerges from such a move is questionable.

## Whither if the tinkering continues?

Surely the time for tinkering has gone. None of the expanded set of governance rules amount to much unless supported by a system of financial disclosure from which the financial consequences of whatever the directors or executives have done and however they have done it, can be determined. Ultimately the financial outcomes of those decisions and actions are the primary basis upon which companies' behaviour in relation to the public interest can be judged. Unless accounting produces a *true* and *fair* statement of financial performance and a *true* and *fair* statement of financial position, corporate regulation and governance generally proceed without direction from an independent system of checks and balances.

In chapter 9 the case for serviceable financial data for corporate groups and other entities is made. It is a case for data that are fit for the uses ordinarily made of them – for data that are serviceable for determining a company's wealth and progress, and for deriving its rate of return on equity and on total assets, for determining solvency, gearing, asset backing, the nature and monetary worth of each of its assets and the nature and amount of its liabilities. It pleads for a system of accounting in which the fiction of deferred tax debits and credits has no part; the judgment necessary for such NPV exercises as in the AIFRSs impairment regime are not part; where depreciation is properly taken to be the decrease in price (*de pretium*) of an asset and not the accountants' nonsensical 'allocation of cost'; where accruals are determined on the basis of the legal recovery of the amount accrued and not on the basis of anticipated future 'related' revenues; where money spent is acknowledged to have gone and is not reported as an asset, as being somehow still possessed; where the system recognises the legal separateness of individual companies, and in which related companies' aggregated data are arranged sensibly to provide the insight into the possible financial implications of the relatedness.

It is not so much the need for a principles-based, as for a *principle*-based accounting that is needed. A general overriding principle underpins this proposal that the data are *serviceable* in the uses ordinarily made of them. A *quality* standard to the effect that the data are *serviceable* in the manner outlined in chapters 6 and 9 meets the now much-contested call for principles-based accounting. That is achieved by a system in which all price and price level changes are brought to account, physical assets are stated at the prices for which they might be sold in the ordinary course of business, tax effect accounting is abandoned, expenditure capitalisation goes, conventional consolidated financial statements are abandoned and with them the unsupportable assumptions underpinning them, and liabilities are stated at their contractual amounts – that is, a system freed of accounting artifacts and the counterfactual.

Were such a system in place the auditor's quality control function becomes possible. And the prospect for recourse to judgment rather than a tick-a-box mentality enhanced.

## Deregulation, serviceability, professionalism

It is reasonable to have expected casual observation would have made it perfectly clear that the present patched-up framework has failed to achieve the overall quality of accounting data, let alone improve it. There isn't a defence of any regulatory framework of compulsory Accounting Standards unless they improve the serviceability of accounting information. In 2003 we wrote:

> One would pursue [more compulsory standards only] with the expectation that the more Standards, the less the complaint and criticism of accounting from consumers, the fewer the instances of creative accounting. We have more prescribed procedures now than at any time in our history, nationally and internationally. One would have thought that there would be evidence of a decline in the dissatisfaction with the data accountants are producing – evidence of less creative accounting. The opposite has occurred (nationally and internationally).

> Against that background it is most curious that ASIC continues its resolve to enforce compliance with the Accounting Standards now the AIFRSs. In 1997 the similar resolve of the (then) ASC was observed – the ASC was determined to 'enforce the rules and apply them strictly as worded', even, it seemed, if 'the ASC might say privately what you have to do does not make sense . . .'. Whether it makes sense, according to the ASC, 'is not the issue'.[5] To the contrary, it was the issue then, and is even more so now – post-HIH, post-One.Tel, post-Harris Scarfe, post-Enron, post-WorldCom, and the rest. Whereas nearly five years ago the ASC passed up the opportunity to be a public voice on consumer protection in respect to financial information, the ASIC now has the responsibility to do so. But, rather than acknowledge the inherent defects in the system, the ASIC has launched into a campaign to enforce compliance with the Accounting Standards. The present large *unexpected* failures have continued the flow of evidence that conventional accounting as it is enshrined in the Accounting Standards is inherently defective. That most of those Standards conform to the current IASs (and possible IFRSs)

suggests that they are equally defective. Thus, it looks as if financial nonsense will continue to be protected in the safe harbour of the Accounting Standards as we move into the new IFRS regime.[6]

Four years after that was written we now have other anomalous cases with allegedly similar features, like Fannie Mae in the US, Parmalat in Italy, and in Australia, Westpoint and Fincorp.

Earlier reference was made to the element of surprise. The unexpectedness of the collapses when those bubbles burst was because the companies' financial disclosures failed to show their trajectory towards failure, and lies more in accounting failure than in audit failure through negligence.

The primary themes of our proposed remedies are that:

- Additional layers of regulation are unnecessary – in any event they will have little impact if the present financial reporting framework continues.
- A clean audit report ought to mean that the financials truly reflect the financial performance and financial position of a company – in terms of a common-sense everyday understanding of those phrases. Currently they do not. Absent of fraud, they are to be read merely as showing that the Accounting Standards have been complied with.
- Complying with the Accounting Standards ought to result in the wealth and progress of a company being shown in the financials. Typically under the present financial reporting regime they are not.
- A clean audit report ought to indicate that the audited data can be used to determine reliably the salient financial characteristics of a company – rate of return, earnings per share, interest times cover, solvency, debt to equity, asset backing, and the like. Typically it does not. Currently, it is not a warrant of quality.
- None of the proposed remedies for the current state of play will improve the quality and serviceability of the data in published financial statements as none address that issue. Indeed, none appear to recognise it.
- Our proposal is a relatively simple approach to implement.
- Were a comprehensive mark-to-market accounting system to be instituted and the true and fair criterion reinstated in practitioners' minds to pre-1992 override status, auditors would potentially have recourse to externally generated, publicly transparent evidence; financial statements would contain data (absent of material fraud) that are fit, *serviceable*, for the uses ordinarily made of them to assess and evaluate the financial state of companies; and, likely as not, most of the mechanisms being proposed to improve the quality of auditing would not be required.
- Contrary to what is implied in many commentaries, it is not failures *per se* that are critical but rather the *unexpected nature* of them. That *unexpectedness* is a

problem relating to what is to be gleaned prior to failure, from the financial data relating to the company's performance and position.

- Quite rightly, independence has been in focus in many commentaries on the current state of play. But, in both its historical and contemporary settings, *auditor independence* properly refers to an auditor having an independent mental attitude when forming his opinion on the *truth and fairness* of the financial representations in the Statement of Financial Performance and the Statement of Financial Position.

- Thus, the notion of independence that has occupied so many in the wake of Bond Corp, Adsteam and HIH, and fuelled by the Parmalat, Enron and WorldCom affairs, has diverted attention from the main problem: that the current system of accounting produces data without recourse to corroborative externally generated evidence (as required everywhere else when the truth of matters is sought). That is, evidence is not sourced outside of that provided by those preparing a reporting entity's financials. The current situation facilitates both accidental misstatement and deliberate financial finagling.

- Data prepared in compliance with the current package of AIFRSs are not conducive to representing a company's financial performance, its financial position or crucial assessments of solvency and firm flexibility in a way remotely consistent with the understanding of those terms in every other setting in which financial calculation and assessment is made.

- As long as the true and fair criterion is deemed subservient to compliance with the Accounting Standards, and deemed to be satisfied by that compliance, the general run of companies' financial statements will be misleading, and the data therein will not be serviceable in the assessments and evaluations ordinarily made with them. Auditors' opinions will not be the product of an independent state of mind and their reports will continue to be largely irrelevant to an assessment of the wealth and progress of companies.[7]

Normative tones are unpopular in analytical work. But the indecent disclosures we have examined here justify an appeal that companies' financials be drafted to 'tell it as it is'. There is need to consider the above to redress the incidence of misleading accounting, accounting facilitating 'commerce without conscience'. For accounting that is misleading without any intent to mislead nurtures collapses equally unexpectedly as accounting deviously crafted to do so. Equally unsettling are the concomitant loss of confidence in the market system, individual losses, and the repeated public bemoaning of the lack of professional ethos by accountants and other business professionals, such as lawyers and valuers.

What is described above is totally consistent with the recommendation of Australia's *CLERP 1*, that conventional historical cost-based accounting be replaced by market value (or what we have called mark-to-market) accounting whereby physical assets are reported at their market selling prices and liabilities

217

at their settlement prices. It draws upon what the 1978 NSW ASRC recommended, without rebuttal from the profession for nearly thirty years. It would provide a more systematic use of market price data than is currently embedded in the mixed cost and other data in listed company's financials (as evident in figure 4.1). The agglomeration of such mixed financial measures produces meaningless aggregates. Any ratio analyses derived from such figures are contestable.

And it is consistent with IFRS moves to have 'fair values' in accounts.

It is reasonable to expect that where the legislatively and professionally endorsed practices are employed, deliberate intent to mislead would be necessary were the financial data presented to the public at large to be misleading. Incongruously, as it is, intent to mislead is unnecessary. Assiduous compliance with the compulsory standards is almost certain to produce most misleading financials. Figure 4.1 illustrates that. The imperative to do something different to mitigate the continuation of indecent disclosures is a major conclusion of our analysis. Time is of the essence as the latest round of private equity buy-out financings in Australia and elsewhere may portend the next merger movement – and ultimately the next round of *unexpected* corporate collapses.[8]

We have considered (especially in chapters 1 to 6) the likely ineffectiveness of current reforms – governmental responses such as Australia's *CLERP 9*, the US *SOX*, Australia's 2001 Ramsay Report, Australia's JCPAA *Report 391* and the federal government's 2006 Independence Review follow-up, as well as new initiatives by government oversight bodies like the US PCAOB, the Canadian Public Accountability Board and self-regulatory reforms like Australia's AQRB audit oversight body. And also, the international accounting and auditing responses – such as the increasing recourse (post-2005) to the IFRSs and the IFAC-endorsed ISA auditing series. These are claimed to have developed measures to mitigate the increasing accounting and auditing difficulties due to the complexity inherent in today's corporate business and financing activities.[9]

However, the latest response of the large accounting firms is still not on point. The vision of the CEOs of the 'international audit networks' in their November 2006 *Global Capital Markets and the Global Economy* (PwC *et al.*) appears as unfocused as ever. Their push is for improved financial reporting. But the XBRL (eXtensible Business Reporting Language) means advocated are more attuned to achieving speed and detail (especially of 'intangibles') than to improving the serviceability of the reported data.

Our assessment (in chapters 4, 5 and elsewhere here) is that most changes made or contemplated relate generally to inputs and processes – to structural issues – rather than to ensuring that the quality of the audit opinion as a quality control device is improved. This story is that all of those reforms are wide of the mark. They fail to address the fundamental problem – *indecent disclosure*. Accounting is the devil of auditing and users of financial statements. Until that is recognised and appropriate reforms developed to address it the history that we have outlined will continue to harbour lessons that are there to be learned, but that are habitually ignored – and we will be doomed to a repeat of that history.

The 1970s Accounting Standards Review Committee (chapter 6) was an opportunity lost. If another comes along, it should be embraced with both hands clapping!

# Notes

Prologue: gilding the corporate lily

1 Unless otherwise stated the context is generally Australian. But, as the accounting and auditing issues are similar in most countries, the criticisms and reforms noted have universal application.

2 As this book goes to press 24 Enron officers have been prosecuted and convicted. Fastow was keen to implicate others, 'fingering' some of the leading banks as being also major culprits in the Enron affair – see Robert Guy, 'Enron exec points finger at banks', *Australian Financial Review*, 28 September 2006, p. 12.

3 S. Jacoby, review of D. Skeel's *Icarus in the Boardroom: The fundamental flaws in corporate America and where they came from* (Oxford: Oxford University Press, 2004), in *Business History Review* (2005, No. 3).

4 See AAP item, '64 face charges as Parmalat case starts', *Australian Financial Review*, 7 June 2006, p. 66. Coincidentally, the circumstances of Calvi's supposed suicide (he was found dead hanging from scaffolding under London's Blackfriars Bridge, with rocks attached to his legs, and with his pockets stuffed with thousands of pounds in cash) are being re-examined in a trial of five persons charged with having murdered him – see *BBC News* as reported BBC News, 18 May 2004; on the web at: <http://news.bbc.co.uk/go/pr/fr/-/1/hi/world/europe/3732485.stm> (downloaded 25 August 2006); and 'Calvi murder trial opens in Rome', *BBC News* as reported BBC News, 06 October, 2005; on the web at: <http://news.bbc.co.uk/2/hi/europe/4313960.stm> (downloaded 20 September 2006). An original inquest of Calvi's death had returned a suicide verdict. See also Raw, *The Money Changers* (1992).

5 T. Lee, 'Clarity comes too late for Cole's liking', *Australian Financial Review*, 29 September 2006, p. 4 and 'AWB's $US8m to be sanitised, deductible', *Australian Financial Review*, 28 September 2006, p. 5. The Cole Report was released in late November 2006, recommending that actions be taken *inter alia* in respect of tax offences, money laundering, terrorist financing, and breaches of the Corporations Law. The allegations of the trucking fees being bribes were not supported. These previously undisclosed matters epitomise the difficulties that persist in Australia's so-called *continuous*, but what still amounts to *indecent* disclosure system. Corporate governance issues were clearly to the fore in the AWB affair.

6 *The Bell Group Limited (In Liquidation) & Ors v Westpac Banking Corporation & Ors* Supreme Court of Western Australia Action No. CIV 1464 of 2000.

7 M. Jacobs, 'Bell fight goes down to the wire as case winds up', *Australian Financial Review*, 19 September 2006, p. 9.

8 Clarke *et al.*, *Corporate Collapse* (2003, especially pp. 248–55), provide details of many other long-running complex Australian corporate cases over the last three decades, including Rothwells, Estate Mortgage, Minsec, Cambridge Credit, Adsteam, HIH.

9  See Dean *et al.*, 'Cross guarantees and the negative pledges: A preliminary analysis' (1995).

10  Anon, *The Advocate*, Connecticut News, 20 September 2006; and anon, 'US Grand Jury indicts former General Re executive', Reuters News, 21 September 2006. This is discussed in B. Masters, *Spoiling for a Fight: The Rise of Eliot Spitzer* (2006) and in M. Gordon, 'SEC sanctions Ernst & Young', *Australian Associated Press*, 27 March 2007.

11  WebCPA staff, 'IRS reaches historic settlement with Glaxo SmithKline', *WebCPA*, 13 September 2006; accessed at <http://wwwwebcpa.com/article.cfn?articleid+ 21816&pg+newsarticles&print+yes>; accessed on 14 September 2006. Also: 'Merck Tax settlement carries $2.3B + ab', *WebCPA*, 15 February 2007.

12  E. Kazi, 'Havens not all bad, says D'Ascenzo', *Australian Financial Review*, 27 September 2006, p. 5. For further taxation issues with groups, especially multinationals, refer to E. Kazi, 'Eye on transfer pricing has directors on their toes', *Australian Financial Review*, 11 September 2006, p. 9.

13  E. Johnston, 'Disclosure proves toughest challenge for insurers', *Australian Financial Review*, 31 July 2006, p. 53.

14  D. Kitney and F. Buffini, 'ASIC offers reprieve on tough reporting rules', *Australian Financial Review*, 7 August 2006, pp. 1 and 11.

15  Consider the following: 'The 24 major European banks analysed ... [exhibit] a wide range of impact by adopting the new rules. . . . Groupe Banques Populaire recorded a gain in the value of the equity on its balance sheet of 22% ... under the same rules Barclays ... an effective decline of 12% . . .. Tony Clifford, partner and IFRS banking specialist at Ernst & Young, says that the introduction of IFRS in 2005 has had the single biggest impact in a generation on the balance sheets of Europe's major banks. . . . [attributing] the complexity of the standards and the consequent volatility in reporting has led to much hair pulling by the banks, regulators, analysts and investment community.' AIA *Accountancy E-News*, 27 October 2006. See also 'Outlook 2007' in BNA Accounting *Policy and Practices Report*, 7 February 2007, which noted: 'A tightening web of complexity in the financial reporting process could ensnare accounting and auditing practitioners'.

16  Clarke *et al.*, *Corporate Collapse* (2003). See also articles in the Special Issue of *Abacus*, Vol. 42.3/4, September/December 2006; and R. Walker, 'Reporting entity concept: a case study of the failure of principles-based regulation' (2007).

17  Benston et al., *Worldwide Financial Reporting* (2006).

18  A special issue of *Abacus*, Vol. 39, No. 3, October 2003 contains several articles that discuss the positive and negative aspects of those national conceptual framework exercises. The current authors were amongst several expressing their views.

19  In an earlier unpublished work, IIR Corporate Governance seminar, October (2002) F. Clarke and G. Dean noted that the word 'governance' is taken arguably from the Greek *cybernetics* (or Latin *gubenatore*) which refers to the ability of the navigator effectively to steer a vessel – a skill that required information about the vessel's current position, the speed it is travelling, sea currents, other vessels' positions, land etc. Information needed was spatial and required continual updating. This was again discussed in Clarke and Dean, 'Corporate governance: A case of misplaced concreteness?' (2005a). Walker and Walker, *Privatisation – Sell Off or Sell Out?* (2000), similarly note that governance has its roots in Greek, where the relevant word can mean 'manage', 'oversee', 'direct' or lead'.

20 For details of the way the use of the corporate veil affected employees' entitlements see Dean *et al.*, 'Corporate restructuring, creditors' rights, cross guarantees and group behaviour' (1999).

21 E. Sexton, 'Nothing to stop another Hardie', *Sydney Morning Herald*, 7 August 2006, pp. 17–18. See also *ASIC Media Release 07–35* 'ASIC commences [civil] proceedings relating to James Hardie', 14 February 2007.

22 Green and Moss, *A Business of National Importance: The Royal Mail Shipping Group, 1902–1937* (1982; especially pp. 141–2), support this claim, noting that the defence 'case made much of the auditor's use of the phrase "after adjustment of taxations reserves" to describe the fortification of the 1926 and 1927 accounts. They were also able to plead that, rightly or wrongly, the secret transfer of inner reserves was a fact of life in large conglomerate companies, particularly in the shipping industry where transfers were an accepted method of ironing out the effects of the business cycle. In this the evidence of Lord Plender was especially persuasive. As a result Kylsant and Morland were cleared of the balance sheet charges.' Notably the complexity of the structure is captured by Green and Moss's reference to the Royal Mail being a conglomerate.

23 Chatov, *Corporate Financial Reporting* (1975). See also David Radler's SEC plea bargain in return for being a witness against Conrad Black (*Australian Financial Review*, 19 March 2007, p.11).

24 Anon, 'Is Jack Grubman the worst analyst ever?', *CNN Money*, 25 April 2002.

25 See AAA Financial Accounting Standards Committee (AAAFASC), 'Evaluating concept-based vs rules-based approaches to standard setting' (2003); K. Schipper, 'Principles-based accounting standards' (2003).

26 This point was demonstrated throughout, using case particulars, in Clarke *et al.*, *Corporate Collapse* (1997 and 2003).

27 D. Catterchina, 'KPMG to be sued for 2 billion by Fannie Mae in the US', *Business Week com*, 12 December 2006; accessed at <<http://www.businessweek.com/ap/financialnews/D8LVJBL00.htm>> on 15 December 2006. Earlier details of the concerns were raised in the Office of Federal Housing Enterprise Oversight, *Report of the Special Examination of Fannie Mae* (Washington: US Government Printer, May 2006).

## 1 Indecent disclosure: omitted factor in unexpected failure?

1 Given it was only five years into the twentieth century, it is most likely Lawson was referring to events during the nineteenth century.

2 Detailed discussion and copious references of such practices are given in Clarke *et al.*, *Corporate Collapse* (2003), especially chapter 2. These include: I. Kellogg and L. B. Kellogg, *Fraud, Window Dressing and Negligence in Financial Statements* (New York: McGraw-Hill, 1991), K. Naser, *Creative Financial Accounting* (London: Prentice Hall International, 1993), H. Schilit, *Financial Shenanigans: How to detect accounting gimmicks and fraud in financial reports* (New York: McGraw-Hill, 1993; 2nd edn, 2002), D. McBarnet and C. Whelan, *Creative Accounting and the Cross-Eyed Javelin Thrower* (Chichester: Wiley, 1999).

3 WorldCom would emerge from bankruptcy in 2004 under the name of MCI, later to be taken over by Verizon Communications after a $US8.44 billion acquisition of the long-distance carrier in early 2006.

4 Lawson, *Frenzied Finance – The Crime of Amalgamated*, p. vii.

5 Arnold, *Folklore of Capitalism* (1937), p.193 (emphasis added).

6 Brooks, *The Royal Mail Case* (1933), p. xv.

7 Clarke *et al.*, *Corporate Collapse* (2003, pp. 248–55).

8 The essence of that chapter is reproduced here as chapter 9 – albeit updated for more recent events, many of which are detailed in chapters 7 and 8. Some recognition of the difficulties in the task of auditing corporate monoliths is recognised in the November 2006 reforms proposed by representatives of a group of major audit firms and regulatory bodies at a Paris Conference. They include the suggestion that auditors should undertake random forensic audits. More on this in chapter 5 below.

9 The 'mission impossible' tag was introduced by the authors in Clarke *et al.*, *Corporate Collapse* (2003). Used as hyperbole it appears to be not too far from the actuality in some cases.

10 Cassidy's prescient *Dot.con: The greatest story ever told* (2002) was just one of many that identified concerns that all was not well. But lamentably, the reported financials of those dot.coms generally suggested otherwise.

11 See annual reports on accounting irregularities and restatements, GAO, *Financial Statement Restatements: Trends, Market Impacts, Regulatory Responses, and Remaining Challenges* (Washington, D. C.: GAO-03-138, 2003, 2004).

12 A brief discussion of Hudson's activities is given in Lee, Clarke, and Dean, 'The dominant senior manager and the reasonably careful, skilful, and cautious auditor' (2007 – forthcoming); S. McCartney and A. J. Arnold, 'George Hudson's financial reporting practices: Putting the Eastern Counties Railway in context', *Accounting, Business and Financial History* 2000; 10 (3) pp. 293–316 and in Valance, *A Very Private Enterprise* (1955).

13 Stoneman, 'The matchless career of Ivar Kreuger – the match king', in *World of Business* (1962) pp. 934–8 and Stoneman, *The Life and Death of Ivar Kreuger* (1932, 1960). See also Flesher and Flesher, 'Ivar Kreuger's contribution to US financial reporting', *The Accounting Review*, July 1986, pp. 421–33 and Shaplen, *Kreuger: Genius and Swindler* (1961; repr. 1990).

14 This analogy is well made in Skeel's *Icarus in the Boardroom* (2004).

15 More examples are given in Clarke *et al.*, *Corporate Collapse* (2003, especially chapter 1).

16 Table 4.1 shows the relative 'losses' for some major failures.

17 This aspect has been the focus of two forums in the accounting journal *Abacus*, September 2003 and June 2006. They straddled the year 2005, when supposedly all would change, company financial reporting data would be greatly improved and would become more comparable as IFRSs became mandatory in many countries from that point onwards (see IASB website for details <www.iasb.org>). Also, several articles in the joint April/May 2006 issue *of Journal of Business, Finance and Accounting* provide evidence to contradict the supposed benefits of adopting IFRSs. Chapter 4 also contains more discussion.

18 See Fabricant, *Capital Consumption and Adjustment* (1936) and Walker, 'The SEC's ban on upward asset revaluations and the disclosure of current values' (1992a).

19 Clarke *et al.*, *Corporate Collapse* (2003).

20 Clarke *et al.*, *Corporate Collapse* (1997), especially chapters 11, 16 and 17.

21 There are many accounts of the Enron failure, including: Fusaro and Miller, *What Went Wrong at Enron?* (2002), Fox, *Enron: The rise and fall* (2003) and (say) Cunningham and Harris, 'Case of the crooked E and the fallen A' (2006). See also the SEC website (<www.sec.gov>) containing details of criminal and civil actions as well as official inquiries and reports on the Enron affair.

22 The issues at Waste Management (the world's largest waste services company) were complex – as outlined in the SEC Complaint, SEC Release No. 1532, 'Waste Management, Inc. founder and five other former top officers sued for massive earnings management fraud' – *Securities and Exchange Commission v. Dean L. Buntrock, Phillip B. Rooney, James E. Koenig, Thomas C. Hau, Herbert A. Getz, and Bruce D. Tobecksen*, Civil Action No. 02 C 2180 (Judge Manning) (ND Ill. 26 March 2002): 'The Securities and Exchange Commission ("Commission") today filed a Complaint charging the founder and five other former top officers of Waste Management, Inc. ("Waste Management" or "Company") with perpetrating a massive financial fraud lasting more than five years. The Commission alleged that, beginning in 1992 and continuing into 1997, defendants engaged in a systematic scheme to falsify and misrepresent Waste Management's financial results and thereby enrich themselves and keep their jobs. The scheme was orchestrated and implemented by Waste Management's most senior officers.'

23 Clarke and Dean, 'Corporate governance: A case of misplaced concreteness?' (2005a).

24 S. Hamilton, 'Tell the truth about CEO pay: Reported salary totals do not reveal all', *Sydney Morning Herald*, 13 November 2006, p. 23.

25 Hawkins, *Corporate Financial Reporting* (1962).

26 Chambers, *Accounting, Evaluation and Economic Behavior* (1966), and Chambers, *Securities and Obscurities: A case for reform of the law of company accounts* (1973b). Others were Sterling, *Theory of The Measurement of Enterprise Income* (1970), and Briloff, *Unaccountable Accounting* (1972). Indeed, possibly up to the early 1970s only Kenneth MacNeal in his plea for *Truth in Accounting* (1939) had hit out strongly against the accounting status quo. And he had brought the might of his profession down upon him – as did Briloff many years later.

27 The evidence of such a state is provided in our other works (Clarke *et al.*, *Corporate Collapse*, 1997, 2003) and is summarised in chapters 4, 5 and 6 below. Our suggested reforms appear in the last two chapters.

28 For the history of this in Australia see Walker, 'Reporting entity concept: A case study of the failure of principles-based regulation' (2007). Observations on the current state of play appear in D. Boymal, Pacioli Society talk reproduced in 'Notes to the Pacioli Society', *Abacus*, March 2007, pp. 107–10.

29 That proposal has many contentious areas – such as reference to 'Statements of Financial Position and Performance', rather than the more conventional, 'Balance Sheet and Profit and Loss Account', a matter that will be explored later when we examine conceptual framework issues in chapter 4. Walker 'Reporting entity concept: a case study of the failure of principles-based regulation' (2007) (appendix) provides a list of different types of entities to which the requirement to produce general purpose reports applies.

30 As reported in F. Buffini, 'Public row over private reporting rules', *Australian Financial Review*, 19 July 2006, p. 25.

31 This was discussed in a letter to the *Australian Financial Review* by K. Alfredson, 'Revolt against new accounting rules', *Australian Financial Review*, 21 July 2006, p. 79; see also his later response to several letters on this issue, letter, 'Accounting concerns still arise on IFRSs', *Australian Financial Review*, 7 August 2006, p. 52.

32 G. Brayshaw, 'No need to account for differences', letter to *Australian Financial Review*, 25 July 2006, p. 57. Interestingly, at the August 2006 meeting of the Sydney University Pacioli Society, leading accountants David Boymal and Bob Walker added other aspects to the differential reporting debate (see Notes to the Sydney University Pacioli Society, 2007).

33 W. Lonergan, letter to *Australian Financial Review*, 'Rules must weigh cost with reporting', *Australian Financial Review*, 22–23 July 2006, p. 62.

34 Editorial, 'Governance can be overdone', *Australian Financial Review*, 22–23 July 2006, p. 62. This was reiterated several weeks later in the same newspaper: and again in US articles; 'Group to examine impact of new [*SOX*] rules', *Business Week Online*, 12 September 2006, and in Robert Guy, 'Benefits seen in easing Sarbanes-Oxley', *Australian Financial Review*, 14 September 2006, p. 13. The latter noted: 'A loosening of some of the [*SOX*] requirements would be a welcome relief for many Australian companies that have endured significantly higher compliance costs since Sarbanes-Oxley was implemented'.

35 Anon, 'Group to examine impact of new [*SOX*] rules', *Business Week Online*, 12 September 2006. Details of US de-listings are given in Foley and Lardner, as reported in I. Ramsay, 'Private equity deals to trigger more de-listings', *Australian Financial Review*, 24 November 2006, p. 83.

36 F. Buffini, 'Local companies not prone to delisting', *Australian Financial Review*, 22 November 2006, p. 16; and I. Ramsay, 'Private equity deals to trigger more de-listings', *Australian Financial Review*, 24 November 2006, p. 83.

37 Editorial, 'Governance can be overdone', *Australian Financial Review*, 22–23 July 2006, p. 62.

38 What follows draws, *inter alia*, on Gower's *Principles of Modern Company Law* (1979) chapters 1 and 2, Ford and Austin, *Principles of Corporations Law* (2006, chapter 2), Hunt, *The Development of the Business Corporation in England, 1800–1867* (1936), Bakan's *The Corporation: The pathological pursuit of power* (2004), chapter 1, Berle and Means' *The Modern Corporation and Private Property* (1932).

39 Evidence of this is provided in W. R. Scott's *magnum opus*, *The Constitution and Finance of English, Scottish and Irish Joint-Stock Companies to 1720* (Gloucester, Mass.: Peter Smith, 1968).

40 L. C. B. Gower, *Principles of Modern Company Law* (see for example, 4th edition, 1979).

41 See accounts by J. Carswell, *The South Sea Bubble* (London: Cresset Press, 1961), L. C. B. Gower *Principles of Modern Company Law* (1979) and (say) Bakan, *The Corporation* (2004), especially chapter 1.

42 The unexpected nature is well described in Clarke and Dean, 'An evolving conceptual framework?' (2003). In essence it refers to the fact that the market had not been privy to the drift in the financial affairs leading to an entity's collapse. As a consequence proper risk/return assessments were not properly informed.

43 Gower, *Principles of Modern Company Law* (1979).

44 See ibid., chapter 1.

45  J. Gleeson, *The Moneymaker: The remarkable true story of John Law – philanderer, gambler, murderer . . . and the father of modern finance* (London: Bantam Books, 1999).

46  See Gower (1979), chapter 1.

47  Kindelberger, *Manias, Panics and Crashes: A history of financial crises* (1989).

48  Consider, inter alia: Bakan, *The Corporation* (2004), Hunt, *The Development of the Business Corporation in England, 1800–1867* (1936), Chambers, *Securities and Obscurities* (1973b).

49  The second, third and fourth merger movements occurred in the 1920s, the 1960s and the 1980s.

50  See Haldane, *With Intent to Deceive: Frauds famous and infamous* (1970), and Valance, *A Very Private Enterprise* (1955).

51  For details see Holtfrerich, *The German Inflation 1914–23* (1986) and Guttmann and Meehan, *The Great Inflation* (1975).

52  Fitzgerald, *The Great Gatsby* (1925).

53  Veblen, *The Theory of the Leisure Class: An economic study of institutions* (1899).

54  For an account see de Bedts, *The New Deal's SEC: The formative years* (1964).

55  See Benston, *Corporate Financial Disclosure in the UK and the USA* (1976), and (say) Chatov, *Corporate Financial Reporting* (1975).

56  Posner, *Economic Analysis of Law* (1977), Zecher and Phillips, *The SEC and the Public Interest* (1981), Cranston, 'Regulation and deregulation: General issues' (1982) and see also the report of an institutional inquiry by the Committee on Interstate and Foreign Commerce, *Report of the Advisory Committee on Corporate Disclosure to the SEC* (1977).

57  What follows is a very brief overview of the changing nature of the regulations affecting corporations since the early 1930s. It draws principally on the summary chapters in the text by Clarke *et al.*, *Corporate Collapse* (chapters, 3, 6, 10 and 14), as well as Zeff's 'Chronology of significant developments in the establishment of accounting principles in the United States, 1926–1972' (1972); and Zeff, 'How the US accounting profession got where it is today: Parts I and II' (2003a and 2003b), pp. 189–205 and 267–86 respectively; Chatov, *Corporate Financial Reporting* (1975) and Dean and Clarke, 'An evolving conceptual framework?' (2003). Some modified extracts from the last piece are reproduced below.

58  'Economic genius' was the term used by J. Bakan, *The Corporation* (2004).

59  These include: Galbraith, *The Great Crash 1929* (1971); Zecher and Phillips, *The SEC and the Public Interest* (1981); Cranston, 'Regulation and deregulation: General issues' (1982); Committee on Interstate and Foreign Commerce, *Report of the Advisory Committee on Corporate Disclosure to the SEC* (1977).

60  In 2002 Spitzer announced that various financial and insurance companies had agreed to make an out-of-court settlement of more than $US1.4 billion. See chapters 4 and 5 of Masters, B., *Spoiling for a Fight: The Rise of Eliot Spitzer* (2006).

61  See Benston, *Corporate Financial Disclosure in the UK and the USA* (1976), Carey, *The Rise of the Accountancy Profession: From technician to professional 1896–1936* (1969), Carey, *The Rise of the Accounting Profession: To responsibility and authority 1937–1969* (1970), Ohlsen, *The Accounting Profession – Years of Trial: 1969–1980* (1982) and Chatov, *Corporate Financial Reporting* (1975), Clarke and Dean, 'Chaos in the counting-house: Accounting under scrutiny' (1992), and Clarke *et al.*, *Corporate Collapse* (2003).

62 See Chatov, *Corporate Financial Reporting* (1975).

63 Federal Trade Conmmision, Staff of, *Economic Report on Corporate Mergers* (1969).

64 Evidence of this is available from the FASB website <www.fasb.org>.

65 This is detailed in Walker *et al.*, 'Infrastructure reporting options' (2000).

66 For some Australian instances see Clarke *et al.*, *Corporate Collapse* (2003, especially chapter 10).

67 McManamy, *The Dreamtime Casino* (1990).

68 Clarke *et al.*, *Corporate Collapse* (2003), Foreword.

69 Previts and Merino, *The History of Accountancy in the United States* (1998) and Zeff, 'Chronology of significant developments in the establishment of accounting principles in the United States, 1926–1972' (1972); Zeff, 'How the US accounting profession got where it is today: Parts I and II' (2003a and 2003b).

70 Clarke and Dean, 'An evolving conceptual framework?' (2003).

71 R. Schmidt's 'Lawsuit targets US Sarbanes-Oxley Act', *Australian Financial Review*, 4 April 2006, p. 12, aptly illustrates this as does M. Gordon, 'SEC approves framework that would ease SOX rules', *Australian Associated Press*, 5 April 2007.

72 R. Guy, 'Benefits seen in easing Sarbanes-Oxley', *Australian Financial Review*, 14 September 2006, p. 13.

## 2 Independence: a misplaced quest for honesty

1 This chapter draws upon ideas and material previously appearing in our work 'Corporate governance: A case of misplaced concreteness' in *Corporate Governance: Does Any Size Fit?* (2005a).

2 This is well captured by Alfred North Whitehead in his *An Enquiry Concerning the Principles of Natural Knowledge* (1919/25) in which he referred to a 'fallacy of misplaced concreteness' for the first time.

3 Many of these cases are discussed in more detail in chapters 7 and 9. As this book goes to press the shareholders of James Hardie NV agreed to fund (over 40 years) approximately $A4 billion in compensation to present and prospective asbestos complainants.

4 Walker, *Consolidated Statements: A history and analysis* (1978).

5 Consider the issues explored in Walker *et al.*, 'Infrastructure reporting options' (2000).

6 The Insull affair provides insight into the way in which assets might be quarantined and is similar to the John Spalvins-led Adsteam empire's exposure of accounting's idiosyncrasies regarding terms, like wealth and income (details appear in Clarke *et al.*, *Corporate Collapse*, 2003, chapter 11).

7 Recall Whitehead's 'fallacy of misplaced concreteness', *An Enquiry Concerning the Principles of Natural Knowledge* (1919/25).

8 Berle and Means, *The Modern Corporation and Private Property* (1932).

9 See Brewster, *Unaccountable: How the Accounting Profession Forfeited a Public Trust* (2003), for the argument that over a long period accounting manipulations have sapped trust in accounting data and the accounting profession. Much the same theme underscores the argument in Berenson, *The Number: Why Companies Lied and the Stock Market Crashed* (2003) – see especially chapter 8, 'Accountants at the trough', pp. 111–28.

10 Berle and Means, *The Modern Corporation and Private Property* (1932).

11 It is arguable that the outcomes of the operations of the Vanderbilts and J. P. Morgan were relatively as significant in their time as globalisation has been in the recent past.

12 See G. Franzini, *Il Crac Parmalat: Storia del crollo dell'impero del latte* (Rome: Editori Ruiniti, 2004), for an outline of events up to February 2004.

13 See R. Smith and J. Emshwiller, *24 Days* (New York: Harper Business, 2003), for example, for a description of the essence of the surprise element of Enron's unwinding over 24 days.

14 The recurring episodes of collapses in the 1960s, 1970s and 1980s are chronicled and discussed in Clarke *et al.*, *Corporate Collapse: Accounting, Regulatory and Ethical Failure* (2003). These should be considered against the background of the *causes célèbres* elsewhere over the same period – of the UK's Robert Maxwell insurance empire (Thompson and Delano, *Maxwell: A Portrait of Power*, 1991); the crisis at Lloyd's insurance (see Gunn, *Nightmare on Lime Street*, 1992); Polly Peck in the UK, BCCI worldwide (Beaty and Gwynne, *The Outlaw Bank*, 1993); Olympia and York in Canada (Foster, *Towers of Debt: The Rise and Fall of the Reichmanns*, 1986); Prudential Insurance (Eichenwald, *Serpent on the Rock*, 1995); the Savings and Loans affair in the US (Pizzo *et al.*, *Inside Job: The Looting of America's Savings and Loans*, 1991, and M. A. Robinson, *Overdrawn: The Behavior of American Savings* (N.Y.: E. P. Dutton, 1990) and, for example, in Italy the Banco Ambrosiano affair (DeFonzo, *St. Peter's Banker*, 1983, and Almerighi, *I banchieri di Dio; il caso Calvi*, 2002).

15 Russell, *Foozles and Frauds* (1978), introduced the notion of a 'foozle' to describe managerial actions deemed to be on the 'grey line' of what is lawful, subsequently followed by clearly more fraudulent ones as the perceived 'short-term' financial problems worsen.

16 McDonald, *Insull* (1962).

17 Clarke *et al.*, *Corporate Collapse* (2003), chapter 11.

18 Culp and Niskanen, *Corporate Aftershock* (2003), p. 50.

19 Walker, 'Gaps in guidelines on audit committees' (2004), identified gaps in audit committees and provided a charter for directors to follow.

20 See United States General Accounting Office, Report to the Chairman, Committee on Banking, Housing, and Urban Affairs, US Senate as at October 2002 and October 2003 (published in 2003, 2004) *Financial Statement Restatements: Trends, Market Impacts, Regulatory Responses, and Remaining Challenges*. For an analysis of those restatements see W. Wallace, 'Auditor changes and restatements', *CPA Journal*, March 2005.

21 *Financial Statement Restatements: Trends, Market Impacts, Regulatory Responses, and Remaining Challenges* (Washington, D. C.: GAO-03–138).

22 GAO-03–395R, *Financial Statement Restatement Database*, 17 January 2003. Sources relied upon in this 2003 GAO Report included Financial Executives International and M. Wu, *Quantitative Measures of the Quality of Financial Reporting*, Internet-Based Special Report (Morristown, NJ: FEI Research Foundation, 2001); M. Jickling, *Accounting Problems Reported in Major Companies Since Enron*, Report for Congress (Washington, D. C.: Congressional Research Service, 2002); Z. V. Palmrose, V. Richardson, and S. Scholz, 'Determinants of market reactions to restatement announcements', Working Paper (Los Angeles, Ca.: University of Southern California, 2002); Huron Consulting Group, *A Study of Restatement Matters*, Internet-Based Report (Chicago, Ill.: Huron Consulting Group, 2002); L. Turner, J. Dietrich, K. Anderson, and A. Bailey, 'Accounting restatements', Working Paper

(Washington, D. C.: Securities and Exchange Commission, 2001); and M. Wu, 'Earnings restatements: A capital market perspective', Working Paper (N.Y.: New York University, 2002). In 2005 the number of restatements had increased to nearly 1100.

23 R. H. Coase produced a series of articles contiguously with B&M in the 1930s and thereafter. These included: 'The nature of the firm', *Economica*, N. S., 1937, pp. 386–405; 'The problem of social cost', *Journal of Law and Economics*, 3, 1960, pp. 1–44.

24 Regarding directors, consider the following comments by David Clark, National Australia Bank, 'I'd like to see some of the black-letter law dismantled . . . and more focus on people who think and act independently rather than the tick-a-box mentality . . .', 15 September 2006, *Australian Financial Review*, p. 13.

25 For example, Baysinger and Butler, 'Corporate governance and the board of directors: performance effects of changes in board composition' (1985), found that US data supported the claim of superior performance with a majority of non-executive directors, though Agrawal and Knoeber, 'Firm performance and mechanisms to control agency problems between managers and shareholders' (1996), and Bhagat and Black, 'The uncertain relationship between board composition and firm performance' (1999), perceived negative performance (measured by Tobin's $q$) to increasing outside directors; Dalton *et al.*, 'Meta-analytic reviews of board composition, leadership structure and financial performance' (1998), reviewing 85 studies variously relating to board composition and 'leadership' found zero relationship with 'performance'; Wood and Patrick, 'Jumping on the bandwagon: Outside representation in corporate governance' (2003) did not identify any linear or non-linear relationship; Laing and Wier, 'Governance structures, size and corporate performance in UK firms' (1999) found little support from UK data, and with Australian data Lawrence and Stapledon, 'Is the board important? A study of listed Australian companies', Working paper (1999), did not find consistent evidence. In contrast, on Canadian data of distressed companies Elloumi and Gueyie, 'Financial distress and corporate governance: An empirical analysis' (2001) noted the distressed companies had a lesser representation of outside directors. It might be noted however, that the different effects of the national accounting rules, and the different concepts of performance used in studies make comparisons contestable. To that end Rhoades *et al.*, 'Board composition and financial performance: A meta analysis of the influence of outside directors' (2000), concluded that the outcomes depended on how the variables of performance were constructed.

26 Interestingly, a similar point is made by long serving Executive Chairman of Macquarie Bank, David Clarke, as reported in F. Buffini, 'Private equity ahead: Clarke', *Australian Financial Review*, 15 September 2006, p. 13, when addressing the need to be independent in mind when a director – and it should not matter if one were a CEO and Chairman of the board. This flushed out several letters and opinion pieces to the Editor critical of Clarke's position (including S. Easterbrook and P. Lee, 'Ticking off Macquarie Bank', *Australian Financial Review*, Opinion, 25 September 2006, p. 63). Our view is that little evidence, and certainly none that is compelling, has been produced to counter Clarke's view. See also U. Rodrigues, 'The fetishization of independence', University of Georgia School of Law Research Paper Series, no. 07–207, March 2007, and F. Clarke and G. Dean, 'Harsh light may shine on non-executives', *Australian Financial Review*, 12 March 2007, p. 63.

27 As reported in F. Buffini, "Private Equity Ahead: Clarke', *Australian Financial Review*, 15 September 2006, p. 13.

28 Institute of Chartered Accountants in Australia and CPA Australia, *Joint Code of Professional Conduct*, Statement F1, Principles 1; replaced in July 2006 by APES 110, *Code of Ethics for Professional Accountants*.

29 This aligns the Australian Code with IESB's *Code of Ethics of Professional Accountants* (New York: IFAC, 2006).

30 Mautz and Sharaf, *The Philosophy of Auditing* (1961)

31 Consider the findings of possible impaired auditor independence in: Citron and Taffler (1992); Geiger *et al.* (1998); Ezzamel *et al.* (1999); Levitt (2000); Carcello and Neal (2003), while contrary findings appear in Simunic (1980); Francis (1984); Francis and Simon (1987), Davis *et al.* (1994) and Geiger and Rama (2003). For full reference details of these sources see working paper by Basioudis *et al.*, 'Audit fees, non-audit fees and auditor-going concern reporting decisions in the UK' (2006).

32 At this point (Report of the HIH Royal Commission, section 21.4) Justice Owen was illustrating how he reasoned the Andersen firm was obliged to meet the 'in appearance and fact' criterion in accord with the then relevant AUP (Statements of Auditing Practice) 202, and AUP 32, paragraph 9, a matter which the firm disputed.

33 Concerns resulting from this relationship have been made by many – S. Turnbull, for example, is a major proponent that this places insurmountable pressures on auditors – see 'Muddled auditing practices', *Board Report*, Journal of the Directors' Association of Australia, no. 906, July 2004; also: S. Turnbull, 'How can auditors lie about being independent?', *News and Views*, Australian Institute of Chartered Secretaries, November 2006, p. 585.

## 3   Governance overload: a contestable strategy

1 Mitchell and Sikkha, *Taming the Corporations* (2005).

2 See, for example, *Accounting Principles and Practices Discussed in Reports of Company Failures*, ASA (1966). An overview of this appears in Clarke *et al.*, *Corporate Collapse* (2003), especially chapter 3.

3 An account of these failures and the profession's responses is given in Clarke *et al.*, *Corporate Collapse* (2003), especially chapter 3 and the references therein.

4 See Haigh, *Bad Company: The Cult of the CEO* (2003), for a balanced discussion of CEOs' invisible handouts, and Flanagan, *Dirty Rotten CEOs: How business leaders are fleecing America* (2003), for a more vitriolic discussion.

5 Toffler, *Final Accounting: Ambition, greed and the fall of Arthur Andersen* (2004), p. 93.

6 See GAO (2003, 2004) and Buckmaster, *Development of the Income Smoothing Literature 1893–1998: A focus on the United States* (2001) for the evidence.

7 The September/December 2006 joint issue of *Abacus* reports the findings of several research papers by leading academics addressing this supposed higher quality of US FASB accounting standards relative to the IFRS.

8 In Clarke *et al.*, *Corporate Collapse* (2003) (especially pp. 34–40), the incidence of these is given regarding the mid to late 1990s and prior reporting practices. There is little reason to expect, and casual observation confirms, that the *ex post* adjustments have been any less frequent in the recent past than they were previously.

9  For illustrations of this kind see Blasi *et al.*, *In the Company of Owners: The truth about stock options* (2003), pp. 79–153.

10  In 1981 President Reagan increased the differential between capital gains tax and income tax, making the capital gains from options trading an attractive tax alternative for option holders, especially for those with options in their 401(K) pension portfolios; in 1993 President Clinton indirectly increased that differential by capping at $US1 million tax deductions to cash components of salaries.

11  That ploy has contributed to the notion that the options are an expense of the issuing company. The process of deducting the 'cost' of the options has the seductive effect of it appearing that such a deduction should be made. Of course, the bottom line would be reduced whenever an amount is deducted – but that does not legitimise the deduction, *per se*. For a summary of the debate, see Frederickson *et al.*, 'The evolution of stock option accounting: Disclosure, voluntary recognition and mandated disavowals' (2006), especially pp. 1073–8.

12  For example, Lambert *et al.*, 'Portfolio considerations in valuing executive compensation' (1991) concluded that what US executives received in the 1970s and 1980s had little relationship to their performances, though a positive impact on shareholder value through stock market effects had been found by Jensen and Murphy, 'Performance pay and top management incentives' (1990) and supported by the United Shareholders Association (1993). The point is that even if executives benefited, so, most importantly, did the shareholders – and that was the point of the exercise. A recent article by Merhebi *et al.*, 'Australian chief executive officer remuneration: pay and performance' (2006, pp. 481–97) provides non-US (Australian) evidence from a sample of 722 firms during 1990–99 that is consistent with an agency theory view that there is a strong positive association between CEO pay (albeit only cash) and performance. This is in contrast to earlier Australian findings: Defina *et al.*, 'What is reasonable remuneration for corporate officers?' (1994), Izan *et al.*, 'Does CEO pay reflect performance?' (1998), O'Neill and Iob, 'Determinants of executive remuneration in Australian organizations: An exploratory study' (1999).

13  See T. Boyd, 'With $92 m in the bank it's not solely about money', *Australian Financial Review*, 5–6 August 2006, p. 5.

14  Support of that proposition by Warren Buffett seems to have taken on the mantle of the official voice from commerce, and by Arthur Levitt, the authoritative voice of accounting expertise.

15  Institutional Shareholder Services, 'Long-term incentives – far from illusory', September 2006; reported on by F. Buffini, 'CEOs coy on options bonanza', *Australian Financial Review*, 4 September 2006, pp. 1 and 4; and S. Washington, 'Tell the truth on CEO pay', *SMH*, 13 November 2006, p. 23.

16  We say *presumed*, for that view tends to ignore the current affinity with corporate stakeholder theory that asserts that corporations have obligations to a considerably wider constituency than merely to shareholders. It also draws upon neo-capitalism perceptions of the purpose and means of commerce. Nonetheless, the legal obligation of companies, as compared with their now claimed social obligations, is to the shareholders.

17  See Blasi *et al.*, *In the Company of Owners: The truth about stock options*, Parts I and II (2003), for the general argument and references to studies supportive of the positive benefits claimed of issuing stock options to employees.

231

18 Ibid.

19 Institutional Shareholder Services' 'Long-term incentives – far from illusory', September 2006 survey confirms this finding in the sample of nearly 50 Australian CEOs' options packages over the period 2001–05.

20 As part of his allegation that 'the Stock Option: [was] the CEO's license to steal', Flanagan, *Dirty Rotten CEOs* (2003) is a good example – whereas he implies a connection between the poor performances Enron and WorldCom disclosed once the accounts were adjusted for the alleged manipulations, in contrast he begrudgingly notes that in respect to Citicorp – while Citicorp did well in 2001 ' . . . Weill did a lot better' (39).

21 See Blasi *et al.*, *In the Company of Owners* (2003), pp. 85–8.

22 Until recent times notable Australian companies, for example, Commonwealth Bank, Westpac, AMP, David Jones, Coles Myer, and Woolworths – 'since the early 1990s' (see R. A. MacDonald, unpublished PhD thesis, 'Corporate modernism . . .', University of Newcastle, 2006) proceeded without the complaint and criticism levelled at the use of options in recent times.

23 Curiously, that would seem to be a stronger argument for declaring the cost of options a 'revenue' to the company, rather than an expense.

24 For an extended discussion of this issue refer CASAC, *Corporate Groups: Final Report* (2000). The relation between the law and accounting in respect of accounting for corporate groups was discussed in Clarke and Dean, 'Law and accounting: The separate legal entity principle and consolidation accounting' (1993).

25 The judgment on this matter in the One.Tel case is not likely to be handed down until late 2007 and a civil action by the liquidator is not likely to be heard till 2008, see V. Carson, 'Packers' lawyers win day, get delay', *SMH*, 29 November 2006, p. 19.

26 *Discussion* rather than *debate* in this context, for there has not been any real debate as to why the similar measures failed to effect good governance in the past, other than to imply that the fault lies with recalcitrant directors, other executives and auditors. This focus is consistent with most of the comment surrounding corporate malpractice and malfeasance. It is what we labelled the 'cult of the individual' – a focus on the individuals diverting attention from systemic defects in corporate regulatory mechanisms – in Clarke *et al.*, *Corporate Collapse* (2003), pp. 14–20.

27 It is worth noting how quickly after the HIH collapse the federal government set up the inquiry into Audit Independence (the Ramsay Report), with what appears to have absolute endorsement from virtually all parties interested in corporate affairs. Perhaps it is not surprising that the necessity for auditor independence almost passed without dissent – the dispute arose more from differences of opinion regarding how to achieve it, and even more so, perhaps, regarding how to have it appear to prevail. Submissions and evidence before the Joint Parliamentary Committee inquiring into the *Independence of Registered Company Auditors* (Hansard, <www.aph.gov.au>) reveal perceptions of how independence is to function as a governance mechanism, similar to that espoused in the Ramsay Report.

28 The inquiry into terrorism shows how what might well be worthwhile activities can become dysfunctional when they lack coordination. There seems to be some strong evidence from the 9/11 Commission in the US, for example, that the different intelligence and other agencies did not know what intelligence on terrorism and Iraq's supposed weapons of mass destruction had been gathered by the others, were unsure of with whom they were to share intelligence, who 'owned' the various bits of

intelligence, who was following-up which leads, and the like. An information 'silo' problem existed. That seems to be the story in the UK and Australia too.

29 More details are provided in E. Johnstone and L. Warwick, 'Directors must begin to ask the right questions', *Australian Financial Review*, 19 January 2007, p. 91.

30 For a discussion of Alfred North Whitehead's notion of misplaced concreteness see Fernside and Holther, *Fallacy: The counterfeit of argument* (1959). It appeared first in Whitehead (1919).

## 4   A very peculiar practice: accounting under scrutiny

1 The beginning of this chapter draws on ideas first penned by the authors as part of the Foreword of Clarke *et al.*, *Corporate Collapse* (2003). Further, ideas from chapter 14 of that work are also relied upon. The material on 'true and fair view' is taken from several pieces including F. Clarke and G. Dean, Editorial, *Abacus*, 2002, and Clarke, 'Introduction: True and fair view – anachronism or quality criterion par excellence' (2006).

2 Clarke and Dean, 'Chaos in the counting house: Accounting under scrutiny' (1992), Clarke *et al.*, *Corporate Collapse* (1997, 2003). This issue was revisited by Federal parliamentarian John Watson's questioning of Jeff Lucy's claim that issues are now being managed better, given Fincorp's unexpected collapse (see R. Harley, 'Crash: a second property empire falls', *Australian Financial Review*, 31 March–1 April 2007, p. 20.

3 Their concerns are reproduced in Demski *et al.*, 'Statement on the state of accounting', mimeo (1991).

4 Demski *et al.*, 'Statement on the state of accounting', mimeo (1991).

5 The iconoclastic Australian accounting academic, Ray Chambers (1999) made similar observations just prior to his death in 1999. Chambers' 1999 work was revisited recently in a Special Issue of *Accounting Education* (March 2005, pp. 1–51).

6 Cases pending in Australia include the 2006–07 Harris Scarfe litigation in the SA Supreme Court where the receiver is seeking $165 million damages against PriceWaterhouseCoopers (C. Milne, 'Harris Scarfe trials claim only one scalp', *Australian Financial Review*, 19 January 2007, pp. 16–27) and the 2004–07 Bell Group case in the WA Supreme Court (see chapter 1).

7 The current head of the IASB, Sir David Tweedie, continues to suggest that the way forward is to move away from a cookbook of rules approach to standards setting, to a principles-based set of standards (see Tweedie, 'IFRSs: View on a financial reporting revolution', 2006, as well as Tweedie, 'True and fair v the rule book: which is the answer to creative accounting?', 1988). We agree. Yet, the Standards handbooks keep getting bigger and the overarching principle of serviceability is still not promulgated.

8 Zeff, 'How the US accounting profession got where it is today', Parts I and II (2003a and 2003b); and by Sullivan, 'Market vs. professions: value added' (2005) and West, *Professionalism and Accounting Rules* (2003).

9 As reported by K. Brice, 'Judgment reserved on the Acacia Part A', *Australian Financial Review*, 27 March 1996, p. 28.

10 *Sons of Gwalia Ltd v Margaretic; ING Investment Management LLC v Margaretic* [2007], High Court of Australia 1, 31 January 2007.

11 Such a scenario had been discussed previously in Clarke *et al.*, *Corporate Collapse* (2003), especially pp. 206–7.

12 Schipper, 'Principles-based Accounting Standards' (2003); SEC Study (2003).

13 See Clarke (2006), Benston *et al.* (2006), Bradbury *et al.* (2006), Kirk (2006) and Alexander and Jemakowicz (2006), all of which appear in a Special Forum issue of *Abacus*, June 2006 – details are in the Bibliography.

14 This section is a modified version of Clarke and Dean, 'An evolving conceptual framework?' (2003), which was based on chapter 14 of Clarke *et al.*, *Corporate Collapse* (2003). What follows here is limited to examining accounting and auditing reforms primarily.

15 See accounts of S. Zeff, *Forging Accounting Principles in Five Countries* (Champaign, Ill.: Stipes, 1971), and Chatov, *Corporate Financial Reporting* (1975).

16 See Chambers, 'Conventions, doctrines and commonsense' (1964); Staunton, 'Exiting intellectual grooves in the reporting of liabilities: An analysis of the reporting of liabilities under Chambers' continuously contemporary accounting' (2006); and Walker, 'Reporting entity concept: A case study of the failure of principles-based regulation' (2007).

17 Walker, 'Reporting entity concept . . .' (2007) questions whether what were referred to in the 1920s and 1930s were really principles; as have many others, including Chambers, 'Conventions, doctrines and commonsense' (1964); R. Sterling, *Theory of The Measurement of Enterprise Income* (Lawrence, KS: University Press of Kansas, 1970).

18 Chatov, *Corporate Financial Reporting* (1975), Clarke *et al.*, *Corporate Collapse* (2003), especially chapters 2, 3, 6, 10.

19 The following section draws upon Clarke *et al.*, *Corporate Collapse* (2003), chapter 14.

20 Respectively: Federal Reserve Chairman, Dr Alan Greenspan (attributed to a speech at the American Enterprise Institute, 5 December 1996), and internationally acclaimed economist, John Kenneth Galbraith (extracted from *The Great Crash 1929* (1971), p. 152).

21 Cassidy, *Dot.con* (2002).

22 For specifics refer to Cassidy, *Dot.con* (2002, especially table 1, p. 293).

23 J. Spinner, 'Sullied accounting firms regaining political clout', *Washington Post*, 12 May 2002, p. A01.

24 Former Federal Reserve Bank Chairman, Volcker, as cited in 'Confused about earnings?', *BusinessWeek*, 26 November 2001.

25 Clarke *et al.*, *Corporate Collapse* (2003), chapter 14, especially table 14.2.

26 A. Hepworth, 'Judges face busy time as watchdogs pounce', *Australian Financial Review*, 11 January 2002, pp. 8 and 9.

27 JCPAA, *Report 391*, p. xvii, 'Terms of reference'.

28 J. Green, 'Fuzzy Law – a better way to "stop snouts in the trough"?', *Company and Securities Law Journal*, June (1991), p. 145.

29 Clarke *et al.*, *Corporate Collapse* (2003), p. 219.

30 A major review of the audit independence literature was undertaken by Wolnizer, *Auditing as Independent Authentication* (1987). He was critical of the overemphasis of the independence of relationships rather than on the auditor's independence of mind when forming an opinion.

31 Chatov, *Corporate Financial Reporting* (1975).

32 In his piece 'Directors and the law', written in the 1960s for an address (reproduced in an Editorial by Dean in *Abacus*, 2005), Ray Chambers presciently noted that this

development would be enormously damaging to the credibility of the profession and to the financial reporting system.

33 JCPAA, *Report 391*, p. iii.

34 In the post-Enron era this was made strongly, amongst others, by leading accounting historian Zeff, 'How the US accounting profession got where it is today', Parts I and II (2003a and 2003b), but interestingly, it had been made equally strongly by another historian, Chatov, in his *Corporate Financial Reporting* (1975) regarding similar problematic activities in the less regulated 1930s and also by Staunton in a PhD thesis, 'Exiting intellectual grooves in the reporting of liabilities: An analysis of the reporting of liabilities under Chambers' continuously contemporary accounting' (2006).

35 For very different reasons G. Benston *et al.*, *Worldwide Financial Reporting* (2006) are also skeptical about the likelihood of IFRSs improving the current state of play.

36 See above and also G. Dean, 'Editorial', *Abacus* (2002) for additional references.

37 Walter Schuetze, former SEC Chief Accountant, would like that to be the case. See Schuetze, 'What are assets and liabilities? Where is true north? (Accounting that my sister would understand)' (2001a), and related monograph, Schuetze, 'A memo to national and international Accounting and Audit Standard Setters and Securities Regulators' (2001b).

38 Botosan *et al.* (2005) discuss the definition, recognition and measurement of liabilities. Staunton, 'Exiting intellectual grooves in the reporting of liabilities' (2006) analyses Botosan *et al.* (2005) and various others who have examined the accounting for liabilities and found tensions due to attempts to provide 'intermingled data – conventional accounting, financial, economic and social – in one report' (Abstract, p. i).

39 M. Marois, 'San Diego settles with SEC over securities fraud claims', *Bloomberg News*, 15 November 2006; p. D03.

40 Nothing is more apt to describe the commercial environment than the Al Gore label for the state of ecological mayhem. It was too good to pass by.


## 5 A most peculiar practice: auditing under the microscope

1 Bartholomeusz, 'Westpoint exposes the soft side of auditing', *SMH* (2006). He noted: 'Westpoint's collapse highlights the continuing inability of the audit function to deliver what the community expects of it. The [recent] reforms might have enhanced the integrity of the audit process but they haven't delivered fundamental improvements in its effectiveness.'

2 F. Clarke and G. Dean, Australian National Audit Office seminar, 'Accounting is auditing's devil', 14 October 2003. While the setting was the public sector, the auditing issues are universal.

3 This section draws on material that the authors have published in recent times: 'Double standards: A different take on true and fair', *Australian Financial Review*, Opinion piece, 11 March 2005; 'True, fair and harder to avoid', *Business Review Weekly*, 5 August 2004, p. 108; and contiguously in an Editorial, 'Principles vs. rules: true and fair and IFRSs', in *Abacus* (G. Dean and F. Clarke, Editorial, *Abacus*, 2004).

4 Chambers and Wolnizer, 'A true and fair view of position and results: The historical background' (1991).

5 We have shown elsewhere that 'creative accounting' is more the consequence of complying with the Standards than deviating from them: Clarke *et al.*, *Corporate Collapse* (2003).

6 Schuetze, 'What are assets and liabilities? Where is true north? (Accounting that my sister would understand)' (2001a), and Dean, 'Editorial', *Abacus* (2002), provide many references in which the 'auditing in crisis' claim is made.

7 Barry, *The Rise and Fall of Alan Bond* (1990), p. 261.

8 R. G. Walker, 'Brought to account: Normal items? Extraordinary!', *Australian Business*, 10 February 1988, pp. 95–6 at 96.

9 An extensive account of the events and accounting at Royal Mail appears in Commentary, 'The Royal Mail Steam Packet Company case', *Canadian Chartered Accountant* (1931).

10 Of course not all auditing problems relate directly to accounting. Client pressures are certainly an issue. But our analysis here is restricted to those that are linked to the problematic nature of accounting (see Beattie *et al.*, *Behind Closed Doors: What a company audit is all about* (2001) and (say) Walker, 'Gaps in guidelines on audit committees' (2004)).

11 Alexander and Jemakowicz, 'A true and fair view of the Principles/Rules debate' (2006).

12 Kirk, 'Perceptions of the true and fair view concept: An empirical investigation' (2006); Alexander and Jemakowicz, 'A true and fair view of the Principles/Rules debate' (2006).

13 This point is well made in Chambers, 'Accounting principles and the law' (1973a), an article published in a leading Australian law journal that draws on accepted ideas in communication theory and the rules of statutory interpretation.

14 In Australia there was the joint ASCPA/ICAA research study and monograph, *A Research Study on Financial Reporting and Auditing – Bridging the Expectations Gap* (1993, 1996) and Trotman, *Financial Report Audit: Meeting the market expectations* (2003), in the US there was the Cohen Commission in 1978, the Treadway Commission in 1987 and the Public Oversight Board (1993); the UK and Canada had their equivalent studies, such as: Auditing Practices Board, *The Future Development of Auditing – A Paper to Promote Debate* (London: APB, 1992) and Canadian Institute of Chartered Accountants, Commission to Study the Public's Expectations of Audits (MacDonald Commission), *Report of the Commission to Study the Public's Expectations of Audits* (Toronto: CICA, 1988). Those studies are discussed in Humphrey *et al.*, *The Audit Expectations Gap in the United Kingdom* (1992), and Humphrey *et al.*, 'Protecting against detection: The case of auditors and fraud' (1993).

15 Teo and Cobbin, 'A revisitation of the "audit expectations gap": judicial and practitioner views on the role of the auditor in late-Victorian England' (2005); and Guy and Sullivan, 'The expectations gap auditing standards' (1998).

16 See Clarke *et al.*, *Corporate Collapse* (2003), especially pp. 19–20 and 319–21.

17 As reported in the JCPAA *Report 391* (2002), p. 79, and drawn from the Mark Liebler *Submission No. 68*, p. S631 to that inquiry.

18 As reported in the JCPAA *Report 391* (2002) p. 8 and drawn from Professor Bob Walker's *Submission No. 41*, p. S384.

19 Gay and Simnett, *Auditing and Assurance Services in Australia* (2006). A similar tone of confidence underpins the 2007 edition of Leung *et al.*'s *Modern Auditing Assurance Services*, especially p. 50.

20 Chambers, *Securities and Obscurities: A case for reform of the law of company accounts* (1973b), pp. 144–5.

21 Proposed IFAC Ethics Code ('Independence – audit and review engagements; independence – other assurance engagements', 2006), covering *inter alia*, independence.

22 Treasury, *Australian Auditor Independence Requirements*, Commonwealth of Australia (2006).

23 Part of this section – on the history of fraud and accounting – is drawn from the conclusion of joint work by the two authors and Tom Lee, 'The dominant senior manager and the reasonably careful, skilful, and cautious auditor', forthcoming in *Critical Perspectives in Accounting* (2007). It was adduced from analyses of numerous cases in the UK, US and Australia from 1844 to the present in that work and cases examined in Clarke *et al.*, *Corporate Collapse* (2003), and Chambers, *Securities and Obscurities* (1973b).

24 Lee, 'The nature of auditing and its objectives', *Accountancy* (1970).

25 See also Clarke *et al.*, *Corporate Collapse* (2003) especially chapter 2.

26 Argenti, *Corporate Collapse: The causes and symptoms* (1976) and Argenti, 'Predicting company failure', *Accountants' Digest No. 93* (1985); and Heimann-Hoffman *et al.*, 'The warning signs of fraudulent financial reporting' (1996).

27 That committee was formed to consider what difficulties would be likely were Australia to adopt the IFRSs given that there had been changes to the Corporations Law (*CLERP 9*) just legislated. Included in that legislation was confirmation that audited accounting data should satisfy the Corporation Law's true and fair requirements.

28 Evans, 'The true and fair view and the fair presentation override of IAS 1' (2003), provides a history of the phrase with a UK focus. Earlier Chambers, 'Accounting principles and the law' (1973a), and later Chambers and Wolnizer, 'A true and fair view of financial position' (1990), Chambers and Wolnizer, 'A true and fair view of position and results: The historical background' (1991) analysed the history of the phrase seeking to draw a distinction between the literal and technical meanings of the phrase within broader Anglo-Saxon accounting and commercial settings. Nobes, 'Is true and fair of over-riding importance' (2000) notes that while the UK has a true and fair view override in theory, in practice it is not employed (a matter disputed by M. Bromwich *et al.*, 'Principles- versus rules-based accounting standards: The FASB's standard setting strategy' (2006). He notes also that the US does not have an override criterion. Finally, in a 2005 article he concludes that the complexity of the existing US rules-based system could be reduced were a 'more appropriate' principle(s) relied upon. Which of course begs the question – how is this 'more appropriate' principle(s) to be determined?, something that Alexander (1999) sought to unravel – as had many more before him – some noted in this footnote. For a compilation of some of these see Parker *et al.*, *Readings in True and Fair* (1996).

29 Nobes, 'Is true and fair of over-riding importance' (2000).

30 See Moroney and Sidhu, 'The reformed "true and fair" test: How often does it trigger additional disclosure?' (2001), Liebler, *Submission to Joint Committee on Public*

237

*Accounts and Audit*, Commonwealth of Australia, 'Review of Independent Auditing by Registered Company Auditors' (2002); available at <www.aph.gov.au>. Service, Response to Question at *Hearings* before the Joint Committee on Corporations and Financial Services (JCCFS) *Report*, as reported in Hansard (7 February 2005); Bromwich *et al.*, 'Principles- versus rules-based accounting standards: The FASB's standard setting strategy' (2006), and Alexander and Jemakowicz, 'A true and fair view of the Principles/Rules debate' (2006).

31 British Financial Reporting Council, *PN 119*, 9 August 2005 at <www/frc.org.uk/press/pub0854.html> accessed 28 August 2006.

## 6   The sound of one hand clapping

1 Some discussion of this appears in the *Accounting Education* Forum discussing Chambers' 'Poverty of accounting discourse', March 2005, pp. 1–51; in Clarke *et al.*, *Corporate Collapse* (2003), and throughout this book.

2 Hein, *The British Companies Acts and the Practice of Accountancy, 1844–1962* (1978) notes that a profit and loss account for companies created by mere registration was not required in the UK until 1928.

3 Financial Reporting Council, *PN 119*, 9 August 2005; <www/frc.org.uk/press/pub0854.html> accessed 28 August 2006.

4 'WorldCom, crushed by its $41 billion debt load, made its filing in the Southern District of New York. With $107 billion in assets, WorldCom's bankruptcy is the largest in US history, dwarfing that of Enron Corp. The Houston-based energy trader listed $63.4 billion in assets when it filed chapter 11 late last year. World-Com's non-US units were not included in the filing.' As cited in Luisa Beltran, 'WorldCom files largest bankruptcy ever – Nation's No. 2 long-distance company in Chapter 11 – largest with $107 billion in assets', *CNN/Money* staff writer, 22 July 2002.

5 Walker, 'SEC's ban on upward asset revaluations and the disclosure of current values' (1992a).

6 This is discussed in Sweeney, *Stabilized Accounting* (1936); Dean and Clarke, 'Schmidt's *Betriebswirtschaft* theory' (1986) and Dean and Clarke, 'Conjectures on the influence of 1920s German *Betriebswirtschaftslehre* on Sweeney's *Stabilized Accounting*' (1989); Clarke, *The Tangled Web of Price Variation Accounting* (1982).

7 Sweeney, *Stabilized Accounting* (1936) and Rorem, *Accounting Method* (1928, repr. 1998).

8 Walker, 'SEC's ban on upward asset revaluations . . .' (1992a), shows, however, that contrary to the conventional wisdom, this had not been mandated by the SEC.

9 HIHRC, *The Failure of the HIH Insurance*, Vol. II (2003), p. 105 *ff.*

10 Based on calculations and material in the HIHRC, *The Failure of the HIH Insurance*, s. 21.5.7, Vol. III (2003), p. 123*ff.*

11 Clarke *et al.*, *Corporate Collapse* (2003), pp. 32–42 provide numerous examples.

12 Waller, *Wheels on Fire: The amazing inside story of the Daimler Chrysler merger* (2001), p. 194.

13 On a comparable basis as various methods are adopted to calculate the numerator and denominators in rate-of-return calculations. In BHP's statistical summary

(p. 150, 1998 Annual Report) the rates quoted appear to correspond with the products of the numerators being the reported Operating (loss) profit attributable to members of the BHP entity and the denominators with an average of the opening and closing shareholders' equity attributable to members of the BHP entity.

14 T. Sykes, 'How a series of poor investment decisions cost BHP $7 billion', *Australian Financial Review*, 30 June 1997, p. 26.

15 See R. Chambers, 'The foundations of financial accounting', Symposium on the Foundations of Financial Accounting, University of California, Berkeley, January 1967, in *Chambers on Accounting. Vol. V: Continuously Contemporary Accounting* (1986).

16 At other times it would be the undervaluation of an entity's assets in takeover plays or when an entity unexpectedly collapses.

17 Chambers, 'A critical examination of company Accounting Standards' (1975).

18 The paper was published posthumously in the Festschrift issue of *Abacus* (October 2000, pp. 321–6) a year after Chambers' death.

19 Inflation statistics for many countries are available on the FASB website <www.fasb.org>.

20 These included Australia, New Zealand and South Africa.

21 Summaries of those professional attempts are given in Clarke, *The Tangled Web of Price Variation Accounting* (1982) and Tweedie and Whittington, *The Debate on Inflation Accounting* (1984).

22 The phrase 'Sydney School' of Accounting was initially used in the 1977 AAA *Statement on Accounting Theory and Theory Acceptance* (1977).

23 The printing style of CoCoA was accidental, in that it was actually suggested by the girl who printed the motto on the match folders (at Sydney's George Street store of the then hardware giant Nock and Kirby) because it 'looked better' than something that might be mistaken for a plug for a popular winter beverage.

24 The unexpected impact provoked the design and printing of drink coasters with the motto 'CoCoA is my cup of tea'.

25 NSW Accounting Standards Review Committee (under chairmanship of Raymond John Chambers), *Company Accounting Standards* (Sydney: NSW Government Printer, 1978).

26 Clarke *et al.*, *Corporate Collapse* (2003, table 6.1).

27 Janetzki, *The Gollin Years* (1989).

28 Clarke *et al.*, *Corporate Collapse* (2003) provides details of these cases.

29 In the first decade of the twenty-first century concern over lack of compliance persists. ASIC announced a crackdown on non-compliance with the AASB standards then in force. Of course, now companies will be penalised for using them rather than the now-endorsed AIFRSs.

30 The Chambers Collection is a collection of correspondence of Ray Chambers that was catalogued and made available in hardcopy, and in summarised digitised form, as part of the University of Sydney Foundation Professors series. In what follows the documents are referred to using the standard style of the Archives Unit at the University of Sydney, namely USA P202, series no, item #. The documents listed in this subsection are all located in one folder under the location USA P202, series 2, item 09491.

31 USA P202, series 2, item 09491 – letter dated 21 November 1977.

32  USA P202, series 2, item 09491.

33  USA P202, series 2, item 09491.

34  USA P202, series 2, item 09491.

35  This White Paper was prepared by the General Council of the ASA. Interestingly, nearly thirty years later IFAC's *Rebuilding Public Confidence in Financial Reporting* (2003) would come to similar conclusions.

36  USA P202, series 2, item 09491 – letter dated 16 February 1981.

37  Chatov, *Corporate Financial Reporting* (1975).

38  USA P202, series 2, item 09491.

39  As an aside, in a letter penned by the Chairman of the Accounting Standards Board, that the authors received after the appearance of the first edition of *Corporate Collapse* (1997), he noted that market prices were being required by the standards setters. One might be excused for thinking that most market participants now agree that current market prices (of which Chambers' exit prices are a subset) are required disclosures in corporate financial reports for some assets and liabilities.

## 7    Commerce without conscience: group enterprise or separate legal entity?

1  This chapter examines the activities of corporate groups in Australia and beyond – experiences at Bond Corporation/Bell Resources (1990–2006), Patrick/MUA (1998), and post-2000 at Ansett/Air New Zealand, HIH, James Hardie, and Enron in the US.

2  Clarke *et al.*, *Corporate Collapse* (1997, 2003).

3  Haigh, *Asbestos House: The secret history of James Hardie Industries* (2006).

4  Some would argue that the separate entity v group enterprise issue has a much longer history. It has permeated trust and equity precedent for many centuries – see Stoljar, *Groups and Entities: An inquiry into corporate theory* (1973) and Webb, *Legal Personality and Political Pluralism* (1958). But there is no doubting its resilience. The latest decision in a ten-year saga between the ATO and Industrial Equity Ltd involving a 1992 complex intra-company dividend shifting arrangement by an IEL subsidiary (Spassked Pty Ltd) is another instance of this issue's continuing relevance (see A. Lampe, 'IEL denied appeal bid over $900 million', *SMH* (13 December 2004) p. 35.

5  This was demonstrated in Clarke and Dean, 'Law and accounting: The separate legal entity principle and consolidation accounting' (1993), p. 246.

6  Ramsay and Stapledon, 'Corporate groups in Australia' (2001), p. 7; for overseas figures see Walker, 'Reporting entity concept: A case study of the failure of principles-based regulation' (2007); in the US and elsewhere the figures are similar.

7  Baxt, 'Corporations law a fragile structure' (2004).

8  Haigh, *Asbestos House: The secret history of James Hardie Industries* (2006), p. 149.

9  The issue was well aired and rejected in the Report of the UK Review Committee (1982).

10  Press speculation is that a situation similar to that alleged at Patrick Stevedores and the other cases noted occurred in the textiles industry in 1990. Employees in a Gazal group company discovered (after a 'major event' – a factory fire) that they were employed by 'a separate company that had no assets and only massive debts'. Allegedly, the employees were frustrated from obtaining suitable financial redress against any specific 'asset-rich' separate legal entity within the Gazal group.

11 Some of these cases are described in Clarke *et al.*, *Corporate Collapse* (1997, 2003).

12 K. Murphy, 'Patrick type tactic targeted', *Australian Financial Review*, 30–31 May 1998, p. 4. The House of Representatives did not accept those amendments. Detailed analysis of the waterfront particulars is given in M. Lee, 'On the waterfront', *The Alternative Law Journal*, Vol. 23 No. 3, 1998, pp. 107–11.

13 Respectively, JCCFS, *Corporate Insolvency Laws – A Stocktake* (2004), CAMAC, *Rehabilitating Large and Complex Enterprises in Financial Difficulties* (2004), Treasury, Corporations (Insolvency) Amendments Bill, 2007 (2006).

14 ASIC Media Release 02/69, 'ASIC's Ansett investigation focuses on financial disclosures by Air New Zealand Limited', March 2002. Interestingly, based on their scheme experiences, the Ansett Group administrator, KordaMentha, has submitted that in such group collapses the assets and liabilities of the group should be 'pooled' (as reported in CAMAC, *Rehabilitating Large and Complex Enterprises in Financial Difficulties* (2004), p. 10.

15 KordaMentha *Research Unit Paper #2*, 'Large and complex administrations: The courts and Ansett', August 2003, Section 4, 'Safety Net'.

16 HIH Royal Commission, *The Failure of HIH Insurance* Vol. III (2003), p. 23.

17 Details of events prior to the collapse are described in Clarke *et al.*, *Corporate Collapse* (2003), chapter 12.

18 Details provided in Clarke *et al.*, *Corporate Collapse* (2003), pp. 178–80.

19 Technically Alan Bond was not convicted of fraud on matters related to the Bond/Bell Resources cash-cow transactions but was found to have failed to act honestly as a director with intent to defraud under the Companies Code (WA) (see Mark Drummond, 'Cases bring Bond saga to a close', *Australian Financial Review*, 27 June 2003, p. 16). Two other members of the Bond inner cabinet were also convicted in relation to the siphoning of funds transaction: Peter Mitchell (a Bond Corp director until 1988 and then director at Bell) for making improper use of his position as director, and Tony Oates, who was released after serving 23 months and 23 days of his 40-month term for his part in the notorious transaction (for more details see B. Cheesman, 'Fraudster Oates out on parole', *Australian Financial Review*, 10–11 September 2005, p. 4.

20 R. Johnson, 'Back-to-back loans: A fraud in transition', *Australian Accounting Review* (2000), p. 67.

21 *The Bell Group Limited (In Liquidation) & Ors v Westpac Banking Corporation & Ors* Supreme Court of Western Australia, Action No. CIV 1464 of 2000.

22 M. Jacobs, 'Bell fight goes down to the wire as case winds up', *Australian Financial Review*, 19 September 2006, p. 9. Summary particulars of the case are provided in interlocutory judgments – 2001, WASC 307; 2001, WASC 317; 2004, WASC 162; 2004, WASC 273; 2004, WASC, 93; 2006, WASC 54.

23 See G. Dean *et al.*, 'Cross guarantees and negative pledges: A preliminary analysis' (1995).

24 G. Haigh, 'UK judge chides Bond over lack of Bell records', *SMH*, 22 July 1989, p. 41.

25 ASIC Media Release, 05–268, 'Antony Oates sentenced', 7 September 2005.

26 This vignette is based on Dean *et al.*, 'Corporate restructuring, creditors' rights, cross guarantees and group behaviour' (1999). See also H. Trinca and A. Davies, *Waterfront: The battle that changed Australia* (Sydney: Doubleday, 2000).

27 An apposite summary by the High Court of Australia of these transactions is provided at *Patrick Stevedores Operations No 2 Pty Ltd v Maritime Union of Australia (No 1)* (1998) 195 CLR 1; 72 ALJR 873. A diagrammatic illustration of the transactions appears in Houghton *et al.*, 'Insolvent corporate groups with cross guarantees: A forensic-LP case study in liquidation' (1999), p. 97. It is reproduced here as Figure 7.1. Corporate groups generally were the focus of the Companies and Securities Advisory Committee, 'Corporate groups', discussion paper, December 1998; *Corporate Groups: Final Report* (May 2000).

28 The 1997 financial year, ended 30 September 1997, represented the first year of Lang Corporation Limited in 'its new operating company status' (1997 Annual Report, p. 1). Previously Lang had been primarily an investor in several groups, including the Patrick Stevedores and Jamison Equity Limited groups.

29 Hill, 'Corporate groups, creditor protection and cross guarantees: Australian perspectives' (1995), provides a summary of the capital boundary problems of corporate trading, financing and liquidation.

30 Contemporary financial commentators generally expressed anxiety over the means used to achieve the seemingly undisputed goal of reform of Australia's waterfronts. For example, both Robert Gottliebsen (*Business Review Weekly*, 18–24 April 1998) and Brian Toohey (*Sun-Herald*, 19 April 1998) expressed reservations in respect of the restructuring. Similar concerns appeared in the *SMH* (17 June 1998, p. 25 which noted that disquiet over certain actions of a feedlot company in the Murrumbidgee Irrigation Area, Ravensworth Pty Ltd (coincidentally it was then a subsidiary of Lang Corporation), 'has similarities to the waterfront imbroglio'.

31 Commentaries on the predecessor NCSC Deed of Indemnity are given in Clarke and Dean, 'Law and accounting – the separate legal entity principle and consolidation accounting' (1993); Dean *et al.*, 'Notional calculations in liquidations revisited: The case of the ASC Class Order cross guarantees' (1993); G. W. Dean, P. F. Luckett and E. Houghton, 'Case note: *Westmex Operations Ltd (in liq) v Westmex Ltd (in liq)*', *Company and Securities Law Journal*, 11(4), December 1993, pp. 45–9; P. F. Luckett, G. W. Dean and E. Houghton, 'Cross debts and group liquidation: a cross claim liquidation model', *Pacific Accounting Review*, December 1995, pp. 73–102; Dean *et al.*, 'Cross guarantees and negative pledges: a preliminary analysis' (1995); as has Hill, 'Cross guarantees and corporate groups' (1992) and Hill, 'Corporate groups, creditor protection and cross guarantees: Australian perspectives' (1995).

32 *ASC Digest*, Update 41, 'Report on the public hearing on accounts and audit relief for wholly-owned subsidiaries' (1991), para. 31

33 *Salomon v Salomon & Co Ltd* [1897] A. C. 22.

34 High Court of Australia, *Patrick Stevedores Operations No 2 Pty Ltd v Maritime Union of Australia* [1998] HCA, 4 May 1998, p. 5.

35 *Patrick Stevedores Operations No. 2 Pty Ltd v Maritime Union of Australia* [1998] HCA 4 May 1998, par. 10.

36 For an outline of the relaxing of the buy-back provisions in Australia since 1989 see H. A. J. Ford and I. Ramsay, *Guide to the First Corporations Law Simplification*, (Sydney: Butterworths, 1996), especially pp. 14–27.

37 I. Verrender, 'An employment tactic to stymie the unions', *SMH*, 10 April 1998, p. 5. This action was voided by Justice North's 8 April ruling.

38 Ibid.

39 'Groupthink' in ensuring firm-specific asset security to the 'group's' bank financiers is implied in Note 13 of the 1997 Annual Report of Lang Corporation. It states that non-current bank loans of approximately $228 million were 'secured by way of mortgages and fixed floating charges, real property mortgages and equitable mortgage over the assets of various *entities within the economic entity*' (p. 25, emphasis added).

40 *Qintex Australia Finance Ltd v Schroeders Australia Ltd* (1991) 3 ACSR 267 at 268; 9 ACLC 109 at 110; *Charterbridge Corporation Ltd v Lloyds Bank Ltd* [1970] 1Ch. 62 at 74; and others (see H. Ford and R. Austin, *Principles of Corporations Law*, Sydney: Butterworths (1997) especially 8.140 *ff.* and Hill, 'Cross guarantees and corporate groups' (1992).

41 *Qintex Australia Finance Ltd v Schroeders Australia Ltd* (1991) 3 ACSR 267 at 268; 9 ACLC 109 at 110.

42 *Wilson v Pipetech Pty Ltd* (1989) 7 ACLC 191.

43 The wider issue of whether generally wholly owned subsidiaries provide a net benefit to society has been addressed in several forums and was assessed in Clarke *et al.*, *Corporate Collapse* (2003), chapters 16 and 17.

44 What follows is based on published materials primarily in James Hardie's financials, Notes to the Accounts (see especially 'Key events since 2001 leading to the signing of the FFA' in the 2006 Notes), newspaper accounts and the 2004 Jackson Special Commission of Inquiry Report (the Jackson Report).

45 E. Sexton, 'A case of who knew what, when', *SMH*, 19 June 2004, p. 48.

46 Haigh, *Asbestos House: The secret history of James Hardie Industries* (2006), especially chapters 13 *et ff*; as well as E. Sexton, 'Smell of rats in moral haze', *Sydney Morning Herald*, 10–11 February 2007, p. 34, which outlined how many, including the ACTU's Barry Robson, reportedly 'smelt a rat' when the restructure in 2001 was announced.

47 James Hardie Industries NV and Subsidiaries, *2006 Financial Statements*, Notes to the Accounts, Note 12, p. 106.

48 As noted in the Jackson Commission Report (Jackson QF (QC)), Report of the Special Commission of Inquiry into the Medical Research and Compensation Foundation (September 2004).

49 This is discussed in I. Ramsay, 'Pushing the limit for directors', *Australian Financial Review*, 5 April 2005, p. 63.

50 For example, consider the common practice of one company within a corporate group, the 'banker', borrowing funds and then on-lending those monies throughout the group. This was well illustrated at Patrick/MUA described earlier.

51 ASIC Media Release 02/69, 'ASIC's Ansett investigation focuses on financial disclo-sures by Air New Zealand Limited', March 2002. The Ansett Group administrator, KordaMentha, has submitted that in such group collapses the assets and liabili-ties of the group should be 'pooled' (as reported in CAMAC, *Rehabilitating Large and Complex Enterprises in Financial Difficulties* (2004), p. 10. Regarding details of the events leading up to and in the Ansett administration, the following draws on KordaMentha Administrator's Reports prepared from 2003 onwards. Extracts from the specific Reports are noted below.

52 Based on extracts from KordaMentha Research Unit Paper 302, 'Large and complex administrations: The courts and Ansett', August 2003.

53 Based on extracts from KordaMentha Research Unit, Paper 305, 'Rehabilitating large and complex enterprises in financial difficulty', December 2003.

54 Based on extracts from KordaMentha Research Unit, Paper 305, 'Rehabilitating large and complex enterprises in financial difficulty', December 2003.

55 The UK Report of the Review Committee (Chairman, Sir Kenneth Cork), *Insolvency Law and Practice* (London: HMSO, 1982) after debating the pros and cons of grouping (for example, contracting-in or contracting-out), rejected both. Interestingly the CASAC (2000) *Corporate Groups: Final report* suggested the opposite approach. An 'opting-in' proposal was suggested for consideration as part of *CLERP 9* reforms. This presumed that all companies be viewed as separate entities unless relevant directors indicated that they opt-in and were to be viewed as a group. Clearly there is uncertainty as to how to resolve this dilemma.

56 F. Buffini, 'Insolvency reforms to protect super', *Australian Financial Review*, 13 November 2006, pp. 1 and 4. Insolvency ED, 'Corporations Amendment (Insolvency) Bill, No XXX, 2007', released for public comment 13 November 2006.

57 Details from HIH *Royal Commission Report* (HIHRC, 2003) and F. Clarke *et al.*, *Corporate Collapse* (2003: especially pp. 222–45).

58 Australian financial commentator Gottliebsen, *10 Best and 10 Worst Decisions of Australian CEOs, 1992–2002* (2003), pp. 184–99 lists HIH's alleged cover-up and FAI takeover by Ray Williams as one of the worst decisions of the period 1992–2002.

59 Chapter 6 refers to some implications of this FAI acquisition as it relates to the 'asset', goodwill appearing in HIH's consolidated accounts.

60 HIH Royal Commission, *The Failure of HIH Insurance* (2003), Vol. III, p. 23.

61 Scandals at Enron, WoldCom and (say) HIH have resulted in numerous academic forums examining what lessons can be learned from these events. Special forum journal issues have resulted, including: *Issues in Accounting Education* (March 2005, pp. 1–53), *European Accounting Review* (November 2005, pp. 341–440), *Accounting History* (November 2005, pp. 5–116), *Accounting Horizons* (November 2006, pp. 345–407). See also Benston and Hargraves, 'Enron: What happened and what we can learn from it' (2002), pp. 105–127.

62 Culp and Niskanen, *Corporate Aftershock* (2003), p. 162. They explain the history of SPEs (pp. 153–73) within a general framework of their being part of a 'structured finance' movement that Enron exploited for its own ends.

63 Partnoy, *Infectious Greed: How deceit and risk corrupted the financial markets* (2003).

## 8 Groupthink: fact or fiction?

1 Clarke *et al.*, *Corporate Collapse* (1997, 2003).

2 CASAC, *Corporate Groups: Final report* (2000).

3 Treasury, *Insolvency ED, Corporations Amendment (Insolvency) Bill No XXX*, 2007, released for public comment 13 November 2006.

4 For a brief discussion on these options refer to CASAC, *Corporate Groups: Final report* (2000), especially chapter 6. Importantly, executing and retaining the deed is a voluntary decision taken by the directors of the closed-group companies. Contrasting with a normal financing institution-administered cross-guarantee instrument, only directors of the relevant closed-group companies are signatories to the ASIC deed.

5 Bosch, *The Workings of a Watchdog* (1990), p. 58. Bosch observed that the introduction of the NCSC Deed of Indemnity was 'the Commission's major [deregulatory]

administrative initiative of the 1980s (p. 58) and further, that '[v]ery large numbers of companies have taken advantage of this decision and great savings have been made . . . the Commission has [not] been made aware of any disadvantage that has been suffered by anyone as a result' (p. 68).

6 Bosch, *The Workings of a Watchdog* (1990), p. 68. Companies originally registered the deed with ASIC for approval, but since June 2004 ASIC only administers the deed. Originally those subsidiaries had to be wholly owned companies, registered in Australia. Revisions to the ASIC Class Order in 1998 (98/14) extended the relief to 'controlled' entities, including foreign registered entities. See also Dean *et al.*, 'Corporate restructuring, creditors' rights, cross guarantees and group behaviour' (1999) n. 39 and 40 for details about previous class orders. The enlarged group is referred to as an 'extended closed group' and companies are now required to provide a consolidated set of reports in the Notes to Accounts on these effectively new reporting entities.

7 Baxt and Lane, 'Developments in relation to corporate groups and responsibilities of directors – some insights and new directions', (1998).

8 The evidence to date on deed usage includes: Dean *et al.*, 'Corporate restructuring, creditors' rights, cross guarantees and group behaviour' (1999); which augmented Ramsay and Stapledon, *Corporate Groups in Australia* (1998) and Ramsay and Stapledon, 'Corporate groups in Australia' (2001).

9 For instance, in possibly Australia's largest liquidation, the HIH administrator had to consider implications of the deed covenants.

10 See Dean *et al.*, 'Corporate restructuring, creditors' rights, cross guarantees and group behaviour' (1999).

11 H. A. J. Ford and R. P. Austin, *Principles of Corporations Law* (Sydney: Butterworths, 7th ed., 1995) p. 776 interpreted McLelland J's solution in the *Westmex* cross-claims case to be what leading lawyers and Debelle J (in the *JN Taylor* case) had described as 'the infinite regress' problem pertaining to cross-claims in a group liquidation: 'The debts, claims and assets to be taken into consideration in ascertaining a shortfall' [for purposes of determining the individual company obligations under the deed] would, according to McLelland J in *Westmex Operations Pty Ltd v Westmex Ltd* (1992) 8 ACSR 146 at 153, be debts, claims and assets *external* to the deed of cross guarantee. It was thought that any other view would deny sensible operation of the deed [the infinite regress issue]: *Re JN Taylor Holdings Ltd (in liq)* 6 ACSR 18; 9 ACLC 1483. For the accounting complexities see Dean *et al.*, "Notional calculations in liquidations revisited: The case of ASC Class Order cross guarantees' (1993), p. 204 (emphasis added).

12 Under the Indemnity Deed the guarantees were unidirectional – that is, between the parent and subsidiary companies only – under the later ASIC Deed of Cross-Guarantee the guarantees are effective against all signatories to the deed.

13 C. Chapman, 'Cross guarantees drown in the pool', *International Financial Review* (September 1990), p. 16.

14 KordaMentha Research Unit, Paper 305, 'Rehabilitating large and complex enterprises in financial difficulty', December 2003 (as noted in chapter 7).

15 In many respects the formal regulatory-approved cross-guarantee instrument has added another dimension to the general common law issue of 'set off' and the related 'guarantee' issues pertaining to cross-claims in group liquidations. The common law

position is well captured in the decision in *Re Amalgamated Investment and Property Co Ltd* [1984] 3 All ER 272 which confirmed the entitlement of a lender to a company within a group with a cross guarantee in place to prove for the full amount of its debt, not only in the liquidation of the group company which is the principal debtor but also in the other guarantor group companies (in liquidation). The caveat is that the creditor cannot receive in aggregate more than 100 cents in the dollar from all admissible claims.

16  In the late 1980s and early 1990s Rogers J made several *obiter* comments suggesting that the operations of wholly owned subsidiaries were presumed by directors to be like the operations of branches of the parent. He observed also that creditors and others were often unaware of which entity within the economic group they were dealing with.

17  These included Hill, 'Cross guarantees and corporate groups' (1992) and Hill, 'Corporate groups, creditor protection and cross guarantees: Australian perspectives' (1995).

18  These figures are preliminary. Compilation and verification is a laborious task. Data obtained from the ASIC Ascot Database has been found to have mistakes due mainly, we believe, to transposition errors when extracting information from the hardcopy of the deed. Ascot information for the period 1999–2002 recently has been obtained but has not been verified. It is expected that the full 1991–2002 verified dataset should be available to researchers generally by the end of 2008.

19  Initial analyses by the authors of the data underpinning figure 8.1 failed to disclose any evidence of closed-group formation responding to economy-wide factors.

20  These numbers vary period by period as revocation, assumption and disposal deeds are executed.

21  Ramsay and Stapledon, *Corporate Groups in Australia* (1998) and Ramsay and Stapledon, 'Corporate groups in Australia' (2001).

22  F. Clarke, G. Dean and E. Houghton, 'Revitalising group accounting: Improving accountability', *Australian Accounting Review*, 58 12 (3) (2002); and Clarke *et al.*, *Corporate Collapse* (2003). This is not just an Australian phenomenon, as is evident by concerns about the lack of serviceability of accounting standards by many informed financial commentators, including Arthur Levitt, Chairman of the US's SEC (see A. Levitt, 'The new numbers game' (remarks delivered at the New York University Center for Law and Business, 28 September 1998) accessed at <http://www.sec.gov/news/speeches/spch220.txt>, and on 18 October 1999, 'Quality information: The lifeblood of our markets' (a plea to those preparing accounting data to give more consideration to their 'quality' in a speech to the Economic Club of New York) <http://www.sec.gov/news/speeches/spch304.htm> and Schuetze (former SEC Chief Accountant), R. J. Chambers Memorial Research Lecture (2001b). For a summary of other US and Australian concerns, refer to Clarke *et al.*, *Corporate Collapse* (2003), especially chapter 2.

23  Details of the questionnaire design and full analyses appear in Clarke and Dean, 'Corporate officers' views on cross-guarantees and other proposals to "lift the corporate veil"' (2005b), pp. 299–320, and Clarke *et al.*, 'Solvency solecisms – corporate officers' views on group solidarity', working paper (2007).

24  In one of the few empirical papers on deed usage, Dean *et al.*, 'Corporate restructuring, creditors' rights, cross guarantees and group behaviour' (1999), mused: 'Why only

20% of Australia's listed companies have taken up the Class Order Deed is not obvious. What makes the deed attractive to some companies but not others of similar size in the same industry is equally unclear. Speculations have intuitive appeal but no solid backing.' An in-depth analysis of issues raised is being undertaken by the authors in an econometric-based modelling paper, Bradbury *et al.* (2007).

25 Ramsay and Stapledon, 'Corporate groups in Australia' (2001).

26 Ramsay and Stapledon, *Corporate Groups in Australia* (1998), especially table 7.

27 Clarke and Dean, 'Corporate officers' views on cross-guarantees and other proposals to "lift the corporate veil"' (2005b), and Bradbury *et al.*, 'Incentives for cross-guarantee in corporate groups' (2007), <www.business.uts.edu.au/accounting/pdfs/conf07bradbury.pdf> have provided tentative explanations of those factors critical in the strategic decision to execute a deed. Their analyses reveal that the deed take-up is clearly a complex issue.

28 Such a view is perhaps influenced by 'grouping' ideas embedded in certain commercial operations, most notably for taxation purposes and workers' compensation laws (see M. Mattera, 'Grouping could affect premiums', *Australian Financial Review*, 18 April 2006, p. 44).

29 See CASAC, *Corporate Groups: Final report* (2000).

30 Consider *ASIC v Rich* (2003) 44 ACSR 341 and *Rich v Australian Securities and Investments Commission* (2004) 209 ALR 271 and newspaper accounts during September and October 2005 of the One.Tel matter in the NSW Supreme Court and articles in the popular press during April 2006, that explained the *ASIC v Rich and Silbermann* case. See also the press commentaries in, say, the *Australian Financial Review* on the Westpoint saga which began when ASIC successfully sought a court-appointed liquidator in February 2006. A brief summary of the Bell case particulars at the end of Australia's longest corporate court case is given in the *Australian News*, 'Banks "took advantage" of Bell Group', 18 September 2006 and also in chapter 7.

31 Victorian *Water Wheel* case: *ASIC v Plymin, Elliott & Harrison* [2003] VSC 123.

32 Observations by ASIC, and by the chair of Australia's AASB, David Boymal on issues of impairment and solvency in justifying dividend decisions, and insurance matters related to solvency in APRA's Financial Condition Reporting Guidelines for Insurers also focus on the importance of understanding what is meant by (in)solvency. See ASIC Media Releases IR 05–42 on withdrawal of PN39 related to impairment of goodwill and IR 05–57 where ASIC clarifies impact of IFRS on dividends. Also, APRA Discussion Paper (2005) on risk and financial management – Media Release No: 05–23; and Finnis, 'Financial reporting for general insurers', *Actuary Australia* (2005).

33 See Margret, 'Insolvency and tests of insolvency: An analysis of the "balance sheet" and "cash flow" tests' (2002), and Mescher, 'Personal liability for company directors for company debts' (1996).

34 A 'schizophrenia' analogy was first introduced into the legal debate on groups when referring to 'Directors' schizophrenia' by Baxt and Lane, 'Developments in relation to corporate groups and the responsibilities of directors'(1998).

35 See also CASAC, *Corporate Groups: Final report* (2000).

36 *The Bell Group Limited (In Liquidation) & Ors v Westpac Banking Corporation & Ors* Supreme Court of Western Australia Action No. CIV 1464 of 2000.

37 CASAC, *Corporate Groups: Final report* (2000). CASAC has changed its name and is now the Corporations and Markets Advisory Committee (CAMAC) – see <www.camac.gov.au>.

38 CASAC, *Corporate Groups: Final report* (2000).

39 R. Baxt, 'Corporations law a fragile structure', *Australian Financial Review*, 19 November 2004, p. 35.

40 The UK Report of the Review Committee (Chairman, Sir Kenneth Cork), *Insolvency Law and Practice* (London: HMSO, 1982) after debating the pros and cons of grouping (for example, contracting-in or contracting-out) cautioned against such a legislative change, noting (paras 1940 and 1952): 1940. 'An alteration in the law would introduce a difference between types of shareholders as regards the fundamental principle of limited liability. An individual shareholder could limit his exposure in a commercial venture by entering into it through the medium of a limited company. A corporate shareholder might no longer have the same facility, or at least not to the same extent. The availability of a limitation on liability may bear significantly on the readiness of an already prosperous company to enter upon a new enterprise. It may quite properly take the view that in the interests of its own shareholders, it should limit its risk. A change in the law may, therefore, affect entrepreneurial activity, whether on a large or a small scale, in commerce and industry . . .'
1952. 'It is impossible to divorce the position in insolvency from the position prior to insolvency, and we have reluctantly come to the conclusion that we should not recommend a fundamental change in company law by means of proposals to effect a change in insolvency law.' See further discussion in Blumberg, *The Law of Corporate Groups* (1983).

## 9 An alternative group therapy to consolidation accounting

1 This chapter draws on: Clarke and Dean, 'Law and accounting: The separate legal entity principle and consolidation accounting' (1993), Clarke and Dean, 'Chaos in the counting house: Accounting under scrutiny' (1992), Dean *et al.*, 'Notional calculations in liquidations revisited: The case of ASC Class Order cross guarantees' (1993) and Clarke *et al.*, 'Improved corporate group accountability' (2002).

2 Hadden, 'The regulation of corporate groups' (1992), p. 72.

3 Hill, 'Cross-guarantees and corporate groups' (1992), 312 at 317 lists some critics.

4 L. C. B. Gower, *Principles of Modern Company Law* (1979), pp. 118–19.

5 *Littlewoods Mail Order Stores Ltd v I.R.C.* 1 WLR [1969], 1254.

6 *D.H.N. Ltd v Tower Hamlets* [1976] 1 WLR, 852 (emphasis added); *Industrial Equity Ltd v Blackburn* (1977), 137 CLR, 567.

7 *Industrial Equity Ltd v Blackburn* (1977), 137 CLR, 567.

8 ASC Media Release 91/64, Issues Paper 29, 'Public hearing: accounting relief for wholly-owned subsidiaries', para. 3.

9 S. Jemison, 'Why not sack Clark, SBSA director asked', *Australian Financial Review*, 22 May 1992, p. 55. Details of the complexity of these off-balance sheet operations were revealed in T. Maher, 'Why the State Bank went south', *Australian Business*, 20 February 1991, pp. 12–16, S. Jemison, 'Counsel turn up the heat as ex-director gives evidence', *Australian Financial Review*, 25 May 1992, p. 48.

10 J. Mason in *Industrial Equity Ltd v Blackburn* (1977), 137 CLR, 567.

11 This is reinforced by the financial imbroglios in 'closed-group' liquidations where attempts to administer regulatory-approved class order cross guarantees have proven nigh impossible. It would seem in respect of 'liquidated' and 'going concerns' a 'state of affairs' presupposes a 'legal' form.

12 The current AIFRS equivalent of AASB 1024 under the AIFRS regime is AASB 127.

13 Walker, *Consolidated Statements: A history and analysis* (1978) documents the numerous functions of consolidated statements. A condensed version appears in R. G. Walker, 'An evaluation of the information conveyed by consolidated statements' *Abacus* (December 1976), pp. 77–115.

14 Hadden, 'The regulation of corporate groups in Australia' (1992), p. 72.

15 Walker, *Consolidated Statements: A history and analysis* (1978), p. 277, emphasis added.

16 Eisenberg, 'Corporate groups' in Gillooly (ed.), *The Law Relating to Corporate Groups* (1993).

17 A somewhat similar, radical move – prohibiting the operation of holding companies across state borders – occurred in the US following the abuses perpetrated by virtue of complex group structures such as Ivar Kreuger's international match labyrinth and Insull-type utility company group structures operating sub/sub holding companies across state boundaries. Many congressmen at the US Congressional Hearings before the Senate Committee on Banking and Practice into the 1920s holding company abuses expressed concerns about complex group structures – some of which are reproduced in Clarke and Dean, 'Chaos in the counting house: Accounting under scrutiny' (1992). J. Farrar, 'The regulation of corporate groups', *Company and Securities Law Journal* (August 1998) acknowledges that while this is an extreme option, it is clearly worth debating.

18 Refer to the Maxwell Communications Investigators' Reports – Thomas and Turner, *Mirror Group Newspapers plc: investigations under Sections 432(2) and 442 of the Companies Act 1985* (2000).

19 See Rogers J. suggestions in several Qintex decisions in the late 1980s.

20 For details of pre-1980 company failures in Australia see Sykes, *Two Centuries of Panic: A history of corporate collapses in Australia* (1988), while more recent controversial consolidation accounting practices are revealed in Walker, 'Off-balance sheet financing' (1992b), Hadden, 'The regulation of corporate groups' (1992) and Sykes, *The Bold Riders* (1996).

21 Chambers, *Securities and Obscurities: A case for reform of the law of company accounts* (1973b), p. 225.

22 *Spedley Securities Limited (in Liquidation) v Greater Pacific Investments Pty Limited (in Liquidation) and Ors, 50177 of 1991: The October Transactions*, p. 10.

23 B. Pheasant, 'Goldberg trust held Brick and Pipe stake', *Australian Financial Review*, 12 February 1992, p. 23.

24 B. Pheasant, 'Backdating gave Goldberg $160 million', *Australian Financial Review*, 14 February 1992, p. 19; and the judgment in the Victorian Supreme Court by Southwell J, *Linter Group Limited v A. Goldberg and Zev Furst and Anors*, No. 2195 of 1990, 4 May 1992; and B. Pheasant, 'Former Goldberg accountant tells of "warehousing"', *Australian Financial Review*, 30 August 1993, p. 4. The latter recounts another deal with the potential to benefit private companies controlled by Goldberg at the expense

249

of the shareholders of public companies. For details of the Rothwells transactions see, McCusker Report, *Report of the Inspector on a Special Investigation into Rothwells Limited Pursuant to Companies Code (W. A.)*, (Perth: W.A. Government Printer, 1989); for details of the Spedley Holdings round robin see J. Manson and T. Sykes, 'Lucky Brian', *Australian Business*, 16 May 1990, pp. 16–19; for the particulars involving Unity Corporation and the private company, Carter Holdings Pty Limited, see C. Fox, 'Carter "siphoned off" $17 million, hearing told', *Australian Financial Review*, 4 February 1992, p. 17.

25 Walker, 'Off-balance sheet financing' (1992b), and Walker, 'A feeling of déjà vu: Controversies in accounting and auditing regulation in Australia' (1993).

26 What follows is our interpretation of Chambers' method, given the advent of computer technology. In the appendix we provide an extended worked example of how this system would apply in practice – especially in a computerised reporting context. The system would be totally compatible with an eXtensible Business Reporting Language accounting system, and would facilitate continuous contemporary disclosures.

27 This approach draws upon a proposal made by R. J. Chambers in 1973. It was first privately illustrated through a worked example by one of the current authors, as part of MBA lecture material at The University of Sydney in 1976.

28 A reviewer of the first edition of *Corporate Collapse* complained that no illustration was given of the alternative we described. Recent events have indicated that if the parent/subsidiary structure is not to be dispensed with, and all the signs are that the impediments remain as strong as ever, a reconstruction of the accounting for intercorporate investments and investments in other entities is long overdue. Accordingly, we provided an illustration of our mechanism in the second edition of *Corporate Collapse* and in the appendix to this chapter and a comparison between it and the metrics of conventional consolidation procedures.

29 These and related issues pertaining to accounting for goodwill are discussed in M. Bloom, Double Accounting for Goodwill, PhD thesis, The University of Sydney, 2005.

30 Hadden, 'The regulation of corporate groups' (1992), p. 72. Importantly, each company within a corporate group normally is required to prepare a separate Annual Return to be lodged with the ASIC.

## 10   'Patching': past, present, prospect

1 D. Skeel, Letter to the Editor, *Wall Street Journal*, 'Recall doing book reports by reading the ending', 31 March 2005, p. A11.

2 Ibid.

3 Chanticleer, *Australian Financial Review*, 22 November 2006, p. 60.

4 Recent press reports imply Australian prosecutors are not as successful as their US counterparts. See, for example, C. Milne, 'Harris Scarfe trials claim only one scalp', *Australian Financial Review*, 12 January 2007, pp. 26–7.

5 T. Boreham, 'Mockers of rules better beware of the watchdog', *Business Review Weekly*, 19 March 1993, pp. 92–3.

6 Clarke *et al.*, *Corporate Collapse* (2003), p. 331.

7 These points are based on ideas first proposed in Dean, Clarke and Wolnizer, 'Submission to JPCAA Inquiry, "Review of independent auditing by registered public companies"', August 2002, www.aph.gov.au.

8 Letters to the Editor, *Australian Financial Review*, 20 December 2006, p. 43 – V. J. Carroll, 'Private equity poses moral hazard' and W. Brown, 'Investors left with junk' – warn of an overheating and impending downturn; also A. Kohler, 'It's different this time, but not different enough, as the tail wags the dog', *SMH*, 22–24 December 2006, p. 55.

9 Gay and Simnett, *Auditing and Assurance Services* (2006), chapter 1. That complexity remains a critical concern for users and regulators and it underpins recent reports of persistent audit problems, for example, K. Drawbough, 'Update 2 – US audit watchdog [PCAOB] flags faults in auditing', *Reuters News*, 22 January 2007 and WebCPA staff, 'Canadian [Public Accountability] Board: Audit firms need to do more', WebCPA, 11 February 2007.

# Bibliography

AAA, *Accounting Principles Underlying Corporate Financial Statements* (Evanston, Ill.: American Accounting Association, 1936).

AAA, *A Statement of Basic Accounting Theory* (Evanston, Ill.: American Accounting Association, 1936).

AAA, *Statement on Accounting Theory and Theory Acceptance* (Florida: American Accounting Association, 1977).

AAA Financial Accounting Standards Committee (AAAFASC), 'Evaluating concept-based vs rules-based approaches to standard setting', *Accounting Horizons*, 17 (1), 2003, pp. 73–89.

Accounting Standards Review Committee, *Company Accounting Standards*, under chairmanship of R. J. Chambers (Sydney: NSW Government Printer, 1978).

Agrawal, A. and C. Knoeber, 'Firm performance and mechanisms to control agency problems between managers and shareholders', *Journal of Financial and Quantitative Analysis*, Vol. 31, 1996, pp. 377–97.

Alexander, A., 'A benchmark for the adequacy of published financial statements', *Accounting and Business Research*, 29, Summer, 1999.

Alexander, A., and E. Jemakowicz, 'A true and fair view of the Principles/Rules debate', *Abacus*, June 2006, pp. 132–64.

Almerighi, M., *I banchieri di Dio: il caso Calvi* (Roma: Editoru Ruiniti, 2002).

Altman, E. I., *Corporate Bankruptcy in America* (Lexington, Mass.: Heath Lexington Books, 1971).

Altman, E. I., *Corporate Financial Distress: A complete guide to predicting, avoiding and dealing with bankruptcy* (New York: John Wiley & Sons, 1983; 2nd edn, 1993).

Altman, E. I., *Bankruptcy, Credit Risk, and High Yield Junk Bonds* (Malden, Mass. and Oxford: Blackwell, 2002).

American Institute of Certified Public Accountants, *The Commission on Auditors' Responsibilities: Report, conclusions, and recommendations* (New York, NY: American Institute of Certified Public Accountants, 1978).

American Law Institute, *Principles of Corporate Governance, Analysis and Recommendations* (New York: American Law Institute, 1992).

Amernic, J. and Craig, R., 'Reform of accounting education in the post-Enron era: moving accountants "out of the shadows"', *Abacus*, 40 (3), October 2004, pp. 342–78.

Argenti, J., *Corporate Collapse: The causes and symptoms* (London: McGraw-Hill, 1976).

Argenti, J., 'Predicting Company Failure', *Accountants' Digest* No. 93 (London: Institute of Chartered Accountants in England and Wales, 1985).

Arnold, A. J. and McCartney, S., *George Hudson: The rise and fall of the railway king* (London: Hambledon, 2004).

Arnold, T. W., *The Folklore of Capitalism* (New Haven: Yale University Press, 1937).

Auditing Practices Board, *The Future Development of Auditing – A Paper to Promote Debate* (London: Auditing Practices Board, 1992).

Australian Accounting Research Foundation, Accounting Theory Monograph No. 10: *Measurement in Financial Accounting* (Melbourne: Australian Accounting Research Foundation, 1998).

*Australian Corporations Act (2001)* (Sydney: Butterworths, 2001).

Australian Securities and Investments Commission (ASIC) Media Releases: 03–118, 'ASIC acts to prevent insolvent trading' (2003); 04–314, 'ASIC urges companies to act early to avoid insolvent trading' (2004); 05–317

Australian Society of Accountants, *Accounting Principles and Practices Discussed in Reports of Company Failures* (Sydney–Melbourne: ASA General Council, 1966).

Australian Society of Certified Practising Accountants (ASCPA) and the Institute of Chartered Accountants in Australia (ICAA), *A Research Study on Financial Reporting and Auditing – Bridging the Expectations Gap* (Melbourne: ASCPA/ICAA, 1993, 1996).

Bakan, J., *The Corporation: The pathological pursuit of power* (London: Constable, 2004).

Barber, D. B., 'Restoring trust after fraud: does corporate governance matter?', *The Accounting Review*, 80 (2), 2005, pp. 539–61.

Barchard, D., *Asil Nadir and the Rise and Fall of Polly Peck* (London: Victor Gollancz, 1992).

Barry, P., *Rich Kids: How the Packers and Murdochs lost $950 million in One.Tel* (Sydney: Bantam Books, 2002).

Barry, P., *The Rise and Fall of Alan Bond* (Sydney: Bantam Books, 1990).

Bartholomeusz, S., 'Westpoint exposes the soft side of auditing', *Sydney Morning Herald*, 13 June 2006.

Basioudis, I. G., Geiger, M. A., Papanastasiou, V., 'Audit fees, non-audit fees and auditor-going concern reporting decisions in the UK', American Accounting Association, paper, Washington, DC, 6–9 August 2006.

Baxt, R., 'Corporations Law a fragile structure', *Australian Financial Review*, 19 November 2004, p. 35.

Baxt, R. and Lane, T., 'Developments in relation to corporate groups and the responsibilities of directors', *Company and Securities Law Journal*, November 1998, pp. 628–53.

Baxter, W. A. and Davidson, S., *Studies in Accounting Theory* (London: Sweet & Maxwell, 1962).

Baysinger, B. and Butler, H., 'Corporate governance and the board of directors: Performance effects of changes in board composition', *Journal of Law, Economics and Organisation*, Vol. 1, 1985, pp. 101–24.

Beattie, V., Fearnley, S. and Brandt, R., *Behind Closed Doors: What a company audit is all about* (Wiltshire: Palgrave/Institute of Chartered Accountants in England and Wales, 2001).

Beaty, J., Gwynne, S. C., *The Outlaw Bank* (New York, NY: Random House, 1993).

Benston, G. J., *Corporate Financial Disclosure in the UK and the USA* (Farnborough, Hants: Saxon House, 1976).

Benston, G., Bromwich, M., Litan, R. E. and Wagenhofer, A., *Worldwide Financial Reporting: The development and future of accounting standards* (Oxford: Oxford University Press, 2006).

Benston, G., Hargraves, A. L., 'Enron: What happened and what we can learn from it', *Journal of Accounting and Public Policy*, 21 (2002), pp. 105–27.

Berenson, A., *The Number: Why companies lied and the stock market crashed* (London: Simon & Schuster, 2003).

Berle, A. A. and Means, G. C., *The Modern Corporation and Private Property* (New York: Macmillan, 1932).

Berle, A. A. and Means, G. C., 'The impact of the corporation on classical economic theory', *Quarterly Journal of Economics*, 79, 1965, pp. 25–40.

Bhagat, S. and Black, B., 'The uncertain relationship between board composition and firm performance', *Business Lawyer*, Vol. 54, No.3, 1999, pp. 921–63.

Blasi, J., Kruse, D. and Berstein, A., *In the Company of Owners: The truth about stock options* (New York: Basic Books, 2003).

Bloom, M., Double Accounting for Goodwill, PhD thesis, The University of Sydney, 2005.

Blumberg, P., *The Law of Corporate Groups* (Boston: Little, Brown and Co., 1983).

Bonbright, J. C. and Means, G. C., *The Holding Company: Its public significance and its regulation* (New York: McGraw-Hill, 1932).

Bosch, H., *The Workings of a Watchdog* (Melbourne: William Heinemann Australia, 1990).

Bosch, H., *Corporate Procedures and Conduct* (Sydney: Institute of Directors, 1991, 1993).

Botosan, C. K., Koonce, L. and Ryan, S. G., 'Accounting for liabilities: conceptual issues, standard setting and evidence from academic research', *Accounting Horizons*, Vol. 19, No. 3, 2005, pp. 159–86.

Bower, T., *Maxwell: The outsider* (London: Mandarin Paperbacks, 1991).

Bradbury, M., Clarke, F. and Dean, G. 'Incentives for cross-guarantee in corporate groups', 2007 University of Technology Sydney Summer Accounting Symposium, 1–2 February 2007, accessed on 2 February 2007 at www.business.uts.edu.au/accounting/pdfs/conf07bradbury.pdf.

Bresciani-Turroni, C., *The Economics of Inflation* (London: Allen & Unwin, 1937).

Brewster, M., *Unaccountable: How the accounting profession forfeited a public trust* (Hoboken, N.J.: Wiley, 2003)

Briloff, A. J., *Unaccountable Accounting* (New York: Harper & Row, 1972).

Briloff, A. J., *More Debits Than Credits: The burnt investor's guide to financial statements* (New York: Harper & Row, 1976).

Briloff, A. J., *The Truth About Corporate Accounting* (New York: Harper & Row, 1982).

Bromwich, M., Benston, G. and Wagenhofer, A., 'Principles- versus rules-based Accounting Standards: the FASB's standard-setting strategy', *Abacus*, June 2006, pp. 165–88.

Brooks, C., *The Royal Mail Case* (Toronto: Law Book Co., 1933).

Buckmaster, D., *Development of the Income Smoothing Literature 1893–1998: A focus on the United States* (JAI Press: Amsterdam, 2001).

Cadbury Committee, *Code of Corporate Governance – Interim and Final* (London: HMSO, 1991, 1992).

Canning, J. B., *The Economics of Accountancy* (New York: Ronald Press, 1929; Arno Press reprint 1978).

Carey, J. L., *The Rise of the Accountancy Profession: From technician to professional 1896–1936* (New York, NY: American Institute of Certified Public Accountants, 1969).

Carey, J. L., *The Rise of the Accounting Profession: To responsibility and authority 1937–1969* (New York, NY: American Institute of Certified Public Accountants, 1970).

Carswell, J., *The South Sea Bubble* (London: Cresset Press, 1961).

Cassidy, J., *Dot.con: The greatest story ever told* (London: Allen Lane, Penguin Press, 2002).

Chambers, R. J., 'Conventions, doctrines and commonsense', *Accountants' Journal*, July 1964, pp. 182–7.

Chambers, R. J., *Accounting, Evaluation and Economic Behavior* (New Jersey: Prentice Hall, Englewood Cliffs, 1966).

Chambers, R. J., 'Accounting principles and the law', *Australian Business Law Review*, June 1973a, pp. 112–29.

Chambers, R. J., *Securities and Obscurities: A case for reform of the law of company accounts* (Melbourne: Gower Press, 1973b); reproduced as *Accounting in Disarray* (New York: Garland Publishing, 1986).

Chambers, R. J., 'A critical examination of company accounting standards', *Abacus*, December 1975, pp. 136–52.

Chambers, R. J., Occasional Paper No. 11, *Current Cost Accounting: A critique of the Sandilands Report* (Lancaster: ICRA University of Lancaster, 1976).

Chambers, R. J., 'Accounting and corporate morality – the ethical cringe', *Australian Journal of Corporate Law*, Vol. I, No. 1, September 1991, pp. 9–21.

Chambers, R. J., *Accounting Thesaurus: Five hundred years of accounting* (London: Elsevier, 1995).

Chambers, R. J., 'Ends, ways, means and conceptual frameworks', *Abacus*, September 1996, pp. 119–32.

Chambers, R. J. and Dean, G. (eds), *Chambers on Accounting, Vol. V: Continuously contemporary accounting* (New York: Garland Publishing, 1986).

Chambers, R. J. and Wolnizer, P., 'A true and fair view of financial position', *Company and Securities Law Journal*, December 1990.

Chambers, R. J. and Wolnizer, P., 'A true and fair view of position and results: The historical background', *Accounting, Business and Financial History*, April 1991.

Chatfield, M. and Vangermeersch, R., *The History of Accounting: An international encyclopedia* (New York: Garland Publishing, 1996).

Chatov, R., *Corporate Financial Reporting* (New York, NY: Free Press, 1975).

Clarke, F. L., *The Tangled Web of Price Variation Accounting* (New York: Garland Publishing, 1982).

Clarke, F. L., 'Deprival value and optimized deprival value in the Australasian public sector accounting: Unwarranted drift and contestable serviceability', *Abacus*, March 1998, pp. 8–17.

Clarke, F. L., 'Introduction: True and Fair view – anachronism or quality control par excellence?', *Abacus*, June 2006, pp. 129–31.

Clarke, F. L. and Dean, G. W., *Contributions of Limperg and Schmidt to the Replacement Cost Debate in the 1920s* (New York: Garland Publishing, 1990a).

Clarke, F. L. and Dean, G. W., *Replacement Cost Accounting and Reform in Post–World War I Germany* (New York: Garland Publishing, 1990b).

Clarke, F. and Dean, G., 'Chaos in the counting house: Accounting under scrutiny', *Australian Journal of Corporate Law*, September 1992, pp. 177–201.

Clarke, F. and Dean, G., 'Law and accounting – the separate legal entity principle and consolidation accounting', *Australian Business Law Review*, Vol. 21, Issue 4, August 1993, pp. 246–69.

Clarke, F. L. and Dean, G., 'An evolving conceptual framework?', *Abacus,* October 2003, pp. 279–97.

Clarke, F. and Dean, G., 'Corporate governance: A case of misplaced concreteness?', *Advances in Public Interest Accounting,* Vol. 11, *Corporate Governance: Does Any Size Fit?* (Elsevier: JAI, 2005a), pp. 15–39.

Clarke, F. and Dean, G., 'Corporate officers' views on cross-guarantees and other proposals to "lift the corporate veil"', *Company and Securities Law Journal,* Vol. 23, 2005b, pp. 299–320.

Clarke, F., Dean, G. and Houghton, E., 'Revitalising group accounting: Improving accountability', *Australian Accounting Review,* November 2002, pp. 58–72.

Clarke, F., Dean, G. and Margret J., 'Solvency solecisms – corporate officers' views on group solidarity', working paper, 2007.

Clarke, F. L., Dean, G. W. and Oliver, K. G., *Corporate Collapse: Regulatory, accounting and ethical failure* (Cambridge: Cambridge University Press, 1997).

Clarke, F., Dean, G. and Oliver, K., *Corporate Collapse: Accounting, regulatory and ethical failure,* rev. 2nd edn (Cambridge: Cambridge University Press, 2003).

Clarke, F. L., Dean, G. and Staunton, J., Letter of comment No. 78, 'On June 2004 FASB ED, Fair Value Measurement', September 2004; accessible on FASB website, <www.fasb.org>

Commentary, 'The Royal Mail Steam Packet Company case', *Canadian Chartered Accountant,* November 1931, pp. 181–94.

Committee on Interstate and Foreign Commerce, *Report of the Advisory Committee on Corporate Disclosure to the SEC* (Washington, DC: Government Printing Office, 1977).

Companies and Securities Advisory Committee, *Corporate Groups: Discussion paper* (Sydney: Australian Securities and Investment Commission, 1998).

Companies and Securities Advisory Committee, *Corporate Groups: Final report* (Sydney: Australian Securities and Investment Commission, May 2000).

Corporations and Markets Advisory Committee, *Discussion Paper: Rehabilitating large and complex enterprises in financial difficulties* (Sydney, NSW: September 2003); final report (same title) (October 2004) available at <www.camac.gov.au>

Couper, C. T., *Report of the Trial of the City of Glasgow Bank Directors* (Edinburgh: Edinburgh Publishing, 1879).

CPA Australia, *The Way Ahead – A New Financial Reporting Framework* (Melbourne: CPA Australia, 2003).

CPA Australia and ICAA, *Auditing and Assurance Handbook* (Sydney: Pearson, 2004).

Cranston, R. F., 'Regulation and deregulation: General issues', *UNSW Law Journal,* Vol. 5, No. 1, 1982, pp. 1–28.

Cronje, S., Ling, M. and Cronje, G., *Lonrho: A portrait of a multinational* (London: Penguin, 1976).

Culp, C. L. and Niskanen, W. A., *Corporate Aftershock* (Hoboken, NJ: Wiley, 2003).

Cunningham, G. M. and Harris, J. E., 'Case of the crooked E and the fallen A', *Global Perspectives in Accounting Education,* Vol. 3, 2006, pp. 27–48.

Dalton, D. R., Daily, C. M., Ellstrand, A. E., and Johnston, J. L., 'Meta-analytic reviews of board composition, leadership structure and financial performance', *Strategic Management Journal,* Vol. 42, No. 6, 1998, pp. 674–86.

Daly, M. T., *Sydney Boom, Sydney Bust: The city and its property market 1850–1981* (Sydney: Allen & Unwin, 1982).

de Bedts, R., *The New Deal's SEC: The formative years* (NY and London: Columbia University Press, 1964).

de Monde, C. W., *Price Waterhouse & Company in America* (New York: privately printed, 1951).

Dean, G., 'Editorial', *Abacus*, February 2002, pp. i–iv.

Dean, G., 'Corporate groups – complexity and reforms in accounting and the law', University of Sydney, Pacioli Society meeting, 14 October 2003, reproduced in *Abacus*, Vol. 40, No. 2, June 2004, pp. 259–64.

Dean, G. and Clarke, F. L., 'Schmidt's *Betriebswirtschaft* theory', *Abacus*, Vol. 22, No. 2, September 1986, pp. 65–102.

Dean, G. W. and Clarke, F. L., 'Anatomy of a failure: A methodological experiment – the case of ASL', in M. Juttner and T. Valentine (eds), *The Economics and Institutions* (Melbourne: Longman Cheshire, 1987).

Dean, G. and Clarke, F. L., 'Conjectures on the influence of 1920s German *Betriebswirtschaftslehre* on Sweeney's *Stabilized Accounting*', *Accounting and Business Research*, Autumn 1989, pp. 1–14.

Dean, G. and Clarke, F., 'Principles vs. rules: true and fair and IFRSs', *Abacus*, June 2004, pp. i–iii.

Dean, G., Clarke, F. and Houghton, E., 'Cross guarantees and negative pledges: A preliminary analysis', *Australian Accounting Review*, May 1995, pp. 48–63.

Dean, G., Clarke, F. and Houghton, E., 'Corporate restructuring, creditors' rights, cross guarantees and group behaviour', *Company and Securities Law Journal*, Vol. 17, 1999, pp. 73–102.

Dean, G., Clarke, F. and Wolnizer, P., 'Submission to the JPCAA Inquiry, "Review of independent auditing by registered public companies"', August 2002 (see www.aph. gov.au).

Dean, G., Luckett, P. and Houghton, E., 'Notional calculations in liquidations revisited: The case of ASC Class Order cross guarantees', *Company and Securities Law Journal*, August 1993, pp. 204–26.

Defina, A. T., Harris, T. C. and Ramsay, L. M., 'What is reasonable remuneration for corporate officers?', *Company and Securities Law Journal*, Vol. 12, 1994, pp. 341–56.

DeFonzo, L., *St. Peter's Banker* (New York: Franklin Watts, 1983).

Demski, J., Dopuch, N., Lev, B., Ronen, J., Searfoss, J., and Sunder, S., 'Statement on the state of accounting', mimeo, 1991, as cited in Mattessich (1995).

Department of Trade and Industry, *Mirror Group Newspapers, plc*, Vols 1 and 2 (London: Stationery Office, 2001).

DeZoort, F. T. and Lee, T. A., 'The impact of SAS No.82 on perceptions of external auditor responsibility for fraud detection', *International Journal of Auditing*, Vol. 2, No. 2, 1998, pp. 167–82.

Edwards, J. R., *A History of Financial Accounting* (London: Routledge, 1989).

Eichenwald, K., *Serpent on the Rock* (New York: HarperBusiness, 1995).

Eisenberg, M. A., 'Corporate groups' in Gillooly (ed.), (1993).

Elloumi, F., and Gueyie, J. P., 'Financial distress and corporate governance: An empirical analysis', *Corporate Governance*, Vol. 1, No. 1, 2001, pp. 15–23.

Evans, L., 'The true and fair view and the fair presentation override of IAS 1', *Accounting and Business Research*, Vol 33 (4), December 2003.

Fabricant, S., *Capital Consumption and Adjustment* (New York: National Bureau of Economic Research, 1936).

FASB, 'Proposed statement of Accounting Standard', *Exposure Draft: Fair Value Measurement* (Stamford, Conn.: FASB, 23 June 2004).

Federal Reserve Board, *Uniform Accounting* (Washington, DC: Government Printing Office, 1917).

Federal Reserve Board, *Verification of Financial Statements* (Washington, DC: Government Printing Office, 1929).

Federal Trade Conmmission, Staff of, *Economic Report on Corporate Mergers* (Washington: US Government Office, 1969).

Fernside, W. and Holther, W. B., *Fallacy: The counterfeit of argument* (New York: Prentice-Hall, 1959).

Finnis, D., 'Financial reporting for general insurers', *Actuary Australia*, May 2005, pp. 18–21.

Fitzgerald, F. S., *The Great Gatsby* (New York: Modern Library, 1925).

Flanagan, W. G., *Dirty Rotten CEOs: How business leaders are fleecing America* (Rowville, Vic.: Five Mile Press, 2003).

Flesher, D. L. and Flesher, T. K., 'Ivar Kreuger's contribution to US financial reporting', *The Accounting Review*, Vol. 61. No. 3, July 1986, pp. 421–33.

Ford, H. A. J., *Principles of Company Law*, 5th edn (Sydney: Butterworths, 1990).

Ford, H. A. J. and Austin, R., *Principles of Corporations Law* (Sydney: Butterworths, 2006).

Foster, P., *Towers of Debt: The rise and fall of the Reichmanns* (London: Hodder & Stoughton, 1986).

Fox, L., *Enron: The rise and fall* (New Jersey: John Wiley & Sons, 2003).

Frederickson, J., Hodge, F. and Pratt, J., 'The evolution of stock option accounting: Disclosure, voluntary recognition and mandated disavowals', *The Accounting Review*, Vol. 81, No. 5, 2006, pp. 1073–93.

Fusaro, P. and Miller, R. M., *What Went Wrong at Enron?* (New Jersey: John Wiley & Sons, 2002).

Galbraith, J. K., *The Great Crash 1929* (London: Pelican, 1971).

Garnsey, G., *Holding Companies and Their Published Accounts* (London: Gee & Co., 1923), reproduced as *Holding Companies and Their Published Accounts: Limitations of a balance sheet* (New York: Garland Publishing, 1982).

Gay, R. and Simnett, R., *Auditing and Assurance Services in Australia*, rev. 3rd edn (Sydney: McGraw-Hill, 2006).

Gillooly, M. A. (ed.), *The Law Relating to Corporate Groups* (Annandale: Federation Press, 1993).

Gottliebsen, R., *10 Best and 10 Worst Decisions of Australian CEOs, 1992–2002* (Camberwell, Vic.: Viking, 2003).

Government Accounting Office, *Financial Statement Restatements: Trends, market impacts, regulatory responses, and remaining challenges* (Washington, DC: GAO-03–138, 2003, 2004).

Gower, L. C. B., *Principles of Modern Company Law*, 3rd edn (London: Law Book Co., 1969); 4th edn (London: Stevens & Co., 1979).

Green, E. and Moss, M., *A Business of National Importance: The Royal Mail shipping group, 1902–1937* (London and New York: Methuen, 1982).

Greising, D. and Morse, L., *Brokers, Bagmen and Moles: Fraud and corruption in the Chicago futures markets* (New York: John Wiley & Sons, 1991).

Griffiths, I., *Creative Accounting: How to make your profits what you want them to be* (London: Allen & Unwin, 1986).

Gunn, C., *Nightmare on Lime Street: Whatever happened to Lloyd's of London?* (London: Smith Gryphon, 1992).

Guttmann, W. and Meehan, P., *The Great Inflation* (London: Saxon House, 1975).

Guy, D. M. and Sullivan, J. D., 'The expectation gap auditing standards', *Journal of Accountancy*, 164 (4), 1998, pp. 36–46.

Hadden, T., 'The regulation of corporate groups in Australia', *UNSW Law Journal*, 15 (1), 1992, pp. 61–85.

Haigh, G., *The Battle for BHP* (Melbourne: Allen & Unwin, 1987).

Haigh G., 'UK judge chides Bond over lack of Bell records', *Sydney Morning Herald*, 22 July 1989, p. 41.

Haigh, G., *Bad Company: The cult of the CEO*, Quarterly Essay 10 (Melbourne: Black Inc., 2003).

Haigh, G., *Asbestos House: The secret history of James Hardie Industries* (Melbourne: Scribe, 2006).

Haldane, A., *With Intent to Deceive: Frauds famous and infamous* (Edinburgh: William Blackwood, 1970).

Hastings, Sir Patrick, 'The case of the Royal Mail', in Baxter and Davidson (1962).

Hawkins, D., *Corporate Financial Reporting* (Homewood: Irwin, 1962).

Heimann-Hoffman, V. B., Morgan, K. P. and Patton, J. M., 'The warning signs of fraudulent financial reporting', *Journal of Accountancy*, 172 (10), 1996, pp. 75–7.

Hein, L. W., *The British Companies Acts and the practice of accountancy, 1844–1962* (New York, NY: Arno Press, 1978).

HIH Royal Commission Report, *The Failure of the HIH Insurance – Vols. I–III: Reasons, circumstances and responsibilities* (Canberra: Commonwealth of Australia; 2003).

Hill, J., 'Cross guarantees and corporate groups', *Companies and Securities Law Journal*, 10, 1992, p. 312.

Hill, J., 'Corporate groups, creditor protection and cross guarantees: Australian perspectives', *Canadian Business Law Journal*, February 1995, pp. 321–56.

Holtfrerich, C.-L., *The German Inflation 1914–23* (Berlin and New York: Walter de Gruyter, 1986).

Horton, J. and Macve, R., '"Fair value" for financial instruments: How erasing theory is leading to unworkable global accounting standards for performance reporting', *Australian Accounting Review*, July 2000.

Houghton, E., Dean, G. and Clarke, F., 'Insolvent corporate groups with cross guarantees: A forensic-LP case study in liquidation', *British Journal of Operations Research*, May 1999, pp. 480–96.

Humphrey, C., Moizer, P. and Turley, S., *The Audit Expectations Gap in the United Kingdom* (London: Institute of Chartered Accountants in England and Wales, 1992).

Humphrey, C., Turley, S. and Moizer, P., 'Protecting against detection: The case of auditors and fraud', *Accounting, Auditing & Accountability Journal*, 6 (1), 1993, pp. 39–62.

259

Hunt, B. C., *The Development of the Business Corporation in England, 1800–1867* (Cambridge, Mass.: Harvard University Press, 1936).

IFAC, *Rebuilding Public Confidence in Financial Reporting* (New York: IFAC, 2003).

IFAC, 'Ethics Code, proposed', 'Independence – audit and review engagements; independence – other assurance engagements' (New York: IFAC, 29 December 2006).

Institutional Shareholder Services, 'Long-term incentives – far from illusory', monograph (Melbourne: ISS, September 2006).

International Federation of Accountants, *Understanding Financial Statements* (Melbourne: Australian Accounting Research Foundation, 1990).

Izan, H. Y., Sidhu, B. and Taylor, S. L., 'Does CEO pay reflect performance?', *Corporate Governance: An international review*, Vol. 6, 1998, pp. 39–47.

Jackson Committee Report (Jackson QF(QC)), Report of the Special Commission of Inquiry into the Medical Research and Compensation Foundation (September 2004).

Jameson, M., *The Practical Art of Creative Accounting* (London: Kogan Page, 1988).

Janetzki, D., *The Gollin Years* (Brisbane: Don Janetzki, privately published, 1989).

Jennings, M. M., *The Seven Signs of Ethical Collapse: Understanding what causes moral meltdowns in organizations* (New York: St Martins Press, 2006).

Jensen, M. C., 'Value maximisation, stakehold theory and the corporate objective function', *European Financial Management*, Vol. 7, No. 3, 2001, pp. 297–317.

Jensen, M. and Murphy, K., 'Performance pay and top management incentives', *Journal of Political Economy*, Vol. 98, No. 2, 1990, pp. 225–65.

Jettner, L. M., *Broadbandits* (Hoboken, New Jersey: John Wiley & Sons, 2003).

Johnson, R., 'Back-to-back loans: A fraud in transition', *Australian Accounting Review*, November 2000; pp. 62–71.

Joint Committee on Corporations and Financial Services, *Report*, 'Accounting Standards tabled in compliance with the Corporations Act, 2001 on 30 August 2004 and 16 November 2004' (Canberra: Australian Government Printing Service, February 2005).

Joint Committee on Public Accounts and Audit, *Report 391, Review of Independent Auditing by Registered Company Auditors* (Canberra: Australian Government Printing Service, August 2002).

Jordanova, L., *History in Practice* (London: Arnold, 2000).

Kellogg, I. and Kellogg, L. B., *Fraud, Window Dressing and Negligence in Financial Statements* (New York: McGraw-Hill, 1991).

Kerry, J. and Brown, H., *The BCCI Affair* (Washington, DC: Committee on Foreign Relations of the United States Senate, 1992).

Kindelberger, C. P., *Manias, Panics and Crashes: A history of financial crises*, 2nd edn (London: Basic Books, 1989).

Kirk, N., 'Perceptions of the true and fair view concept: An empirical investigation', *Abacus*, June 2006, pp. 205–35.

Klein, A., 'Likely effects of stock exchange governance proposals and Sarbanes-Oxley on corporate boards and financial reporting', *Accounting Horizons*, 17 (4), 2003, pp. 343–55.

Laing, D. and Wier, C. M., 'Governance structures, size and corporate performance in UK firms', *Management Decision*, Vol. 37, No. 1/2, 1999, pp. 46–51.

Lambert, R., Larker, D. and Verrechia, R., 'Portfolio considerations in valuing executive compensation', *Journal of Accounting Research*, Vol. 29, 1991, pp. 129–34.

Lawrence, J. and Stapledon, G., 'Is the board important? A study of listed Australian companies', working paper, University of Melbourne, 1999.

Lawson, T. W., *Frenzied Finance – The Crime of Amalgamated* (New York: Ridgway-Thayer, 1905).

Lee, T. A., 'The nature of auditing and its objectives', *Accountancy*, 34 (4), 1970, pp. 292–6.

Lee, T. A., Clarke, F. and Dean, G., 'The dominant senior manager and the reasonably careful, skilful, and cautious auditor', *Critical Perspectives in Accounting*, 2007; forthcoming.

Leung, P., Coram, P. and Cooper, B., *Modern Auditing Assurance Services* (Milton, Qld: John Wiley & Sons, 2007).

Levit, A. and Dyer, P., *Take On the Street: What Wall Street and corporate America didn't want you to know* (New York: Pantheon Books, 2006).

Liebler, M., *Submission to Joint Committee on Public Accounts and Audit*, Commonwealth of Australia, 'Review of independent auditing by registered company auditors', 2002; available at <www.aph.gov.au>; last accessed on 10 February 2005.

Loftus, J. and Miller, M., *Reporting on Solvency and Cash Position*, Accounting Theory Monograph No. 11 (Melbourne: Australian Accounting Research Foundation, 2000).

McBarnet, D. and Whelan, C., *Creative Accounting and the Cross-Eyed Javelin Thrower* (Chichester: John Wiley & Sons, 1999).

McCartney, S. and Arnold, A. J., 'George Hudson's financial reporting practices: Putting the Eastern Counties Railway in context', *Accounting, Business and Financial History*, 10 (3), 2000, pp. 293–316.

McDonald, F., *Insull* (Chicago, Ill.: Chicago University Press, 1962).

McManamy, J., *The Dreamtime Casino* (Melbourne: Schwarz & Wilkinson, 1990).

Macve, R., Letter of Comment No 6, 'On June 2004 FASB ED, "Fair value measurement"', September 2004; accessible on FASB website, <www.fasb.org>.

Maher, T., *Bond* (Melbourne: William Heinemann, 1990).

Malik, O., *Disconnected: Inside the $750 billion telecom heist* (Hoboken, NJ: Wiley & Sons, 2003).

Mantle, J., *For Whom the Bell Tolls: The scandalous inside story of Lloyd's crisis* (London: Mandarin Paperbacks, 1993).

Margret, J. E., 'Insolvency and tests of insolvency: An analysis of the "balance sheet" and "cash flow" tests', *Australian Accounting Review*, Vol.12, No. 2, 2002, pp. 59–72.

Masters, B. A., *Spoiling for a Fight: The Rise of Eliot Spitzer* (New York: Times Books, Henry Holt and Company, 2006).

Mattessich, R., *Critique of Accounting: Examination of the foundations and normative structure of an applied discipline* (Westport, CT: Quorum Books, 1995).

Mautz, R. K. and Sharaf, H. A., *The Philosophy of Auditing* (Evanston, Ill.: American Accounting Association, 1961).

May, G. O., *Twenty-five Years of Accounting Responsibility: 1911–1936* (New York, NY: Price Waterhouse & Co., 1936).

May, G. O., 'Kreuger and Toll' in May (1936); reprint (Lawrence, Kan.: Scholars Book Co., 1971), pp. 104–11.

261

Merhebi, R., Pattenden, K., Swan, P. and Zhou, X., 'Australian chief executive officer remuneration: pay and performance', *Accounting and Finance*, September 2006, pp. 481–97.

Mescher, B., 'Personal liability for company directors for company debts', *Australian Law Journal*, Vol. 70, October 1996, pp. 837–50.

Mescher, B., 'Directors and accountants and the obligation to ensure proper accounts are kept', *Financial Reporting, Regulation and Governance*, Vol. 4, No. 2, 2005, pp.1–25.

Mitchell, A. and Sikkha, P., *Taming the Corporations* (London: Basildon, Association for Accountancy & Business Affairs, 2005).

Monks, R. A. G. and Minnow, N., *Corporate Governance*, 3rd edn (Oxford: Blackwell Publishing, 2004).

Moroney, R. and Sidhu, B. K., 'The reformed "true and fair" test: How often does it trigger additional disclosure?', *Accounting Research Journal*, Vol. 14, No. 1, 2001.

Murford, C. W. and Cominsky, E. E., *The Financial Numbers Game: Detecting creative accounting practices* (New York: John Wiley & Sons, 2002).

Naser, K. H. M., *Creative Financial Accounting* (London: Prentice Hall International, 1993).

National Commission on Fraudulent Financial Reporting, *Report of the National Commission on Fraudulent Financial Reporting* (Washington, DC: AICPA, 1987).

National Companies and Securities Commission, *A 'True and Fair View' and the Reporting Obligations of Auditors* (Canberra: Australian Government Printing Service, 1984).

Nobes, C., 'Is true and fair of over-riding importance?', *Accounting and Business Research*, 30 (Autumn), 2000.

Nobes, C., 'Rules-based standards and the lack of principles in accounting', *Accounting Horizons*, March 2005.

Notes to the Sydney University Pacioli Society, *Abacus*, March 2007, pp. 107–10.

OECD, *OECD Principles of Corporate Governance* (Geneva: OECD, 1999).

Office of Federal Housing Enterprise Oversight, *Report of the Special Examination of Fannie Mae* (Washington: US Government Printer, May 2006).

Ohlsen, W., *The Accounting Profession – Years of Trial: 1969–1980* (New York: American Institute of Certified Public Accountants, 1982)

O'Neill, G. L. and Iob, M., 'Determinants of executive remuneration in Australian organizations: An exploratory study', *Asia-Pacific Journal of Human Resources*, Vol. 37, 1999, pp. 65–75.

Parker, R. H., Wolnizer, P. W. and Nobes, C., *Readings in True and Fair* (New York: Garland Publishing, 1996).

Partnoy, F., *Infectious Greed: How deceit and risk corrupted the financial markets* (London: Profile Books, 2003).

Pecora, F., *Wall Street Under Oath: The story of our modern money changers* (New York: Simon & Schuster, 1939).

Pizzo, S., Ricker, M. and Muolo, P., *Inside Job: The looting of America's savings and loans* (New York, N.Y.: HarperPerennial, 1991).

Posner, R., *Economic Analysis of Law* (Boston and Toronto: Little, Brown and Company, 1977, 2nd ed.)

Previts, G. J. and Merino, B. D., *A History of Accountancy in the United States: The cultural significance of accounting* (Columbus, OH: Ohio State University Press, 1998).

Public Oversight Board, 'Issues in confronting the accounting profession', report by Public Oversight Board of the SEC Practice Section (Stamford, CT: AICPA, 1993).

PwC, KPMG, DeLoitte, E&Y, BDO and Grant Thornton, *Global Capital Markets and the Global Economy: A vision from the CEOs of the International Audit Network* (Paris: Global Public Policy Symposium, November 2006).

Ramage, R. W., *The Companies Acts: Table A 1856–1981* (London: Butterworths, 1982).

Ramsay, I. and Stapledon, G., *Corporate Groups in Australia* (Melbourne: Centre for Corporate Law and Securities Regulation, University of Melbourne, November 1998).

Ramsay, I. and Stapledon, G., 'Corporate groups in Australia', *Australian Business Law Review*, Vol. 29, No. 1, 2001, pp. 7–32.

Raw, C., *Slater Walker* (London: Andre Deutsch, 1977).

Raw, C., *The Money Changers: How the Vatican Bank enabled Roberto Calvi to steal $250 million for the heads of the P2 Masonic Lodge* (London: Harvill, 1992).

Report of the Review Committee (Chairman, Sir Kenneth Cork), *Insolvency Law and Practice* (London: HMSO, 1982).

Rhoades, D. L., Rechner, P. L. and Sundarmurthy, C., 'Board composition and financial performance: A meta-analysis of the influence of outside directors', *Journal of Managerial Issues*, Vol. 12, Iss. 1, 2000, pp. 76–88.

Rorem, C. R., *Accounting Method* (1928; repr. New York: Garland, 1998).

Rothchild, J., *Going for Broke: How Robert Campeau bankrupted the retail industry, jolted the junk bond market and brought the booming eighties to a crashing halt* (New York: Simon & Schuster, 1991).

Russell, H. F., *Foozles and Fraud* (Altamone Springs: Florida: Institute of Internal Auditors, 1978).

Sanders, T. H., Hatfield, H. R. and Moore, U., *A Tentative Statement of Accounting Principles* (New York: American Institute of Accountants, 1938).

Schilit, H., *Financial Shenanigans: How to detect accounting gimmicks and fraud in financial reports* (New York: McGraw-Hill, 1993; 2nd edn, 2002).

Schipper, K., 'Principles-based Accounting Standards', *Accounting Horizons*, 17 (1), 2003, pp. 61–72.

Schuetze, W. P., 'What are assets and liabilities? Where is true North? (Accounting that my sister would understand)', *Abacus*, February 2001a, pp. 1–25.

Schuetze, W. P., 'A memo to national and international accounting and audit standard setters and securities regulators', *The R. J. Chambers Research Lecture*, November 2001b.

Scott, W. R., *The Constitution and Finance of English, Scottish and Irish Joint-Stock Companies to 1720* (Gloucester, Mass: Peter Smith, 1968).

Securities and Exchange Commission, *Research Study*, 'Study pursuant to Section 108(d) of the *Sarbanes-Oxley Act* of 2002 on the adoption by the United States financial reporting system of a principles-based accounting system' (Washington, DC: Securities and Exchange Commission, 25 July 2003).

Service, J., Response to question at Hearings before the Joint Committee on Corporations and Financial Services, *Report*, 'Accounting Standards tabled in compliance with the *Corporations Act, 2001* on 30 August 2004 and 16 November, 2004', as reported in Hansard (7 February 2005).

Shaplen, R., *Kreuger: Genius and Swindler* (1961; repr. New York: Garland Publishing, 1990).

Skeel, D., *Icarus in the Boardroom: The fundamental flaws in corporate America and where they came from* (Oxford: Oxford University Press, 2004).

Smith, T., *Accounting for Growth: Stripping the camouflage from company accounts* (London: Century Business, 1992).

Spacek, L., *A Search for Fairness: In financial reporting to the public* (Chicago: Arthur Andersen, 1969).

Staunton, J., 'Exiting intellectual grooves in the reporting of liabilities: An analysis of the reporting of liabilities under Chambers' continuously contemporary accounting', PhD thesis, University of Sydney, November 2006.

Sterling, R., *Theory of The Measurement of Enterprise Income* (Lawrence, Kan.: University Press of Kansas, 1970).

Stoljar, S. J., *Groups and Entities: An inquiry into corporate theory* (Canberra: Australian National University Press, 1973).

Stoneman, W., *The Life and Death of Ivar Kreuger* (Indianapolis: Bobs Merrill Co., 1932, 1960).

Stoneman, W. H., 'The matchless career of Ivar Kreuger – The Match King', in *World of Business* (New York, NY: Harvard Business School, Simon & Schuster, 1962) pp. 934–8.

Sullivan, W., 'Markets vs. professions: value added', *Daedalus*, Summer 2005, pp. 19–26.

Sweeney, H., *Stabilized Accounting* (New York: Harper & Brothers, 1936).

Sykes, T., *The Money Miners: Australia's mining boom 1969–70* (Sydney: Wildcat Press, 1978).

Sykes, T., *Two Centuries of Panic: A history of corporate collapses in Australia* (Sydney: Allen & Unwin, 1988).

Sykes, T., *The Bold Riders* (Sydney: Allen & Unwin, 1994; 2nd edn 1996).

Taylor, M. H., DeZoort F. T., Munn, E. and Thomas, M. W., 'A proposed framework emphasising auditor reliability over auditor independence', *Accounting Horizons*, 17 (3), 2003, pp. 257–66.

Teo, E. and Cobbin, P. E., 'A revisitation of the "audit expectations gap": Judicial and practitioner views on the role of the auditor in late-Victorian England', *Accounting History*, 10 (2), 2005, pp. 35–66.

Thomas, R. J. L. and Turner, R. T., *Mirror Group Newspapers plc: Investigations under Sections 432(2) and 442 of the* Companies Act 1985 (London: Department of Trade and Industry; 2000).

Thompson, P. and Delano, A., *Maxwell: A portrait of power* (London: Corgi, 1991).

Toffler, B. L. with Reingold, J., *Final Accounting: Ambition, greed and the fall of Arthur Andersen* (New York: Currency, Doubleday, 2004).

Treasury, *Australian Auditor Independence Requirements, Commonwealth of Australia* (Canberra: Australian Government Printing Service, November 2006).

Treasury, 'Corporate and Financial Services Regulation Review Proposals' paper (Canberra: Australian Treasury) 16 November 2006.

Trotman, K., *Financial Report Audit: Meeting the market expectations* (Sydney: ICAA, 2003).

Truell, P. and Gurwin, L., *BCCI – The Inside Story of the World's Most Corrupt Financial Empire* (London: Bloomsbury Publishing, 1992).

Tweedie, D., 'True and fair v the rule book: which is the answer to creative accounting?', *Pacific Accounting Review*, December 1988, pp. 1–21.

Tweedie, D., 'IFRSs: View on a financial reporting revolution', pp. 35–8, as reported in KPMG, *International Financial Reporting Standards: Views on a financial reporting revolution* (London: KPMG, 2006).

Tweedie, D. and Whittington, G., *The Debate on Inflation Accounting* (Cambridge: Cambridge University Press, 1984).

US Congress, *Hearings before the Senate Committee on Banking and Currency, Stock Exchange Practices*, 73rd Congress, Part 4, 1933, pp. 1146–395.

Valance, A., 'Lucifer descending' in Valance (1955), pp. 155–66.

Valance, A., *A Very Private Enterprise* (London: Thames & Hudson, 1955).

Veblen, T., *The Theory of the Leisure Class: An economic study of institutions* (New York: Macmillan, 1899).

Waddock, S., 'Hollow men and women – hollow accounting ethics?', *Issues in Accounting Education*, 20 (2), 2005, pp. 145–50.

Walker, R. G., *Consolidated Statements: A history and analysis* (New York: Arno Press, 1978a).

Walker R. G., 'Disclosure rules – the 1929 Companies Act and the Royal Mail case' in Walker, *Consolidated Statements* (1978b), pp. 83–98.

Walker, R. G., 'The SEC's ban on upward asset revaluations and the disclosure of current values', *Abacus*, September 1992a, pp. 3–35.

Walker, R. G., 'Off-balance sheet financing', *UNSW Law Journal*, Vol. 15, No. 1, 1992b, pp. 196–213.

Walker, R. G., 'A feeling of déjà vu: Controversies in accounting and auditing regulation in Australia', *Critical Perspectives in Accounting*, Vol. 4, 1993, pp. 97–109.

Walker, R. G., 'Gaps in guidelines on audit committees', *Abacus*, June 2004, pp.157–92.

Walker, R. G., 'Reporting entity concept: A case study of the failure of principles-based regulation', *Abacus*, March 2007, pp. 49–75.

Walker, R. G., Clarke, F. L. and Dean, G. W., 'Infrastructure reporting options', *Abacus*, June 2000, pp. 123–59.

Walker, R. G. and Walker, B. C., *Privatisation – Sell Off or Sell Out?: The Australian experience* (Sydney: ABC Books, 2000).

Wallace W., *Trial of the City of Glasgow Bank Directors* (Glasgow and Edinburgh: William Hodge and Co.; 1905).

Waller, D., *Wheels on Fire: The Amazing Inside Story of the Daimler Chrysler Merger* (London: Hodder & Stoughton, 2001).

Webb, L. C., *Legal Personality and Political Pluralism* (Melbourne: Melbourne University Press, 1958).

Weisman, S. L., *Need and Greed: The story of the largest ponzi scheme in American history* (Syracuse: Syracuse University Press, 1999).

West, B. P., *Professionalism and Accounting Rules* (London: Routledge, 2003).

Whitehead, Alfred North, *An Enquiry Concerning the Principles of Natural Knowledge* (Cambridge: Cambridge University Press, 1919, 1925).

Wolnizer, P., *Auditing as Independent Authentication* (Sydney: Sydney University Press, 1987).

Wood, C. and Patrick, T., 'Jumping on the bandwagon: Outside representation in corporate governance', *Journal of Business and Economic Studies*, Vol. 9, No. 2, 2003, pp. 48–53.

Zecher, J. R. and Phillips, S., *The SEC and the Public Interest* (Cambridge, Mass.: MIT Press, 1981).

Zeff, S. A., 'Chronology of significant developments in the establishment of accounting principles in the United States, 1926–1972', *Journal of Accounting Research*, Vol. 10, No. 1, Spring 1972, pp. 217–27.

Zeff, S. A., 'How the US accounting profession got where it is today: Part I', *Accounting Horizons*, September 2003a, pp. 189–205.

Zeff, S. A., 'How the US accounting profession got where it is today: Part II', *Accounting Horizons*, December 2003b, pp. 267–86.

Zekany, K. E., Braun, L. W. and Warder, Z. T., 'Behind closed doors at WorldCom: 2001', *Issues in Accounting Education*, Vol. 19, No. 1, 2004, pp. 101–17.

# Index